FISCAL POLICY AND ECONOMIC REFORM

In an era of rapid and extensive economic reform, what is the appropriate role for fiscal policy? Is there a residual role of government after socialism and dirigisme?

Following *Macroeconomic Dimensions of Public Finance*, this is the second volume of essays in honour of Vito Tanzi. It focuses on the importance of fiscal policy on the wholesale economic reforms that are sweeping the advanced, less developed and formerly communist countries. Issues analysed include:

- the role of fiscal and budgetary policies in the process of reform;
- the impact of privatization on the exchequer and the dilemmas for social policy in times of fiscal austerity;
- the paradox of post-socialism and post-dirigisme that an efficient and harmonic move to a decontrolled, liberal market economy involves active state intervention; and
- the methodological aspects relating to the proper assessment of selected fiscal policy mechanisms.

This collection of essays will contribute to understanding the channels and transmission mechanisms of fiscal policies in the context of major economic reforms.

Mario I. Blejer is Senior Adviser at the International Monetary Fund (IMF). He holds an economics Ph.D from Chicago and has taught at Hebrew, Boston and New York universities. He has published extensively on monetary and fiscal issues and transition economies.

Teresa Ter-Minassian holds degrees in law and economics from Rome and Harvard. She reached the grade of Division Chief at the Bank of Italy before taking a permanent position at the IMF, where she is currently Deputy Director of the Fiscal Affairs Department.

ROUTLEDGE STUDIES IN THE MODERN WORLD ECONOMY

1 INTEREST RATES AND BUDGET DEFICITS
A study of the advanced economies
Kanhaya L. Gupta and Bakhtiar Moazzami

2 WORLD TRADE AFTER THE URUGUAY ROUND
Prospects and policy options for the twenty-first century
Edited by Harald Sander and András Inotai

3 THE FLOW ANALYSIS OF LABOUR MARKETS
Edited by Ronald Schettkat

4 INFLATION AND UNEMPLOYMENT
Contributions to a new macroeconomic approach
Edited by Alvaro Cencini and Mauro Baranzini

5 MACROECONOMIC DIMENSIONS OF PUBLIC FINANCE
Essays in honour of Vito Tanzi
Edited by Mario I. Blejer and Teresa Ter-Minassian

6 FISCAL POLICY AND ECONOMIC REFORM
Essays in honour of Vito Tanzi
Edited by Mario I. Blejer and Teresa Ter-Minassian

FISCAL POLICY AND ECONOMIC REFORM

Essays in honour of Vito Tanzi

Edited by
Mario I. Blejer and Teresa Ter-Minassian

Advisory Board Members

Professors Richard M. Bird, Arnold Harberger, Richard Musgrave and Sweder Van Wijnbergen

London and New York

First published 1997
by Routledge
11 New Fetter Lane, London EC4P 4EE

Simultaneously published in the USA and Canada
by Routledge
29 West 35th Street, New York, NY 10001

Typeset in Times by Solidus (Bristol) Limited
Printed and bound in Great Britain by
TJ Press (Padstow) Ltd, Padstow, Cornwall

British Library Cataloguing in Publication Data
A catalogue record for this book is available from the British Library

Library of Congress Cataloguing in Publication Data
Fiscal policy and economic reform : essays in honour of Vito Tanzi /
edited by Mario I. Bléjer and Teresa M. Ter-Minassian.
p. cm. – (Routledge studies in the modern world economy.
Includes bibliographical references and index.
1. Fiscal policy. 2. Economic policy. I. Tanzi, Vito.
II. Bléjer, Mario I. III. Ter-Minassian, Teresa. IV. Series.
HJ192.5.F57 1997
336.3–dc20 95-497778
CIP

ISBN 0–415–13739–X (hbk)

CONTENTS

List of figures ix
List of tables xi
List of contributors xiv
Preface: Vito Tanzi – The Economist and the Man xv

1 INTRODUCTION AND OVERVIEW: THE ROLE OF FISCAL POLICIES IN PROMOTING ECONOMIC REFORMS 1
M.I. Blejer and Ter-Minassian

Part 1 Fiscal policies, privatization, and structural reforms

2 THE BUDGETARY IMPACT OF PRIVATISATION 9
David M. Newbery

3 MACROECONOMIC CONSTRAINTS AND THE MODALITIES OF PRIVATIZATION 32
Peter Heller, Richard Hemming, and Rupa Chakrabarti

4 A FISCAL APPROACH TO LIBERALIZATION POLICY 50
Miguel A. Fernández-Ordoñez and Carlos Ocaña

Part II Fiscal policy and the promotion of sustainable growth

5 EMPIRICAL EVIDENCE ON THE IMPACT OF RECENT TAX REFORMS ON SAVINGS, INVESTMENT, AND GROWTH 67
Krister Andersson

Part III Fiscal policy and the environment

6 FISCAL AND MACROECONOMIC ASPECTS OF ENVIRONMENT TAXES 93
David C.L. Nellor

Part IV Fiscal policies, poverty alleviation, and the social safety net

7 POVERTY ALLEVIATION IN A FINANCIAL PROGRAMMING FRAMEWORK: AN INTEGRATED APPROACH 113
Sheetal K. Chand and Parthasarathi Shome

8 ECONOMIC REFORMS, SOCIAL SAFETY NETS, AND THE BUDGET IN TRANSITION ECONOMIES 134
Ke-young Chu and Sanjeev Gupta

9 CONSUMER PRICE REFORMS AND THE SAFETY NET IN TRANSITION ECONOMIES 164
Ehtisham Ahmad and Liam Halligan

Part V Fiscal policy reforms and the transition from central planning

10 EXCESS WAGES TAX 181
Alan A. Tait and S. Nuri Erbas

11 THE FISCAL COMPONENT AND THE FIRST RUSSIAN STABILIZATION EFFORT, 1992–3 223
Piroska M. Nagy

12 TAXATION AND FOREIGN DIRECT INVESTMENT: THE EXPERIENCE OF THE ECONOMIES IN TRANSITION 246
David Holland and Jeffrey Owens

Part VI List of selected publications by Vito Tanzi

SELECTED PUBLICATIONS BY VITO TANZI 293

Index 299

FIGURES

2.1	Share of public enterprise in GDP, 1986–91	10
2.2	Public enterprise share in investment, 1986–91	11
2.3	PE relative capital intensity: ratio of investment to output, 1986–91	12
2.4	Tariffs and returns of ESIs in World Bank countries	14
2.5	Inefficiencies in electricity in developing countries	15
2.6	UK public and industrial/commercial cost, net surpluses and rates of profit	19
2.7	Shares in GDP at current factor cost, UK public and private sectors	21
2.8	Gross domestic capital formation, UK public and private sectors	22
2.9	UK public and private net capital stock, fixed assets share of GDP	23
2.10	Net worth of the public sector as percentage of GDP	24
5.1	Tax revenues (per cent of GDP)	68
5.2	Household savings rate (per cent of disposable income)	71
5.3	Bank lending to private sector (stock) (percentage change year on year)	73
5.4	Household gross debt (per cent of disposable income)	74
5.5	Credit losses in the banking sector (per cent of total credit)	75
5.6	Total turnover in the Swedish foreign exchange market (per cent of GDP)	76
5.7	Taxes on corporate income (per cent of GDP)	78
5.8	Unemployment (per cent of labour force)	80
5.9	Profit share in business sector (gross rate of return from production income on capital stock)	81
5.10	Gross capital formation (per cent of GDP)	82
5.11	GDP growth (index end 1969 = 100)	83
5.12	General government fiscal balances (per cent of GDP)	85
6.1	Pigouvian taxes	95
9.1	A simple representation of rationing	167

9.2 Kinked budget constraint in the absence of arbitrage 169
9.3 Quota relaxation and arbitrage possibilities 170
9.4 Ration resale and effective demand for a rationed good 171

TABLES

2.1 Growth and profit measures of PEs 16
2.2 Investment and balances of PEs 17
2.3 Fiscal impact and welfare gains from privatisation 27
3.1 Privatization proceeds, 1989–92 40
4.1 Budget for restrictions on competition 60
5.1 Top marginal tax rates for individuals 69
5.2 Corporation income tax rates 70
5.3 Some average amounts for persons over 17 years of age in Norway 70
5.4 Interest deductions in per cent of average income in Denmark 71
5.5 Effect of abolishing taxes on capital income in Sweden, 1984 72
7.1 Simulation results 126
8.1 Demographic structure and living standards in selected transition economies, 1992 136
8.2 Pre- and post-reform subsidies and cash transfers in selected transition economies (as per cent of GDP) 138
8.3 A hypothetical country: annual expenditures of an average individual in non-poor and poor households 145
8.4 A hypothetical country: budgetary cost of subsidies 146
8.5 The overall budgetary position and the extrabudgetary fund 147
8.6 Summary of budgetary impact of policy and other exogenous developments in the stylized economy 148
8.7 Effect on the cost of living of the non-poor and the poor 149
8.8 Summary of budgetary impact of social protection reform options in a stylized economy 153
A8.1 Average consumption per person in selected transition economies 159
10.1 Some examples of EWTs, 1992–4 184
10.2 Tax arrears relative to taxes due (in per cent) 201
10.3 Average wages for selected months (thousands of zlotys per worker) 202
10.4 PPWW per worker (thousands of zlotys) 202

TABLES

11.1 Russian Federation: summary of main economic indicators, 1991–3 229
11.2 Russian Federation: summary of fiscal indicators, 1992–3 232
11.3 Comparison of structure of revenues between the Russian Federation and the USSR 235
11.4 Subsidization in the USSR and Russia 236

CONTRIBUTORS

Ehtisham Ahmad, International Monetary Fund, Washington, DC 20431, USA

Krister Andersson, Economics Department, Central Bank of Sweden, S-10337 Stockholm, Sweden

Rupa Chakrabarti, 120 Valentine Place, Apt 2001, Ithaca, NY 14850, USA

Sheetal Chand, International Monetary Fund, Washington, DC 20431, USA

Ke-young Chu, International Monetary Fund, Washington, DC 20431, USA

Nuri Erbas, International Monetary Fund, Washington, DC 20431, USA

Miguel Angel Fernández-Ordoñez, Tribunal de Defensa de la Competencia, 28016 Madrid, Spain

Sanjeev Gupta, International Monetary Fund, Washington, DC 20431, USA

Liam Halligan, Centre for Economic Performance, LSE, Houghton Street, London WC2A 2AE, UK

Peter Heller, International Monetary Fund, Washington, DC 20431, USA

Richard Hemming, International Monetary Fund, Washington, DC 20431, USA

David Holland, Fiscal Affairs Division, OECD, 2, rue Andre Pascal, 75775 Paris CEDEX 16, France

Piroska Nagy, International Monetary Fund, Washington, DC 20431, USA

David Nellor, International Monetary Fund, Washington, DC 20431, USA

David Newbery, Department of Applied Economics, University of Cambridge, Sidgwick Avenue, Cambridge CB3 9DE, UK

Carlos Ocaña, Comisión del Sistema Eléctrico Nacional, Marqués del Duero, 4, 28001 Madrid, Spain

Jeffrey Owens, Fiscal Affairs Division, OECD, 2, rue Andre Pascal, 75775 Paris CEDEX 16, France

Parthasarathi Shome, International Monetary Fund, Washington, DC 20431, USA

Alan Tait, International Monetary Fund, Washington, DC 20431, USA

PREFACE

Vito Tanzi: the economist and the man

This book is one of the two volumes of essays especially written to honor Vito Tanzi. The articles included in this volume and in its companion (*Fiscal Policies and Economic Reforms*) were selected from more than 60 papers submitted for this project by many renowned world specialists in public finance. The selection of papers was performed with the help of an Advisory Board composed of Professors Richard M. Bird, Arnold Harberger, Richard Musgrave, and Sweder Van Wijnbergen. The prominence of the scholars who accepted to serve on the board, as well as the fact that so many distinguished colleagues submitted their contributions, and that those which were accepted could be divided naturally into two volumes covering quite different dimensions of fiscal policies, are all testimonies of the respect, admiration, and affection that Vito Tanzi elicits from his friends, colleagues, and associates, as well as of the broad span of subjects covered by his work.

Vito Tanzi's contribution to economics in general, and to public finance in particular, has, indeed, taken many forms. As a scholar, he has been extremely creative and productive; as a policy adviser, he has combined practicality and realism with breadth of vision and innovativeness, and his recommendations have had a lasting impact on the design of fiscal policies in many countries; and as a teacher and mentor he has always been inspiring and encouraging.

Tanzi's work has encompassed practically all aspects of modern public finance, from the technical analysis of tax and expenditure policies and incidence to the thorough investigation of the causes for the emergence of an underground economy and the economics of corruption. His research has provided important insights which are relevant for both developing and industrial countries. His studies have systematically analysed the implications of tax policies, government expenditures, and deficit financing on savings, growth, investment, and income distribution. More recently he has devoted much attention to the interaction between fiscal policies and economic liberalization and reforms and, in particular, to the budgetary consequences of the post-socialist transition. His studies have always combined the development of a rigorous conceptual framework with the practical implications derived from his keen observation of reality or from detailed empirical analysis.

A most salient feature of Vito Tanzi's scholarly research has been, however, his deep interest in the linkages between public finance and macroeconomic policies and the implications of these linkages for the proper design of fiscal policies. His numerous writings dealing with the interactions between inflation, the exchange rate, taxation, spending, and deficit financing have made a lasting contribution to our understanding of the channels through which budgetary developments affect, and in turn are affected by, macroeconomic upturns. Indeed, much of what today is conventional wisdom in this field derives from Tanzi's original thinking. His now classic 1977 and 1978 articles, 'Inflation, Lags in Collection, and the Real Value of Tax Revenue', and 'Inflation, Real Tax Revenue, and the Case for Inflationary Finance: Theory with an Application to Argentina',[1] provided the analytical and empirical base for what is now well known as the 'Tanzi effect', i.e. the erosive consequences of inflation on the real value of tax revenues. It would not be an exaggeration to affirm that the consideration of this effect (and the 'reverse Tanzi effect' as inflation recedes) has become standard practice in the design of stabilization strategies.

But Tanzi's contribution to the understanding of the close association between public finance and macroeconomic analysis has gone much further. From the many other examples of his innovative thinking in this area, we could mention his pioneering work in the area of interest rate determination. His views that taxation affects the manner in which inflationary expectations are transmitted to nominal interest rates, and that therefore the Fisher equation should be corrected accordingly, were published early in 1976[2] and empirically tested in 1980.[3] As happened with the 'Tanzi effect', this innovation rapidly became an accepted and generalized element of macroeconomic analysis.

Vito Tanzi is the author of numerous books and articles (a selective list of his contributions appears at the end of this volume). His work is invariably marked by creative and perceptive insights, by a judicious awareness of the manner in which people and institutions respond to economic incentives, and by a deep historical knowledge of economic developments. His standing in the public finance field is virtually unchallenged, and he has earned vast professional respect all over the world. But, probably more important, he is a thoughtful and supportive colleague, a wonderful friend, and an outstanding human being. For all these attributes he has gained the esteem, admiration, and affection of all those fortunate enough to know him. As Vito celebrates his 60th birthday, these volumes are a partial reflection of this affection.

NOTES

1 *IMF Staff Papers*, Vol. 24, No. 1, Washington DC 1977, and Vol. 25, No. 4, Washington, DC 1978.
2 'Inflation, Indexation and Interest Income Taxation', *Banca Nazionale del Lavoro Quarterly Review*, Rome, March 1976.
3 'Inflationary Expectations, Economic Activity, Taxes, and Interest Rates', *American Economic Review*, March 1980.

1

INTRODUCTION AND OVERVIEW

The role of fiscal policies in promoting economic reform

Mario I. Blejer and Teresa Ter-Minassian

The Festschrift for Vito Tanzi is composed of two volumes. While the companion volume to this book explores various aspects of the macro-economic impact of fiscal policies, this volume focuses on the role of these policies in the process of economic and structural reform. Both dimensions of fiscal policy have been emphasized in Vito Tanzi's scholarly, as well as applied, economic policy work. Indeed, the issue of structural reforms has probably predominated, especially in recent years, when, as Director of the Fiscal Affairs Department of the International Monetary Fund (IMF), Tanzi spearheaded the policy advice and technical assistance of the IMF to the implementation of reforms in the fiscal area in industrial, developing, and former socialist countries.

As with those in the companion volume, the chapters in this book span a quite broad range of topics, reflecting the varied interests and professional experiences of the authors, several of whom have been directly involved, as policymakers or policy advisers, in the reforms discussed in the chapters. This involvement is reflected in the policy relevance and practical orientation of the analyses.

A common theme that runs through the variety of topics addressed is the evolving role of the state in a process of economic reforms that is aimed at promoting efficient market mechanisms around the world. Over the last fifteen years or so, an increasing number of countries have moved – more or less speedily and decisively – towards liberalization, deregulation, privatization, and generally reducing state intervention in economic life, while opening the economy to external trade and factor movements. Frequently, these economic reforms have paralleled a process of political democratization, decentralization and, in many instances, more participatory and transparent governance. These trends have been most evident in the ongoing process of transition to market economies by formerly centrally planned countries in Eastern Europe, Asia, and the former Soviet Union, but 'the silent revolution'

– as it is sometimes referred to – has progressed to various degrees in other parts of the world as well.

Does this process of reduced intervention of the state in economic life mean a virtual end to the role of fiscal policy, or rather its redirection? What are the fiscal dimensions of privatization and deregulation? Can tax policies still be used to promote savings, investment, and foreign capital flows? Can they be used to promote environmental objectives? Increased reliance on market mechanisms involves substantial redistributive effects across income groups. What should be the role of expenditure and other fiscal policies in alleviating these effects on the more vulnerable groups of society?

These are some of the questions that the chapters in this book explore, drawing in particular on specific country experiences.

Part I explores the fiscal dimensions of privatization and deregulation. In Chapter 2 'The budgetary impact of privatization', David Newbery develops an analytical framework for assessing the budgetary effects of sales of public enterprises, comparing the cash proceeds of the sales, plus the present value of the future tax receipts from the privatized enterprises, with the loss of transferred profits from the former state-owned firms. An estimation of these magnitudes for a sample of privatized enterprises in the United Kingdom, Chile, Malaysia, and Mexico suggests that in several instances the loss of transferred profits broadly offsets the gain from the taxation of the privatized enterprise, leaving the net sale proceeds as the main benefit from privatization. The implication is that mass privatization through vouchers is unlikely to provide significant benefits to the budget, although it may be the only effective mechanism for quick privatization of large, nonprofitable firms, especially in transition economies characterized by a dearth of private domestic capital.

This latter point is supported by the analysis of 'Macroeconomic constraints and the modalities of privatization', by P. Heller, R. Hemming, and R. Chakrabarti. This chapter explores macroeconomic aspects of privatization. It notes that the macroeconomic effects of privatization depend both on how the private sector finances its acquisition of the public assets, and on how the government utilizes the proceeds of the assets sales (e.g. to redeem public debt outstanding, increase public spending, or reduce taxes). The chapter develops a comprehensive taxonomy of various models of assets sales and use of proceeds, and provides supporting empirical evidence of its conclusions, drawing on a sample of country experiences.

The chapter by A. Fernández-Ordoñez and C. Ocaña, 'A fiscal approach to liberalization policy', draws attention to the major political economy obstacles to liberalization and deregulation efforts. It notes that regulations which restrict competition are basically quasi-fiscal instruments, involving an implicit subsidy to the protected producers, matched by an equivalent implicit tax on the consumers of the relevant goods. The chapter notes that removal of these implicit taxes and subsidies tends to be made difficult by the fact that the benefits of liberalization are small and diffuse, while the costs are concentrated on a small (often vocal and powerful) group, and, for those affected, are likely to be substantial. The chapter points to the crucial role that broad dissemination of information on such costs and benefits can play in overcoming the opposition to liberalization policies. It advocates the preparation of an annual 'Budget of restrictions on competition', presenting estimates of the costs of such restrictions, based on the extra margins charged by firms sheltered from competition. The chapter reflects the experience of the authors, who are senior officials of the anti-monopoly authority in Spain.

Chapter 5 by K. Andersson discusses recent experiences with tax reform in the Scandinavian countries. These countries were characterized, from the 1960s to the early 1980s, by a relentless growth of the tax burden, necessitated in turn by a steady growth of public spending, especially in the social sphere. The chapter discusses the adverse side effects of the rising tax burden, especially the stimulus that it provided to debt accumulation by households and firms in an environment of financial deregulation, leading eventually to an asset price bubble and to speculative capital flows.

Tax reforms – involving, in particular, limitation of interest deductions for the income taxes, the replacement of the global income tax with schedular taxes, with reduced rate for income from capital, and a shift towards increased indirect taxation – were implemented in all Scandinavian countries in the late 1980s. The chapter analyzes their effects on households' savings, labor supply, enterprise borrowing, and asset prices. It concludes that the reforms reduced distortions and contributed to macroeconomic stabilization, in particular by moderating consumption. Their effects could have been, however, more significant if they had been more timely and supported by tighter financial policies.

Chapter 6 by D. Nellor discusses the fiscal and macroeconomic effects of environmental taxes. Going beyond the traditional Pigouvian analysis of such taxes as instruments to discourage pollution by raising its price to match the social cost of environmental damage, the chapter focusses on the case for using environmental taxes for revenue-raising purposes as well. In this perspective, it compares environmental taxes to alternative instruments such as a broad-based consumption tax (e.g. VAT). It concludes that the macroeconomic costs (in terms of output and employment), as well as the distributional costs of environmental taxes, are likely to exceed those for broader-based taxes. This suggests that the optimal rate of environmental taxation should continue to be set on purely Pigouvian criteria. Among various types of environmental taxes, the chapter finds that a tax on energy consumption is preferable on welfare grounds to a tax on energy production (such as the tax on BTU advocated by some in the United States).

Part IV focusses on the distributional impact of economic reform policies, and on options available to policymakers to alleviate the adverse effects of these policies on the more vulnerable groups of society.

In their chapter, S. Chand and P. Shome expand the financial programming framework, frequently utilized in the design of macroeconomic adjustment programs supported by the IMF resources, to incorporate the constraint that policies utilized should not lead to an increase in poverty beyond a certain level. Through this expanded framework they simulate the impact of different policy mixes – in response to an adverse external shock – on a poverty index, and conclude that a combination of real exchange rate depreciation and financial tightening has less adverse impact on poverty than a policy of financial restraint alone. They also trace the effects on poverty of delayed or disorderly adjustment, and conclude that, although these policies may well cushion the impact of an adverse external shock on the poor in the short run, they are unlikely to safeguard their living standards over the longer term.

The chapter by K.Y. Chu and S. Gupta explores in some detail, and with supporting empirical evidence from a variety of transition economies, the adverse effects, particularly in the initial phase, of price liberalization and restructuring of state enterprises, policies that are at the core of the transition process. They show that the specific distribution of these effects among different groups of society depends, in particular, on the specific mix and sequencing of the policies adopted, and on the demographic structure and initial living standards of the country in question. They then proceed to analyze, with the help of a stylized model, the effects of alternative remedial steps that can be taken to provide a safety net to the most vulnerable groups. They analyze, in particular, the differential costs and benefits of generalized price subsidies versus targeted cash benefits, alternative reforms of the pension, unemployment and other welfare benefits, and of the payroll taxes which provide the main source of financing of these benefits. From this analysis, a number of interesting policy conclusions are drawn. In particular, the chapter points to the substantial scope for budgetary savings and improved equity through targeting of social benefits, although it recognizes the practical difficulties of implementing effective targeting mechanisms.

The chapter by E. Ahmad and L. Halligan develops further a particular form of social safety net, aimed at mitigating the impact of price liberalization on the poor. Specifically, it examines the theoretical underpinnings and practical features of the provision at below market prices of marketable ration coupons for essential commodities, the prices of which are sharply increased or liberalized. This scheme, which involves the coexistence of quantity-constrained markets (with below-equilibrium, administered prices) with free markets for the same commodities, is seen as a feasible and cost-effective short-term mechanism of social protection in the early phases of transition.

The final part of the book discusses other selected aspects of the transition process. The chapter by A. Tait and N. Erbas analyzes the effects of a tax-based income policy instrument (the excess wage tax) which has been used extensively in transition economies to promote wage restraint during the period of price liberalization. These effects are analyzed under alternative models of enterprise behavior (profit maximization and maximization of workers' incomes). The authors find that in the first case, the tax can be effective in curbing wage growth but only at the cost of a decline in output. In the second case, the impact of the excess wage tax is found to depend on the degree of 'hardiness' of the enterprises' budget constraint. The chapter also finds that the revenue effects of this tax are generally small and that its distortionary consequences (in particular the labor market and the wage structure) can be significant.

Chapter 11, by P. Nagy, reviews the evolution of budgetary policies in the final period of the Soviet Union and the early phases of Russia's stabilization effort. It notes the difficult initial conditions facing the Russian authorities at the outset of stabilization: political chaos, lack of consensus on the reform strategy, uncertainty regarding the future of the ruble zone, collapsing output, and escalating price pressures. These conditions, and the continued reliance on the traditional methods of a command economy (e.g. exclusive focus on cash expenditures of the budget rather than on commitments, pervasive use of extrabudgetary funds, directed credits to enterprises), made fiscal and consequently macroeconomic adjustment very slow during the early 1990s. Nevertheless, important initial steps were taken in structural reforms, in particular price liberalization and privatization of small and medium enterprises, which were instrumental in laying the basis for an improved macroperformance. Although the jury is still out on the extent and durability of the latter, hopeful signs of recovery in economic activity and price deceleration, in a context of firmer financial policies and a reduction of public sector deficits, are beginning to emerge.

The chapter by D. Holland and J. Owens discusses the use and effectiveness of tax incentives in attracting foreign direct investments to transition economies. The chapter is based on the findings of consultations conducted by staff of the OECD with the authorities of a wide range of transition economies. Following a review of the objectives pursued by these countries in seeking to attract foreign investments, and of the nontax factors likely to affect such investments, the chapter presents a comprehensive analysis of both the general features of a tax system that can be expected to have a bearing on foreign investments, and of the specific forms that the tax incentives for foreign investment may take. The respective costs and benefits of alternative schemes are discussed in detail. On balance, the authors' judgment on the cost-effectiveness of tax incentives for foreign investment is rather negative. They stress that a transparent and agile regulatory framework for such investments, a tax system broadly patterned on international standards, with relatively low rates and broad bases (as well as other economic considerations relating to cost advantages, size of market, and availability of key infrastructures), is likely to prove more effective in attracting a stable flow of productive capital than tax incentives. Among the latter, tax holidays are found to be the least cost effective, and investment allowances and credits – offered at moderate rates with clear and transparent features, including defined 'sunset provisions' – are regarded as clearly preferable.

We hope that this brief overview of the varied contributions of this volume to the debate on the role of fiscal policies in economic reform will stimulate the readers' interest in a close examination of these contributions, as well as induce further academic and applied policy work on these issues.

Part I

FISCAL POLICIES, PRIVATIZATION, AND STRUCTURAL REFORMS

2

THE BUDGETARY IMPACT OF PRIVATISATION*

David M. Newbery

Vito Tanzi's extensive publications range over issues of taxation, debt, deficits and the importance of fiscal reform for nurturing sustainable economic growth. His recent studies of fiscal policy for transitional economies bring many of these themes together (Tanzi, 1992, 1993). In soviet-type economies public finance is almost indistinguishable from the organisation of production, accumulation and distribution, managed through the planning system and carried out by large enterprises under ministerial direction. The transition to a market economy raises sharp questions of the role of the state in promoting and undertaking capital accumulation. When assets are privatised, their profits no longer directly return to the exchequer, but nor does the responsibility to finance their investment. With the transfer of assets to private ownership, the state loses the tangible asset backing to its liabilities, of which an important part are future social security and pension obligations. Clearly, privatisation has important effects on the national balance sheet, and thus the national debt, as well as on current government revenue and expenditures. A study of the fiscal effects of privatisation therefore sits happily within the issues that continue to concern Vito Tanzi.

IMPORTANCE OF PUBLIC ENTERPRISES

Public enterprises are state-owned production units that market their output, and are thus directly involved in the market process, unlike the state provision of roads, defence, law and order, which are provided, not marketed. World Bank (1995) has collected data on public enterprises in developing countries for the period 1978–91, significantly updating the earlier study of Short (1984) that presented data for the late 1970s. Figure 2.1 shows the share of public enterprises (PEs) in GDP, averaged for the period 1986–91, and graphed against real income per head in 1988 measured using purchasing power parities, taken from Summers and Heston (1991).[1] The graph shows the weighted average shares for the world (actually a subset of the developing countries plotted), Latin America (LA, also a subset of the larger countries), Africa and Asia. There is no correlation between income and PE share, and

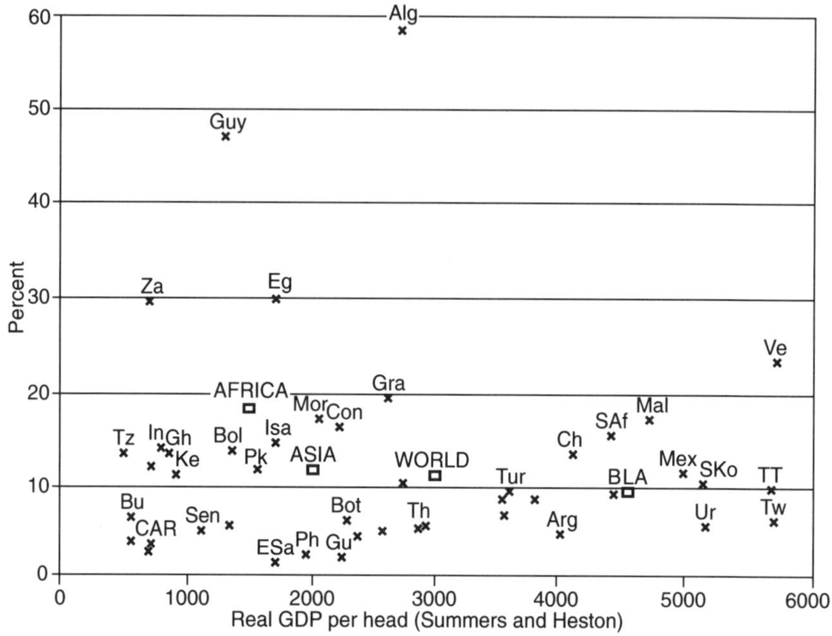

Figure 2.1 Share of public enterprise in GDP, 1986–91

the world average shown is almost identical to the average using Short's data, which also includes developed countries (Newbery, 1992, fig. 2). PEs have a larger share in Africa than Asia, which exceeds that in Latin America. Developed countries (at least in the 1970s) would be similar in share to Latin America on average.

Figure 2.2 shows that PEs have a relatively larger share of total investment than they do of GDP, and this is confirmed by Figure 2.3, which plots the ratio of the investment to output for the PE sector divided by the non-PE sector (defined as the residual). The average relative PE capital intensity is twice that of the non-PE sector, rather higher in Asia and lower in Africa. This is partly explained by the concentration of public ownership in the capital-intensive power, telecommunications, railways and extractive industries, but possibly also by the tendency of PEs to underprice their output in many countries. There is again no correlation between PE investment shares and income, in contrast to the weak negative correlation found in Short's data (Newbery, 1992, fig. 1 and fn. 2).

Short (1984) was able to study the sectoral allocation of public enterprises and found that developing countries are not so different from developed countries in the pattern of public ownership across sectors. There are good economic reasons to expect public ownership of enterprises in network

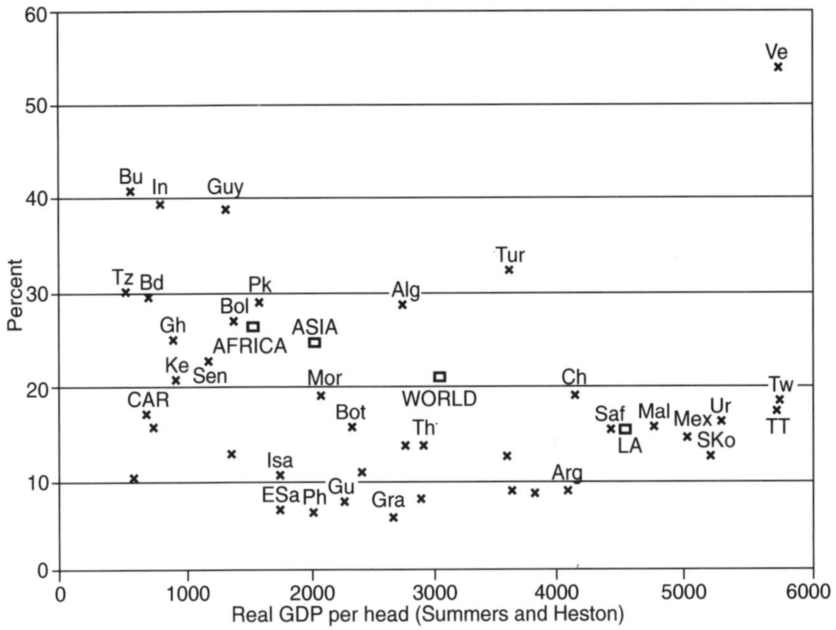

Figure 2.2 Public enterprise share in investment, 1986–91

industries such as post and telecommunications, rail, gas, electricity, and in other natural monopolies such as ports. Natural monopolies will inevitably be subject to price regulation if in the private sector, which makes the investor vulnerable to opportunistic behaviour by the regulator. In most cases capital, once sunk, cannot be removed, and the government may be tempted by domestic consumer interests to hold down prices to unremunerative levels. Fearing this, private investors will be reluctant to invest unless they are confident in the commitment of the regulatory process to fair rates of return. As a result in many developing countries, public ownership was the only viable option.

In developed countries this argument is less convincing as the United States has demonstrated the viability of regulating investor-owned network industries. Germany has investor-owned electricity utilities, and the UK has recently privatised telecoms, gas, water and electricity. Many European countries nationalised network industries after the Second World War, in some cases to overcome the impediments to coordination created by dispersed municipal ownership, in other cases for a mixture of ideological reasons or the belief that mobilising the high rates of investment after the devastation of the war required government finance.

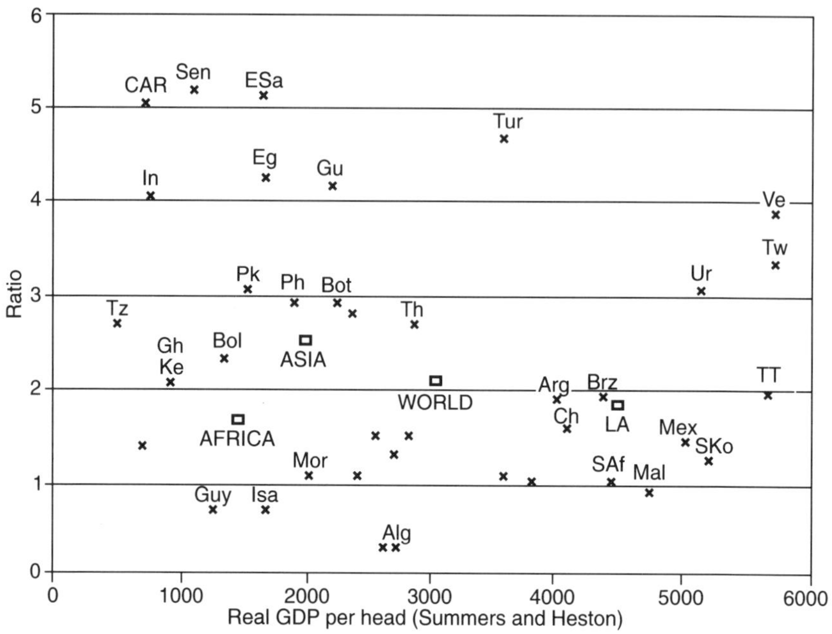

Figure 2.3 PE relative capital intensity: ratio of investment to output, 1986–91

In the European communist bloc countries before the transition of the late 1980s, most non-agricultural industry was in state ownership. Apart from the ideological reasons, one argument for state ownership was the apparent ability to raise the rate of investment and growth by using profits to finance investment, rather than distributing profits as dividends to be consumed. Another way to put this same argument is that a government concerned to redistribute income through the tax system is limited by the distortionary costs of taxation. In a private capitalist economy taxes on capital are likely to have high deadweight costs (the more so the more internationally mobile is capital). If the state owns the capital, then taxation is not necessary, as the profits can be returned to the owner, in the form of the central planning office, to be allocated to where they would be most productively employed – either as transfers to the current poor (notably, pensioners), or to future generations via investment.

This kind of social cost–benefit analysis is brought out very clearly in Little and Mirrlees (1974), and it may be that these objectives can be achieved under capitalism, providing consumption out of profits is sufficiently low, and the productivity of investment under private ownership is adequately high compared with the alternative of public ownership. One mechanism to encourage adequate investment and redistribution in a capitalist economy is compulsory saving for retirement in fully funded pension schemes. But it is important to realise that the case for public ownership cannot be simply based on a comparison of the current productivity of capital under public or private ownership, unless the distribution of income between individuals and over time is considered satisfactory, for public ownership offers the prospect of acquiring additional resources in the form of profits for such redistributive purposes. This can be measured by the social value of public funds, relative to the same funds held in private (capitalist) hands, which will normally be greater than unity.[2]

While this argument would have been considered quite persuasive in the 1970s, as handbooks of social cost–benefit analysis were being written for various international aid agencies such as the OECD (Little and Mirrlees, 1968), UNIDO (Dasgupta *et al.*, 1972), and the World Bank (Squire and van der Tak, 1975; Ray, 1984), the mood of the 1980s has changed, with growing disillusionment by welfare economists that governments pursue the objectives postulated by these rather utopian visions of the social good. The evidence continues to accumulate that governments frequently fail to invest adequately, that they often have a lower rate of savings out of public profits than private corporations, and that they underprice the output of public corporations leading to low rates of return, and hence lower rates of reinvestment and a higher dependency on external borrowing than would be the case for private corporations.

The electricity industry provides a good example, as it accounted for nearly one-quarter of total public investment in a sample of middle-income countries in the 1980s (World Bank, 1994a, figs. 1.1, 2) – an annual power sector investment of about \$80 billion in developing countries (see Figure 2.5 below).

Performance was frequently unimpressive, particularly in the high-inflation period after the oil shocks of the 1970s. Prices were normally below long-run marginal cost, often despite excess demand, so that investment could not be adequately financed out of profits, as in many developed countries. Figure 2.4 shows that average real power tariffs declined to below 4 US cents/kW h (1986 constant \$) for a sample of 60 World Bank countries in 1989, while the rate of return on revalued net fixed assets also declined to below 4 per cent for a sample of 360 actual financial rates of return recorded for 57 World Bank countries (World Bank, 1993), well below the 10 per cent rate of return normally taken as the test discount rate by international agencies. Only 60 per cent of power sector costs were covered by revenue (Besant-Jones, 1993), while self-financing ratios fell to only 12 per cent of investment requirements in 1991 (World Bank, 1993, p. 12).[3] Newbery (1992) noted similar problems for Asian countries. Figure 2.5 shows the magnitude of the problem. Underpricing electricity resulted in a heavy fiscal burden estimated at \$90 billion annually or about 7 per cent of total government revenues in developing countries, larger than annual power investment requirements of

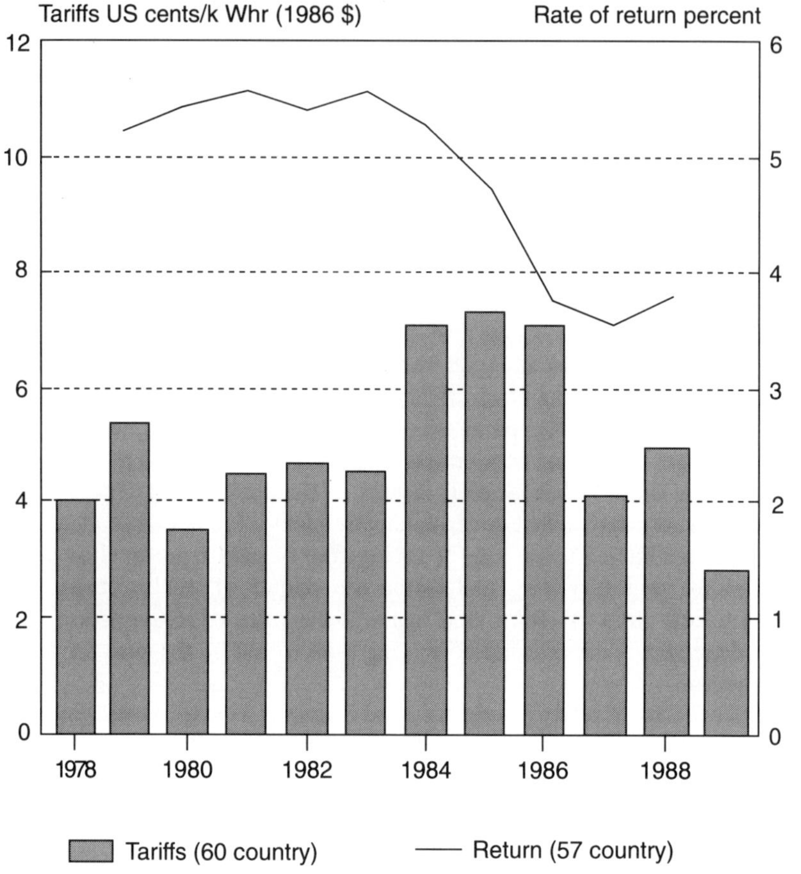

Figure 2.4 Tariffs and returns of ESIs in World Bank countries (for 60 and 57 countries)
Source: World Bank (1993)

about $80 billion, while technical inefficiencies caused true economic losses of nearly $30 billion annually (World Bank, 1994a, table 6.7).

We can use World Bank (1995) data to investigate further the contributions of PEs to the government budget, which gives the average public enterprise savings–investment gap in 46 developing countries from 1978 to 1991 (though there are gaps in many of the data series). The savings–investment gap, or balance, is defined as the difference between the current surplus (revenues excluding transfers *less* costs excluding dividends) and gross investment (including stock changes). A negative number implies that the PEs needed to receive net external transfers to finance investment. For the weighted average of these countries, the balance was –1.3 per cent of GDP

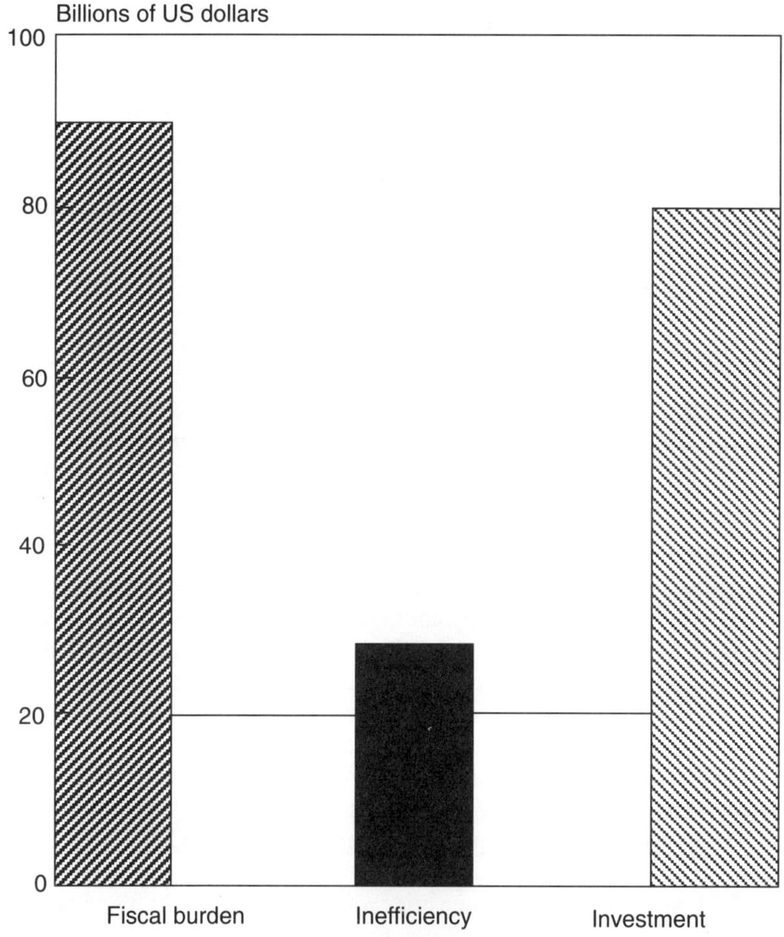

Figure 2.5 Inefficiencies in electricity in developing countries
Source: World Development Report (1994, fig 5)

for the whole period, but improving from –2.3 per cent to zero. The improvement came partly from reduced investment and partly from increased savings due to raising output prices. He found that the balance moved closely with fiscal and current account deficits, and that the PE deficit was highly correlated with each.

Tables 2.1 and 2.2 present data for the larger countries in the sample for which a reasonably long time series of data were available. Table 2.1 gives the growth rates of GDP and PEs over the decade[4] showing a correlation between the two, as would be expected. The next three columns give estimates of the capital–output ratio. The period ICOR or incremental (gross) capital

Table 2.1 Growth and profit measures of PEs

Country	*GDP growth rate (% p.a.) 80–90*	*PE growth rate (% p.a.) 80–90*	*Period ICOR 79–91*	*Capital–output Av (ratios) 79–91*	*Capital–output Av (ratios) 85–91*	*av. RoR (% p.a.)*	*100 ICOR (% p.a.)*
Argentina	–0.4	–4.0	–10.1	9.7	9.5	–5.6	–9.9
Brazil (c)	2.2	6.2	11.6	11.2	7.7	3.0	0.6
Chile	3.2	2.2	10.0	2.7	2.6	32.1	10.0
Colombia	3.4	5.2	8.0	3.9	4.4	8.8	12.6
Mexico (e)	1.6	2.2	12.4	3.8	4.3	13.5	8.1
Venezuela	1.0	2.0	20.1	6.0	5.1	17.2	5.0
Bangladesh (e)	3.7	7.9	11.8	5.4	6.4	2.8	8.5
India (e)	5.6	9.2	7.4	4.9	4.9	8.7	13.6
Indonesia (e)	5.5	2.4	9.4	3.3	3.1	3.2	10.7
Turkey (e)	4.9	10.1	9.6	1.0	0.8	33.6	10.4
Average (unwted)	3.1	4.3	9.0	5.1	4.9	11.7	7.7

Notes and *source*: See Table 2.2

output ratio is computed as the average ratio of the share of investment in PE output to the average rate of growth of PE output. An estimate of the capital stock was constructed using the perpetual inventory method of adding successive gross investments to an assumed initial capital stock and depreciating the resulting capital at 4 per cent per annum. The initial capital stock was chosen to produce a smoothly varying capital–output ratio over time, and does not have too much influence on the average for the period 1985–91. The last two columns give measures of gross profitability – the average RoR is the gross rate of return, defined as gross profits divided by gross capital stock, and the resulting annual rates were averaged over the period. The inverse of the ICOR expressed as a percentage is a rather cruder measure of returns to additional gross investment. Table 2.1 reveals high capital intensities and low rates of profit for most of these countries, consistent with either low productivity of public enterprises and/or underpricing of the output.

Table 2.2 compares the profit, investment, and the savings–investment gap to the output (i.e. value added) of the PEs. The first three columns give gross profits as a share of value added, in most cases high consistent with the high capital intensity of these PEs. What is perhaps more surprising is the high share of gross investment to value added, which, because it exceeds the share of profits in most cases, implies the need for external financing shown in the largely negative balances. The unweighted averages are heavily influenced by Venezuela, which is probably heavily influenced by the oil sector. Table 2.2 illustrates the finding that profits have risen and investment has fallen to give a declining net burden on the budget and the table therefore demonstrates both the possibility of improvement and the remarkably poor performance of these enterprises in the early subperiod. What is particularly surprising is the high rate of investment, with low achieved rates of growth, with, if anything,

Table 2.2 Investment and balances of PEs (percentages)

Country	*Profit/value added*			*Investment/VA*			*Balance/VA*			*Balance/ GDP*
	78–85	*86–91*	*78–91*	*78–85*	*86–91*	*78–91*	*78–85*	*86–91*	*78–91*	*78–91*
Argentina	–44	–21	–34	55	30	40	–99	–52	–93	–4.0
Brazil (c)	–4	57	22	117	39	72	–121	19	–32	–0.8
Chile	70	92	77	22	23	23	48	67	59	8.7
Columbia	24	51	36	42	37	42	–23	14	6	0.1
Mexico (e)	48	48	48	55	25	27	17	23	21	2.6
Venezuela	80	80	80	42	41	40	38	39	39	9.2
Bangladesh (e)	7	19	13	53	120	93	–46	–101	–76	–2.2
India (e)	44	29	37	79	61	68	–35	–19	–19	–2.4
Indonesia (e)	6	18	10	26	16	22	–20	2	–11	–2.0
Turkey (e)	24	17	21	142	81	97	–118	–64	–73	–5.4
Average (unwted)	25.5	39.0	31.0	63.3	47.2	52.4	–36.9	–7.2	–19.1	0.4

Notes: Shares in value added (VA) are computed from real GDP on an annual basis from shares of PE categories in GDP
ICOR is average share of investment in PE output divided by rate of growth of PE output
Capital output ratio is computed yearly from an estimate of PE capital stock
PE capital stock is estimated from a permanent inventory (adding successive gross investment) assuming 4% depreciation and sensible initial *K/Y*
Gross profit is balance plus investment
RoR is gross rate of return on capital stock as a percentage from gross profit/capital stock
Balance is savings less investment
(c) Financial sector PEs also included
(e) See country notes in Galal (1994); major points to note:
Mexico – directly controlled NFPEs only; Bangladesh 85–91 data for 10 large PEs. 81–84 for five large PEs only
India – NFPEs owned by central, state and local governments; Turkey includes PEs under privatisation schemes
Source: World Bank (1995); IMF database for GDP

a slightly negative relation between these two.

The evidence from at least this sample of developing countries is that far from contributing to improved economic performance, public investment in PEs appears to earn a low net rate of return, and to require net transfers to these enterprises, rather than generating net contributions to the government. We should not expect that the rate of return to investment in developing countries lies below the rate of growth of output, and so it should be possible for investment to more than finance itself out of retained profits and, indeed, to provide dividends to its owner, the state. At least in the period 1978–85 this was generally not the case, and despite heavy economic pressures to improve the performance of PEs, even the second subperiod suggest a precarious balance between savings and investment, with little net contribution to the budget.

A large part of the fiscal case for privatisation in developing countries is the belief that sustaining improvements in performance, pricing and finance of these enterprises in the public sector will be difficult and perhaps impossible, and that they should therefore be privatised to reduce the fiscal and current account burden of the enterprises on the economy. This claim is explored in more detail below.

PUBLIC ENTERPRISE PERFORMANCE IN DEVELOPED COUNTRIES

If the performance of PEs in developing countries has been unimpressive and burdensome, what has been the case in developed market economies? It would be too large an undertaking to evaluate systematically the experience even in Western Europe, and instead I shall concentrate on the UK. The Conservative government under Mrs Thatcher argued that the public sector was inefficient and should be privatised, and it may be that other countries have had a more successful public sector. Nevertheless, the UK is an obvious choice given the importance of privatisation and the potentially large impact this had on the wealth and income generating potential of the public sector.

Figure 2.6 presents data for public and private corporations (the latter restricted to industrial and commercial corporations) for their surplus and net rates of profit. The surplus is defined as the gross trading surplus plus rent excluding subsidies and before taxes *less* gross investment, and shown as a percentage of value added. It is a measure of the surplus available to the economy after investment. The net rate of return is computed as the surplus net of depreciation and excluding subsidies, before taxes, as a percentage of the net capital stock. Figure 2.6 shows that private corporations earn a net return of about 15 per cent, and generate a surplus of a similar amount, whilst public corporations essentially make a zero net rate of return and impose large deficits on the economy, though this improved after 1977 (and has been adversely affected by the recession from 1989–92, or possibly from

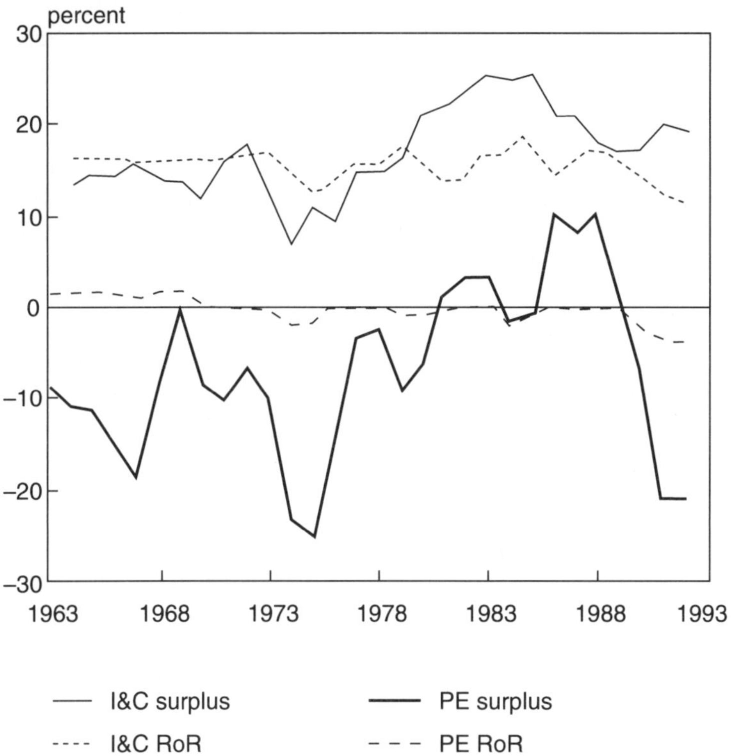

Figure 2.6 UK public and industrial/commercial companies, net surpluses and rates of profit
Source: Blue Book (1993)
Notes: Surplus = gross profit–investment. RoR is net profit before tax/net capital

transferring the family silver to the private sector). It would seem that UK PEs are not so different from those in developing countries.

THE EXTENT OF PRIVATISATION

World Bank (1995) was particularly concerned to measure the extent of divestiture of public enterprises in developing countries, and whether privatisation had diminished their importance in recent years. Citing evidence from Sader (1993), he gives the estimated total number of privatisation transactions worldwide between 1988 and 1992 as 1100, and the revenue generated from divestiture as $185 billion. Excluding Eastern Europe, developing countries realised $52 billion from 498 transactions in the period 1988–92, mostly concentrated in a small number of countries (Chile, Jamaica, Brazil, Mexico, Guinea, Côte d'Ivoire, Togo and Niger). The larger fraction of worldwide revenue came from developed countries, dominated by the UK (62 entities for $48 billion), followed by Canada ($5.7 billion), Italy ($6.6 billion), New Zealand ($6.3 billion) and Australia ($6.2 billion).

Privatisation in Central and Eastern Europe has accelerated since 1990. The Treuhandanstalt, charged with privatising enterprises in the former East Germany, completed its task at the end of 1994 with the transfer of some 13,000 PEs. The Czech Republic has undertaken mass privatisation of a significant fraction of its state-owned enterprises, though privatisation is moving more slowly in Hungary and Poland. Russia has nominally transferred a large fraction of state assets to private ownership, usually to former managers and workers of the enterprises, with some shareholding involvement of the population through mass privatisation. The economic logic of such mass privatisation is fundamentally different from privatisation in market economies, where normally the state is concerned to sell the assets at a high fraction of their market value, though one might claim that in both cases the objective was to maximise the social value of the assets. Newbery (1991) argued that more attention should be paid to maintaining the net worth of the public sector, bearing in mind the large remaining pension liabilities of the state, which could be thought of as backed by the assets to be privatised. Tanzi (1993) notes the fiscal problems associated with the transition to a market economy.

The leading example of a privatising market economy is the UK, and Figures 2.7–2.10 demonstrate how extensive that process has been. Figure 2.7 gives the share of the public and private sectors in GDP since 1963 (with the same definitions as in Figure 2.6), showing that PEs (shown as PCs using UK terminology in the figures) have fallen from just below 20 per cent of the total corporate sector to about 5 per cent in the last decade. Figure 2.8 shows a similar decline in investment shares, while Figure 2.9 shows that PEs have declined from about 40 per cent of net capital stock to about 10 per cent.

Figure 2.10 shows the impact of this on the net worth of the public sector, updating work by Hills (1989). The net worth of each sector is defined as the value of tangible assets, as far as possible measured at market prices, *plus* the value of financial assets, *less* the value of financial liabilities.[5] The public sector as a whole had negative net worth until 1964, but thereafter it increased steadily until 1975, the first year for which the CSO started producing annual estimates. If the PEs to be privatised had been sold at their market value, and had the proceeds been used to decrease the national debt, then the net worth of the public sector should not have been adversely affected. As it is, PEs were sold at a discount of about 25 per cent, and council houses sold to tenants were also discounted (though were already shown in the accounts as having a below-market value as they lacked vacant possession).

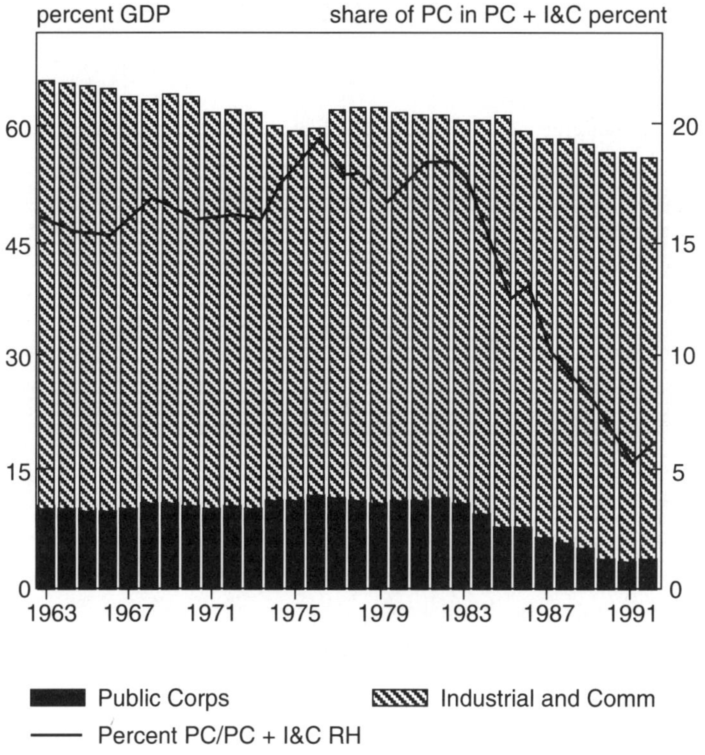

Figure 2.7 Shares in GDP at current factor cost, UK public and private sectors

MEASURING THE IMPACT OF PRIVATISATION ON THE BUDGET

Jones *et al.* (1990) set out a cost–benefit methodology for evaluating privatisation proposals, and implement this for 12 case studies in Galal *et al.* (1994). As with all cost–benefit analyses, one first measures the quantitative impact on the world with the project (privatising a PE) relative to the counterfactual of the world without the project (the PE remaining in public ownership), and then values the impact, breaking this down into its component parts:

$$\Delta W = \Delta S + \Delta \pi + \Delta G + \Delta L + \Delta C, \qquad (2.1)$$

where ΔW is the present value (PV) of the change in welfare, ΔS is the PV of the change in consumer surplus, $\Delta \pi$ is the PV of the change in private net profits of the new owners, ΔG is the change in government net receipts, ΔL

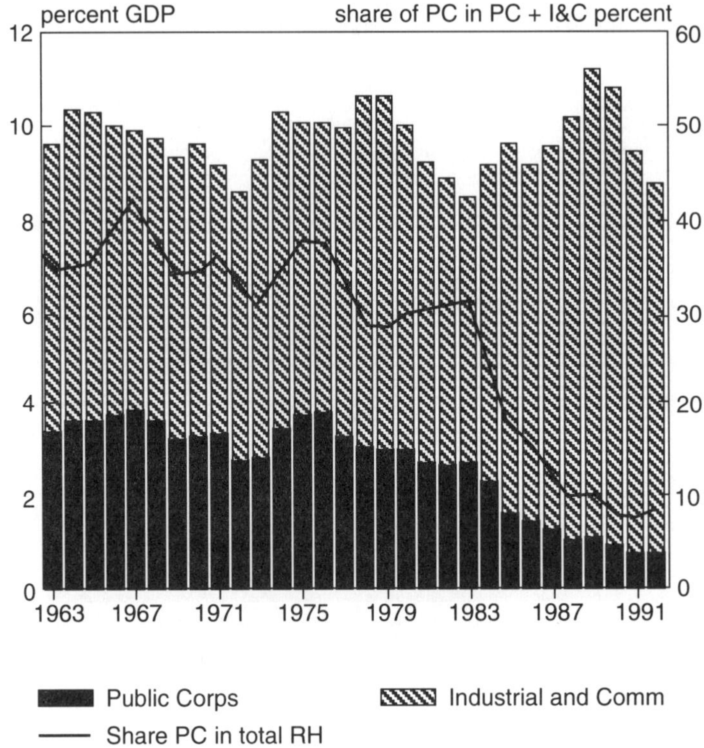

Figure 2.8 Gross domestic capital formation, UK public and private sectors
Source: Blue Book (1993)

is the change in the PV of net benefits to workers (i.e. their extra surplus), and ΔC is the change in the PV of competitors' net benefits.

For present purposes, we are concerned with the narrower question of the impact on the budget, ΔG, rather than the impact on total social welfare, ΔW, and the two can move in different directions. The PV of future returns to the budget under public ownership needs to be forecast under the counterfactual, and can be illustrated for a PE with net capital at date t of K_t, net profit R_t (defined as revenues less costs and less depreciation, but before taxes and subsidies), net investment I_t, and net surplus $S_t = R_t - I_t$. Then if

$$R_t = rK_t, \quad I_t = sR_t, \quad dK/dt = I, \tag{2.2}$$

revenues and the surplus transferred to the budget will grow at rate $g = sr$ determined by the rate of return and the rate of reinvestment, giving the current PV of future budget receipts of V_0, discounting at the public sector discount rate i:

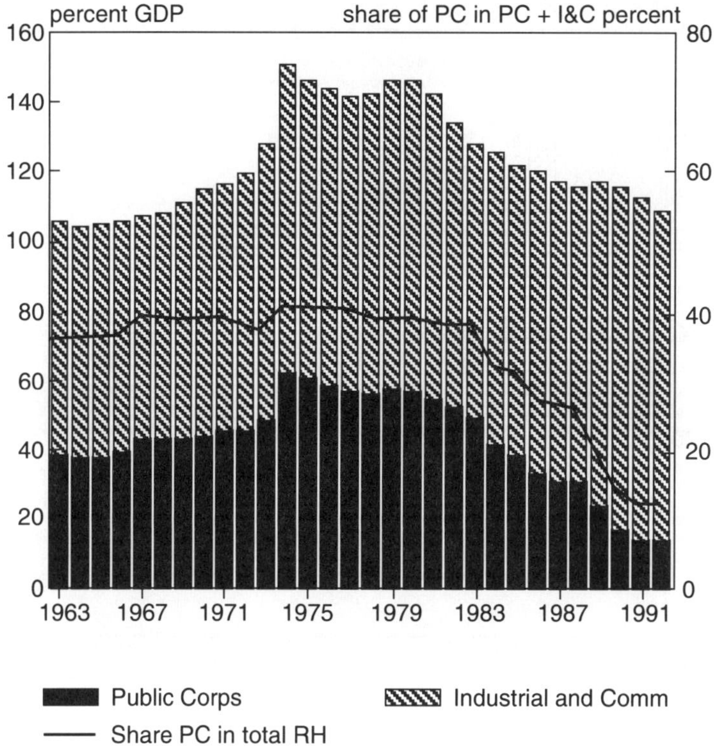

Figure 2.9 UK public and private net capital stock, fixed assets share of GDP
Source: Blue Book (1993)

$$S_t = (1-s)\, rK_0 e^{gt}, \quad V_0/K_0 = (1-s)\, r/(i - rs). \tag{2.3}$$

Suppose that the PE is sold at a price (net of selling costs) of θK_0, and the receipts are then used to reduce the national debt, on which the real rate of interest paid is b. The private sector then succeeds in earning a net rate of return of ρ (net of depreciation, before tax), and pays taxes on these net returns at rate τ. If the rate of net reinvestment is σ out of these net returns (not necessarily in the same enterprise), and if reinvestment earns the same returns and pay the same taxes,[6] then the PV of the impact on the budget is

$$\frac{\Delta G}{K_0} = \frac{b\theta}{i} + \frac{\tau\rho}{i - \rho\sigma} - \frac{(1-s)\, r}{i - rs}. \tag{2.4}$$

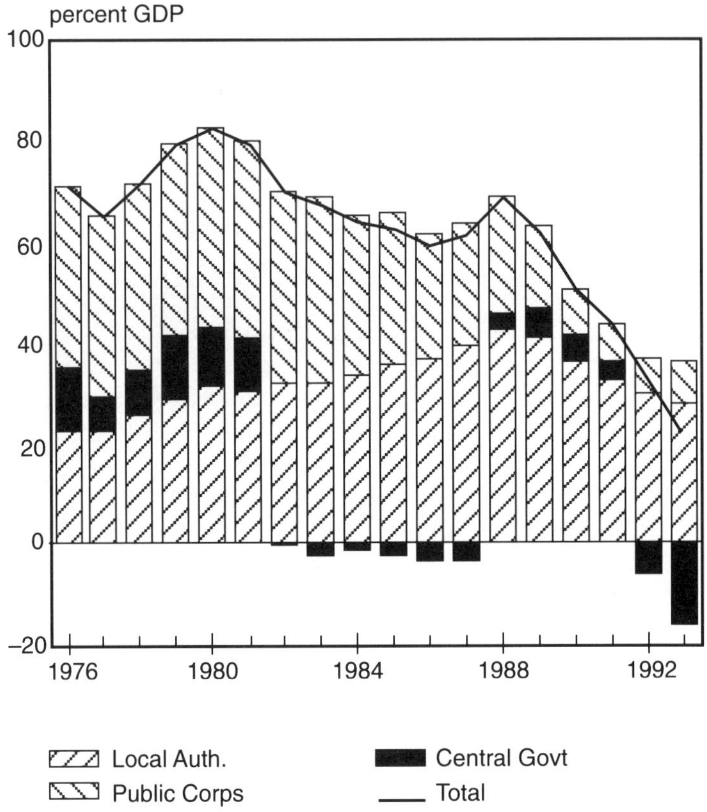

Figure 2.10 Net worth of the public sector as percentage of GDP
Source: Blue Book (1994)
Note Deflated by GDP deflator

The first term on the right-hand side is the value of the net sales proceeds. The second term is the PV of the extra tax receipts resulting from privatisation, and the third term is the loss in quasi-rents or net transfers to the budget from continued public ownership. Galal *et al.* (1994) break down the impact on the government sector into the same components, though their estimates are based on detailed modelling of the enterprise in question without assuming steady growth and constant parameters as in this shorthand expression. Nevertheless, equation (2.4) indicates that the budgetary impact is more likely to be positive the higher are τ, ρ and σ relative to $(1 - s)$, r and s, and the higher is θ (i.e. the closer the sales value approaches the market value of the enterprise).

Most of the elements in (2.4) can be estimated from past history and/or deduced from the counterfactual. One of the more problematic elements is the tax rate, τ, which is the *extra* tax revenue resulting from the transfer of the assets to the private sector. They include all taxes on the profit income above those that would have been paid on the national debt that was sold to raise the funds to acquire the asset (an amount higher than θK_0 by the selling costs). It should *exclude* (most of the) indirect taxes paid on the sales of the enterprise. Even if sales increase, perhaps because of a fall in relative prices, consumers will switch from buying other (taxed) goods, and it is only the increase in total tax revenue that should count. This might be approached by estimating the increase in GDP caused by privatisation (the extra productivity of inputs, not any price changes), and then estimating the net tax revenue associated with this increase, adjusting for the tax revenue already counted from the extra profit income. To the extent that real consumer expenditure increases (and this will include some increased wage income), tax paid will rise, though so will some government expenditures (e.g. on roads, and as a result of a general increase in the real income and hence cost of public sector employees). To a large extent, the public sector acts as an insurance system, transferring incomes from people when rich to people when poor, and a substantial part of this would be effectively via taxes to finance future pensions. Thus increased tax revenue arising from higher GDP might be entirely transferred as increased expenditure to the same kind of people when they retire, with no increase in uncommitted revenue.

It is thus hard to know what the net fiscal gain from increased GDP would be, and even whether it would be positive. In the short run, an above-trend increase in GDP would normally be associated with rising revenues relative to expenditures, and thus to either a fall in the budget deficit or a rise in the surplus. Thereafter, either taxes would be cut, or, more probably, expenditure increased. Certainly there seems no tendency for the share of government to fall with rising real GDP per head. One could certainly defend the view that there was zero net indirect fiscal gain (i.e. excluding the extra profits tax revenue) from any increased productivity gain caused by privatisation.

The methodology illustrated in the case studies reported in Galal *et al.* (1994) follows the approach outlined above, without counting either the indirect taxes on extra sales or any estimated tax revenue from increments to GDP. Consider the case of the privatisation of BT (British Telecom) in 1984. Using a (rather high) public discount rate of 9 per cent real, the authors estimate that privatisation increased world welfare (ΔW) by £10 billion at 1985 prices, of which the UK received £9 billion, which was divided between the government (ΔG = £2.2 billion), domestic shareholders ($\Delta \pi_d$ = £2.7 billion), competitors (ΔC = –£0.1 billion), and consumers (ΔS = £4.2 billion). These large numbers can be put into perspective by noting that the total is less than 2 per cent of the PV of welfare generated by BT, and 12 per cent of annual sales revenue in 1983.

The fiscal impact of £2.2 billion was made up of extra taxes of £2 billion, net sales revenues of £3.6 billion, and reduced quasi-rents (i.e. transfers to the government) of –£3.4 billion The gain in productivity associated with privatisation derives primarily from enhanced labour productivity (£6.9 billion, a considerable part of which is passed on to consumers as lower prices). Much of this improvement in real GDP accrues as higher profits and is thus already counted in the fiscal gain. Lower public sector discount rates would raise the PV of the welfare gain, but would reduce the PV of the fiscal gain, as the loss in future quasi-rents is larger than the extra tax revenues, and both increase relative to the sales receipts as the discount rate falls. The chosen discount rate of 9 per cent real is higher than the current (and then prevailing) public sector discount rate of 6 per cent real. Galal *et al.* (1994) summarise by noting that the increased social profit (the increased social welfare less the increased consumer surplus) was split 40:60 between the public and private sectors.

The other two UK case studies presented in Galal *et al.* (1994) are British Airways and National Freight. The welfare gains for British Airways (BA) are (at 1987 prices), using the notation of equation (2.1) are:

ΔW = £680 million, of which the UK received £550 million
ΔG = £315 million
$\Delta \pi_d$ = £646 million, $\Delta \pi_f$ = £126 million (subscripts d, f for domestic, foreign)
ΔC = –£84 million
ΔS = –£323 million

Again, the relative sizes are small, and less than 2 per cent of BA's 1987 revenue. The benefits derive from cost cutting, and the synergies of merging with BCal, though the resulting increase in market power had adverse effects on consumers. Again, increased profitability led to more taxes (PV = £346 million), the loss of quasi-rents from the change of ownership of –£874 million, compensated by net sales proceeds of £843 million. Again, a lower public discount rate would reduce the budget gain, for the same reasons as with BT.

The final UK example, National Freight, had an adverse budget impact:

ΔW = £225 million, all domestic (at £1982), 4 per cent of the PV of 1982 revenues
ΔG = –£11 million
$\Delta \pi$ = £41 million
ΔL = £194 million (as shareholders)
$\Delta C = 0 = \Delta S$

The budgetary impact was made up of sales receipts of £53 million, forgone quasi-rents of –£112 million, and extra tax revenue of £48 million, so lower public discount rates would have made the budgetary impact more adverse.

The adverse budgetary impact was primarily caused by underpricing the sale of assets, and the welfare gain resulted from improved productivity and associated increases in investment, both attributable to privatisation.

In terms of equation (2.4), these evaluations effectively take $b = i = 9$ per cent, and derive most of their beneficial impacts from a slightly higher private sector productivity ($\rho > r$) and associated rate of growth of profits. Much then turns on the difference between the tax rate τ and the dividends forgone, with the latter higher in the three UK cases than the former. Selling the assets for a good fraction of the market value was the primary way of benefiting the budget, and when this failed to occur, as with National Freight, the budget suffered.

The results of these and the other case studies are presented in Table 2.3, which shows that the budgetary impacts were adverse for two (both electricity companies) of the three Chilean divestitures. In both cases the loss in budgetary quasi-rents exceeded the modest tax gains and the value of the sales proceeds, and would have been more costly still at lower discount rates. In the case of the telephone company, CTC, the loss in quasi-rents was less than the sale proceeds, and tax revenue also increased. The main sources of welfare gain varied by company, but demand and investment changes were the largest

Table 2.3 Fiscal impact and welfare gains from privatisation (percentage of annual sales in predivestiture year)

Country/enterprise	*Government*	*Other domestic*	*Foreign*	*Total*
United Kingdom				
British Telecom	2.7	8.1	1.2	12.0
British Airways	0.9	1.2	–0.1	1.6
National Freight	–0.2	4.5	0.0	4.3
Chile				
CHILGENER	–1.4	2.1	1.4	2.1
ENERSIS	–1.6	6.2	0.6	5.2
CTC	8.0	137.0	10.0	155.0
Malaysia				
Malaysian Airline Systems	5.2	–0.6	17.4	22.1
Kelang Container Terminal	37.6	12.8	3.0	53.4
Sports Toto Malaysia	13.6	–2.7	0.0	10.9
Mexico				
Teléfonos de México	13.3	–6.6	43.0	49.5
Aeroméxico	62.3	9.4	–4.4	48.5
Mexicana de Aviación	3.5	–5.9	–4.6	–7.0

Source: Galal *et al.* (1994, Table 23.1, p. 528)

sources, with modest productivity gains in CHILGENER and rather larger in CTC.

In Malaysia, the partial financial divestiture of the airline generated a sales value more than twice the size of the PV of forgone quasi-rents, and extra taxes had an even greater value. The improved decision making resulting from a larger share of private shareholders led to considerable gains, mostly transferred to foreign shareholders and customers. In the case of the container terminal, the sales price was relatively small compared with the additional tax revenue, whose PV exceeded that of forgone quasi-rents (and which would thus be more attractive at lower discount rates). Domestic shareholders gained at the expense of competitors, as, to a lesser extent did foreign shareholders and customers relative to foreign competitors, all as a result of better management.

The final country chosen for case studies was Mexico, where again all three divestitures produced a beneficial impact on the budget, even though one produced a negative overall gain, and two had negative impacts on the rest of the domestic sector. In the case of the telephone company, the loss in quasi-rents was only slightly larger than the additional tax revenue, leaving the net sales proceeds as a beneficial budgetary impact (almost exactly the same value as the loss in quasi-rents). The main gains were derived from moving prices up to welfare-improving efficient levels, adversely affecting consumers and benefiting foreign shareholders, though labour productivity also grew rapidly.

Aeroméxico is an interesting case with a zero sales price as the government placed the firm into bankruptcy to quell militant unions and terminate consistent losses. The main budgetary gains came from improved quasi-rents and additional tax revenue, both of which would increase as the discount rate falls. The rise in prices mainly impacted on foreign consumers but both foreign and domestic shareholders gained. By contrast, selling Mexicana de Aviación as an attractive going concern but retaining a large shareholding stake was timely, in that the subsequent losses were transferred to private shareholders. The losses resulted from an excessively ambitious investment programme which failed to produce additional profit.

LESSONS FROM THE CASE STUDIES

In a majority of cases, the loss of profits from ownership was only partially compensated by the increased tax revenues on the privatised enterprise, and the overall impact on the budget then depended sensitively on the sales receipts from privatisation. The implication is that mass privatisations in Eastern Europe are almost certain to affect the budget adversely. In some cases, the improvement in performance is sufficient to offset the loss in profits, though this happened in the case study examples less frequently than might have been expected.

One of the problems of fiscal accounting is that the public sector rarely produces a complete balance sheet showing liabilities associated with pension obligations. Hills (1989) discusses the issues involved and produces an assessment for the UK to demonstrate the potentially large effect this has. His estimates for 1987 show that the net worth of the public sector moves from 75 per cent of GDP (see Figure 2.10 above) to –70 per cent of GDP if pension liabilities already accrued are included, together with deferred corporation tax liabilities and future oil revenues. Moving from narrower to wider definitions of the public sector balance sheet involves (for 1987) a move from financial liabilities (conventional national debt) of 32 per cent of GDP (i.e. apparent net worth of –32 per cent), to +75 per cent if tangible public sector assets are included, to the final figure of –70 per cent with these additional liabilities. Different definitions thus dramatically alter the apparent solvency of the public sector.

World Bank (1994b) argues that old-age security systems are in trouble worldwide, and the present public provision of pensions is unsustainable, in that the net worth of the public sector is inadequate to provide for future pensions without implausibly high and costly tax rates on workers. Chile provides an interesting example of how the receipts from privatisation helped finance the transition to a funded social security system (World Bank, 1994b, Box 8.5, p. 267). The UK, in contrast, appears not to have used privatisation receipts to improve the net worth of the public sector, even on the narrow definition excluding pension liabilities shown in Figure 2.10. Most East European countries face an even more serious pension funding problem (World Bank, 1994b, Box 4.7, pp. 142–3) and are either unwilling or unable to realise significant receipts for the sale of PEs that might be used to fund the pension liabilities. In some countries, the state has transferred a (usually small) fraction of the shares in PEs to the social security fund (10 per cent in the case of Hungary) but one certainly could argue for a considerably larger transfer of such shares (Newbery, 1991).

Looking at the case studies, the PEs that seem to generate the most favourable budgetary impact are mismanaged commercial operations that are sold at a competitive price to new owners well placed to realise the potential market value. Selling public utilities seems less likely to generate a beneficial impact on the budget, although in some countries the fiscal deficits caused by such utilities and the improbability of reforming these enterprises may make divestiture attractive.

The main problem in improving the budgetary position appears to arise from an accounting confusion between flows and stocks, that is between income and balances, a failure to account adequately for all the liabilities of the public sector, and the resulting temptation to use privatisation receipts to fund current expenditures. In such cases, even successful privatisations may have only a temporary effect on the budgetary position of the government.

NOTES

*Support from the British Economic and Social Research Council under the project R000 23 3766 *The Impact of Electricity Privatisation on the British Energy Markets* is gratefully acknowledged. I am indebted to Ahmad Galal for preliminary access to his statistical material, without implicating him in the use to which I have put it.

1 Detailed notes on the sources of and qualifications for the data are to be found in World Bank (1995).
2 It is important to specify the numeraire carefully when discussing distributionally sensitive shadow prices. Optimal tax theory, as exemplified by Atkinson and Stiglitz (1980) or Diamond and Mirrlees (1971), often takes as a convenient numeraire the social value of $1 distributed equally as a lump-sum (after-tax) transfer to the entire population. It then follows that the social value of government funds is normally equal to unity, since it is usually open to the government either to increase or reduce such lump-sum transfers. When comparing the social value of government funds available for investment or redistribution, compared with private profits also available for such purposes, one must take account of the higher average wealth of profit recipients compared with the whole population, leading to a lower social value of their income. See e.g. Little and Mirrlees (1974).
3 The power sector would be able to finance all investment at an unchanged gearing ratio if the financial rate of return exceeded the rate of growth of capacity. The average annual rate of growth of power was about 7 per cent p.a. for middle-income countries between 1960 and 1990, compared with an average *economic* (but not financial) rate of return on World Bank projects of 11 per cent (World Bank, 1994a, fig. 3 and table 1.2). Had the financial rate of return been raised to the economic rate of return, financing should not have been a problem.
4 The initial and terminal dates were taken as 3-year moving averages.
5 The methodology is set out in *Economic Trends*, CSO, May 1987, 92–119.
6 It may be that initially, the private enterprise earns a different return on the apparent value of the transferred capital than the market rate of return, ρ. This should properly be captured by an appropriate revaluation of K_0, with suitable adjustments to θ and the other parameters of (2.2). Reinvestment ought to be subject to a market test and thus earn the normal private rate of return.

REFERENCES

Atkinson, Anthony B. and Joseph E. Stiglitz (1980) *Lectures on Public Economics*, New York: McGraw-Hill.

Besant-Jones, J.E. (ed.) (1993) ‘Reforming the Policies for Electric Power in Developing Countries’, World Bank, Industry and Energy Department, Washington, DC.

CSO (1994) *United Kingdom National Accounts: The CSO Blue Book 1994 Edition*, London: HMSO.

Dasgupta, P.D., S. Marglin and A.K. Sen (1972) *Guidelines for Project Evaluation*, New York: UNIDO.

Diamond, P.A. and J.A. Mirrlees (1971) ‘Optimal Taxation and Public Production, Part 1: Production Efficiency’, *American Economic Review*, **61**(1), 8–27.

Galal, A., L. Jones, P. Tandon and I. Vogelsang (1994) *Welfare Consequences of Selling Public Enterprises: An Empirical Analysis*, Oxford: Oxford University Press.

Hills, John (1989) 'Counting the Family Silver: The Public Sector's Balance Sheet 1956 to 1987', *Fiscal Studies*, **10**(2), May, 66–85.

Jones, L., P. Tandon and I. Vogelsang (1990) *Selling Public Enterprises: A Cost Benefit Methodology*, Cambridge, MA: The MIT Press.

Little, I.M.D. and J.A. Mirrlees (1968) *Manual of Industrial Project Analysis*, Vol. 2, Paris: OECD Development Centre.

Little, I.M.D. and J.A. Mirrlees (1974) *Project Appraisal and Planning for Developing Countries*, London: Heinemann.

Newbery, D.M. (1991) 'Reform in Hungary: Sequencing and Privatisation', *European Economic Review*, **35**, May, 571–80.

Newbery, D.M. (1992) 'The Role of Public Enterprises in the National Economy', *Asian Economic Review*, **10**(2), 1–34.

Ray, A. (1984) *Cost-Benefit Analysis: Issues and Methodologies*, Baltimore, MD: Johns Hopkins University Press for the World Bank.

Sader, F. (1993) 'Privatization and Foreign Direct Investment in the Developing World, 1988–92', Policy Research Working Paper 1202, The World Bank, Washington, DC.

Short, R.P. (1984) 'The Role of Public Enterprises: An International Statistical Comparison', in R. Floyd, C. Gary and R. Short (eds) *Public Enterprises in Mixed Economies: Some Macroeconomic Aspects*, Washington, DC: IMF.

Squire, L. and H.G. van der Tak (1975) *Economic Analysis of Projects*, Baltimore, MD: Johns Hopkins University Press for the World Bank.

Summers, R. and A. Heston (1988) 'A New Set of International Comparisons of Real Product and Prices for 130 Countries, 1950–1985', *The Review of Income and Wealth*, Series 34, No. 1.

Summers, R. and A. Heston (1991) 'The Penn World Table (Mark 5): An Expanded Set of International Comparisons, 1950–1988', *Quarterly Journal of Economics*, **106**(2), 327–68.

Tanzi, V. (ed.) (1992) *Fiscal Policies in Economies in Transition*, Washington, DC: IMF.

Tanzi, V. (1993) 'The Budget Deficits in Transition: A Cautionary Note', *IMF Staff Papers*, **40**(3), 697–707.

World Bank (1993) *The World Bank's Role in the Electric Power Sector*, Washington, DC: World Bank.

World Bank (1994a) *World Development Report 1994*, New York: Oxford University Press for World Bank.

World Bank (1994b) *Averting the Old Age Crisis*, New York: Oxford University Press for World Bank.

World Bank (1995) *Bureaucrats in Business: The Economics and Politics of Government Ownership*, New York: Oxford University Press for World Bank.

3

MACROECONOMIC CONSTRAINTS AND THE MODALITIES OF PRIVATIZATION

Peter Heller, Richard Hemming, and Rupa Chakrabarti

INTRODUCTION

A recurring pattern in the privatization experience of some East European economies has been the tendency to abandon principal reliance on traditional privatization through market sales and to move toward various modes of 'mass privatization'. In such countries as Bulgaria and Poland, initial attempts at the traditional approach faltered against the background of inadequate local capital markets and the small size of the local savings base. The failure of the traditional approach in economies where a significant proportion of the economy's assets are to be privatized illustrates a central point about the process of privatization.

In effect, the traditional mode of privatization involving the sale of assets of an enterprise at a market-related price is only feasible in macroeconomic terms in an economy with financially deep markets, where private sector financial asset holdings are substantial (as a share of total assets), and where the implied financial transfer is small in terms of the overall size of the economy. Once the privatization process entails the sale of state-owned assets which are quantitatively large relative to either the size of the economy and its financial markets or the capacity of the population to finance asset purchases, it becomes necessary to modify the traditional approaches, to include 'giveaways' or voucher privatization. A slowing of the pace of a privatization program and significant foreign investment in privatized assets may also be entailed.

In this chapter, we explore these issues in more depth. The next section reviews the channels through which a traditional privatization program exerts its macroeconomic influence, and explains how the scale of a program may prove impractical or yield adverse macroeconomic effects. It notes that the macroeconomic impact is likely to be influenced by the way in which the government utilizes the proceeds from privatization, the way in which the private sector finances the purchase of privatized assets, and the extent of foreign participation. The next section then indicates the way in which alternative modalities of privatization can be a means to alleviate these macroeconomic effects or to render the process more feasible in institutional terms. The following section reviews the modalities of privatization that have been adopted by countries where the privatization of significantly large elements of the economy has been attempted. This includes both countries in Eastern Europe and the former Soviet Union. It notes the types of adaptations that have been made to modalities of privatization for both enterprises and land, the foreign participation that is allowed, and the approach taken by governments in utilizing the proceeds of privatization. Finally, the last section looks at the lessons from the theory and country experiences for other countries contemplating large-scale privatization.

TRADITIONAL APPROACHES TO PRIVATIZATION

In what follows, privatization is defined as the sale of state-owned assets to the private sector (which may or may not include participation by foreign buyers). Such assets will typically take the form of equity shares in an enterprise, although direct sale of the physical assets of an enterprise may also be the case, particularly in countries with poorly functioning capital markets. In cases where land has been owned by the state, the sale or long-term lease of land may also be an important form of privatization. The traditional process of sale is through an auction or a tender, where an attempt is made to obtain a market-related price for the asset. Normally, the government would seek full receipt of the proceeds of privatization up-front. In this traditional case, it is also assumed, for the present, that the net equity of the firm to be privatized has a positive value.

The following analysis abstracts from the gains in productive and allocative efficiency due to privatization. Handing an enterprise over to the private sector and opening it up to the forces of competition is likely to lower costs and to result in greater responsiveness to consumer demand. In turn, this could lead to an increase in the rate of growth of output and stimulate exports and increase the competitiveness of the economy. Similarly, the subsidization of a loss-making enterprise out of general taxation can be prevented through privatizing potentially profitable enterprises. Any government revenue that results can be directed to social spending or to profitable projects. There is therefore a sense in which privatization can relieve macroeconomic constraints.

In the short term at least, the source of any macroeconomic effects of privatization would arise from the impact of this transfer of financial or physical assets from the public to the private sector. Abstracting from the case of foreign purchases, the private sector acquires additional equity or physical capital in exchange for a reduction in its cash balances and/or an increase in its outstanding liabilities. The government's portfolio is correspondingly affected, with a reduction in equity or physical capital (which in some countries may be highly illiquid) and, initially, an increase in its cash balances.

Several obvious questions arise in evaluating the macroeconomic effects of the transfer. First, how does the private sector respond to this shift in its portfolio in terms of its short-term (and possibly medium-term) consumption or investment behavior? Does the shift in its portfolio of assets and liabilities affect its demand for credit from the banking system? Are there different effects which depend upon whether the private sector finances the asset purchase from its own resources or by increased debt? Second, what does the government do with the receipts of the asset sale? Does it permanently increase its cash balances? Does it provide a temporary tax cut or increase in expenditure? Does it reduce its outstanding debt?

Answering these questions may shed light on whether the asset transfer would give rise to a significant shift, in the short term, in the demand for goods and factors of production across the different sectors of the economy and whether this would have an effect on output, prices, and the balance of payments. It may also determine whether the asset transfer leads to crowding out in the financial system. In this connection, it is also relevant whether monetary and fiscal policy are conducted responsibly in the context of a privatization program. Specifically, can one assume that the overall monetary program allows for monetary expansion compatible with nominal GDP targets and the projected demand for money and taking account of the targets for external reserve accumulation? Can one assume that fiscal policy is 'rational' in the sense that one-shot receipts from privatization do not give rise to a permanent cut in tax rates or an increase in recurrent budgetary outlays (in excess of the annuity value of privatization receipts)?

As already indicated, the initial impact of the private sector's acquisition of public assets will be a shift in its portfolio, with reduced cash balances and/or increased debt, which would have a contractionary effect on consumption demand. While investment demand would be inhibited to the extent that the private sector's capacity to assume additional debt would be reduced, it is also likely that the acquisition of privatized enterprises would be associated with an increase in demand for plant and equipment to rationalize or modernize the privatized enterprise. Acquisition of vacant land would also be expected to stimulate additional investment, particularly if efforts were made to limit purchases for speculation.

Whatever the net impact on domestic demand, the acquisition of privatized assets through a reduction in cash balances is more contractionary than acquisition through additional bank credit. In the former case, both base money and broad money would be reduced. Only the net credit position of the government would improve. In the latter case, there would be a reduction in base money but broad money would remain unchanged. Increased credit to the private sector would be matched by an improvement in the net credit position of the government. However, where credit expansion by commercial banks is constrained by an overall monetary target, the demand for credit to purchase privatized assets will crowd out new investment, either directly or through higher interest rates.

There may also be a second-order relative price effect arising from the change in the stocks of equity and other assets. The increase in the supply of equity in the portfolio of the private sector lowers the price of equity and hence increases the rate of return on equity. Other assets become less attractive, and the rate of return on them may increase to restore portfolio balance, which in turn implies that there may be an increase in the general rate of interest. This could lead to a reduction in private investment demand.

Ultimately, however, the impact on the private sector cannot be assessed independently of a knowledge of the government's likely response to the receipt of privatization proceeds. The simplest and most obvious case would be to assume that the government fully utilizes the proceeds to reduce temporarily capital taxation. While unlikely, this case illustrates the possibility of a negligible macroeconomic effect, as the financial position of private purchasers of public assets would be fully restored. Utilization of the receipts for a redemption of government debt with the public at large (as opposed to the banking system) has a similar effect. In contrast, a reduction in taxes – or an equivalent increase in transfers – that is heavily weighted toward low-income groups would increase aggregate consumption.

A temporary increase in government expenditure (most readily achievable through an increase in nonrecurrent capital spending) would also tend to have an expansionary effect on aggregate demand. However, the character of the expenditure increase would be critical in assessing whether it was likely to give rise to a significant shift in sectoral demand in the economy or to affect adversely the balance of payments. In this case, an initial monetary contraction would not necessarily be fully offset by increased government expenditure. This will depend upon the composition of demand as between local goods and imports. Real resource crowding out could emerge to the extent that the government's increased demand for resources (and the reduced purchasing power of the private sector) absorbs inputs previously used for the production of private sector consumption or investment goods. Financial crowding out could emerge to the extent that a combination of increased private sector credit (for the purpose of acquiring the privatized assets), and government utilization of the privatization receipts for expenditure, reduced the available room for additional credit expansion to the private sector.

Another possible scenario is where the government increases its deposits in the commercial banking system or reduces its outstanding debt with the banking system. Thus a monetary contraction would accompany the aggregate demand contraction deriving from the private sector (as indicated above). However, this scenario also offers the prospect of some subsequent crowding in of the private sector, with the possibility of reduced interest rates and commercial banks seeking to add to their loan portfolio.

The above analysis can be modified to allow for the possibility of foreign purchases of privatized assets. The key issue once again becomes the response of the government to the increase in its financial assets in the short run. Utilization of the privatization receipts for government expenditure or tax cuts would directly augment aggregate demand, and in the context of a monetary program, limit potential credit expansion to the private sector, thus giving rise to financial and real resource crowding-out effects. If the government reduces its external debt liability, the macroeconomic impact would largely be felt in the future, as the government's future fiscal and external account position is strengthened with a reduction in its debt service obligations. If the funds are used to reduce the government's domestic debt, the short-run impact is equivalent to the effect of a foreign private capital inflow (as the government uses the resources to repay domestic creditors), with a corresponding increase in broad money. Alternatively, the government could sterilize the monetary impact of the higher foreign exchange receipts by increasing government deposits or holding more foreign nonmonetary assets.

In the above discussion, it has been presumed that the asset to be privatized has a positive net present value. Yet as one considers the possible macroeconomic implications of privatization in many formerly centrally planned economies, it is also necessary to consider the possibility that the market value of the enterprise is negative. The combination of an outmoded capital stock and past outstanding debt obligations may imply that under the traditional approach, the government would need to pay the private sector some amount to acquire the assets. This could be the case where the government sought to engineer a restructuring of the corporation to enhance its productivity following privatization or where the government expected the purchasers of an enterprise to make some commitment with regard to employment or new investment. Indeed, some additional government outlay may result from its assumption of the debt obligations of the firm to be privatized, or the payment of severance pay to employees who are to be retrenched prior to sale, or other forms of restructuring.

Such a case represents, in effect, a variant of the earlier scenarios, but one where the cost to the private sector is nil and the government spends more than it received in order to effect the desired privatization. In effect, it is the macroeconomic equivalent of an increase in deficit-financed government outlays. The greater the outlays required to effect the privatization, the more expansionary the privatization process would become and, within the context of a monetary program, the more the crowding out implied.

Two points become obvious in the above discussion. First, the government's approach to the utilization of its receipts from privatization will critically influence the likely macroeconomic effects. The greater the extent to which the government offsets the withdrawal of purchasing power from the private sector by utilizing the receipts to reinject purchasing power into the economy, the greater (weaker) the net expansionary (contractionary) effect.

Second, the size of the financial transfers involved will determine whether the privatization program has a significant impact on consumption or investment aggregates and on the distribution of demand across sectors. In a large market economy, where the assets to be divested are relatively small and the corresponding effect of shifts in the portfolio of the private sector is limited, there is not likely to be much of a net impact on consumption and investment. It is also unlikely that there will be a shift in the relative rates of return on the various assets that could lead to a change in the rate of interest. Similarly, it is reasonable to make the assumption that there is sufficient underlying demand in the private sector to absorb the transfer of assets at a price that would appear reasonable in terms of market values.

In contrast, in a small and relatively closed economy or an economy where public sector assets are substantial as a percentage of total assets, the magnitude of the transfers associated with privatization could readily lead to significant effects on the portfolios of the private and public sector, give rise to a significant shift in consumption and investment by both sectors, and have an impact on relative asset prices. This is most obvious in economies where the private sector is fairly underdeveloped, and where the magnitude of the transfers that are potentially possible could far outstrip the private sector's financial capacity (either in terms of own resources or debt absorption capacity) to finance the transfers. This could make it difficult to achieve the financial transfer of privatized assets other than at prices which would be regarded as unacceptable by the government.

The scale of the program could also be excessive in a situation where the costs of restructuring exceed the government's fiscal capacity; reliance on traditional modes of privatization would force the government to pay the private sector to induce it to accept and operate the enterprises. This may lead the government to look for alternative modes of privatization that bypass the issue of the government having to finance the inevitable restructuring of the enterprise or the costs of retrenching workers. However, the costs to the government are unlikely to be independent of the privatization strategy, except in the short run.

Institutional factors also underscore the importance of alternative approaches to privatization. In addition to limits on the private sector's capacity to finance asset purchases or the government's capacity to finance restructuring, the size of transactions can also prove a bottleneck in terms of the institutional requirements for executing financial transfers. In many economies, particularly in developing countries and economies in transition, the capacity of financial markets (broadly defined to include all institutions used to intermediate the sale of state-owned assets) will set clear limits on the magnitude of the financial transfers that are feasible during any given period. A commitment to rapid privatization of the economy in such cases may necessitate alternative approaches to privatization that do not rely on financial transfers at market-related prices.

NONTRADITIONAL APPROACHES TO PRIVATIZATION

The above analysis hints at approaches to minimize macroeconomic effects where these are perceived as significant, or to address limitations in the private (government) sector's capacity to finance asset purchases (restructuring). The future impact is clearly lessened when the government seeks to give back the receipts or transfer privatized assets at a significant discount to the private sector. Similarly, efforts by the government to allow the purchase of the privatized assets to take place over a long period of time reduce the scale of transfers in any given period, limit the intermediation burden on the financial sector, and reduce the potential financial crowding-out effects. Slowing the pace of the privatization program by limiting the amount of assets to be divested in any time period is another obvious way of minimizing the associated macroeconomic impact.

The methods of privatization observed in most of the formerly centrally planned economies involve significant elements of such modifications to the traditional approach. They include (a) mass distribution, at low or negligible cost, of vouchers which may be used for the purchase directly of equity shares either in enterprises to be privatized or in financial intermediaries (e.g. forms of mutual investment funds) which utilize the vouchers to accumulate a significant stake in a number of enterprises; (b) allowing workers or management of firms to be privatized to acquire a specified share of the equity at a significantly reduced price; (c) allowing the buyers of the assets of an enterprise to direct a significant share of the purchase price into investments in the enterprise (in effect, an earmarking of the government's receipts back to the privatized firm); and (d) returning assets or land to the original owners. In the case of land, countries that have sought to maintain formal state ownership of land have in some cases allowed peasant farmers or owners of structures in urban areas full and long-term rights to use land at limited or negligible cost.

The essence of most of these approaches is that the transfer of assets takes place with only limited, and at times, zero compensation to the government. In the pure 'giveaway' case, explicit equity rights are transferred to the private sector, resulting in an augmentation of the wealth of the private sector. The presence of these new assets in the private sector's portfolio can create a perception of greater wealth which may encourage consumption through a running down of precautionary balances. If the equity shares can be redeemed or exchanged for cash, the likelihood of an expansion in consumption is greater. Individuals with a higher marginal propensity to consume are likely to exchange their shares for cash with those interested in having a larger equity share in their portfolio; the latter are likely to be those with a lower marginal propensity to consume. The net effect would be an increase in aggregate consumption demand. The voucher case is largely analogous, particularly if vouchers are tradeable; if not, the increase in consumption demand would likely be more limited, reflecting only the perception of increased wealth and a willingness to reduce precautionary balances.

Another difference in the macroeconomic impact of the voucher relative to targeted giveaway approaches is the extent to which they affect the likelihood of a meaningful restructuring of the enterprise in the future. This will depend upon the nature of the governance of the firm that emerges post-privatization. In the pure case where a voucher system leads to a widespread, relatively egalitarian distribution of equity shares, the enhanced wealth of the private sector is not likely to result in a significant increase in consumption (through a reduction in precautionary financial balances). Neither would the transfer of ownership provide additional capital resources to finance new investment or the restructuring of the enterprise. In the case where vouchers may be pooled in an investment fund, the prospects for more focussed enterprise restructuring may lead to more aggressive efforts either to secure additional bank credit or to tap into additional financial resources of large shareholders.

In contrast, targeted giveaways to the workers and management may again provide for a more focussed effort in terms of approaches to secure additional capital or credit to restructure the enterprise's operations. Alternatively, it may also contribute to stasis, where the types of restructuring (including retrenchment) necessary to energize an enterprise may not be feasible. This might be the case, for example, if financial markets provide fewer resources to employee-run enterprises because of a perception that employee–owners maximize wages rather than profits.

As noted above, an interesting half-way approach in a few countries has been for the government to seek to sell the assets of an enterprise at a market-related price, but with the explicit provision that a share of the receipts would be plowed back into the enterprise for investment purposes. In effect, this is a variation of the case where the private sector asset purchase is accompanied by government expenditures. However, the contractionary effect associated with additional borrowing or reduced financial balances of the private sector is offset to the extent of the additional investment in the enterprise.

RECENT COUNTRY EXPERIENCES WITH PRIVATIZATION

In most well-established market economies that have undertaken the traditional modes of privatization in the last decade, it is apparent that the magnitude of financial transfers to the government has not been large as a share of GDP (Table 3.1). Over the four year period 1989–1992, the annual average proceeds rarely exceeded 1 percent of GDP. In some individual years in some countries (notably Argentina (1992), New Zealand (1989, 1992), Sweden (1989), United Kingdom (1991), Malaysia (1992), and Mexico (1990–1992)), it has reached nearly 3 percent of GDP in one year (and 4 percent of GDP in Venezuela in 1991), but except in the case of Mexico, it has rarely been sustained at that high a level.

However, the largest transfers have been negative, relating to outlays of the government of the Federal Republic of Germany in connection with the privatization and restructuring of the economy of the former Democratic Republic of Germany. The principal privatization entity, the Treuhand, has incurred substantial deficits during the last several years. It is estimated that

Table 3.1 Privatization proceeds, 1989–92, (Annual average, in percent of GDP)

Argentina	1.0
Australia	0.3
Brazil	0.7
Canada	0.2
Chile	0.2
Czechoslovakia	0.3
FRG	0.2
Greece	0.3
Hungary	0.9
Ireland	0.3
Israel	0.2
Jamaica	1.1
Malaysia	1.1
Mexico	1.7
Netherlands	0.2
New Zealand	1.2
Philippines	0.5
Poland	0.3
South Africa	0.3
South Korea	0.2
Sweden	0.6
Turkey	0.2
United Kingdom	1.1
Venezuela	1.0

Source: Staff estimates

between July 1990 – the beginning of the privatization program – and the dissolution of the privatization agency at the end of 1994, the Treuhand will have spent about US$140 billion which compares to revenues of only US$26 billion. Almost 80 percent of all expenditures are related to enterprise restructuring and the absorption of company debt.[1] Little quantitative data is available on the magnitude of transfers in the East European countries and the former Soviet Union, given that privatization initiatives have been relatively recent. In principle, were these countries to have attempted significant privatization using the traditional market sales approach, the magnitudes of the transfers would probably have been significantly higher.[2] In reality, both the pace and approaches used have been such that the gross proceeds have been kept to more modest levels, as indicated for the few countries for which data was available.

In this section, we look at some of the prevailing methods of enterprise privatization that have been used in Eastern Europe. We also look at the case of land privatization specifically, as this has been a major issue in countries in Eastern Europe and is emerging as an issue elsewhere, for example in Ethiopia. Given the importance of the way in which privatization proceeds are used by a government to any macroeconomic assessment, we also review the experience in this regard as well.

In reviewing the empirical experience, certain obvious patterns emerge. First, and most noteworthy, most countries have used a blend of methods, either concurrently or as the privatization program has evolved. Even the countries that have most heavily relied on 'mass privatization' techniques have also utilized traditional sales for certain types of enterprises or sectors. In some cases, a portion of the shares of an enterprise has been sold, while the remainder has been distributed in some way to the population or employees and management. Second, revenue considerations have been a principal consideration in market economies where the traditional approach is perceived as viable. In Eastern Europe in particular, the interest in generating substantial revenue to meet fiscal needs has often proved in conflict with the macroeconomic issues discussed above (*inter alia* the absence of adequate capital markets and domestic savings and the difficulties associated with the valuation of enterprises) or has been subordinated to other objectives of the program.

Third, while macroeconomic considerations emerge as an obvious constraint inducing alternative approaches to privatization, other considerations have also been critical in determining which of the possible alternatives have been chosen. These include (a) a concern for equity, namely to ensure that the value of the wealth implicit in the government's enterprise asset portfolio is shared widely and equally by the population at the initial stages of the privatization program; (b) a desire to build mass support for the privatization initiative by ensuring a widespread distribution of ownership within the population; (c) a concern for ensuring a successful transition by the privatized enterprise to a more productive operating position and to ensure strengthened governance of the enterprise; such concerns have led to schemes to increase the likelihood of significant new investments in the privatized enterprises (through active management groups, such as investment funds, foreign investors, etc.); (d) a desire to prevent significant cutbacks in employment in the privatized enterprises; (e) a desire for speed and momentum in the program, presumably out of a fear that delays may encourage opposition from entrenched insider interests and weaken public support; (f) a need to take account of the interests of insider groups (management, employees) who have sought to ensure preservation of their position in the enterprise; (g) wanting the enterprise management and employees to have a significant input into the privatization approach to be adopted; (h) the impact of legal and institutional issues relating to ownership rights, local interests separable from those of the central government, political opposition, etc.; and (i) a desire by some countries to encourage foreign investment.

Sale of assets

Several of the economies in transition have sought to sell the assets of state enterprises. In most cases, privatization was preceded by a process of corporatization, in which attenuated property rights were respecified and transferred to the government, which was then in a legal position actually to dispose of the assets by the establishment of the necessary legal and regulatory framework, and by the development of a stock market. Corporatization in particular has provided a legal basis for the acquisition of ownership stakes by domestic and foreign investors.

In the case of *Hungary*, privatization of enterprises has almost exclusively relied on sales rather than giveaways. The initial focus was on the smaller enterprises. Particularly in the early years of the process (through 1990), considerable scope was allowed for management and investor-initiated privatizations, particularly for the state-owned small- and medium-sized firms, which were transformed into joint-stock companies (Hare and Grosfeld, 1991). It was expected that most of these firms would be sold through the stock exchange, whereas the weaker firms would be reorganized or entirely liquidated. Privatization of the larger state enterprises has proved slower than originally envisaged. While the Hungarian approach has relied on the traditional privatization approach, it should be noted that subsidized credit facilities were nevertheless used heavily and significant efforts were made to encourage foreign participation through tax and foreign exchange incentives. Efforts to engage in a fully traditional sales approach did not prove very successful.[3,4]

In *Bulgaria*, the State Privatization Agency has been responsible for the sale of state-owned commercial companies with assets valued at more than Leva 10 million (US$444,444). It has sought to use a variety of methods of sale such as the public auction of shares or a publicly invited tender (Frydman *et al.*, 1993). However, sales have proceeded extremely slowly, reflecting the unwillingness of investors to buy enterprises with significant outstanding debts, the lack of well-defined property rights, the undeveloped capital market, and a limited domestic financial capacity to finance purchases. It now appears that Bulgaria will move more toward a mass privatization approach. As in Hungary, preferential sales (at a 50 percent discount on purchases up to a specified amount) to employees and retirees (up to 20 percent of the shares) were anticipated.

In the case of the former *Democratic Republic of Germany*, the Treuhand's policy has been to pursue three objectives simultaneously: (a) to maximize privatization receipts; (b) to protect jobs; and (c) to secure future investments. Among the three, the most weight was given to employment.[5] Since revenue maximization was not the ultimate objective, the Treuhand has discarded any public offerings and direct auction methods and this despite well-functioning capital markets in Germany. Instead, it relied on private tenders as a mode of privatization and approached competitors directly to assure that industry-relevant know-how is transferred. In the case of small companies, management buyouts have been encouraged. The strong emphasis on maintaining employment and the restructuring of companies – at the expense of revenue as an objective of the program – has led the Treuhandanstalt to absorb large amounts of outstanding enterprise debt and to provide guarantees to banks associated with the borrowing of liquid funds by the newly privatized enterprises.

In *Russia*, the first phase of privatization relied mostly on vouchers and concessionary terms for enterprise work collectives (see below) and hence did not generate much revenue for the federal and municipal budgets, and did not provide much impetus for investment. However, for small nonfarm businesses (with a labor force under 200 and a January 1992 book value of less than Rub 1 million), enterprises were sold at auction or by tender with the divestiture process managed by regional and local governments.[6] The second phase (which was passed in July 1994 through a Presidential Decree and in spite of significant parliamentary opposition) was expected to rely more heavily on sale by auctions of equity shares in large joint-stock companies created from state and municipal enterprises. Shares are to be sold for cash, with 51 percent of the proceeds transferred into special enterprise accounts which are to be used for investment in the enterprise (post-privatization). Thus, a new enterprise owner needs to pay the state only about half the market value (Oxford Analytica Daily Brief (OADB), 1994c). The remainder of the receipts would be received by the federal and local government. The second phase also anticipated reduced concessionary benefits to employees of privatized enterprises. Foreign capital inflows for equity purchase have proved limited, reflecting an uncertain attitude of both expatriate investors and nation holding foreign exchange abroad.

In *Poland*, the traditional approach to sales has been constrained by the lack of a developed local capital market and by the limited financial savings of the private sector. However, as with the FRG, the government has been concerned to ensure that the transfer of ownership will bring about a sufficient improvement in governance to achieve significant restructuring and improve the efficiency of enterprises after privatization. By allowing management and employees a significant voice in the decision as to whether and when to engage in the privatization process, it has been allowed to proceed slowly. As in other countries, the process has moved more quickly for smaller enterprises (particularly in the services sectors), with many sales or leases to management and workers. Privatization in industry and for larger enterprises has lagged, which has led to the consideration of mass privatization approaches.

In the former *Czechoslovakia*, traditional sales through auctions were used for the privatization of small businesses in the service sector. Total cumulative receipts derived from sales though 1992 amounted to no more than 1 per cent of GDP in 1992. In the two privatization waves that were programmed for 1992 and 1994 (involving roughly 2500 of the larger enterprises in each wave, with a combined book value in each wave of just under half of 1992 GDP), approximately two-thirds of the enterprises were to be sold, in principle, by conventional direct sales methods (auctions, tenders and direct sales, as well as by transfers free of charge to municipalities).[7] However, it appears that in the first wave (as of June 1992) two-thirds of the book value of the enterprises privatized occurred through vouchers (equivalent to about one-third of GDP in purported value). The book value of enterprises to be sold through more conventional methods would then be about 10–15 percent of GDP, but actual receipts proved significantly less.

Vouchers and giveaways

The most notable voucher schemes have been in *Russia* and in the former *Czechoslovakia*. In both cases, citizens were free to decide whether to use the vouchers to purchase shares in companies directly or to invest them in investment funds. The idea behind the voucher scheme has been to disperse economic power among the population at large and to create a class of people with a vested interest in the success of the transition to capitalism.

In the former *Czechoslovakia*, the authorities sought a fast-track privatization program that took account both of equity considerations and the limited capacity of the local financial market. In addition to the traditional approach discussed above, 'giveaway' elements of the program included restitution in kind of expropriated property to former owners, transformation of cooperatives (principally in agriculture) into private business entities (with ownership assigned both to employees and individuals entitled to restitution), and a voucher scheme, whereby all adult citizens were allowed to purchase vouchers which could be used to bid for shares in auctions. Effectively, the purchase price of the vouchers allowed for purchases at only a small fraction of the book value (less than 5 percent) or the market value of the shares at the voucher auctions. Vouchers could be used directly to bid for shares or they could be entrusted to Investment Privatization Funds.

In *Russia*, from October 1992 to January 1993, Russian citizens were able to obtain vouchers, each with a face value of 10,000 rubles, at local branches of the State Savings Bank.[8] By the end of 1993, nearly 5000 medium and large-scale enterprises were privatized through voucher auctions (OADB, 1993b). One of the reasons for the success of the Russian voucher scheme was that in addition to using their vouchers to bid directly for shares in companies or to invest in private investment funds, Russian citizens had the option of selling their vouchers for cash. Tradeability of vouchers enabled citizens who were not interested in becoming shareholders to receive immediate benefits from the privatization program by cashing in their vouchers. It also allowed interested investors to accumulate large blocks of vouchers which could then be used to bid for a sizable equity share of a company. In general, it also gave citizens an incentive to participate, building support for the reform process. Evidence also suggests that the privatization process was associated with a significant undervaluation of industrial assets, with the real value of equity shares significantly in excess of the amounts 'paid' (albeit through vouchers or other concessionary terms) by the new owners.

Russia's privatization program also offered generous concessions to enterprise managers and workers, who could acquire 40 to 51 percent of the shares in their enterprise on preferential terms (including use of vouchers as well as retained profits and cash, significantly discounted shares, and concessional payment terms) before shares were auctioned to the public. Hence most companies went into the voucher auctions with a majority of shares already owned by employees. Finally, one unfortunate aspect of the Russian program has been that it has not yet tackled the difficult issues associated with industrial restructuring; many of the privatized enterprises continued to rely on soft credit terms from the banking system in order to maintain their operations.

While not moving as fast as privatization in Russia, the program in *Estonia* is every bit as successful and in many respects more so. It differs significantly from that of Russia in that it has achieved the transfer of controlling stakes in enterprises to workers and managers. By mid-1994 about one-half of the state-owned enterprises and businesses had been privatized using a wide variety of methods – restitution, auctions, and tenders, leasing, joint ventures, and a voucher program. The voucher program is different in certain respects. The program is biased toward long-term residents and native Estonians, additional vouchers are issued as compensation to those whose property was expropriated and cannot be retrieved and to those deported during the Soviet era, and vouchers can be exchanged for residential property and land. It is expected that about two-thirds of all vouchers will be used to obtain property and land. Privatization revenue is being used primarily to clear enterprise debt (World Bank, 1994).

In some other countries of the former Soviet Union (e.g. Kazakhstan, Kyrgyzstan, Moldova, Ukraine), voucher schemes and concessionary sales to workers have also been attempted, although with much less success than in Russia (OADB, 1993b).

There have also been cases of distribution of equity shares of enterprises; in *Hungary*, shares were distributed to the Social Security Fund. Although similar to the distribution of vouchers, the shares were less marketable and could not be distributed prior to the privatization process getting started.

In *Poland*, the authorities passed legislation for a 'mass privatization program' of some larger enterprises utilizing a voucher-based scheme. Such enterprises were first to be transformed into joint-stock companies. Ten percent of the shares were to be given to workers in the enterprises and another share was allocated to pensioners. Investment funds were to receive half of the shares, with the government retaining a percentage of the shares. Investment fund shares were eventually to be purchasable with vouchers, the latter which were to be freely distributed among citizens, workers, the Social Security Fund, and other financial intermediaries. One argument for this approach was to ensure that although ownership was widely distributed (through shareholdings in the investment funds), enterprise management would be subject to the scrutiny of managers (domestic and foreign) of the principal investment funds.

Privatization of land

Privatization of real estate has been clearly perceived by most East European and FSU countries as involving considerable more difficulties than for the non-real estate assets of enterprises. The issue of ownership has been a key difficulty, with many former owners seeking either a return of the real estate or restitution for the current market value of the land. The problem of the uncertainty of land prices and the likelihood that privatizing land would substantially increase the cost to potential buyers has also been a factor in leading privatization agencies not to include the underlying land in privatization sales.

In *Hungary*, in a significant percentage of cases, real estate was not sold, with the sale focussed on the business, equipment, the brand name, and the lease of premises for a ten year period. In the small-scale privatization program of the former *Czechoslovakia*, real estate was only infrequently sold, with leases more the norm. In *Russia*, the enterprise privatization efforts to date have not included land, which remained under the ownership of the local authorities and for which lease agreements were negotiated. Only in the most recent second phase of the enterprise privatization effort is it contemplated to include sales of land as well as buildings and other structures (OADB, 1994c).

Macroeconomic and equity considerations also emerged in the evolution of *Ethiopia*'s efforts to formulate a policy with respect to land, which had been largely nationalized by the previous regime in the mid-1970s. For the present, the new government has committed itself that for rural land, the state would continue to own the land, but peasant farmers and their families would have full use rights, which could be passed on through inheritance. For urban land, the government recently sought to introduce a market-based 'land-lease' system for the allocation of urban land, almost all of which was owned by the state. The land-lease system was seen as a way of eliminating the previous system of land allocation at zero cost through administrative discretion. Under the proposed new system, leases on vacant land parcels were to be auctioned to the highest bidder. Subject to administratively set floor prices, the auctions were also to be used for the valuation of land with existing structures (excluding owner-occupied housing), and the owners of the structures were expected to purchase the land-lease rights to the underlying land. Receipts from land-lease sales were to be earmarked to municipalities for the purpose of constructing urban infrastructure and housing.

Soon after this proposal was devised, it became apparent that the magnitude of the potential financial transfer from the private to the public sector could be substantial relative to the total output of the economy. Moreover, limits on the income and financial assets of much of the population would have prevented most citizens from acquiring land-lease titles, and the demand for mortgage financing of the land-lease titles would have swamped the financial capacity of the only commercial bank in the economy, crowding out loans for non-land investments. Both the institutional impracticality of the proposal and the potentially adverse macroeconomic effects were such as to lead the government drastically to revise the program by not requiring the land-lease system to be immediately applied with respect to land with existing structures.

USES OF PRIVATIZATION PROCEEDS

Although most countries proclaim good intentions with regard to the use of the proceeds of privatization, it is in reality quite difficult to assert with any confidence whether the funds have been genuinely used as indicated. In the absence of an analytic and empirical approach that can identify the counterfactual (namely, the fiscal outcome in the absence of the privatization receipts), one cannot readily know the extent to which other revenues are lower or expenditures higher as a consequence of receipts from asset sales. In addition, most of the privatization programs in the economies in transition have not gotten fully underway; and since many of them involve giveaways, there have not been substantial revenues generated. Most countries, however, have indicated their intentions to use the proceeds for debt repayment and investment purposes, both at the state and municipal level. As noted above, in some cases a significant portion of the proceeds is to be retained by the enterprise itself. For example, in *Bulgaria*, the privatization law specified that for cases of small-scale privatization, 40 percent of the sales proceeds was to be retained by the companies involved in the program for investment purposes, 30 percent was to be channelled to a state or municipal investment fund, and 30 percent was to be targeted for the settlement of foreign debt. In *Hungary*, roughly half of the receipts were expected to be returned to the enterprise, 5-15 percent were to be directed to the municipal or local government, and the remainder were to be used by the central government, with the exact proportions to be determined on a case-by-case basis (reflecting the needs of the enterprise for new investments). Some countries have sought to ensure (even to the extent of earmarking provisions in the legislation underlying privatization) that the funds are used for investment purposes. For example, in *Ethiopia*, the land-lease legislation earmarks 95 percent of the land-lease receipts to the municipality for low-income housing and local infrastructure investments.

CONCLUSION

While privatization has not generated substantial amounts of revenue, in contrast to some of the early claims made of it, the process of the transfer of ownership of assets from the government to the private sector is underway in the case of both industrial enterprises and land. The macroeconomic implications of privatization depend critically on the actual method of transfer of assets, the use of the proceeds, and the means by which the private sector finances the purchase. The government can maximize the revenue it gets by selling an asset at market price. However, given a lack of savings to finance large-scale privatization, this is not always feasible. Therefore, to keep privatization moving, the government can use a combination of sales and giveaways. Introducing a giveaway element into a privatization program necessarily reduces revenue. But is it any different in its other macroeconomic effects?

Large-scale asset sales, involving a sizable financial transfer from the private sector to the government, have the potential to crowd out private investment and to be inflationary. Indeed, alternative methods of privatization not involving such large transfers may in fact be a response to these potential macroeconomic problems. In contrast, if the government uses privatization sales proceeds to retire debt with the private sector, this may lower interest rates and crowd in private investment. And if the government reduces foreign indebtedness, this may help to attract more foreign investment in the economy. Through judicious use of the proceeds, the privatization process can therefore be used to promote wider objectives than enterprise restructuring.

NOTES

1 Treuhandanstalt. Daten und Fakten zur Aufgabenerfüllung der Treuhandanstalt. Berlin 1994.

2 Some sense of the scale of the possible initiatives can be obtained from the proposed privatization initiatives in the former Czechoslovakia, where each of the two waves of privatizations involved enterprises with book values equivalent to almost half of 1993 GDP.

3 In the first active privatization program announced in September 1990, the authorities sought to value (at international standards) and sell twenty of the larger state enterprises. The auctions proved unsuccessful as the authorities were perceived as seeking unrealistically high prices, particularly in the context of the collapse of COMECON trade (Frydman *et al.*, 1993, p. 134).

4 Some sense of scale of the effort can be gleaned from the following. In 1991, total proceeds of the SPA from privatization amounted to Ft 39.2 billion (from which Hungarian private investors represented about Ft 7 billion). This represented about 1.5 percent of 1991 GDP.

5 As of January 1994, the Treuhand privatized about 13,500 enterprises or 98 percent of its portfolio, secured 1.5 million jobs and received investment commitments of about US$119 billion. The Treuhand can legally enforce about US$65 billion of the investment commitments and can hold the buyers accountable for 921,000 jobs.

6 Under alternative scenarios, employees received a significant share (approximately 30 percent) of the receipts (either in the form of a bonus, or, in the case of employee purchases, a 30 percent discount off the purchase price).

7 The amounts offered for the firm could, in principle, be significantly below the book value (reflecting the perceived market value).

8 Approximately 148 million vouchers were issued (OADB, 1994c).

REFERENCES

Frydman, R. *et al.* (1993) *The Privatization Process in Central Europe*, London: Central European University Press.

Hare, P. and I. Grosfeld (1991) *Privatization in Hungary, Poland and Czechoslovakia*, Centre for Economic Policy Research, Discussion Paper No. 544, London.

Oxford Analytica Daily Brief (OADB) (1993a) *CIS: Mass Privatization*, November 9, 1993.

———(1993b) *CIS: Mass Privatization*, November 10, 1993.

———(1994c) *Russia: Privatization Controversies*, July 19, 1994.

World Bank (1994) *Transition*, Vol. 5, No. 6, July–August, Washington, DC: World Bank.

4

A FISCAL APPROACH TO LIBERALIZATION POLICY[1,2]

Miguel A. Fernández-Ordoñez and Carlos Ocaña

There are two types of foe that liberty faces, namely: the vested interest of the few and the ignorance of the many.

(Francisco Cabarrús, 1978)

INTRODUCTION

Liberalization[3] policies are booming. The last GATT round negotiations that were closed in Marrakesh have almost completed the liberalization of industrial goods trade that was initiated after World War II. They have also created some possibilities of trade liberalization in agriculture, still a highly protected sector all around the world. In contrast with trade liberalization, the vast liberalization of the international movement of capital has developed without special negotiations at an international level; however, it owes a great deal to the profound liberalization reforms of the domestic financial system adopted in many countries during the last decades. Finally, labor market regulations are under review in those countries – mainly European – which have disproportionate unemployment rates.

In spite of this liberal trend, a huge amount of legal restrictions to competition are still present in many countries. The USA still allows cartel organizations in the shipping industry and maintains some outdated monopolies like postal services. In Germany, architects' fees – which are insensitive to their qualifications or seniority – are periodically approved by the Parliament. In the UK, barristers escaped the Thatcher reforms and maintain their monopoly in the British Isles. In Spain, funeral services are still city monopolies, while in France, long-distance calls continue to be a monopoly and there are no prospects of change before 1998.

These examples suggest that it is in the services sector that most legal restrictions to competition are still concentrated. Although there are differences among countries, service markets all over the world continue to be rigidly regulated, in sharp contrast with the rules that govern industrial goods markets. Legal restrictions to competition also dominate in real estate markets that only very recently (Kennedy, 1994; Brittan, 1994a, b; Government of

Japan, 1994) have begun to draw the attention of economists.

Yet the liberalization of service markets is a crucial task of economic policy for at least three reasons. First, as a consequence of the large and increasing weight of services in the national output, an improved performance of the services sector has become a necessary condition for growth (Krugman, 1994). Second, the potential gains in productivity are enormous in many service markets relative to potential gains in manufacturing and other activities. A small amount of competition has large effects in traditionally rigid markets. In some particular markets like telecommunications, these potential productivity gains are greatly enhanced by the ongoing technological revolution. The increase of competition will help to accelerate the adoption of new technologies. And third, in an increasingly open economy the role of other policy instruments, namely monetary and fiscal, is necessarily reduced. In this context, microeconomic – liberalization – policies become more important than ever for growth.

This chapter contains some considerations that could help to implement the long-postponed reforms in the service and real estate markets. In the next section, we discuss the reasons why the liberalization of the service sector is particularly difficult. In the following section, we argue that some interesting insights can be gained by analyzing the structural reforms of the service sector as a case of fiscal reform. The final section contains some examples of the contribution of fiscal policy to market liberalization.

THE DIFFICULTIES OF IMPLEMENTING LIBERALIZATION POLICY[4]

For centuries economists have been trying to convince policy makers and the general public about the beneficial effects of competition and the welfare loss caused by monopolies and all other types of restrictions to competition. Their success has only been relative. Entire sectors and countries have remained isolated from competition. The Spanish 'enlightened' politician Cabarrús, quoted at the beginning of this chapter, wondering two centuries ago why Spaniards did not adopt free trade policies, came to the conclusion that the main obstacles to market liberalization were 'the vested interests of the few' and 'the ignorance of the many'. His claim fits well the problems faced by today's policy makers when they try to liberalize their economies. In this section we elaborate on these two obstacles.

'The vested interests of the few'

Although most economists agree that competition increases social welfare, the perception among particular groups of citizens is often different. Even if the total benefits of competition to all consumers are large, the benefit to each one of them may be so small as to make it negligible. On the other hand, the introduction of competition is – at least in the short run – detrimental to the interests of those who until then had produced goods or provided services under monopoly (or near monopoly) conditions. Even if the damage done to this group – 'the few' – is small when compared to the consumers' total gain, the individual damage may be large because it must be shared among a relatively small group.

This unequal distribution of the positive and negative effects of competition among economic agents determines their reaction when the reform is announced. This reaction must be identified in advance if a reform is to be implemented successfully. It is difficult to organize consumers, because, although there are many of them, each one sees him- or herself as hardly affected at all. In this sense, consumers often are free-riders of the benefits of market liberalization. Each individual consumer lacks the incentives to incur the costs of lobbying for market competition even if he or she would like to have more competition. However, it is relatively easy for 'the few' who see themselves as deeply affected by the liberalization to get organized. These are the so-called interest groups, who will use everything in their power to defend this 'status quo'. This explains why, paradoxically, reforms which benefit almost everybody are defended by almost no one and, nevertheless, fiercely attacked by a few.

Very often, reluctance to change is found not only in the owners of the company but among a wider circle. The reason is that the rents generated by monopolies and other restrictions to competition are distributed among all the people linked to the protected firms. Thus, the monopoly rents do not always materialize in the monopoly's profit account. The extraordinary income is frequently shared among directors, employees, suppliers, etc., pushing the costs of monopolistic firms up over those of companies that have to face competition. The result is that, despite the higher prices monopolies charge their customers, their end-of-year figures may not be better than those of companies in the competitive economy. In such cases, it is not the shareholders – either public or private – who oppose reform, so much as the directors, employees, and suppliers of the firm (Leibenstein, 1966; Vives, 1993).

'The ignorance of the many'

The small benefit obtained by each individual consumer can explain the lack of interest of the population in liberalization policies, but it does not explain why in many cases the majority of the population – 'the many' – is not just indifferent to liberalization policies but fiercely oppose them. Very frequently liberalization policies are seen as policies enacted to benefit 'rich people' or aimed to encourage private profits, or regarded as not being consistent with the achievement of public or social goals. In particular, solidarity or redistribution goals are sometimes presented as opposed to competition.

Certainly these concerns can be counteracted by explaining that competition reduces the profits achieved by those who have not increased the welfare of society. Under competitive conditions it is nearly impossible for someone to make a profit without benefiting consumers. By contrast, a monopoly can obtain undeserved profits while treating clients badly, or selling low-quality products; in short, it is possible for a monopolist to act against the social interest and still make money.

There are, however, other arguments in favor of legal restriction to competition that create confusion in the minds of most people. Monopolies and legal restrictions to competition are presented as the unique tool to achieve redistribution of income or other public objectives like health, safety, environmental protection, etc. Public utility monopolies – for instance, telephone monopolies – frequently proclaim that if the provision of their services were opened up to competition, no one would take the trouble to provide such services in the least developed regions. The idea to be transmitted is that these social goals can only be achieved if competition is restricted. However, there is a fallacy built into this. If a monopoly can be forced to provide an extended coverage, then the same requirement can be imposed on any number of competing firms. The same objective – the subsidization of a particular consumers' group – can be obtained be means of a canon imposed to other groups of consumers in a system with various competing firms. In short, there are other and (more efficient) ways to subsidize consumer groups than resorting to a monopoly.

The case of architects in Europe or airlines in the USA before deregulation is a good example of how interest groups present the trade-off between safety and competition. These two groups often claim that competition would result in a decrease in safety levels that would risk the lives of their clients. As the US airline deregulation experience shows, this trade-off need not exist. Safety, health, and environmental standards can be imposed on a competitive industry provided that enough resources are devoted to monitoring compliance of the rules. In summary, most criticisms of free competition are based on a link between competition and the insufficient protection of social goals. The examples given above suggest, however, that such a link need not exist.

In order to counteract all these criticisms it is important to identify those who benefit and those who do not from the lack of competition, to quantify the social cost and benefits of anti-competition regulations, and to make all this information available to the public. An interpretation of liberalization policies as a process of fiscal reform can help in this task.

THE LIBERALIZATION PROCESS SEEN FROM THE FISCAL PERSPECTIVE

Restrictions on competition as a system of taxes and subsidies

Historically, monopolies and border duties were created to raise revenue in a world in which other means of public financing were ineffective, or too expensive, or nonexistent. Today, the 'regulation for revenue' motive (Altashuler and Gómez-Ibáñez, 1993) is still important in most activities like, for instance, the financing of local services by means of regulations on urban land use. However, in many activities there are other public objectives implicit in regulations like, for instance, setting security or quality standards, and cross-subsidizing particular consumer groups.

Regardless of the alleged objective, regulations that have the effect of restricting competition – as granting monopoly rights, creating barriers to entry, allowing or promoting collective price fixing, etc. – generally raise prices above the competition level (i.e. above the price that would prevail in the absence of the regulations). Many regulations are not anti-competition in the sense of having the final effect of raising prices. Commercial laws and quality standards, for instance, usually promote both efficiency and competition (reducing information gathering and transaction costs). Other regulations – like standards on health, environmental effects, or safety – increase prices, but as long as all companies are obliged to reach the same standard and the increase in price reflects an increase in quality, regulations cannot be regarded as anti-competition. From now on we will be concerned only with anti-competition regulations, like, for instance, limits on the number of firms allowed to operate in a market, restrictions on prices (price floors, administered prices, etc.), or production quotas. Anti-competition regulations could be defined as those that, in the absence of legal exemption, would be prosecuted by anti-trust authorities.

The basic premise of this chapter, first developed in Posner (1971) and extended in a number of articles (see Bird (1991) for a survey), is that the objectives and effects of anti-competition regulations are, in principle, similar to the objectives and effects of fiscal policy. Specifically, the extra price paid by consumers as a consequence of an anti-competition regulation is similar to a tax levied by the suppliers of the good or service and paid by the buyers of the good. Restrictions on competition are equivalent to a tax on consumption of a given good or service because they force the consumer to pay more than he or she would have to if there were free competition. The size of the implicit tax is measured by the price increase caused by the regulation. On the other hand, from the point of view of the recipients of the tax, this constitutes a subsidy since it is an income that is not obtained in a free market in exchange for the provision of some additional good or service. In a slightly more general context, these rent transfers have been named 'regulatory subsidies' (EEC Commission, 1991).

Another similarity between legal restrictions on competition and taxes is that the revenue generated by that surcharge is theoretically earmarked to address public needs. Although in practice most of the income generated by restrictions on competition is not used to satisfy social needs, this was usually the argument employed to justify the introduction of restrictions on free competition. For example, when a country gave a monopoly to an airline, it was supposed to make enough profit from frequently flown routes to keep routes open between cities with less traffic.

This similarity between taxation and the surcharge derived from restrictions on competition is not a new idea, since the history of monopolies is intimately related to taxation of one kind or another. Royal privileges and prerogatives, for instance, were concessions of monopolies granted by the king to certain citizens or companies, in exchange for which those who ran the monopolies paid a rent to the Crown, to finance royalty's expenses. More recently, Posner (1971) studied the (internal) cross-subsidies implicit in most regulatory measures. He concluded that an explicit accounting of regulatory subsidies should be practiced and proposed an efficiency analysis of these to determine whether the same ends could be attained at a smaller cost by means of external subsidies. This chapter elaborates on the practical meaning and implementation of Posner's suggestions. Specifically, we discuss how an explicit account of subsidies could be developed and analyze some aspects of internal regulatory subsidies from the point of view of fiscal policy.

In the context of international trade Hetzel (1994) developed a similar argument by noting that protectionism is equivalent to a tax on consumers. From this perspective he analyzed some characteristics of the tax implicit in tariffs, quotas, and other forms of trade discrimination and found it to be inefficient, regressive, and off budget. A similar argument is developed in the following pages for the case of regulations that limit competition.

Before going any further with this analogy between taxes and monopolies it is important to determine its limits. In particular, it is important to ask whether there are other reasonable objectives, different from the aforementioned revenue-raising motive, guiding the adoption of anti-competition regulations. This question is tantamount to considering in which cases it is possible to increase the efficiency of a market by means of anti-competition regulation.

The concept of market failure is fundamental for answering this question. There is a relatively long list of potential market failures, that is of instances in which the operation of a market is not efficient. This list includes externalities and public goods, information asymmetries, transaction costs, and economies of scale. In any of these circumstances one form or another of market intervention has the potential of improving the efficiency of the market as a resource allocation mechanism. The relevant question, however, is to determine in which cases a necessary intervention obliges limiting the number of firms operating in the market or requires limiting their capacity to independently set prices or quantities. In fact there is only one – even if important – case in which allowing competition among firms necessarily yields an inefficient market outcome: when there are economies of scale, or more generally, when the technology originates a natural monopoly, then a single firm is potentially the most efficient arrangement of the supply side of the market. The theory of contestable markets gives a detailed account of the conditions under which monopoly or oligopoly configurations are technically more efficient than the competitive benchmark (Baumol *et al.*, 1982). If, in addition, the monopoly is not sustainable, then it is justifiable for public authorities to prohibit entry. In the rest of the cases of market failure, some form of regulation could improve social welfare but competition itself is not the problem and consequently the restriction of competition to solve market failures is an inadequate recipe.

The distinction between *market* and *competition* is thus crucial. A large number of market failures can be found but there is only one case in which allowing competition among firms is detrimental: namely, the natural monopolies. Consequently, market failures, *per se*, are not enough to justify the adoption of anti-competition measures. With these two qualifications – not every regulation is anti-competition and not every market failure can be solved by limiting competition – we can now return to the fiscal analysis of anti-competition regulations.

Restrictions on competition as a hidden tax-subsidy system

Despite the similarities, there is an important difference between legal restrictions on competition and taxes: while the latter are annually quantified and reviewed in the process of drafting the national budget, the former are not. Restrictions on competition are like 'hidden budgets', that is they are forced rent transfers that are not accounted for in any budget at all. Notice that these 'hidden budgets' fail to be included in the national budget, as in the case of the 'off-budgets' considered in related literature. But even these off-budget expenditures are more transparent than restrictions to competition. For instance, the off-budget financing of certain activities by the central bank can be calculated from its annual accounts. However, the extra income obtained from a restriction on competition does not appear in the budget of any institution. The income is not only 'off' but also 'hidden'.

The lack of transparency of these 'hidden budgets' has some negative consequences. First, a 'hidden budget' is difficult to quantify. This makes it hard or even impossible to evaluate the costs and benefits of anti-competition regulation. In order to facilitate decision making, the expected income to be generated by every tax is forecasted and included in every year's budget. The fact that these numbers are mere approximations does not preclude them from being brought into the budget. There is no compelling reason to explain why monopolistic rents should not be treated similarly.

Second, the possibilities of the practical control of 'hidden' budgets by parliament are diminished because they are excluded from the control procedures imposed by the budgeting process. This facilitates rent seeking among the beneficiaries of the restriction. Even if there were well-defined public goals at the time a restriction on competition is approved, rent seeking tends to substitute private for public goals. And third, because of the lack of an annual budgetary review, hidden budgets tend to self-perpetuate.

THE CONTRIBUTION OF FISCAL POLICY TO MARKET LIBERALIZATION

The above criticisms suggest that, in the tradition of sound fiscal principles, 'hidden budgets' should be quantified and included in the national budget. Even if quantification is difficult, it is possible to argue about the significance, in terms of fiscal policy, of this yet-to-be-drafted budget. Both lines of thinking – how to quantify the hidden budget and what its policy implications are – are developed below.

The budget of restrictions on competition

The first lesson to be learnt from the fiscal approach to liberalization policies is that the hidden costs of legal restrictions on competition should be budgeted and put under parliamentary control. The origins of parliament as a body that decides on taxes are well known: people revolted against despotic royal power and demanded that all exactions of private rents – taxes – should be authorized by parliament and reviewed periodically, with regard to both the level of taxation and the use of tax revenue.

The permanent temptation for politicians has been to behave in exactly the opposite way. Since democratic parliaments were established, nearly all governments have sought ways to raise income without parliamentary approval. The most common and destructive method has been to issue money to finance government expenditures or, in other words, to use inflation as a tax. Governments not willing to ask parliament for authorization to raise taxes, or issue debt paper, have chosen to finance their expenditures by resorting to their central bank. Finance agencies and public enterprises have also played a similar role.

Fiscal experts very early detected these maneuvers and named them 'off-budget' techniques. They have shown that, in many cases, an off-budget can be more destructive than an increase in the public deficit (Joulfaian and Marlow, 1991).

Restrictions on competition play the role of off-budgets; that is, revenue is accrued without going to the parliament. The list of different subterfuges used to 'hide the budget' is as immense as human imagination: cross-subsidies in public monopolies, obligations to buy from national industries, regulations that force TV stations to finance national movies, legalized cartels, etc. The objective in setting a *Budget of Restrictions on Competition* is to make transparent to parliaments and governments the amount of income extracted by force of law (the hidden taxes) and the use of that money; that is, how much of it goes to finance social or public goals and how much goes to the pockets of those benefiting from the restriction on competition. In summary, the idea is to add the costs of legal restrictions to competition to the national budget.

In this way governments would be obliged to submit to the parliament every year not just the explicit taxes and expenditure items contained in the budget, but also the taxes and expenses implicit in restrictions on competition. Every year, the national budget sanctions certain public expenditures and makes an estimate of how much revenue is expected. The same should apply to the income and expenditure generated by legal restrictions on competition. Every year a document, namely a *Budget of Restrictions on Competition*, should list the income derived from restrictions and indicate how it will be spent. This budget would have the same two basic advantages as ordinary budgets in a democratic system: it would be annual and it would be transparent.

A similar scheme was adopted in many countries with respect to the so-called 'fiscal expenses'. The proposal was to calculate the benefits accrued by certain citizens from lower taxes, tax breaks, and so on, and to include them in a separate document which accompanies the budget. With the help of this technique it has been possible to lower those benefits over time and, in any case, to measure them precisely because they were explicit and assessed periodically. Gradually, those that were not justified economically or socially have been suppressed, leaving only those with sufficient social or economic justification. The same would happen if a *Budget of Restrictions on Competition* was sent to the parliament every year. Slowly, public awareness of these restrictions and their transparency would lead to some of them being maintained, while other unnecessary restrictions would be gradually suppressed. Periodic debate would, undoubtedly, encourage suggestions of ways in which social goals might be achieved without resorting to monopolies or having to restrict competition, and, therefore, social goals could be obtained at a lower cost to the public.

We will not discuss in detail the calculation of this budget. There are, however, two points we want to make. First, in practice the sophisticated economic approach has some weaknesses. Second, for our purposes, all that is usually needed is an estimate based on international or intersectoral price comparisons. Let us consider each point in turn.

The textbook recipe for calculating the welfare losses of monopolies is, simply stated, to measure the extra profit made by the corresponding firms in excess of the normal rate of return. This is the procedure first used in

Harberger (1954) and, with several refinements, it is also the basic method employed later in the empirical literature on deregulation; see Winston (1993) or Joskow and Rose (1989) for a survey. There are two main problems with this approach. First, it disregards the fact that a large part of the social costs of monopoly power occurs in the forms of inefficient management (Leibenstein, 1966) and rent seeking (Tullock, 1967). In these cases, restrictions on competition do not result in higher profits but in higher costs. As a consequence, many estimates of monopoly profits are just a lower bound of the monopoly premium paid by consumers. Second, on the practical side, the required amount of information and calculation involved in estimating welfare losses is very large. As a matter of fact, the complexity of these calculations makes it a hard research problem, thus limiting its usefulness for policy implementation.

The *Budget of Restrictions on Competition*, being less ambitious than welfare loss estimates, tries to overcome both difficulties. The basic idea is that in order to measure the extra margin charged by firms sheltered from competition, it is often possible to take the reference of another country or state, or even of another sector in the same country. Let us consider two examples taken from the Tribunal de Defensa de la Competencia studies of the Spanish economy.

In the case of telecommunications, basic telephone services are offered by a monopoly in Spain (and most other countries in continental Europe) while some degree of competition exists in the USA, UK, etc. Thus it seems reasonable to compare Spanish tariffs to UK tariffs. Direct comparison reveals that Spanish consumers were paying in 1992 an extra 240 billion pesetas for their long-distance calls (i.e. they would have saved this amount if the same calls had been charged at UK prices). The 240 billion pesetas are the hidden tax of the telecommunications monopoly. There is also a subsidy to local calls, which are cheaper in Spain than in the UK, that amounted to 110 billion pesetas, approximately. The difference between these two amounts can be interpreted as unjustified monopoly profits. Table 4.1 shows how the *Budget of Restrictions on Competition* might look. The items in this table have been taken from the Tribunal de Defensa de la Competencia studies of the Spanish economy and cover telecommunications, pharmaceutical products, and coal mining.

Consider as another example the distribution of pharmaceutical products. Prices are regulated in most European countries and, in any case, it is hard to figure out average prices because there are many different pharmaceutical products. Thus, it is difficult to compare different countries. Alternatively, there is a similar enough sector that can be used as a benchmark. The distribution of nonpharmaceutical drugs and cosmetics is an unregulated activity in Spain and it is very similar to the distribution of pharmaceutical products. The average mark-up in the former is 32 per cent while the fixed mark-up charged (by force of law) by pharmacies in Spain is 42 per cent. The

Table 4.1 Budget for Restrictions on Competition (sample summary)

	Monopoly income (millions of pesetas)	
1	Long-distance and international phone calls	239,964
2	Distribution of medicines (pharmacies)	53,297
3	Protection of national coal (through the electricity bill)	135,000
etc.		
Total . . .		

	Expenditure (public necessities attended to by monopolies) (millions of pesetas)	
1.1	Subsidies to local calls	112,704
1.2	Various telephone services (rural, maritime, etc.)	10,000
2	Upkeep of pharmacies in remote areas	5,000
3	Coal mining subsidies	135,000
etc.		
Total . . .		

extra margin of 10 per cent does constitute the monopolist surcharge which amounts to some 50 billion pesetas per year. The only subsidy to consumers in this case would be the cost of keeping pharmacies in remote areas.

In any case, the important contribution of the *Budget for Restrictions on Competition* is that it would provoke discussion, and as a result of that discussion, the restrictions that make sense would be maintained, while those that do not, and which are harmful, would gradually disappear.

Optimal taxation and restrictions on competition

Once restrictions on competition are budgeted as taxes, at least conceptually, a fiscal analysis of these taxes seems appropriate. The question we want to examine is whether the system of taxes and subsidies built into the restrictions on competition is an efficient way for redistributing income. The answer suggested below is that it is indeed a grossly inefficient system.

In order to illustrate this approach let us consider the well-developed analysis of excise taxation; see Stiglitz (1992) as a textbook reference. We know from it that excise taxes are not generally optimal from the point of view of social welfare. Other forms of taxation are less distortionary in many contexts. A general income tax, a sales tax or a value-added tax, for instance, is in many cases less welfare decreasing than an excise tax generating the same revenue. Since the tax implicit in a restriction on competition is by definition an excise tax, it can be inferred that, in general, monopolies impose inefficient taxes. The same revenues can be obtained in less distortionary ways. Both excise and general taxes decrease disposable income. However, the excise tax also changes relative prices by increasing consumption of the other goods while decreasing consumption of the taxed good. Since in an efficient market system prices convey information about the relative scarcity of each good, distorted prices must necessarily yield a worse final allocation. In this view, market reform is equivalent to a fiscal reform substituting a set of taxes for another, more efficient system.

A preliminary analysis of the effects of restrictions on competition on the distribution of income can also be easily done in certain cases. Specifically, when there are no cross-subsidies among consumers the analysis is immediate. This is essentially the case if the good is sold at a uniform price.

It is known that differential taxation of goods with inelastic demands tends to be regressive. Since anti-competition regulations tend to proliferate, at least in Europe, in markets with a low price and income elasticity of demand (energy, pharmaceutical, basic telecommunication services, etc.), it must be inferred that anti-competition regulations are regressive in many cases.

While this line of reasoning will not be developed in further detail in this chapter, it highlights the potential of the analogy between taxes and anti-competition regulations.

The role of fiscal policy in smoothing the transition to a competitive market

Finally, the experience of fiscal policy also offers some guidance on how to organize the transition to a more competitive market. As we argued above, a conflict between competition and public protection of social goals need not exist. Indeed, once it is assumed that monopolies are not necessary to subsidize particular groups, the process of eliminating restrictions on competition can be divorced from the process of eliminating subsidies. It is possible to allow competition to work and at the same time maintain the cross-subsidies implicit in the restrictions to competition. Cross-subsidies can be gradually dismantled thus giving time to the consumers and firms involved to reorganize. Let us consider some examples.

Telecommunications monopolies are responsible, in some European countries, for providing what is called 'universal service'. However, there are many ways to obtain universal service in a competitive situation. The former monopoly can be forced to provide it as long as its market share is large enough; this was done in the UK. It is also possible to finance universal service by means of a canon imposed on all telecommunications operators or to finance it from a general tax, etc. Any of these methods allows competition to work while keeping the redistribution of income unchanged. While this is, admittedly, a second-best policy it is, in any case, a better policy than granting a monopoly right. At least the benefits of competition are obtained this way. A similar approach could be taken in real state markets where the 'regulation for revenue' approach is nowadays dominant in many countries. It consists, in essence, in buying from the authorities the modification of zoning regulations in exchange for the financing of public infrastructures and buildings. It is easy to imagine other ways of financing public investments without virtually closing the urban land market. A general tax, a property tax, or any other charge on urban land owners could provide the same amount of money without impeding the role of supply and demand to allocate land to its different uses.

It can be argued that cross-subsidies are (almost) always inefficient and therefore should be abolished at the same time restrictions on competition are eliminated. However, it is more realistic to begin by dismantling monopolies and suppressing legal restrictions on competition and to follow by eliminating subsidies. In this way the coalition among the vested interests (groups interested in maintaining the restrictions) and the group of consumers interested in maintaining the subsidies is broken. In this gradual approach, restrictions on competition are first eliminated while maintaining subsidies. Something is gained in this scenario with respect to the original situation: the subsidy is financed in a more efficient way because competition is allowed to work.

CONCLUDING REMARKS

There is a tendency to consider the adoption of liberalization policies as sectoral problems. In this view, market reforms must proceed case by case and must be entrusted to experts in each sector. Consequently, reforms tend to proceed slowly and results are unequal across markets. The bottom line of this chapter is that liberalization policies should not be treated exclusively as a sectoral problem. Instead, liberalization policies must be considered as an economy-wide problem that has to be treated with the same tools applied to other economic policy problems. This chapter shows how the models of fiscal theory and the tools of fiscal policy are useful to implement market liberalization. Hopefully this could facilitate a more rapid and homogeneous development of liberalization policies.

NOTES

1 In the early 1990s and at the request of the Spanish Government, the Tribunal de Defensa de la Competencia (the Spanish Antitrust Commission) prepared some reports including numerous proposals to increase competition in services (transportation, telecommunications, professional services, local monopolies, energy, professional services, etc.) and urban land markets. This chapter greatly reflects that task and consequently we are indebted to all the people who made it possible.

2 We are indebted to Vicente Salas for many helpful comments. However, the contents of this chapter only reflect the authors' views and opinions.

3 We selected this term for policies that aim to create or increase competition in the markets by suppressing legal restrictions. We discarded the more common expression 'deregulation policy' because this term has a wider significance and usually implies the suppression of regulations with a different purpose than increasing competition, like those protecting health or safety. Other possible terms are either horrible – like 're-regulation' – or confusing, like 'competition policy', whose conventional use has become identical to anti-trust policy.

4 The importance and slow progress of the liberalization of services in western countries have moved us to focus this chapter on these particular sectors. Nevertheless, the advantages of adopting 'a fiscal approach' in designing and implementing liberalization policies extend to other sectors and countries. In particular, the profound process of liberalization launched in ex-communist countries calls for a more prominent role of fiscal policy in defining and implementing that process.

REFERENCES

Altashuler, Alan A. and José A. Gómez-Ibáñez (1993) 'Regulation for Revenue: The Political Economy of Land Use Exactions', The Lincoln Institute of Land Policy.

Baumol, W., J. Panzar and R. Willig (1982) 'Contestable Markets and the Theory of Industry Structure', San Diego: Harcourt Brace Jovanovich.

Bird, R. (ed.) (1991) 'More Taxing than Taxes: An Introduction', *More Taxing than Taxes*, San Francisco: ICS Press.

Brittan, S. (1994a) 'Nimbyism: The Growing Cost', *Financial Times*, March 24, Economic Viewpoint.

Brittan, S. (1994b) 'How "Nimbies" will curb Recovery', *Financial Times*, July 7, Economic Viewpoint.

EEC Commission (1991) 'Economic Rationale for Subsidy Control', Chapter 3, Part I: Fair Competition in the Internal Market: Community State Aid Policy, *European Economy*, No. 48, September.

Government of Japan (1994) 'Draft of the Deregulation Program'.

Harberger, A. (1954) 'Monopoly and Resource Allocation', *American Economic Review*, Vol. XLIV, No. 2, pp. 77–87.

Hetzel, R. (1994) 'The Free Trade Debate: The Illusion of Security versus Growth', *Economic Quarterly*, Richmond Federal Reserve Bank.

Joskow, P. and N. Rose (1989) 'The Effects of Economic Regulation', in *Handbook of Industrial Organization, Vol. II*, ed. M. Schmalensee and R. Willig, Amsterdam: North-Holland,

Joulfaian, D. and M. Marlow (1991) 'The Relationship between on-budget and off-budget Government', *Economic Letters*, Vol. 35, No. 3, pp. 307–310.

Kennedy, N. (1994) 'Household Saving and Real House Prices: An International Perspective', Bank for International Settlements, Working Paper No. 20.

Krugman, P. (1994) 'Competitiveness: A Dangerous Obsession', *Foreign Affairs*, Vol. 73, No. 2.

Leibenstein, H. (1966) 'Allocative Efficiency vs. "X-Efficiency"', *American Economic Review*, Vol. 56, pp. 392–415.

Posner, R. (1971) 'Taxation by Regulation', *Bell Journal of Economics*, Spring, Vol. 2, No. 1.

Stiglitz, J. (1992) *La Economía del Sector Público*, Barcelona: Antoni Bosch.

Tullock, G. (1967) 'The Welfare Costs of Tariffs, Monopolies and Theft', *Western Economic Journal*, Vol. 5, No. 3, pp. 224–232.

Vives, X. (1993) 'La competencia en la Perspectiva Europea', *Papeles de economía española*, No. 57.

Winston, C. (1993) 'Economic Deregulation: Days of Reckoning for Microeconomists', *Journal of Economic Literature*, Vol. XXXI, pp. 1263–1289.

Part II

FISCAL POLICY AND THE PROMOTION OF SUSTAINABLE GROWTH

5

EMPIRICAL EVIDENCE ON THE IMPACT OF RECENT TAX REFORMS ON SAVINGS, INVESTMENT, AND GROWTH

*Krister Andersson**

INTRODUCTION

The Scandinavian countries are well known for their high taxes and extensive welfare systems. In the latter half of the 1980s and early 1990s, Sweden, Norway and Denmark have all undertaken major tax reforms resulting in considerably lower tax rates and broader tax bases. Since the tax rates used to be very high, and therefore presumably highly distortive, the tax reforms in these countries serve as illustrative examples of the effects of tax changes on economic activity and growth.[1] The most significant lesson to come from the Scandinavian experience with tax reform is the timing of tax reforms and other structural reforms as well as the need for appropriate macro-economic policies to obtain the full benefit of a tax reform.

This chapter is structured in the following way. First, reasons behind the tax reforms are analyzed. Domestic factors in particular, but also international considerations, played a role. The importance of the macro-economic environment in which the new tax system is to operate is then discussed. When evaluating the effects of a tax reform on savings, investment and growth, it is important also to consider the effects of other structural reforms and the sequencing of reforms. These aspects are discussed and the policy conclusions are drawn in the final section.

DOMESTIC REASONS BEHIND THE TAX REFORMS

Background

The tax to GDP ratio in the Scandinavian countries increased throughout the 1970s and the first half of the 1980s. By the mid-1980s, the Scandinavian countries had a tax to GDP ratio above 50 percent, a much higher level than that in other countries. In Sweden, the ratio increased to around 56 percent in 1987 (see Figure 5.1). Critics claimed that large inefficiencies were created and that the growth of the public sector stifled the economy. However, no major attempts were made to lower the overall tax burden significantly. The high marginal tax rates in Scandinavia also meant that tax deductions were valuable.

The tax systems became more comprehensive and complex in order to raise the necessary tax revenue. However, with each amendment to the tax code, numerous new loopholes were created. In the 1970s, the number of people who went to great efforts to plan their taxes started to grow rapidly. As the inflation rate increased, more and more people took advantage of the large benefits to be gained from interest deductions and investments in assets with a low taxable yield. When credit markets were liberalized in the 1980s, credit became available to everyone, and tax planning activities grew at an ever increasing rate.

Interest deductions increased in all of the Scandinavian countries and revenues from taxes on capital decreased.[2] The response to the tax-induced incentives was so large that the government would have raised more tax revenues if capital income had been exempt from taxation. The reason was that the deductions exceeded reported income, especially for high-income earners. Capital income taxation no longer contributed to an equalization of after-tax incomes (on the contrary).

Tax reforms undertaken elsewhere in the 1980s were also an impetus to

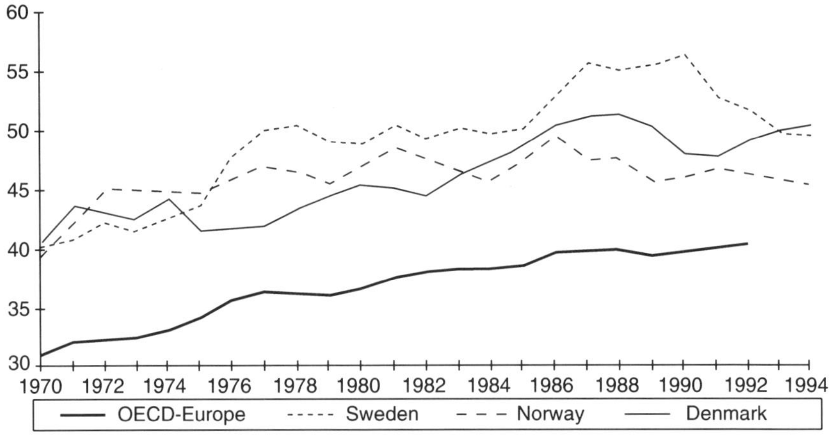

Figure 5.1 Tax revenues (percent of GDP)
Sources: OECD Revenue Statistics and OECD Economic Outlook Database
Notes: Figures for 1993 and 1994 are OECD forecasts

reform. The Scandinavian countries are small open economies and they have traditionally followed developments in other countries. The arguments that tax reduction led to growth and thereby expanded tax revenues[3] were debated in Scandinavia but were not taken seriously and were not the principal reason for reforms. However, as capital markets became more and more integrated, and financial markets were deregulated, the need for tax reform increased. Furthermore, the emigration of highly trained persons and the reluctance of people with high marginal tax rates to work overtime, alerted policy makers of the need to reform the tax system. The recent tax debate continues to put little emphasis on international pressures, even as the process of economic integration proceeds. As the economies recover further from the recent recession, international factors may, however, once again play a role in the tax reform efforts.

The tax structure in the Scandinavian countries

The changes in the top marginal tax rates and corporate tax in the Scandinavian countries in the 1980s could perhaps be viewed as small compared to some other countries (see Tables 5.1 and 5.2). However, a decrease of 15 to 20 percentage points in the top marginal tax rate is significant in its potential effects on incentives, especially given the very high levels of marginal rates before the tax reforms. It seems reasonable to assume that the costs of the distortions decrease proportionately more for each percentage point reduction in the marginal tax rate at very high tax rates, compared to lowering at low tax rates.[4]

Considerable changes have been made in corporate taxes. Both the rates and the tax bases have been modified in all three countries. The corporate tax rates have been lowered to highly competitive levels. By lowering the statutory corporate tax rates, the subsidies to debt financing through the corporate tax system decrease. The relative disincentive to equity financing in the corporate sector therefore also tends to decrease. The corporate tax rates, during the 1980s and so far during the 1990s, are given in Table 5.2.[5]

Table 5.1 Top marginal tax rates for individuals

	1980	*1985*	*1989*	*1994*
Sweden[1]	85.0	80.0	72.0	50.0
Denmark[2]	70.0	73.0	68.7	67.5
Norway[3]	75.4	66.9	53.8	41.7

[1] At a local tax rate of 30%.
[2] At a local tax rate of 28%.
[3] At a local tax rate of 21%.
Sources: *European Tax Handbook*, International Bureau of Fiscal Documentation and various national sources

Table 5.2 Corporation income tax rates

	1980	*1985*	*1989*	*1994*
Sweden	58.0	52.0	52.0	28.0
Denmark	40.0	50.0	50.0	34.0
Norway	50.8	50.8	50.8	28.0

Sources: *European Tax Handbook*, International Bureau of Fiscal Documentation and various national sources

Taxation of capital income and savings

The Scandinavian countries applied the general income tax where capital income was added to wage income and taxed at the marginal tax rate. Nominal interest income and dividends were taxable, which meant that, in the 1980s, the real after-tax rate of return was often negative. During the first half of the 1980s, the average inflation rate declined from double figures to around 6 percent in 1985. Since nominal interest payments were deductible at very high marginal tax rates, the subsidy to debt financing was considerable. As a consequence, household savings rates in the Scandinavian countries declined and became negative for several years in the second half of the 1980s in both Norway and Sweden (see Figure 5.2). The decline in the savings rate partly reflected the effects of the tax system, partly the deregulation of financial markets which was undertaken (see below).[6]

Individuals in the three countries responded to the tax-induced incentives by debt-financing asset holdings with a low taxable return. The strains on the global income tax became more and more evident as time progressed.

In Norway, interest payments were fully deductible against the marginal income tax rate until 1987. While taxable capital income grew only slowly, deductions for interest payments quadrupled between 1979 and 1986 (see Table 5.3).

The growth rate of interest deductions was considerably higher than the growth rate for wage income. Furthermore, the average interest deduction for

Table 5.3 Some average amounts for persons over 17 years of age in Norway (thousands of kroner)

	1979	*1982*	*1984*	*1985*	*1986*
Wages	39.9	53.8	60.5	66.7	77.0
Capital income	2.0	2.7	3.6	4.2	5.7
Interest deductions[1]	3.0	5.4	8.2	9.5	13.0

[1] The average interest deduction for wage earners was, according to the National Budget for 1989, equal to NOK18,200 in 1986.
Source: Author's calculations based on material presented in the Norwegian National Budget for 1989

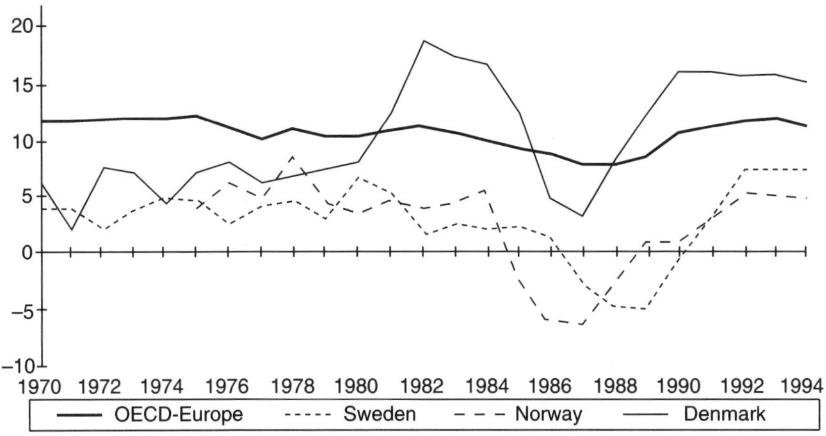

Figure 5.2 Household savings rate (percent of disposable income)
Source: OECD Economic Outlook
Notes: OECD-Europe excluding Greece, Iceland, Ireland, Luxembourg, Portugal and Turkey. Figures for 1994 are OECD forecasts

wage earners was higher in relative terms for high-income earners than for low-income earners.

The situation was similar in Denmark. Interest deductions as a percentage of wage income increased substantially during the 1970s and early 1980s. High-income earners had larger interest deductions relative to their income than low-income earners (see Table 5.4).

In Sweden, the tax base, as defined by the tax code, had become negative and the government lost revenues from taxing capital income. In 1982, the tax base for capital income was estimated to have been *minus* SEK9.3 billion or some 1.5 percent of GDP.[7] Furthermore, while low-income earners reported positive capital income, high-income earners reported negative capital income. Even the top 2.5 centiles showed negative capital income (taxable).

Table 5.4 Interest deductions in percent of average income in Denmark (DKK)

Gross income (thousands DKK)	*2–300*	*3–400*	*4–500*	*>500*	*Total*
Average income in the interval	236.2	339.9	442.5	825.5	
Interest deduction in % of av. income	23.4	27.7	30.8	34.7	15.4

Source: Author's calculations based on *Indkomster og Formuer 1983 og 1984*, Danmarks statistik, 1988, table 11B

If capital income had been tax exempt, high-income earners would have paid *more* in taxes (see Table 5.5).

The tax reform efforts in the Scandinavian countries all focused on lowering capital income taxes while trying to maintain a large public sector by taxing labor income and consumption relatively heavily. As a consequence, all three countries came to the conclusion that it was not appropriate to maintain the global income tax, and schedular taxation was introduced.

It is interesting to note that the Scandinavian countries are among the first western economies to abandon the global income tax. The reason is not administrative concerns or international pressures, but efficiency and equity considerations and the resulting low growth rate. The problems with a global income tax may be worth examining for those countries engaged in tax reform in Eastern and Central Europe. Vito Tanzi has pointed out important administrative problems which a global income tax will have for these countries:

> For example, the attempt to introduce a global income tax, a pet idea of many western economists, would almost surely lead to disappointment. A global income tax would require large-scale filing and complex administrative procedures for which these countries are not prepared.
>
> (Tanzi 1992, p. 19)

Besides the administrative problems, efficiency and equity considerations could be added, in particular if the tax rates are high.

In conclusion, it should be stressed that the Scandinavian tax systems needed to be changed for domestic reasons. Generous provisions for deductions for interest payments created large distortions in the economies and slowed the growth rate of the economies. The tax systems even

Table 5.5 The effect of abolishing taxes on capital income in Sweden, 1984 (SEK)

Decile	*Taxable income*	*Differences in taxes paid*
1	–22,300	–75
2	22,300–29,700	–839
3	29,700–37,700	–1,110
4	37,700–47,200	–976
5	47,200–58,700	–458
6	58,700–69,500	–978
7	69,500–79,200	+109
8	79,200–90,200	+1,305
9	90,200–108,800	+3,385
10	108,800–	+5,065
Top 2.5%	156,500–	+7,617
All		+571

Source: 'Sweden' by K. Andersson in *Comparative Tax Systems, Europe, Canada, and Japan*, edited by J. Pechman, Tax Analysts, 1987, p. 90

contributed in an adverse way to social objectives like a more even distribution of income. These effects existed before financial markets were deregulated but they became more noticeable and the consequences for tax revenues became a matter of concern after deregulation.

The importance of financial deregulation

In the Scandinavian countries, financial markets had for decades been heavily regulated, creating distortions and an inefficient allocation of resources. The timing of financial deregulation was somewhat different in the three countries but few lessons, if any, were drawn from neighbors' experiences.

Denmark was the first country to embark on financial deregulation. Norway followed and finally Sweden started to deregulate financial markets in the mid to late 1980s.

In all three countries, bank lending to the private sector expanded rapidly (see Figure 5.3). The level of indebtedness, which already was higher than that in the largest industrial countries, increased drastically (see Figure 5.4).

The deregulation of financial markets was necessary in order to improve the functioning of the economies. However, the combination of somewhat freer access to capital markets for ordinary citizens and a financial system unused to evaluating credit risks resulted in a widespread expansion of credit without proper collateral. The tax systems still favored borrowing by allowing very generous deductions for interest payments and, furthermore, there was a habit to undertake primarily domestic investments and foreign portfolio diversification expanded slowly. This resulted in very large price increases on

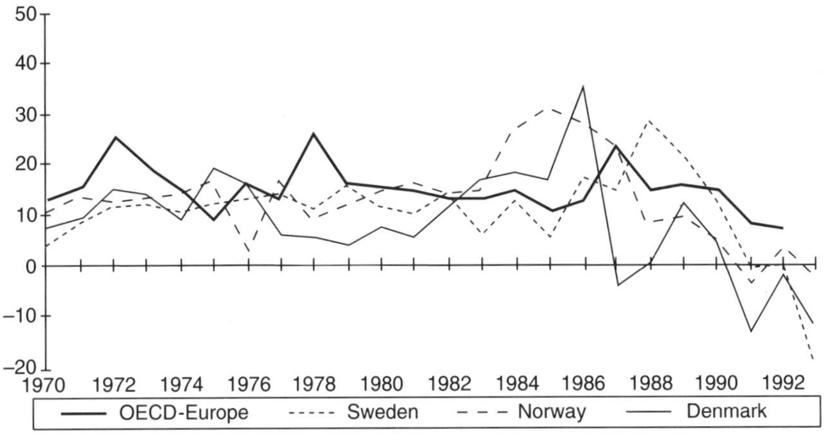

Figure 5.3 Bank lending to private sector (stock) (percentage change year on year)
Source: International Financial Statistics, IMF
Note: OECD-Europe includes Denmark, Finland, France, Germany, Italy, Norway, Sweden and United Kingdom

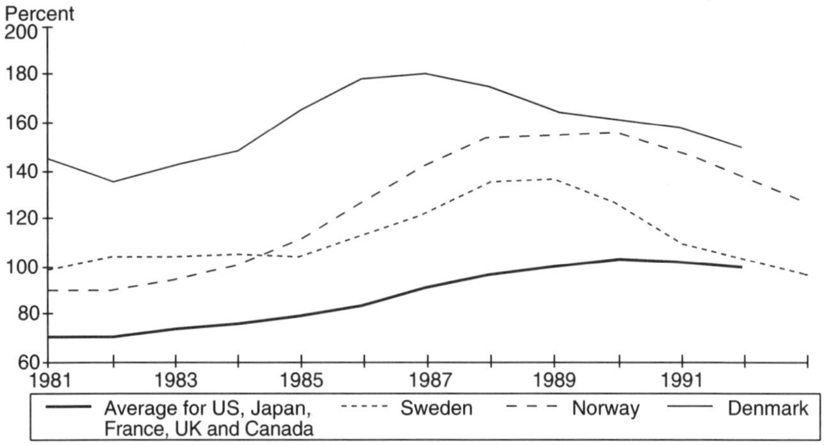

Figure 5.4 Household gross debt (percent of disposable income)
Sources: United States, Japan, France, United Kingdom and Canada: OECD Economic Outlook; Denmark: Ministry of Economic Affairs; Norway: Statistics Norway and Norges Bank; and Sweden: Statistics Sweden

domestic assets in general, and on commercial real estate in particular.

Unfortunately, the stance of macro-economic policies was lax and in the inflationary environment which still prevailed, asset bubbles were created. Toward the end of the decade, and in Sweden in the early 1990s, the bursting of the asset bubbles resulted in large losses in the banking sector (see Figure 5.5). The factors behind the bank problems are sometimes described as 'bad luck, bad policies and bad banking'.

An important lesson from Scandinavia is that tax reform efforts cannot been seen as isolated from other structural changes or the overall stance of macro-economic policies. The sequencing of reforms is crucial in order to avoid other problems; this may be very costly to tax payers and may even force governments to reverse the tax reform owing to heavier revenue requirements. Even if the tax reform is not reversed, expectations of some backscaling may take away important effects of the reform such as a positive investment response.[8]

INTERNATIONAL FACTORS BEHIND THE TAX REFORMS

As capital markets became increasingly integrated, the need for tax coordination or tax harmonization started to influence tax policies. The Scandinavian countries are small open economies and have a large foreign sector. However, capital flows, other than investments through firms, were restricted, and portfolio investment in particular was often limited to the domestic market.

Inward foreign direct investment was around 1 percent of GDP in all three

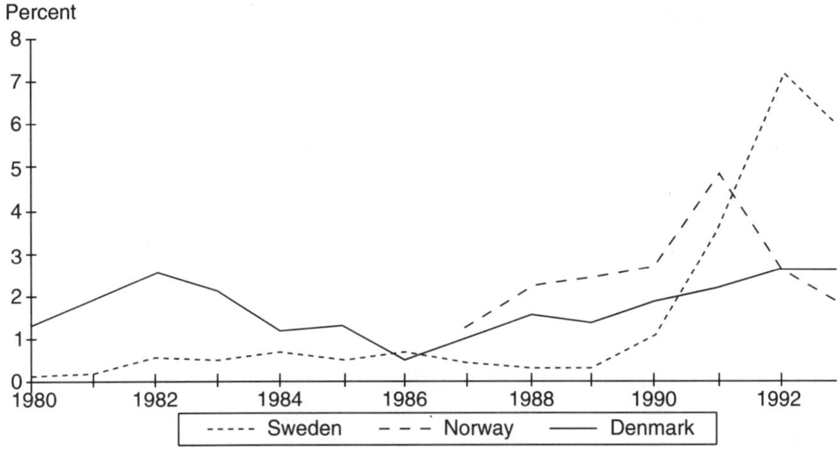

Figure 5.5 Credit losses in the banking sector (percent of total credit)
Sources: Denmark: Danmarks Nationalbank; Norway: Norges Bank; and Sweden: Sveriges Riksbank

countries during the second half of the 1980s. Outward foreign direct investment tended to be higher, and in Sweden it reached a level above 5 per cent at the end of the decade. Tax factors may have played a role in this process but most analyses point to other factors, like the wish to establish a branch or subsidiary inside the European Community, as being far more important.[9]

The liberalization of credit markets and rules concerning foreign portfolio investments resulted in portfolio adjustments and large capital movements. The turnover in the Swedish foreign exchange market can be viewed as an indicator of the increased integration of the Scandinavian countries into the world capital market: it more than doubled from 700 per cent of GDP in 1987 to 1,400 per cent in 1993 (see Figure 5.6). In April 1992, the turnover of the Swedish foreign exchange market in relation to GDP was roughly twice as high as in France or Germany.[10]

The closer integration of capital markets clearly played a role in the tax reform efforts. In particular, it reinforced the need to reform capital income taxation. To assess to what extent a tax system creates incentives to allocate the capital to certain assets or to move abroad, a methodology of calculating user cost of capital may be applied.[11]

By using this methodology[12] it is possible to evaluate to what extent the Scandinavian tax systems fulfilled the requirement of export neutrality and import neutrality of capital.

Calculations show that even before the tax reform, the corporate tax treatment in Sweden was favorable, partly due to very generous provisions for depreciation allowances.[13] However, the high tax rates on capital income meant that an equity-financed investment carried a heavy tax load for the

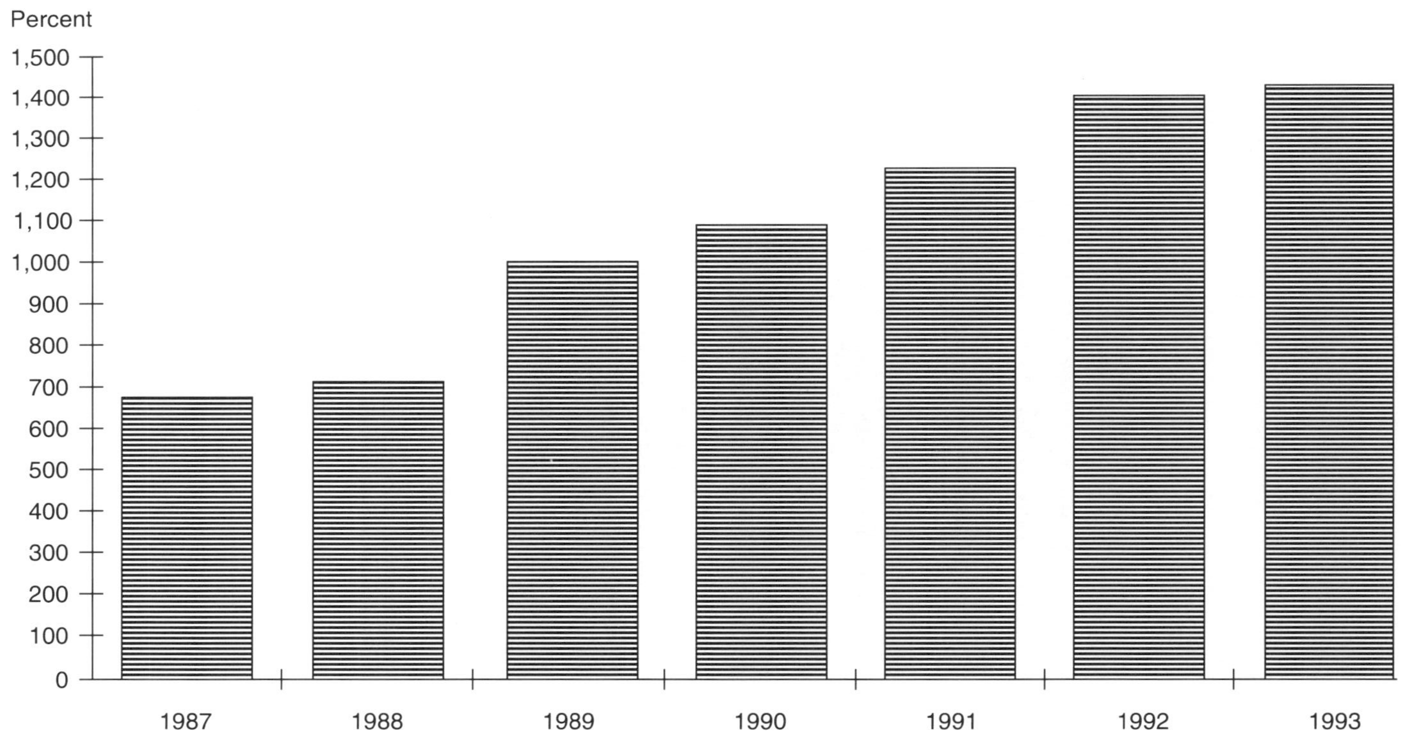

Figure 5.6 Total turnover in the Swedish foreign exchange market (percent of GDP)
Source: Sveriges Riksbank

investor while a debt-financed investment was taxed much more lightly. For foreign investors, with low capital taxes on dividends and capital gains, the effect of favorable corporate tax treatment in the Scandinavian countries was highly advantageous. The Scandinavian tax systems therefore tended to favor foreign holding of Scandinavian equities while domestic owners faced incentives to specialize in debt financing. One can therefore conclude that not even within a country tax neutrality prevailed between different modes of financing, and across countries tax neutrality was not upheld. Furthermore, Scandinavian investors faced a heavier tax burden on their savings than investors in most other countries.

In Sweden and Denmark, the overall tax revenues from corporate income have remained at 2 percent or less of total tax revenues (see Figure 5.7). Moreover, the lack of integration of the corporate and individual taxes, in conjunction with relatively high capital taxes before the tax reforms, resulted in a sizable total tax wedge for domestic households.

CORE FEATURES OF THE TAX REFORMS

From the description above, it is obvious that capital income taxation has been at the core of tax reform efforts in Scandinavia. The Scandinavian countries all faced considerable problems with their tax structure and tax reforms were needed for domestic economic reasons. The large deductions for interest payments created distortions and eroded the trust in the tax system as equitable. It was considered far too costly to lower the overall tax rates to levels where capital income taxes needed to be to limit the incentives to debt financing and to limit tax evasion and capital flight. All three countries therefore chose to tax labor income and capital income separately. The global income tax had to be abandoned. It is worth pointing out that the reasons behind abandoning the global income tax were primarily domestic rather than international. At very high marginal tax rates, the distortions had become so large that it was difficult to maintain a global income tax. Savings were taxed too heavily and borrowing had gotten to be so advantageous as to induce serious distortions in the investment pattern.

Limiting interest deductions

The three countries came up with different methods for keeping a large public sector and having relatively high marginal tax rates while at the same time limiting the value of deductions. However, limiting deductions created problems in two ways. If self-employed persons would also face a limitation on deductions, different kinds of businesses would not be treated in the same way. No limitations on deductions for interest payments for incorporated businesses were considered. On the other hand, if there was no limitation for self-employed persons on their deductions, they would be in a better situation

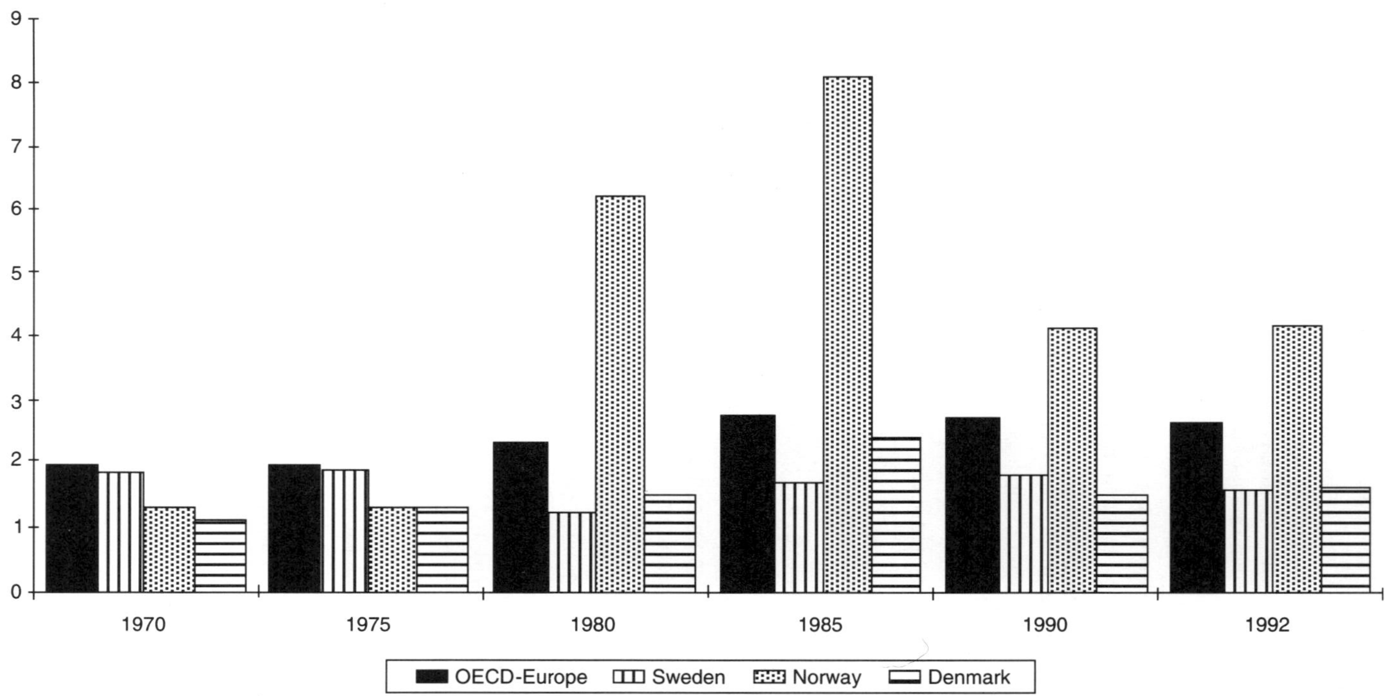

Figure 5.7 Taxes on corporate income (percent of GDP)
Source: OECD Revenue Statistics

than wage earners. It would be possible for self-employed persons to borrow as a business and use the money for private consumption. A substantial part of the tax reform efforts in Scandinavia was devoted to this question.

Norway decided to introduce a new tax base, a gross income tax base, and to levy a tax on gross income (top tax) as well as keeping the old income tax on net income. The marginal tax rate on net income was lowered considerably and deductions were basically only allowed when calculating the net income. In addition, high-income earners have to pay taxes on their gross income. Full imputation was introduced in the tax reform of 1991 and no taxes are due on dividend income (the corporate tax rate is 28 percent). In computing capital gains from the sale of shares, the shareholder's acquisition cost of each share is increased annually by the company's retained profits.

Denmark decided to separate labor and capital income. The Danish example is very interesting, although somewhat complicated. Interest deductions now have a limited value of 51 percent while the top marginal tax rate is 67.5 percent. The value of interest deductions is scheduled to be gradually reduced to 37.5 percent in 1998, at a time when the top marginal tax rate is expected to be 59.5 percent. Dividends are tax exempt if the market value of the stocks held by an individual is below $15,000 (DKK100,000) and the holding period exceeds three years. If not, the tax rate is 30 percent if total dividend income does not exceed approximately $5,000 (DKK31,700). Dividends above this limit are taxed at 40 percent (before 1993, 45 percent).

Sweden first decided (in the mid-1980s) to introduce two tax schedules instead of one, limiting the value of deductions for interest payments corresponding to a marginal tax rate of 50 percent. However, the 1990–1991 tax reform lowered the marginal tax rate on labor income to 50 percent and capital income is now taxed separately at a flat rate of 30 percent.[14]

Through these changes, the Scandinavian tax systems tended to limit the disadvantage for domestic holders of corporate shares.

EFFECTS ON INVESTMENTS, SAVINGS AND GROWTH OF THE TAX REFORMS

Effects on labor supply

The aim of the tax reforms was to be revenue neutral but to raise the revenue in a less distorting way. The shift from very high marginal tax rates on labor income to top marginal tax rates of around 50 percent was intended to boost labor supply. However, as the economies went into a recession in the early 1990s, it is hard to assess the impact on employment. Between 1989 and 1993, the unemployment rate went up in all three countries, but mostly in Sweden where the unemployment rate went from less than 2 percent of the labor force to 8 percent. The rate of increase in Denmark paralleled that of OECD–

Europe while Norway has experienced a considerably slower rate of increase (see Figure 5.8).

One of the ways the tax reforms were financed was by scaling back basic deductions and lowering the zero bracket. In Sweden, the zero bracket before the tax reform was already very small compared to that in most other countries: an annual income of around $1,500 was indeed taxed at a marginal tax rate of 30 percent. Despite the fact that no single individual can survive on such a low income, the tax reform meant that even lower incomes were made taxable. At the same time, these individuals were eligible for substantial subsidies and transfers from the public. The tendency to tax low-income earners more heavily is, however, not unique to the Scandinavian countries. For instance, the average tax rate on low-income workers increased somewhat in the United States in the second half of the 1980s.[15]

For high-income earners, the top marginal tax rate was reduced and their expected after-tax wage income rose. They instantaneously experienced a capital gain on their human resources, and the payoff to higher education was expected to promote additional investments in human capital.

Taxes clearly affect the choice between labor and leisure time but many other factors influence that decision as well. Taxes in this regard should also include payroll taxes and social security contributions to the extent that they do not reflect an actuarial payment for benefits to be received later on in life. Furthermore, transfers to the household sector may be linked to taxable income. In Scandinavia, rent subsidies may decrease as incomes increase and the marginal effective 'tax' rate for low- and middle-income earners may still be in the range of 70 to 80 percent, if the effect of income increases on means-tested benefits is taken into account.

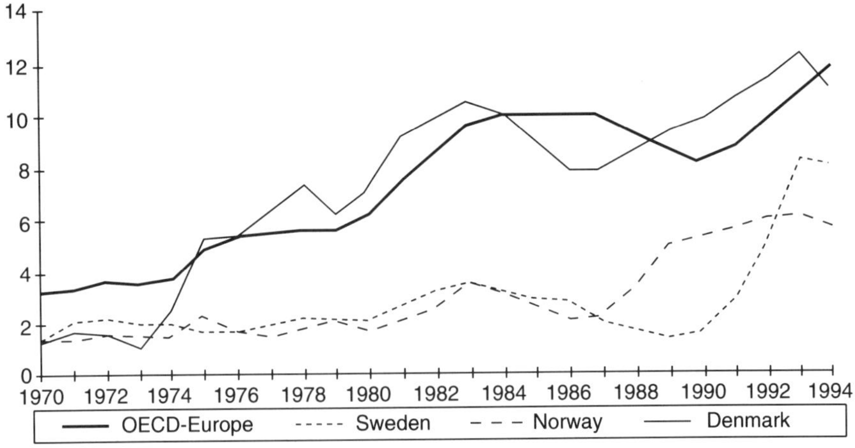

Figure 5.8 Unemployment (percent of labour force)
Source: OECD Economic Outlook
Notes: National definitions. Figures for 1994 are OECD forecasts

However, the business cycle and the flexibility of wages are probably the most important factors in determining demand and supply for labor. The biggest impact on labor supply from a tax reform is actually likely to come from changes in capital taxation and the treatment of corporate income. If investments increase, the demand for labor will also tend to go up.

As part of reforming the taxation of capital income in the Scandinavian countries, the value of deductions for mortgage interest payments was cut in half or even more (in Sweden the value has gone from 80 percent in the early 1980s to 50 percent in the mid-1980s to 30 percent in 1991). As a consequence, the demand for large houses or a second or third house has decreased substantially and a third of the labor force in the construction sector is out of work. This is sometimes viewed as a negative impact of the tax reform, disregarding that tax-induced overconsumption of housing has diminished. It has also resulted in considerably lower prices on construction material and therefore a price decline of up to 30 percent on newly built houses. However, it should be recognized that a shift toward a more neutral tax treatment of different forms of capital income may induce huge swings in asset prices which have macro-economic implications.

Effects on investment and growth

In the latter half of the 1970s and the beginning of the 1980s, the profit share in the business sector was below the OECD–Europe average (see Figure 5.9).[16] In Sweden, the policy response was to devalue the currency by 10

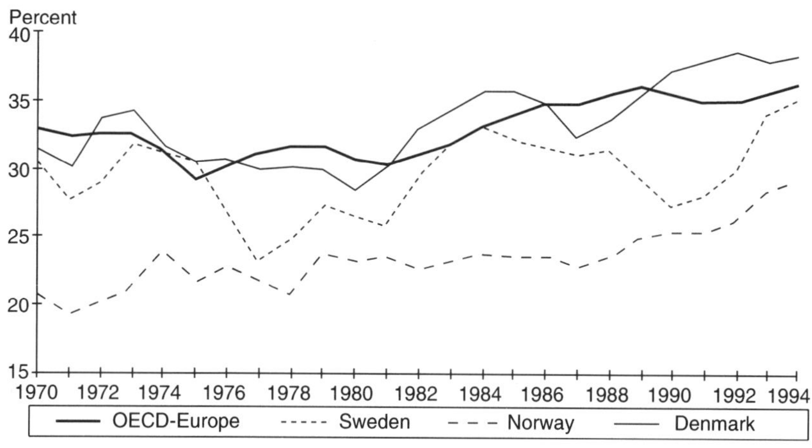

Figure 5.9 Profit share in business sector (gross rate of return from production income on capital stock)
Source: OECD Economic Outlook Database
Notes: Europe excluding Greece, Iceland, Luxembourg, Portugal and Turkey

percent in 1981 and an additional 16 percent in 1982. Despite the very large depreciation, Swedish industries only gained market shares in one single year, in 1983, and profitability only reached the European average in 1984 before a substantial decline occurred.

Since the reforms of the corporate tax systems aimed to keep the corporate tax burden unchanged, changes in the profit share were derived from a more competitive environment induced by the tax reform, and the overall macroeconomic policies pursued in the countries. As can be seen from the chart, the profit share rose substantially in Denmark and exceeded the European average at the end of the 1980s and in the 1990s. The increase in profitability in Sweden in 1991 and 1992, that is before the Swedish krona was allowed to float on November 19, 1992, partly reflects a more uniform taxation of various sectors brought about by the tax reform.

While Norwegian businesses have experienced the lowest profitability, investment levels have outpaced the European average and the investment level in Sweden and Denmark (see Figure 5.10). After the tax reforms were enacted, the investment ratio declined in all three countries. The aggregate numbers are, however, somewhat misleading. In the second half of the 1980s, in conjunction with the deregulation of financial markets and before the tax systems were reformed, investments in residential housing increased drastically, resulting in an increase in the overall investment ratio, despite falling industrial investments. The effect of reduced incentives to debt financing and opening up of markets has been a levelling of the field, and the share of nonresidential investments in the overall investment level has increased. However, the recession meant that the response was mitigated. It is obvious

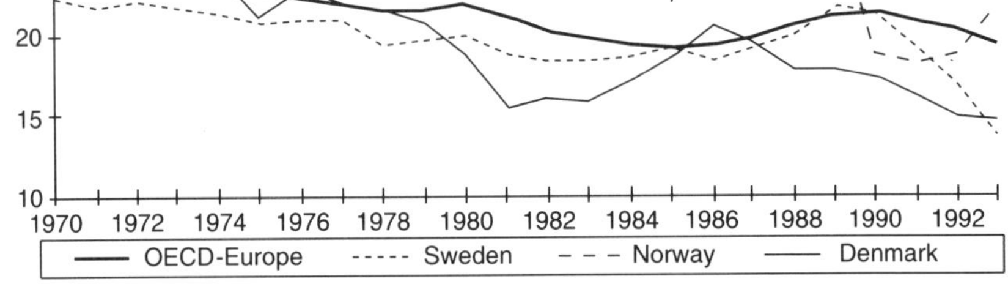

Figure 5.10 Gross capital formation (percent of GDP)
Source: OECD National Accounts

that a more uniform tax treatment for businesses alone is not sufficient for creating a favorable investment climate.[17]

The growth rate in Denmark and Sweden was lower than the OECD average during the 1970s and the 1980s. The same goes for Norway if the oil sector is excluded. It is difficult to see any decisive impact of the tax reforms by just looking at a chart depicting growth rates (see Figure 5.11). However, with the increased flexibility in the labor market due to lower marginal tax rates and mitigated lock-in effects of capital in the corporate sector, the potential growth rate of the economies is believed to have increased by a quarter to half a percentage point. Such an increase in the potential growth rate is very important in order to achieve sustainable growth without inflationary pressures. It is also believed that some of the so-called dynamic effects will materialize as the economies continue to expand after the recession in the early 1990s. However, some of these effects could easily be reversed if the tax reforms are not perceived as politically sustainable in the future. Accumulated large budget deficits, partly due to government support for the banking sector, may also exert economic pressure and may lead to a reversal of the reforms with higher marginal tax rates as a consequence.

Effects on household savings and tax revenues

One of the main aspects of the tax reforms was to reduce incentives to borrowing and to increase national savings, in particular household savings. As noted earlier, the household savings rate in the Scandinavian countries had been relatively stable during the 1970s, although considerably below the

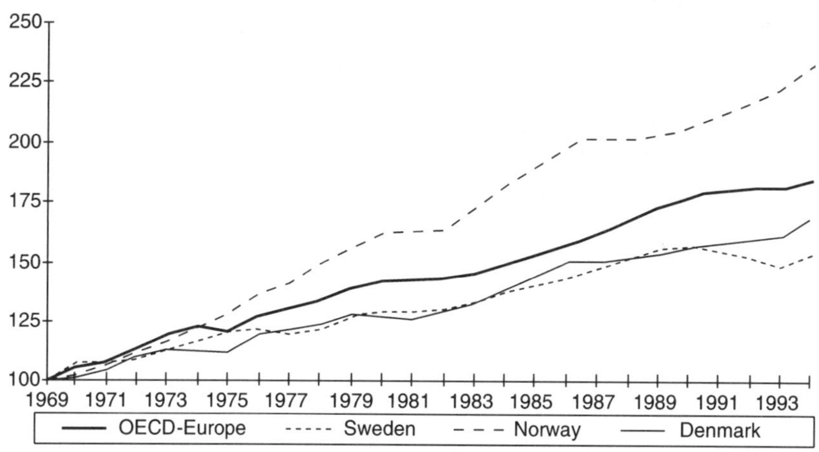

Figure 5.11 GDP growth (index end-1969 = 100)
Source: OECD Economic Outlook
Notes: Figures for 1993 are OECD forecasts

average in the OECD countries in Europe. The Danish savings rate rose drastically in the early 1980s at a time when the budget deficit had risen to very high levels (in 1982, the government in its budget document envisaged a budget deficit of 12 percent of GDP in 1982 and 15 percent in 1983). As decisive budget consolidation measures were undertaken (reducing the budget deficit by a quarter in a single year), the household savings rate started to decline. During this period financial deregulation took place in all three countries and the savings rate declined sharply and became negative in both Norway and Sweden.

When financial markets were deregulated, tax reforms were not yet enacted and the tax systems still favored borrowing, especially since real after-tax interest rates were negative. As a result debt accumulated in all sectors. While the savings rate declined, the economies were growing at, or above, their potential growth rate. The overconsumption resulting from the decline in the savings rate made some structural problems, like a structural budget deficit, less obvious. As the savings rate declined, fiscal balances improved sharply, owing to comprehensive taxation of consumption of goods and services. The picture is very similar in Denmark and Sweden, although Denmark was a couple of years ahead of Sweden in this development. In Norway, fiscal balances deteriorated despite the higher level of consumption. Here again, oil revenues play a major role and tend to blur the picture of the situation in the mainland economy.

The decrease in the savings rate in the wake of financial deregulation, with its resulting overconsumption, holds several important pieces of information for other countries. First, it is important to have an adequate tax structure at the time of financial deregulation. If the tax system favors consumption and borrowing, asset prices will increase and severe problems in the banking sector may follow. Second, the risk that the tax reform will be underfinanced is greater the more overheated the economy becomes at the time of reform. This is especially the case if the existing level of consumption is taken as the norm for a normal level of consumption, and therefore indirect taxes, particularly VAT, are expected to bring in large revenues to the Treasury. In all three countries, direct taxes on income were lowered and indirect taxes on consumption were increased. To avoid a worsening of any structural imbalances in the central government accounts, it is important to anticipate an increase in the savings rate to more normal levels and therefore to realize that tax revenues from consumption will be lower under a more sustainable growth rate.

There is also an inherent political risk when fiscal deficits temporarily improve owing to overconsumption. The ambition to reduce tax rates too much for the chosen expenditure level is obvious. Therefore, to the politicians, it may appear possible to combine low tax rates with a large public sector. However, the very purpose of the tax reform has been to enhance savings, and lower taxes on capital income will tend to increase household

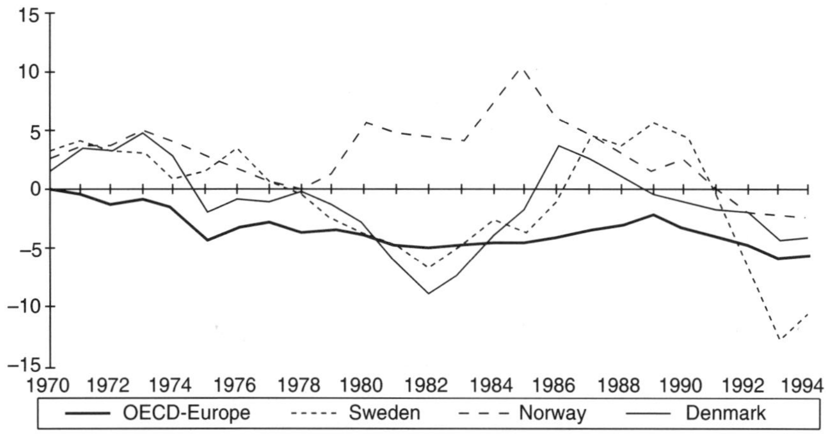

Figure 5.12 General government fiscal balances (percent of GDP)
Source: OECD Economic Outlook
Notes: Figures for 1994 are OECD forecasts

savings. If the budget deficit increases at the same time, the savings rate will go up even further in anticipation of future tax increases and cuts in transfers. This will tend to make any structural deficit highly visible and the need for early action against the budget deficit becomes crucial if the spiral of weak demand and ever increasing deficits is to be broken.

Sweden is an obvious example of a country that overestimated tax revenues from consumption taxes, assuming that the high level of consumption would prevail also after the tax reform. As real interest rates rose in the beginning of the 1990s, asset prices started to decline and savings rose. This meant that tax revenues fell sharply and the budget deficit reached 13 percent of GDP in 1993 (see Figure 5.12). The tax reform certainly made financial savings less tax disadvantaged but the increase in the savings rate depended to a large extent on the increased uncertainty about the future direction of economic policies and the level of taxation in the future.[18]

In all of the Scandinavian countries, the household savings rate appears to have levelled off at a historically high level. It is likely that macro-economic developments explain most of this development, in particular the decline in the inflation rates from double figures in the early 1980s to around 2 percent in 1994. The lower tax rates have contributed to the higher real after-tax interest rates and therefore clearly contributed to this development. The abolition of the general income tax in favor of a schedular taxation of capital income, at internationally relatively low levels, has changed the incentives for borrowing and savings. Unfortunately, the Scandinavian countries all learned the hard way how costly this can be with a combination of high tax rates, generous deductibility of interest payments and high inflation rates. It led to an asset price bubble and after the bubble burst, tax payers had to bail out the banking system.

CONCLUSIONS

Domestic reasons for changing the tax systems in the Scandinavian countries became increasingly urgent in the early 1980s. Scandinavian tax systems were characterized by very high marginal tax rates and very generous provisions for deducting interest payments. These elements caused weak growth rates and a tendency toward overconsumption. Furthermore, the deregulation of credit markets allowed consumers to take full advantage of the favorable tax treatment of borrowing resulting in a sharp increase in bank lending and asset prices.

Because of these developments, all three countries chose to tax labor income and capital income separately. The reasons behind abandoning the global income tax were almost entirely domestic ones rather than international. At the very high tax rates in the Scandinavian countries, it was difficult to maintain a global income tax since both efficiency and equity suffered.

It is too early to say what the overall effect of the tax reforms on productivity and savings will be. There are indications that the benefits from these reforms will be considerable. Owing to the alleviation of tax-induced rigidities in the labor market and of lock-in effects for capital, the potential growth rate of the economies is believed to have increased by a quarter to half a percentage point. Private savings have increased in all three countries while asset prices are returning to normal levels. In Sweden, these savings are providing risk capital for small businesses which was lacking before. Changes in the tax system have also increased the returns on education, an investment which yielded low returns with the old system. This in turn should contribute to productivity growth over time.

However, it is very clear that the benefits of the tax reform in the short term are much lower than they would have been if the reforms had been undertaken with an eye on the macro-economic environment and on changes in other sectors. In all three countries, costly misallocation of capital would have been avoided if the tax reforms had been implemented before the liberalization of capital markets. Moreover, these tax reforms were constructed without regard for the fact that the economies were experiencing an unusual boom. Calculations of tax revenues made in these times of overheating and overconsumption have proven to be overoptimistic. An important lesson from Scandinavia is that tax reform efforts, however economically sound they may be, cannot be undertaken in isolation from other structural changes or the overall stance of macro-economic policies.

To conclude, the Scandinavian countries are evidence that the global income tax may have to be abandoned in order to decrease efficiency and equity repercussions of the tax system. A separate and lower tax on capital may be necessary for domestic economic policy reasons, rather than purely for international considerations.

NOTES

*I would like to thank Per Hedfors, Leif Mutén and Erik Offerdal for very helpful comments on an earlier version. The views expressed are those of the author and do not necessarily reflect those of the Riksbank or the IMF.

1 The role of the level of taxation is discussed in Tanzi (1990).
2 The implications for tax revenues are by no means unique to industrialized countries. For a discussion on the impact on tax revenues, see Tanzi (1989).
3 See e.g. Gandhi *et al.* (1987).
4 The classic discussion about the size of the excess burden of taxation can be found in Harberger (1962) and Musgrave (1959).
5 These rates are nominal. Through different reserve provisions etc., the effective rate measured on the base of an economic concept will have been rather much lower – indeed, the Swedish rate reduction from 52 percent to 30 percent turned out to be a small increase in the effective rate and new reserve provisions were introduced to replace some of the old provisions which were abolished.
6 Individuals channeled their savings toward purchase of real assets, including consumer durables, for which the tax treatment on the economic rate of return was very low. This effect is mentioned in Tanzi (1989) as a likely consequence of high inflation.
7 *Utgiftsskatt – Teknik och Effekter*, Betänkande av utgiftsskattekommittén, SOU 1986:40, Bilaga 2, p. 21.
8 For a discussion of the political constraints in tax reform efforts, see Tanzi (1992a).
9 Modén (1995) found that a 1 percentage point increase in the effective marginal Swedish corporate tax rate would, *ceteris paribus*, lead to an extra outflow of direct investment of about half a percentage point. The measure is expressed in terms of the ratio between the volume of investment expenditure abroad and value added at home.
10 The *daily* average turnover as a fraction of the yearly GDP was 2.9 percent in France, 3.4 percent in Germany and 5.9 percent in Sweden (see Study of G10, April 1992).
11 This approach was presented, although not fully formalized, in Mutén (1968) For an extension to cross-country portfolio investments, see Bovenberg *et al.* (1989).
12 For a description of assumptions, see Andersson (1992a).
13 See Andersson (1992b).
14 For a description of the Swedish tax system, see Andersson and Mutén (1994).
15 See Steuerle (1992, p. 125).
16 The profit share is gross return on productive capital, defined as total sales in relation to the capital stock (exclusive of inventory, land, natural resources and residential real estate).
17 As pointed out in Feldstein (1983) macro-economic policies leading to a high rate of inflation reduce the long-run capital intensity of production.
18 Berg (1994) estimates that a decrease in the marginal tax rate on labor by 1 percentage point increases the financial savings ratio in the household sector by 0.1 percentage points, mainly because of decreased preference for savings in real assets. An increase in the real interest rate by 1 percentage point is estimated to result in an increase in the financial savings ratio by half a percentage point. The large increase in real after-tax interest rates and the higher unemployment level

are estimated to give rise to a long-run savings rate in the household sector of 6.5 percent. The tax reform is only attributed a minor part of this drastic increase.

REFERENCES

Alworth, J. (1988) 'Capital Mobility, the Cost of Capital under Certainty and Effective Tax Rates in Europe,' *Finnish Economic Papers*, Vol. 1.

Andersson, K. (1992a) 'Efficiency Considerations in Tax Policy', in *Fiscal Policies in Economies in Transition*, ed. Vito Tanzi, Washington, DC: International Monetary Fund.

Andersson, K. (1992b) *Svensk beskattning i ett integrerat Europa*, Report No. 2 to the Swedish Medium Term Survey (SOU 1992:19), Stockholm.

Andersson, K. and L. Mutén (1994) 'The Tax System of Sweden', *Tax Notes International*, October 10, pp. 1147–1163.

Berg, L. (1994) *90-talets systemskifte och hushållens sparande*, Ekonomiska Sekretariatet, Nordbanken.

Bovenberg, L., K. Andersson, K. Aramaki and S. Chand (1989) 'Tax Incentives and International Capital Flows: The Case of the United States and Japan', in *Taxation in the Global Economy*, ed. A. Razin and J. Slemrod, NBER, Chicago: University of Chicago Press.

Devereux, M. and M. Pearson (1989) *Corporate Tax Harmonisation and Economic Efficiency*, The Institute for Fiscal Studies, Report Series No. 35, Cambridge: Woodhead-Faulkner.

Feldstein, M. (1983) *Inflation, Tax Rules and Capital Formation*, NBER, Chicago: University of Chicago Press.

Gandhi, V. P. *et al.* (1987) *Supply-Side Tax Policy – Its Relevance to Developing Countries*, Washington, DC: International Monetary Fund.

Gordon, R. (1986) 'Taxation of Investment and Savings in a World Economy,' *American Economic Review*, Vol. 76, No. 5 (December).

Group of Ten (G10) (1992) *International Capital Movements and Foreign Exchange Markets – A Report to the Ministers and Governors by the Group of Deputies*, April.

Harberger, A. C. (1962) 'The Incidence of the Corporation Income Tax', *Journal of Political Economy*, Vol. 70, pp. 215–240.

King, M. and D. Fullerton (eds) (1984) *The Taxation of Income from Capital; A Comparative Study of the United States, the United Kingdom, Sweden and West Germany*, Chicago: University of Chicago Press.

Lodin, S.-O. (1993) 'The Nordic Reforms of Company and Shareholder Taxation – A Comparison', The Legal Association of Finland.

Modén, K.-M. (1995) 'The Impact of Tax Reform on Foreign Direct Investment', Paper presented at the Tax Evaluation Conference, January 9–10, 1995, Eklundshof, Uppsala.

Musgrave, R.A. (1959) *The Theory of Public Finance*, New York: McGraw-Hill.

Mutén, L. (1968) *The Corporation Income Tax and The Cost of Capital* (in Swedish with a summary in English, Stockholm: Almquist & Wicksell).

Mutén, L. and K.O. Faxén (1966) 'Sweden', in *Foreign Tax Policies and Economic Growth*, A Conference Report of the NBER and the Brookings Institution, NBER, New York: Columbia University Press.

Pechman, J.A. (ed.) (1987) *Comparative Tax Systems – Europe, Canada, and Japan*, Tax Analysts, Arlington, Virginia.

Sinn, H.W. (1987) *Capital Income Taxation and Resource Allocation*, Amsterdam: North-Holland.

SOU (1986) *Utgiftsskatt – Teknik och Effekter*, Betänkande av utgiftsskattekommittén (SOU 1986: 40), Stockholm.

Steuerle, E. (1992) *The Tax Decade*, Washington, DC: The Urban Institute Press.

Tanzi, V. (1980) 'Inflationary Expectations, Economic Activity, Taxes, and Interest Rates', *American Economic Review*, Vol. 70 (March), pp. 12–21.

Tanzi, V. (1989) 'The Impact of Macroeconomic Policies on the Level of Taxation and the Fiscal Balance in Developing Countries', *IMF Staff Papers*, Vol. 36, No. 3 (September).

Tanzi, V. (1990) 'The IMF and Tax Reform', *IMF Working Paper*, No. 39.

Tanzi, V. (1992a) 'Theory and Policy: A Comment on Dixit and on Current Tax Theory', *IMF Working Paper*, No. 15.

Tanzi, V. (1992b) 'Financial Markets and Public Finance in the Transformation Process', *IMF Working Paper*, No. 29.

Tanzi, V. and L. Bovenberg (1990) 'Is There a Need for Harmonizing Capital Income Taxes Within EC Countries?', *IMF Working Paper*, No. 17.

Part III

FISCAL POLICY AND THE ENVIRONMENT

6

FISCAL AND MACROECONOMIC ASPECTS OF ENVIRONMENT TAXES*

David C.L. Nellor

INTRODUCTION

The use of taxes to address environmental concerns is the familiar policy recommendation based on Pigou's contribution to modern welfare economics. Pigou characterized environmental damage in terms of a divergence between marginal social net product and marginal private net product and suggested how this difference might be bridged.[1] This analysis of how to attain social efficiency did not, however, examine the feasibility or implications of the policy by considering its consequences for the public finances and the macroeconomy. The point of departure of this chapter is to consider environment taxes from this broader perspective.

In relation to *fiscal policy*, a vigorous pursuit of environmental objectives might imply a trade-off between revenue and environmental goals. The restructuring of prevailing energy taxes into carbon taxes in Sweden, for example, was intended to meet environmental objectives but subject to the constraint that budget revenues were not threatened. Recognizing these other objectives, there are circumstances when efficiency reasons warrant environment tax rates that are higher than justified by environmental considerations. Moreover, the optimal environment tax rate depends on the public expenditure side of the budget. One reason is that the environment tax rate determines the provision of a public good, namely a cleaner environment, and this public good may, for example, be complementary to other public goods. In any event, the optimal rate of environment tax is likely to differ from that justified on environment grounds alone.

In relation to *distributional goals*, concerns that environment taxes, such as carbon taxes, are vertically inequitable imply a trade-off between distributional and environmental objectives. As noted above, the environment tax rate is linked to the provision of the cleaner environment public good and thus, in some respects, implies that environment taxes are earmarked. This earmarking is at the heart of the equity costs of environment taxes because it means that the distribution of costs of producing the public good are not independent of its production.

In relation to *macroeconomic objectives*, there have been suggestions that environment taxes will be costly, but it has also been suggested that environment taxes might be used to promote macroeconomic goals. In the former case, the European Commission carbon tax proposal, intended to stabilize European carbon dioxide emissions at 1990 levels by the end of the decade, is one example.[2] The Commission made special provisions to minimize the loss of international competitiveness of firms even though this implied that environmental targets would be secured less effectively.[3] The special provisions limit the magnitude of the tax on tradable goods and shift the tax burden from producers toward final consumption. From an environmental perspective, however, the tax must be levied on use of fossil fuels at all stages, including on productive inputs, otherwise the environmental effectiveness of the tax is reduced. It has been suggested elsewhere that output and employment objectives can be promoted by substituting environment taxes for prevailing taxes on labor. We find that this does not apply despite the conventional result that a lower social cost of taxation will boost output.

Examining the implications of tax policy in a wider fiscal and macroeconomic context lies very much within the spirit of the important contributions of Vito Tanzi to the public finance literature and its practice in many countries. There are many examples of work in this vein including Tanzi (1969), which relates individual income taxation to the issue of economic growth; the relationship between taxation, inflation, and interest rates (Tanzi, 1980); and the impact of tax collection lags on the fiscal balance in an inflationary environment (Tanzi, 1989).

The chapter is organized as follows. The next section provides a brief exposition of the standard welfare case for using environment (Pigouvian) taxes. The section after that examines environment taxes in a fiscal context looking at revenue, expenditure, and distributional aspects. The following section examines environment taxes in the context of macroeconomic goals. The final section provides conclusions.

THE ENVIRONMENTAL RATIONALE FOR TAXATION

Pigouvian-type environment taxes raise the price of polluting to reflect social costs by imposing specific rate taxes on units of environmental damage.[4] For example, if environmental damage results from waste emissions into the atmosphere, the tax rate is set equal to marginal social cost at the socially efficient level of waste emissions. The socially efficient level of emissions, in turn, is defined by an equality of marginal cost and marginal benefit in the conventional fashion: the marginal cost is the sum of the costs incurred by individuals resulting from the waste emissions and the marginal benefit is the polluter's gain from emitting waste. Pigouvian taxes thus ensure that polluters face the private *and* social costs of their actions.

Pigouvian taxes are illustrated in Figure 6.1. The marginal benefit to firms from various levels of emissions is shown by the MB schedule. Marginal benefit is defined as the savings earned by the firm from being able to emit waste. Because firms will emit waste as long as the benefit exceeds the private cost, they will emit waste to the point, shown by B, where any further emission fails to yield benefits (in the absence of environmental policy). The marginal social cost of emissions damage is shown by the MSC schedule. The socially optimal emission level is identified by the equality of the MB and the MSC schedules. The waste emitted, shown by point B, exceeds the socially optimal level identified as point A in the chart. The Pigouvian solution, of a per unit of pollution tax equal to the marginal social cost at the socially optimal level, is a tax equal to AC per unit of waste emitted. This tax reduces the marginal benefit to firms from emitting waste by the tax rate and thus shifts the marginal benefit schedule to MB′. Firms then optimize by emitting waste to point A which coincides with the socially efficient emission level.

Pigouvian taxes ensure that polluters face the private and social costs of their actions and also secure a cleaner environment at lowest possible cost. First, taxes may reduce the cost of environment policy because they rely on the price system in contrast to the administrative costs that characterize command and control policies. Second, Pigouvian taxes reduce pollution in

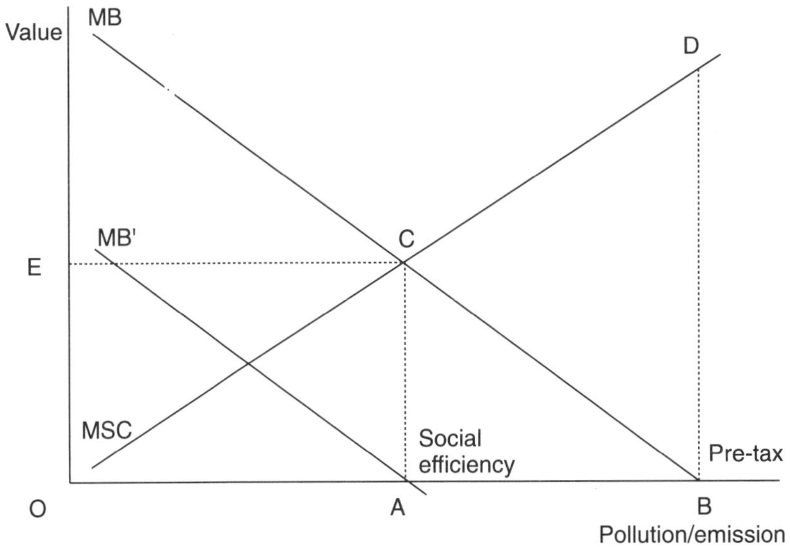

Figure 6.1 Pigouvian taxes

the least cost manner by encouraging the greatest pollution abatement by firms able to adjust at lowest cost as well as least cost abatement by each firm. Thus, firms reduce waste emissions by determining the combination of lower output, changes in inputs, and investment in new technology that reduces emissions at least cost.[5]

ENVIRONMENT TAXES: A PUBLIC FINANCE PERSPECTIVE

The fiscal and distributional implications of environment taxes are examined in this section. On the revenue side, the role for environment taxes from an efficiency perspective is explored. On the expenditure side, the discussion recognizes that, unlike other types of taxes, environment taxes are linked to the provision of a public good (a cleaner environment) and thus have particular implications for public expenditure. Finally, with respect to fiscal equity, the section identifies why environment taxes often have harmful equity implications.

The revenue side of the budget

The case for using environment taxes remains intact when environment taxes are examined from a revenue perspective. But, the rate of environment tax depends on other factors including how the environment tax revenues are used as well as the general equilibrium consequences of environment taxes for other tax revenues and public goods demand. Environment tax rates should be raised – perhaps substantially in some circumstances – to levels that cannot be justified on environment grounds alone.

The optimal environment tax rate – in a public finance framework – is a function of the benefits and costs, or welfare implications, of the tax relative to alternative taxes. The problem posed in the literature is how to raise a given level of revenue in the most efficient manner by setting various consumer good tax rates when lump-sum taxes are not available.[6] Environmental damage is associated with the consumption of one of these goods. The optimal tax rate on the consumption of the environmentally damaging good has two parts: the Pigouvian tax – which imposes no marginal welfare costs – and an additional tax defined by the tax rate equating the marginal welfare cost across alternative taxes.

In the case of independent demands (which we consider for reasons of illustrative simplicity), the rate of tax on a good x, that is *not* associated with environmental damage, is defined as the tax, t_x, divided by the price of the good, P_x,

$$t_x/P_x = (1-\mu)(-1/\eta_x) \quad \text{for } x \neq y. \tag{6.1}$$

The tax on good y, the good that is associated with environmental damage, is levied at a rate of

$$t_y/P_y = (1-\mu)(-1/\eta_y) + \mu(-nU_{y+1}/U_y). \tag{6.2}$$

The terms $(-1/\eta_x)$ and $(-1/\eta_y)$, in expressions (6.1) and (6.2) respectively, reflect the familiar result, from optimal tax theory, that tax rates across goods should be set reflecting the inverse relationship between the rate of tax and the elasticity of demand for the good (η_x and η_y); the more inelastic the demand for the good the higher the tax rate. The term, μ, is interpreted as the marginal rate of substitution between private and public incomes.[7] The term $(-nU_{y+1}/U_y)$ is the Pigouvian tax which reflects the marginal social damage as the sum of the marginal rates of substitution of the n identical consumers between good y as a private good and as a public good.

In the case of the environmentally damaging good, the optimal tax rate is thus comprised of the Pigouvian tax and the additional tax reflecting the welfare cost of raising revenue from other goods. The relative importance of these two taxes is a function of the term, μ. The higher is the value of μ, the higher is the marginal value of private income compared to public income and thus the lower is the aggregate tax revenue requirement. In this circumstance, relatively lower importance is placed on the additional optimal tax term and there is greater importance placed on the Pigouvian tax on good y. This also reflects the fact that revenue is first raised from the environmentally damaging good (where welfare costs do not arise) and, in the case when $\mu = 1$, all revenues are raised from the Pigouvian tax and the tax on other items falls to zero. This analysis examines the use of a tax on a consumption good that is related to environmental damage. A Pigouvian tax is, however, levied on emissions. If, as an example, fresh air is the consumer good, it follows from the preceding analysis that a Pigouvian tax should be imposed on emissions that damage fresh air as well as an additional tax that will satisfy the preceding conditions.[8]

The so-called 'double dividend' of environment taxes rests on the preceding result.[9] Environment taxes are said to provide a double dividend because (a) they provide environmental benefits by reducing externalities; and (b) they raise revenue that permits the reduction of other taxes which impose welfare costs. The double dividend of environment taxes is evident in the chart. First, the reduction in pollution results in a net social gain, shown by the area BCD, reflecting the difference between the gross gain of beneficiaries of lower pollution, ACDB, and the abatement cost incurred by polluters of ABC. Second, revenues, shown by the area OACE, are raised without imposing any marginal social excess burden. The preceding discussion suggested, however, that the rate of tax should perhaps be increased to a rate higher than AC – leading to a lower level of pollution than optimal – even though the marginal social gain, looking at the pollution alone, would be negative. Such increases in the tax rate – which bring about a greater reduction in environmental damage – will impose social costs equal to the difference between the marginal social cost and the marginal benefit schedules.

The double dividend is unlikely to hold in most practical policy situations. First, the double dividend presumes that revenues from environment taxes are used to finance reduced rates of other taxes rather than for deficit reduction or additional expenditure. Second, the partial equilibrium analysis of the double dividend fails to recognize that the imposition of environment taxes may have implications for other taxes. It may be necessary, for example, to increase the rates of other distorting taxes if the introduction of the environment tax causes other tax bases to contract.[10] Third, there is no double dividend to be exploited if environment taxes have already been implemented although the benefits may be gained if prevailing environment tax rates are less than optimal. Fourth, public goods implications – discussed below – may mean that the double dividend benefits are not available.

In sum, revenue objectives do not unambiguously justify greater use of environment taxes. Nevertheless, the argument for using environment taxes remains intact and there are some circumstances when the rate of environment tax should be higher than levels justified on environment grounds alone. The consequence of environment taxes for revenue also depends, *inter alia*, on the general equilibrium consequences for other taxes.

The expenditure side of the budget

Environment taxes differ from other taxes in several respects. The first factor differentiating the environment tax from other taxes is the link between the tax and expenditure sides of the budget. The environment tax rate should be assessed in relation to the expenditure side of the budget because the tax rate determines the provision of the environment public good.[11] This stands in contrast to an examination of other taxes where, in effect, the revenue and expenditure sides of the budget are separate. The efficiency of these other taxes is assessed independently of the expenditure side of the budget: the optimal level of public goods provision is determined and, subsequently, the issue of financing this provision is addressed.[12] By contrast, environment taxes are linked directly to the expenditure side of the budget because environment taxes induce taxpayers to produce the public good of a cleaner environment.

A second factor differentiating analysis of environment taxes from conventional public finance is that the normal distinction between *public provision* and *production* of public goods does not apply to a cleaner environment. The public goods literature emphasizes that the provision of public goods must be undertaken by government in order to overcome the market failure associated with the jointness and nonexcludability characteristics of public goods. The production of public goods can, however, be undertaken by either the government or the private sector.[13] In cases where environment taxes are used, a cleaner environment is *provided* by the government because it imposes the taxes. The environmental public goods are, however, *produced* only by the private sector via the responses of producers and consumers to these taxes. Consequently, environment taxes promote efficient production of the cleaner environment public good because they are produced by profit-maximizing producers or utility-maximizing consumers. In fact, in production efficiency terms, it is possible that the environment public good should be provided in greater quantities, relative to other public goods, because the marginal cost of other public goods is equal to the tax (resource) cost plus the opportunity cost of any inefficient public resource use – the latter cost does not apply to the environment public good.

Overall public expenditure efficiency may, however, be difficult to secure because the link between environment taxes and the provision of a cleaner environment makes aspects of earmarking unavoidable. Proposals to link revenues from particular taxes to the financing or provision of particular public goods – or earmarking – are, as a general rule, inefficient. Earmarking is only efficient in the unlikely circumstance of a coincidence between the revenue raised from the earmarked tax and the required amount of a public good. The tying of specific revenue sources to the provision of particular public goods also makes it difficult to implement public expenditure priorities. In the case of environment taxes, the tax rate determines how much of the cleaner environment public good is provided. In a first-best world, optimality could be achieved by a Pigouvian tax. The argument that environmental damage reduction should be set at the level defined in the Pigouvian analysis does not hold, however, in a second-best world where other public goods are not provided at levels satisfying the Samuelsonian efficiency conditions.

A third factor differentiating environment taxes from other taxes is their impact on the marginal cost of public funds. Public goods provision may be influenced by the impact of environment taxes on the marginal cost of public funds. The direct effect of environment taxes on the marginal cost of public funds is like that of any tax, but, in the case of environment taxes, this effect can be modified by the complementarity or substitutability of the clean environment with other public goods. The link between the environment tax and the provision of a public good means that it is indeterminate whether a lower marginal cost of public goods provision implies an increase in demand for public goods. A lower marginal cost of public funds will increase the level of public goods demand whenever demand for environment damage reduction and other public goods are separable. But, more generally, the provision of the cleaner environment may influence demand for public goods that could offset, or reinforce, the incentives created by the environment-tax-induced change in the marginal cost of funds. For example, a cleaner environment may raise the demand for national park services and justify use of taxes that impose higher welfare costs. The outcome thus depends on the substitutability or complementarity of a cleaner environment with other public goods.

In sum, the design of environment taxes could be modified when examined in terms of their implications for the expenditure side of the budget. Owing to the link between environment taxes and the provision of the public good there may be a need to reassess the level of environment taxes. This assessment will depend on the production efficiency of various public goods as well as the complementarity of the cleaner environment with other public goods.

Equity aspects of environment taxes

The equity aspects of environment taxes have been examined extensively with the finding, albeit subject to various caveats, that these taxes are often vertically inequitable.[14] It is not our purpose to evaluate these studies but to inquire why equity concerns have been such an important impediment to the use of environment taxes. A key reason is that environment taxes fail to satisfy a criterion of other taxes that play a role in the Allocation Branch of Musgrave's multi-branch budget framework. The reason for this failure rests with the link between the tax and the production of the cleaner environment public good. To make environment taxes comparable to other taxes, it would be necessary to accompany the environment taxes with lump-sum subsidies.

The Allocation Branch of the budget, as outlined by Musgrave, is responsible for provision of public goods and resolution of environmental and other externalities. Taxes imposed by the Allocation Branch are designed to cover the cost of these public services by identifying the tax base and setting rates of tax to cover the cost of public goods perhaps according to the income elasticity of these social wants.[15] The key characteristic of these taxes is that they separate provision of resources for public goods production from the distribution across taxpayers of these resource costs. In other words, 'For the Allocation Branch, the need for securing a cost distribution independent of the particular resource transfer is the function and raison d'etre of taxation.'[16] Environment taxes, although used to pursue allocative goals, fail this test because of their earmarking features.

Musgrave (1959) illustrates the independence of public goods production from the sharing of the production costs. He notes that if

> the government wishes to obtain a battleship, and steel is needed, steel may be commandeered and transferred from the production of passenger cars, and labor may be conscripted and transferred from other uses to produce more steel. This would accomplish the purpose of securing the battleship for government use, but it would place the entire cost on the producers of steel.
>
> (Musgrave, 1959, pp. 15, 16)

This commandeering of resources is the same, in its effect, as the environment tax. The tax leads polluters to produce the public good of a cleaner environment by providing real resources to reduce the damage caused by their production or consumption decisions. For example, the owners of a coal-fired power plant may, in response to a tax on emissions, invest in a coal scrubber, adjust its capital equipment, utilize more expensive low-sulphur coal, and reduce output. An alternative to commandeering resources – in the conventional public goods case – is to impose taxes to transfer resources from the private to the public sector and to use these to purchase the factors of production to produce the public good such as the battleship.

> The desired result of resource transfer is obtained in both cases, but the distribution of cost is now independent of the particular resources that are transferred. . . . The tax-purchase mechanism as a means of resource transfer thus permits a cost allocation quite independent of the ownership distribution of the resources that are to be transferred.

It is the lack of independence between the distribution of costs and the resource costs of producing the public good that is at the heart of the perceived equity costs of environment taxes.[17] Thus, government may, for example, be reluctant to tax the users of energy because the incidence of the production costs falls disproportionately on poor consumers. This outcome could only be avoided by using compensatory lump-sum transfers alongside the environment tax.

ENVIRONMENT TAXES: A MACROECONOMIC PERSPECTIVE

The implications of environment taxes for macroeconomic goals are examined in this section. One issue is whether environment taxes thwart macroeconomic objectives. Even if macroeconomic costs of environment taxes are incurred, however, public policy priorities may deem these costs to be acceptable. Some environment tax proposals go further, however, and suggest that environment taxes are the preferred tax instrument when revenue-raising measures are required for macroeconomic reasons. This issue, of whether environment taxes are the best available tax from a macroeconomic perspective, is the second issue examined in this section. The section concludes that environment taxes can be costly from a macroeconomic perspective. Moreover, the output and employment costs of environment taxes will, as a general rule, exceed those of broad-based taxes, like value-added taxes (VAT), making them an inferior fiscal policy for securing macroeconomic objectives.

Macroeconomic policy objectives

Macroeconomic policy objectives have been used both as a rationale to justify as well as to impede the introduction of environment taxes. On the one hand, there have been various proposals to replace nonenvironment taxes by environment taxes in order to pursue more effectively macroeconomic objectives of output and employment. Examples include a European Commission carbon tax proposal and the proposed introduction of the British Thermal Unit (BTU) tax in the United States. The Commission of the European Communities (1993a) suggested that employment prospects can be improved by reducing charges on labor, such as social security contributions, and compensating these revenue losses by increases in other taxes, including environment-targeted energy taxes. The United States Administration proposed an energy tax, in the form of a tax based on BTUs, as part of its deficit reduction plan in early 1993. On the other hand, specific environment tax proposals have either been vetoed or redesigned for the same macroeconomic reasons; it is suggested that such taxes harm competitiveness and thus impose costs on output and employment.

The proposal to use environment taxes to secure macroeconomic objectives is usually based on the double dividend proposition outlined previously. The first dividend of environment taxes is the reduction of externalities, and the second is the revenue raised which permits lower nonenvironment tax rates thereby reducing distorting effects on labor supply, investment, or consumption. This view suggests that environment taxes are the best available tax instrument because they will boost economic activity by imposing lower social costs on the economy compared to alternative tax measures. In other words, taxes which impose low social costs should be adopted because they impose lower output costs. This link in the argument – that lower social costs imply lower output costs – does not apply to environment taxes; a low tax-induced social cost may impose significant negative output effects.

Economic output

Economic output would be promoted by a reduction in the effective private sector tax burden. Broad-based taxes, such as VAT, are likely to be more effective in reducing the tax burden than a revenue-neutral substitution of environment taxes for existing taxes. This is not to say that environment taxes could not reduce the tax burden by replacing certain (high excess burden) taxes but rather that environment taxes are not the best tax instrument to achieve this objective.

The conjectured superiority of environment taxes in promoting economic output is based on the observation that environment taxes impose a lower (theoretically a zero) excess burden. Environment taxes may well impose a lower social cost but this arises from the net effect of two components – a benefit to those suffering the externality that outweighs the cost of abatement to polluters. It is the cost of abatement, however, that matters for the output implications of the tax; this is the cost of producing the public good of a cleaner environment. Environment taxes are like any tax: if imposed on productive factors they lead taxpayers to modify production decisions and change the cost of capital goods; if imposed on consumer goods they lead taxpayers, *inter alia*, to change their pattern of consumption. In the case of an environment tax, excess burden arises because the private sector is encouraged to reduce use of environmental resources. The excess burden takes the form of the abatement costs incurred by the taxpayer.[18] In the chart, discussed earlier, this excess burden is equal to ABC. This adjustment, after all, yields the environmental benefits that are anticipated to flow from the environment tax.

There are several considerations which influence the relative output consequences of using environment taxes versus other taxes. In many practical circumstances these factors mean that a broad-based tax is preferable to environment taxes although case-by-case examination is needed to assess the effect on the private sector's tax burden.

A broad-based tax will generally impose a lower excess burden than narrow-based taxes. A broad-based tax will not change relative prices and thus is less likely to encourage taxpayers to modify their production or consumption behavior compared to an environment tax. A broad-based consumption tax could influence the choice between consumption and leisure whereas an environment tax influences choices on a number of margins: consumption, production inputs, saving and investment, as well as consumption leisure choices. Consequently, it is reasonable to presume that a broad-based consumption tax, such as a VAT, will impose a lower excess burden than an environment tax.

The excess burden of a tax increases more than proportionally with its tax rate subject to the nature of pre-existing distortions.[19] An environment tax will require a tax rate considerably higher than an equal revenue broad-based consumption tax and, consequently, the broad-based tax is likely to impose a lower excess burden than the environment tax. This result would not hold, however, if the taxed environmental activity is subject initially to relatively low taxation. To take one example, if energy is being subsidized – as it has been in many countries – there is probably a strong efficiency case for eliminating those energy subsidies, and perhaps imposing environment taxes, rather than imposing other types of taxes.[20]

Empirical studies support the presumption in favor of broad-based taxes and against environment taxes when the policy choice is defined by the implications for economic output. The empirical results are usefully considered in two stages. First, there is scope for use of environment taxes to reduce the social cost of the tax system. Goulder (1992) quantifies a double dividend from using a carbon tax in the United States.[21] The carbon tax revenues are used to finance a reduction in marginal tax rates of personal or corporate income taxes and this reduces the excess burden of a carbon tax by 25 percent to 32 percent compared to when the carbon tax revenues are returned to taxpayers in lump-sum form. Second, and more importantly, however, other types of taxes are, by a large margin, more effective than environment taxes in reducing the social cost of the tax system (Goulder, 1993). For example, the output costs of employing the BTU tax and a tax on gasoline consumption (proposed in the US deficit reduction debate) exceed by a significant margin the costs of increasing personal income taxes and, by a bigger margin, the use of a broad-based consumption tax. A key factor driving the results is the relative narrowness of the energy tax bases – most of the higher output costs of the BTU tax flow from its relatively narrow base and the balance is attributable to the fact that the tax is levied on gross output rather than on final or net output.

Employment

This section examines whether environment taxes can promote employment by replacing taxes on labor. The European Commission envisages that use of energy taxes will result in substitution of labor for capital/energy. It suggests that nonwage labor costs, such as social security payments – particularly for unskilled workers – be reduced and the revenue loss compensated for by increases in excise duties on energy products and introduction of a carbon/ energy tax.[22]

Using environment taxes in place of taxes on labor is unlikely to promote employment prospects. There are two avenues by which employment could potentially be promoted. First, employment could be promoted via a tax-induced output effect. But environment taxes are likely to impose greater output losses than alternative tax measures according to the previous section and thus, if anything, are likely to have negative implications for employment of labor. Second, employment could be promoted via a substitution of labor for other factors of production if labor becomes relatively more attractive than other production factors.[23] It is difficult, however, to shift taxes away from labor and this suggests that this avenue by which environment taxes might promote employment is also likely to prove ineffective. Nevertheless, it is the incidence of environment taxes which will determine ultimately whether the replacement of nonwage taxes on labor by environment taxes reduces the cost of labor. The incidence of environment taxes, and thus whether employment will become relatively more attractive, depends on a number of factors. Some considerations are summarized below.

Taxes on inputs

An environment-oriented energy tax will likely include taxation of energy as an input. Two cases are identified in considering the incidence of such taxes: when goods, produced using taxed energy inputs, are tradable and when they are nontradable. In the tradable case, labor is likely to bear most of the energy tax burden. Factors of production, and not consumers, will bear the tax burden because prices for the tradable final output will be set on world markets. Factors of production will bear the tax according to their elasticity of supply which means, in effect, that factors which are least mobile will bear the tax. Both capital and energy factors are mobile even though, in the short run, physical capital is likely to be immobile. This leaves labor as most likely to bear much of the energy tax. As a result, employment prospects are not likely to be promoted by the substitution of environment taxes. In the case of nontradable goods, domestic consumers are likely to bear the tax burden. Consequently, if the environment tax is limited to nontradable goods, then there is a greater chance that employment can be promoted by the tax substitution.[24] Just because the tax is borne by consumers, however, does not ensure that employment prospects are promoted. Taxes that fall on consumers are discussed next.

Taxes on final consumption

Consumers are likely to bear the burden of a tax levied on final energy consumption. The tax is borne by capital income earners and transfer recipients in addition to labor income earners. In this case, it is possible that taxation of labor income earners, a subset of consumers, can be reduced. Taxes that raise consumer prices, however, interact with taxes on labor income adding to the distortion that reduces labor supply and discourages employment. Real wages are reduced by consumer energy taxes because they increase consumer good prices that are used to deflate nominal after-tax wages; the after-tax real wage is $(1 - t_I)w/(1 + t_i)p$ where t_I is the marginal income tax rate, w is the nominal wage, t_i the average indirect tax rate, and p the price level – a higher value of p resulting from the energy tax reduces real wages and interacts with the labor income tax wedge $(1 - t_I)$. Labor reduces its supply in response to lower real wages. The labor supply distortion introduced by energy taxes (or other taxes influencing the price level) is a function of $(1 - t_I)/(1 + t_i)$.[25] Thus, taxes on final energy consumption, although falling on consumers, may do little to help or may even harm employment prospects.

International aspects of environment tax incidence

The tax burden could be borne to some degree by energy-producing countries if, following a European proposal, the major OECD countries introduced carbon taxes or similar measures. These OECD countries, as a group, are major oil importers and by imposing energy taxes jointly they could shift part of the tax burden to energy producers. Thus, an increase in energy taxes could, subject to supply elasticity, result in a decline in oil prices. The countries imposing the tax could record improved terms of trade and employment at the expense of energy producers. This outcome, while serving the employment prospects of OECD countries, does not provide the environmental benefits of an energy tax.

Internationally mobile capital can be forced to bear a greater share of the tax burden if there is international coordination of tax policies. However, it is not clear that shifting the tax burden to capital, even if the requisite international cooperation is deemed feasible, would improve employment prospects. The environment tax would, if borne by capital, increase the price of capital goods with the consequence that capital formation would decline and this might well result in a reduction in labor productivity.[26] A decline in labor productivity could, depending on the flexibility of the labor market, worsen unemployment.

At the outset of this section, two issues were posed: first, whether environment taxes thwart macroeconomic objectives and second, whether environment taxes are the best tax when revenue-raising fiscal measures are required for macroeconomic reasons. In sum, environment taxes may thwart output and employment objectives. Moreover, although environment taxes may reduce output costs compared to some other taxes, it seems unlikely that environment taxes are the best available tax instrument to pursue macroeconomic objectives. This, of course, is not to say that environment taxes should not be used but rather emphasizes that they should be directed to meeting environmental objectives. This reflects the general principle that policy instruments should be assigned to specific policy objectives and rarely can multiple policy goals be achieved with a single instrument.

CONCLUSIONS

The policy discussion of environment taxes has focussed not so much on their environmental implications but on their implications for the budget, equity, economic activity, and employment. The US Government proposed an energy tax, and implemented a gasoline tax, as a revenue-raising policy that was part of its deficit reduction plan. Environmental objectives were used to justify the use of energy taxes although opponents to these measures pointed to the harmful equity aspects of energy taxes. The European Commission has suggested that environment taxes be used to replace taxes on labor because environment taxes will impose lower social costs boosting economic activity and promoting employment.

Policymakers have multiple policy goals and the hypothesized double dividend of environment taxes has raised the specter that more than one of these goals can be achieved simultaneously by the use of the one environment tax policy instrument. In our view, such a policy 'free lunch' is not available. The double dividend of environment taxes is that environment taxes reduce environmental damage (the first dividend) and provide revenue without loss of efficiency that characterizes other taxes because of their environmental benefits (the second dividend). The double dividend is valid only in limited circumstances and, even where it does hold, says nothing about whether environment taxes are the best policy instrument to achieve various non-environmental policy objectives.

The problem for policymakers is that the second dividend is made up of two parts – an excess burden or cost, perhaps in the form of lower output and employment – and offsetting this burden is an 'excess benefit' in the form of lower environmental damage. Policymakers who are concerned with economic activity, employment, and equity issues are interested primarily with the 'excess burden' aspect of the environment tax. There is a reasonable presumption that environment taxes will impose a greater excess burden than alternative taxes such as broad-based consumption taxes. Moreover, it is unlikely that shifting from taxes on labor to energy taxes will substantially reduce the relative tax burden on labor. This chapter therefore concludes that environment taxes should be targeted to environmental goals where they may be the appropriate policy instrument and that environment taxes are less efficient than alternatives in promoting various nonenvironmental policy objectives.

NOTES

*The views expressed are those of the author and do not necessarily represent the views of the International Monetary Fund.

1 See Pigou (1920).
2 See Commission of the European Communities (1992).
3 The proposal provides for (a) graduated tax reductions for energy-intensive firms that may be disadvantaged relative to international competitors; (b) tax incentives and temporary exemptions for firms embarking on energy-saving investment; and (c) introduction of the tax was conditional on other OECD countries introducing comparable taxes or measures. Other carbon taxes have similar provisions. For example, the Danish carbon tax provides tax refunds to VAT-registered firms with high energy consumption.
4 Baumol and Oates (1988) discuss the literature on Pigouvian taxes.
5 Environment-targeted taxes may take a variety of forms other than Pigouvian taxes. For example, taxes may be levied on goods whose use is related to environmental damage or some general taxes may have provisions – such as rate variation or exemptions – that are targeted to achieve environmental goals. These

taxes are only as effective as Pigouvian taxes when their use is linked directly to the emissions or environmental damage. McMorran and Nellor (1994) discuss these other forms of environment taxes.

6 Setting the optimal rate of tax on an environmentally damaging good has been examined by Sandmo (1975) and the following reflects the results developed in that paper.

7 More specifically, the term μ is equal to the negative of the marginal utility of income over the marginal impact of an increase in the tax revenue requirement on social utility.

8 The efficiency gains from raising environment tax revenues could be significant. Browning (1987), for example, shows that the marginal cost of taxes on wages in the United States might lie in the range of \$1.32 to \$1.47 although estimates of the marginal cost of public funds are highly sensitive to a number of parameter values.

9 On the double dividend see, for example, Pearce (1991).

10 See Bovenberg and de Mooij (1992).

11 A cleaner environment is a public good because it can be consumed jointly and consumers cannot be excluded from its consumption.

12 One exception to this sequential characterization of budget determination is the benefit tax approach. Moreover, in the sequential exercise of determining public goods provision and then determining taxes, it is recognized that raising revenues could generate social costs that should influence the level of public goods provision.

13 See Musgrave (1959).

14 For example, see Poterba (1989) and Smith (1992).

15 See Musgrave (1959, p. 12).

16 See Musgrave (1959, p. 16).

17 These arguments apply equally at the domestic level and the international level. In the latter case the debate on the use of carbon taxes to address the global externality of global warming often stumbles on the equity aspects of the costs of adjustment that would be borne by developing countries.

18 This discussion assumes that environmental externalities have no implications for productivity. If productivity is harmed by environmental damage, environment taxes can raise productivity and output to the extent that they alleviate damage. In these circumstances, the excess burden incurred by taxpayers should reflect both abatement costs and improved productivity.

19 In his classic article Harberger (1964) shows that the excess burden increases as the square of the tax rate. Subsequent literature indicated that the relationship of excess burden to the tax rate was complicated by the presence of other distorting taxes.

20 The form of the environment tax will influence the relative costs imposed on the economy. Thus, for example, the US policy of using a gasoline tax on final consumers may well be more efficient, in a macroeconomic context, than the proposed BTU tax that it replaced (albeit not as effective from an environmental perspective). A tax on final gasoline consumption, unlike the BTU tax, does not influence producer input or savings and investment choices. A broad-based consumption tax is still likely to be preferable to a tax on final gasoline consumption.

21 The excess burden of the carbon tax is 15 percent lower than otherwise on account of the pre-existing low relative taxation of fossil fuel industries in the United States, illustrating that part of the tax eliminates a pre-existing distortion.

22 The European Commission QUEST model concludes that a carbon/energy tax is superior to a VAT because it encourages greater substitution of labor for energy than would a VAT. There are no details provided regarding incidence of the taxes.

See Commission of the European Communities (1993b).

23 Even if relative prices change in favor of increasing employment it does not necessarily follow that this will boost employment. A key issue is the appropriate form of modeling labor market behavior. For example, in an 'insiders' type of model the increase in labor demand may be reflected in increasing real wages of the insiders without any net change in employment.

24 There will be other social costs from the distortions encouraged by this substitution.

25 See Bovenberg and de Mooij (1992), and Poterba (1993).

26 It has often been pointed out that the sharp increase in oil prices that took place in the 1973 oil price shock coincided with the sharp decline in productivity recorded in many industrial countries.

REFERENCES

Baumol, William, and Wallace Oates (1988) *The Theory of Environmental Policy*, Cambridge: Cambridge University Press.

Bovenberg, A. Lans, and Ruud A. de Mooij (1992) 'Environmental Taxation and Labor Market Distortions', University of Tilburg Working Paper 9252, Center for Economic Research, The Netherlands.

Bovenberg, A. Lans, and Frederick van der Ploeg (1992) 'Environmental Policy, Public Finance and the Labor Market in A Second-Best World', Center for Economic Policy Research, Working Paper 745, London.

Browning, Edgar (1987) 'On the Marginal Welfare Cost of Taxation', *American Economic Review*, Vol. 77 (March), pp. 11–23.

Commission of the European Communities (1992) 'The Commission Adopts Proposal on Carbon/Energy Tax', *Information Note*, Brussels, May 27.

———(1993a) 'Growth, Competitiveness, Unemployment', White Paper, *Bulletin of the European Communities*, Supplement 6/93, Brussels.

———(1993b) *Taxation, Employment and Environment: Fiscal Reform for Reducing Unemployment*, Brussels: Directorate General of Economic and Financial Affairs.

Goulder, Lawrence H. (1992) 'Do the Costs of a Carbon Tax Vanish when Interactions with other Taxes are Accounted for?', NBER Working Paper No. 4061, Cambridge, Massachusetts: National Bureau of Economic Research.

———(1993) 'Energy Taxes: Traditional Efficiency Effects and Environmental Implications', NBER Working Paper No. 4582, Cambridge, Massachusetts: National Bureau of Economic Research.

Harberger, Arnold (1964) 'Taxation, Resource Allocation and Welfare', in *The Role of Direct and Indirect Taxes in the Federal Revenue System*, NBER Other Conference Series No. 3, Cambridge, Massachusetts.

McMorran, Ronald, and David Nellor (1994) 'Tax Policy and the Environment: Theory and Practice', International Monetary Fund Working Paper WP/94/106, Washington, DC.

Musgrave, Richard (1959) *The Theory of Public Finance*, New York: McGraw-Hill.

Pearce, David W. (1991) 'The Role of Carbon Taxes in Adjusting to Global Warming', *Economic Journal*, Vol. 101, pp. 938–48.

Pigou, Arthur C. (1920) *The Economics of Welfare*, London: Macmillan (4th edition, 1932).

Poterba, James M. (1989) 'Lifetime Incidence and the Distributional Burden of Excise Taxes', *American Economic Review Papers and Proceedings*, Vol. 97, No. 2 (May), pp. 325–30.

———(1993) 'Global Warming Policy: A Public Finance Perspective', *Journal of*

Economic Perspectives, Vol. 7 (Fall), pp. 47–63.

Sandmo, Agnar (1975) 'Optimal Taxation in the Presence of Externalities', *Swedish Journal of Economics*, Vol. 77, pp. 86–98.

Smith, Stephen (1992) 'The Distributional Consequences of Taxes on Energy and the Carbon Content of Fuels', in *Commission of the European Community, European Economy*, Vol. 1, pp. 241–68.

Tanzi, Vito (1969) *The Individual Income Tax and Economic Growth*, Baltimore: Johns Hopkins University Press.

———(1980) 'Inflationary Expectations, Economic Activity, Taxes, and Interest Rates, *American Economic Review*, Vol. 70 (March).

———(1989) 'The Impact of Macroeconomic Policies on the Level of Taxation and the Fiscal Balance in Developing Countries', *Staff Papers*, International Monetary Fund (Washington, DC), Vol. 36 (September).

Part IV

FISCAL POLICIES, POVERTY ALLEVIATION, AND THE SOCIAL SAFETY NET

7

POVERTY ALLEVIATION IN A FINANCIAL PROGRAMMING FRAMEWORK

An integrated approach

Sheetal K. Chand and Parthasarathi Shome[1]

INTRODUCTION

In recent years, country stabilization and structural adjustment programs supported by the International Monetary Fund (IMF) have been criticized for ignoring their effects on the poor even while their impact may have been positive for the balance of payments (see, among many others, Cornia and Stewart, 1993; EISSEAS, 1994). Increasingly, country financial programs have attempted to recognize the importance of ensuring that the poor and vulnerable are not made worse off as a consequence of the adjustment measures incorporated in the financial programs (see Heller *et al.*, 1988; Tanzi and Chu, 1989; and Nashashibi *et al.*, 1992). In the discussion surrounding these attempts, it is recognized that there are potentially important trade-offs between policy objectives giving rise to the policy mix problem (see various recent reports issued by the Development Committee, for example 1990). It is also recognized that the use of various instruments has to reckon with possible adverse side effects, and that how measures are sequenced can make a big difference to the attainment of the poverty alleviation objective, in particular. However, the issue of how to take account of the poverty alleviation objective in the Fund's financial programming framework has yet to be resolved.

The programs often explicitly propose measures to alleviate social stress subject, of course, to available resources. Because much of the focus of this work is on how to economize on the limited resources available when promoting poverty alleviation goals, the emphasis is on the design of selective measures for the more cost-effective targeting of economically vulnerable groups (see Gupta and Nashashibi, 1990; Chu and Gupta, 1993). The resulting poverty alleviation measures, better defined as social safety net mechanisms, are 'added on' to the financial programs insofar as the underlying stabilization and adjustment targets remain unaffected.[2]

While there is much to be said for the operational and analytical convenience of this additive approach, often the critique of financial adjustment programs stems from the exclusion of a poverty constraint as an integral part of the underlying model. Indeed, adopting an integrated approach could make it evident whether, and to what extent, different macropolicy prescriptions result compared to those emerging from the traditional model.

The extent to which the overall design characteristics of a financial program itself may need to be modified to support a poverty alleviation objective depends on the economic structure. A particular economic structure could impose significant trade-offs between the different objectives. Indeed, that is likely to be the case. It is possible that by adopting an 'integrated' approach, whereby the settings of the program instruments are selected in such a way as to minimize adverse implications for poverty, the likelihood of success, both with regard to the stabilization objective of balance of payments viability as well as the poverty alleviation objective, is increased.[3] Such an approach should help address some of the concerns expressed by certain critics of Fund-supported financial programs that the programs have an excessively deflationary and pro-poverty bias (Cornia and Stewart, 1993). They argue not only that the programs constrain output growth, which adds to the ranks of the poor, but that the poor are further hit by the mandatory curtailment of overall fiscal outlays for stabilization purposes.[4]

The stabilization-induced decline in output growth could cause revenue to fall, forcing the government to cut back overall outlays in order to preserve its stabilization-oriented fiscal target, which further depresses output. This process of declining output is likely to be accompanied by declining social outlays, which are often the first expenditures to be cut. While the additive approach reallocates expenditure and puts in place targeted poverty programs, which cushion the poor to some extent,[5] nevertheless, a mutually reinforcing vicious circle could result. Some have, therefore, concluded that the outcome for the poor could be even more adverse than what is shown by indices of output decline, owing to the inevitable curtailment of public goods that support minimum living standards, which serves to aggravate social stress (Anand and Revallion, 1993).

An integrated approach that may be better able to limit the adverse ramifications on the poor by explicitly incorporating a poverty constraint, than the additive approach which relies only on supplemental poverty alleviation programs, therefore, should be considered. Such an investigation is the objective of this chapter. The chapter proceeds by first setting up, in the next section, a general version of the financial programming model that can be used to explore possible trade-offs between targets for the balance of payments, output growth, and inflation.[6] Alternative measures of poverty are reviewed in the following section, with a view to determining which ones may be included in the financial programming models along with macroeconomic indicators typically used as performance criteria by them. The penultimate section presents a simulation of the financial programming model under the influence of an external shock followed by typical program-related policy responses, and considers implications for the poverty alleviation objective. Concluding comments are presented in the final section.

THE MODEL

In the financial programming approach, central reliance is placed on a predictable demand for money function and the means for supplying the money needed to fulfill that demand, whether through domestic credit creation or international reserve movements (see IMF Occasional Paper No. 55). Programming in this context consists of determining, by reference to the economic objectives and, in particular, the balance of payments target, the appropriate rate of credit expansion as a key policy instrument. Typically, the models assume that there is an underlying rate of growth of output and of inflation that are separately determined, either as trends or as targets, which determine the incremental demand for money. It is also assumed that these are not affected by the solution for the rate of credit expansion that is consistent with the projected incremental demand for money and the balance of payments targets. The version of the financial programming model set out here, while continuing to be driven by monetarist underpinnings – in that the incremental demand for money plays a central role – is more general, from which the basic model falls out as a special case (see Chand, 1989). This permits exploring possible trade-offs between targets for the balance of payments, and nominal output growth, in particular.

The model, containing a number of particularly simple behavioral expressions, is set out here in annotated form and distinguishes four sectors:[7,8]

Monetary sector

- demand for money

$$M^{d} = \frac{1}{v} PY \tag{7.1}$$

- incremental money supply

$$\Delta M^{s} = \Delta D_{g} + \Delta D_{p} + E\Delta F, \tag{7.2}$$

- incremental demand for money

$$\Delta M^{\mathrm{d}} = \left(\frac{\Delta P}{P_{-1}} + \frac{\Delta Y}{Y_{-1}}\right) M_{-1} = \frac{1}{v} \Delta PY, \tag{7.3}$$

- distribution of credit

$$\Delta D = \Delta D_{\mathrm{g}} + \Delta D_{\mathrm{p}}. \tag{7.4}$$

External sector

- incremental supply of foreign exchange (in domestic currency terms, with E the exchange rate and taking account of trade, net external transfers and capital flows)

$$E\Delta F^{\mathrm{s}} = P_{\mathrm{x}}X - EP_{\mathrm{f}}Z + ETr_{\mathrm{g}} + ETr_{\mathrm{p}} + E\Delta K_{\mathrm{g}} + E\Delta K_{\mathrm{p}}, \qquad (7.5)^{9}$$

- import demand function

$$EP_{\mathrm{f}}Z = z(e)PA, \tag{7.6}$$

where $z = eb(e)$ and $b'(e) < 0$. PA refers to absorption and is defined as

$$PA = PC_{\mathrm{p}} + PI_{\mathrm{p}} + PG. \tag{7.7}$$

Private sector

- income and borrowing flows and their allocation

$$PY_{\mathrm{d}} + ETr_{\mathrm{p}} + E\Delta K_{\mathrm{p}} + \Delta D_{\mathrm{p}} = PC_{\mathrm{p}} + PI_{\mathrm{p}} + \Delta M^{\mathrm{d}}, \tag{7.8}$$

- consumption function

$$PC_{\mathrm{p}} = cPY_{\mathrm{d}}, \tag{7.9}$$

- disposable income definition

$$PY_{\mathrm{d}} = PY - PT + PG_{\mathrm{po}}, \tag{7.10}$$

where PG_{po} denotes government transfers to the poor,

- tax function

$$PT = tPY, \tag{7.11}$$

- investment function

$$PI_p = PY_d - PC_p + (ETr_p + E\Delta K_p + \Delta D_p - \Delta M^d). \qquad (7.12)$$

Government sector

- budget constraint

$$PG + PG_{po} - (PT + ETr_g) = E\Delta K_g + \Delta D_g. \qquad (7.13)$$

Some consolidations

Imports are assumed to be a function of desired absorption A by residents. The sum of expenditures represented by the latter equals the consolidated flow of the private and government sector's income, to which is added any net transfers received by these two sectors and the proceeds from borrowing, and from which the desired accumulation of money balances is subtracted. This demonstration begins with equation (7.7), where absorption is defined as the sum of private consumption and investment demands and government outlays. Then equation (7.8) is used to substitute for consumption, and equation (7.13) to substitute for government expenditure, which on manipulation will yield

$$PA = PY + (ETr + \Delta D + E\Delta K) - \Delta M^d. \qquad (7.14)$$

The reduced reform solution

The equilibrium conditions for financial and physical flows in this model are developed by adding up the three sectoral constraints (7.5), (7.8) and (7.13), placing goods on the left-hand side (LHS) and financial items on the right-hand side (RHS) to generate

$$PY - PC_p - PI_p - PG - (P_x X - EP_f Z) = (\Delta M^d - \Delta M^s). \qquad (7.15)$$

The solution of the model is provided in terms of nominal income by equating either the LHS or the RHS of the conditions stated in (7.15) to zero. Equating the RHS of (7.15) to zero, and substituting for the incremental demand and supply of money by using equations (7.2) and (7.3), yields

$$\Delta PY = v(\Delta D + E\Delta F). \qquad (7.16)$$

The reduced form solution for the change in nominal income can be obtained by using equation (7.5) to substitute for the $E\Delta F$ term in equation (7.16), drawing on equations (7.6) and (7.14) to substitute for the import term, and utilizing the property $PY = (PY)_{-1} + \Delta PY$:

$$\Delta PY = \frac{v}{(1 - z + zv)} [(1 - z)(\Delta D + ETr + E\Delta K) + P_x X - z(PY)_{-1}]. \qquad (7.17)$$

To understand this solution, note that if there is an excess supply of money from additional domestic credit creation, absorption will increase and both nominal income and imports will rise. This contrasts with the basic formulation of the financial programming model, where an excess money supply is eliminated only through a deterioration in the balance of payments (see Chand, 1989), given that nominal income is exogenously determined. This result is easily generated in the present model by pegging ΔPY and noting that exports now function as a slack variable that automatically adjusts to preserve it. As before, absorption is raised by the additional domestic credit creation, but is now entirely met by a diversion of some exports to domestic use and an increase in imports, thereby generating the one-to-one relationship between additional credit creation and the balance of payments deterioration of the basic model.[10]

The solution for nominal income can be subdivided into its respective output and price components by noting that

$$(1 + \Delta PY/PY_{-1}) = (1 + p)(1 + y) \qquad (7.18)$$

where lower case letters denote growth rates.

By building in more structure so as to determine endogenously a rate of price inflation p, or alternatively output growth y, the nominal income solution can be decomposed into its price and output components which, in turn, would facilitate the assessment of output growth and inflation trade-offs. However, this decomposition is not needed in what follows. The approach here, as will be evident subsequently, is to use a purchasing power criterion that can be conveniently expressed in nominal terms. On a heuristic basis, movements in nominal GDP can sometimes be used to derive inferences about the underlying price and output components as is illustrated subsequently.

Finally, it should be noted that the solution presented above is for an interval of time. For a proper dynamic analysis, a sequence of such intervals will need to be examined that allows for the effects of capacity-affecting policies to take place. Such an analysis, however, is beyond the scope of this chapter, which focusses on shorter-term responses during which the bulk of the adverse poverty effects is likely to occur. Beneficial supply-enhancing effects of the stabilization and structural adjustment policies generally take hold over a longer interval.

SELECTED POVERTY MEASURES

With the objective of seeking a feasible poverty index or criterion that could be incorporated within the financial programming framework, this section surveys various alternatives in the literature and seeks to select a couple that could be usefully employed. Feasibility in this context should comprise two factors: first, that the criterion used adequately addresses the issue of poverty; and second, that its application be based on easily available data so that it would be amenable for use in individual country programs.

A comprehensive survey of the literature on poverty measures has been carried out by Blackwood and Lynch (1994). The definition of poverty could be linked to concepts of well-being, opulence, utility of a predefined variety or income (see Anand and Revallion, 1993). Nevertheless, the most practical definition of poverty – especially in terms of the feasibility criterion defined above – has to be based on income. Below we consider the pros and cons of selected possibilities.

Poverty line and head count

These are the most rudimentary poverty measures. As a beginning, a minimum income level required to meet basic needs could be used to establish a poverty line (o). Of course basic needs and their costs would vary among different economies; nevertheless, an attempt might be made to estimate it individually by country[11] and to ensure that it is kept constant in real terms over time. A typical financial programming exercise could relatively easily incorporate a binding constraint ensuring a minimum income level at the poverty line. Also, a before-and-after head count of the people as a percentage of the population under the poverty line could be used as an index. The problem, however, is that the poverty line, being an income level, is a discreet measure even though poverty cannot quite be conceived as terminating at a particular marginal dollar for all individuals. Also, the head count is a simplistic measure which fails to recognize the extent of poverty as a criterion. Therefore, it may be necessary to incorporate somewhat more sophisticated measures of poverty, building on the poverty line and head count, in the financial programming model. Some possible measures are discussed below.

Poverty gap

If the income shortfall from the poverty line, of the average poor with mean income $\bar{m}$, is denoted by Δk, then the aggregate income shortfall or the poverty gap is:

$$(\Delta k)n = (o - \bar{m})n \tag{7.19}$$

where n is the size of the population below the poverty line o. Conceptually, it should be possible to reduce $(\Delta k)n$, given o, within the financial programming model. This can happen if the financial program results in a reduction in the number of poor. While a reduction in the poverty gap could certainly be incorporated in a financial programming framework as a performance criterion, its shortcoming lies in that it would ignore income distribution among the poor.

Lorenz curve and Gini coefficient

The Lorenz curve (L) is well known. Its concomitant concept, the Gini coefficient (GI) incorporates income distribution. L relates, in a square diagram, the cumulative shares of income to the cumulative percentages of the population. Thus

$$GI = \frac{\text{area between } L \text{ and diagonal line}}{\text{area between diagonal and horizontal axis}}, \quad 0 \leq GI \leq 1.^{12} \qquad (7.20)$$

Larger values of GI imply higher inequality. GI could be estimated for any segment of the population, for example for only the poor (GI_{po}). Then measures of GI_{po} under the poverty line, before and after a policy change, would indicate how the distribution of income among the poor was affected by that policy.[13]

Nevertheless, the GI is not flawless in that it fails to order income distributions completely. For example, two Ls with dissimilar shapes could yield the same GI. This is because the numerator in the above expression of GI may result from populations with vastly different concentrations in income. It therefore fails to indicate the intensity of poverty.

Composite poverty indices

The poverty measures considered, so far, have the positive property of simplicity but, for the reasons cited above, they are not fully indicative when used by themselves. For this reason, composite poverty indices that incorporate more properties have been proposed. Two such indices that are also feasible are the Sen poverty index (S) and the generalized Lorenz curve (GLC).

Sen poverty index (S)

S incorporates the number of poor (head count h), the degree of poverty $\Delta k'$ (poverty gap Δk as a ratio of the poverty line level), and the distribution of income (GI_{po}) among the poor. Thus

$$S = h[\Delta k' + (1 - \Delta k')GI_{\mathrm{po}}]. \qquad (7.21)$$

$\Delta k'$, already defined above, is

$$\Delta k' = \left[\sum_{i=1}^{n} (o - m_i) \right] / \, no \qquad (7.22)$$

where m_i is the income of the ith household under the poverty line o.

The following properties of S may be observed. First, it is an index that focusses only on the poor rather than on their relative position *vis-à-vis* the rich. Second, it is negatively related to the incomes of the poor.[14] Third, income transfers even within the poor – which can be regressive or progressive – affect the value of S.

If S were to be included as a constraint in a typical financial programming model, then the additional information that would be required would include: o, Σm_i, n, h, G_{po} (pro-poor government transfers) and GI_{po}. While this certainly adds to data requirements, the nature of the data reveals that it should not be impossible to assemble them.

Nevertheless, S could be argued to possess some shortcomings. It is biased toward improving h more than Δk or GI_{po}. This implies that S would improve most by first bringing across people from just below to just over o. It would improve least as a result of policies that focus on the most destitute first. Therefore, the use of S in the framework of financial programming models does involve a value judgment.

Generalized Lorenz curve (GLC)

By weighting the L by the average income of the distribution, Shorrocks (1983) introduced the *GLC*. Thus, focussing only on the poor,

$$GL_{\mathrm{po}} = \bar{m}L_{\mathrm{p}}(m_i, \ldots, m_n, n). \qquad (7.23)$$

The weighting allows two identical income distributions – but with different average incomes – that would have yielded the same L to result in two *GL*s, that is in two different poverty measures. This simple procedure thus makes it feasible to track not only the income distribution among the poor but also the degree of poverty.

Incorporating GL_{po} into a financial programming framework requires information similar to that of S. However, unlike the latter, the former does not involve a head count of the poor that could be of some interest to policymakers. Other than that, *GL* and S are similar indices. Given the slightly greater information available from using S, it should be usually preferable to use it over GL_{po}.

SOME EXPERIMENTS WITH THE INTEGRATED MODEL

This section first considers some of the connections or interface points between the financial programming model and the Sen poverty index as the preferred poverty index. Subsequently, a simulation is undertaken of the integrated model.

Integrating poverty into the model

Even at the macroeconomic level of the financial programming model, there are several ways in which the selected poverty index can be affected, either by the outcomes of the model with respect to output and inflation, or by the policy measures that may be enacted such as a devaluation or fiscal consolidation.

The first, and probably the most important influence on the poverty index, concerns the growth in output in the face of a growing population. If for some reason output contracts, while population continues to grow, average per capita output levels could decline fairly sharply. Does this imply an increase in the poverty index? Even if the relative distribution of income remains unchanged, which in itself is a strong assumption – as the more likely outcome is for it to shift in favor of the stronger and less vulnerable – the decline in average per capita output will have caused a number of persons to cross over to below the poverty line. The 1990 *World Development Report* (WDR) (World Bank, 1990) took US$370 in purchasing power equivalent as the measure of the poverty line. According to that report about one-third of the population of the developing countries falls below that line. While more detailed information is needed to infer the distribution of a population across the income range, it is likely that a reduction of say 10 per cent in the mean real per capita income in a poor country, which could easily occur in a year of bad harvest or deteriorating terms of trade, would push a significant additional part of the population below the poverty line.[15]

Second, a real depreciation of the exchange rate, which implies some reduction in the real purchasing power of the economy, could also involve an increase in the poverty index; just as with the decline in real per capita output, more persons would be pushed below the poverty line. However, it is now possible, depending on the differential effects of the devaluation, that exporters and producers of exportables gain, and importers lose, so that even though the purchasing power of the economy as a whole is reduced, there may be a change in relative incomes such that the poverty index declines. This would be the case if, for example, producers of exportables were primarily peasant farmers earning below the poverty line, while consumers of imports were primarily urban dwellers earning above the poverty line. In the apparently more typical situation, however, significant numbers of both urban dwellers and peasant farmers continue to earn below the poverty line after the devaluation with the consequence that the poverty index may rise. Nevertheless, insofar as the depreciation eases the balance of payments constraint, and the supply of imports improves, the economy could benefit.

A third manifestation of the model that could affect the poverty index concerns inflation. While the effect of inflation is not to change, at least directly, the amount of output or purchasing power available to the economy, there is a strong presumption that those who have less recourse to indexation, in particular, people such as pensioners on fixed incomes or unorganized labor, will lose relative to other income groups. The poverty gap, or the difference between the incomes of the poor and more vulnerable and the poverty line would widen. Measures would then have to be taken to counter the impact of inflation on the poverty index.

Fourth, policies that involve fiscal consolidation could affect the poverty index adversely, although the outcome will depend on a balancing of effects. Typically, the most poor tend to be subsistence farmers who are usually less affected by government spending and tax programs. Nevertheless, a sufficiently sharp retrenchment of the budget could push other occupation groups from above to below the poverty line. In addition, it could worsen the distribution of income for those already below that line. However, insofar as fiscal consolidation succeeds in reducing the rate of inflation, the poor may be benefited, as they would from any resulting crowding in of investment that raises the growth rate, although all these effects will have to be set against a possible shorter-term economic contraction. Such conflicting tendencies are likely to make it more difficult to assess the overall effects on the poverty index of fiscal consolidation.

While the preceding discussion concerns possible deflationary macroeconomic effects of fiscal consolidation, any pro-poor outlays that are eliminated or reduced, for example transfers or subsidies, will directly impact on the poor who will suffer an equivalent income loss. Once again, some balancing is involved between the economy's efficiency gains from the pursuit of less distortive policies and the direct loss sustained by the poor.

To sum up, by reference to factors inducing a change in the poverty index and with a view to containing their effect, the preferred short-term macroeconomic outcome of an adjustment program would be for (a) the rate of growth of output not to be unduly depressed; (2) the balance of payments to be improved; (3) inflation to be reduced; and (4) fiscal outlays, especially with a pro-poor bias, not to be unduly suppressed. Some aspects of sequencing have to be kept in mind. In the short run, alleviating a particularly severe balance of payments constraint may be an overriding concern and growth may have to decline even more leading to a bigger increase in the poverty index. The important question examined next is that of how to observe the overriding (balance of payments) constraint, while choosing that package of adjustment measures that minimizes the rise in the poverty index.

Incorporating the Sen poverty index (S) in the financial programming model

Of the three components in S, at least two are likely to be directly influenced by movements in macroeconomic aggregates: the head-count ratio h and the poverty gap Δk. The GI for the poor (GI_{po}), which measures the distribution of income amongst the poor, is subject to several, less well-understood complex forces whose relationship to shorter-term fluctuations in macroeconomic aggregates may in any case be limited. In the analysis that follows we will assume that this coefficient is set at a constant value and focus on the first two components in S.[16]

Key influences on the head-count ratio would obviously include the measure of the poverty line. Employing the World Bank criterion of US$370 for the poverty line and expressing it in local currency terms gives the first point of reference. This is assumed to be an absolute standard whose local valuation in an import-dependent economy depends on the level of the exchange rate. Should the latter appreciate, the head-count ratio would fall, and conversely for a depreciation. Fluctuations in the exchange rate are thus taken into account in the local currency valuation of the poverty line. The combined effects of inflation and output growth are captured by movements in nominal GNP which, given the size of the population, affect average per capita income. If the latter rises relative to the poverty line, some of the poor will be lifted above the line, with the number depending on the underlying distribution of income. This feature is conveniently expressed as a response elasticity of the head-count ratio with respect to the gap between the per capita income for that economy and the poverty line:

$$
\begin{aligned}
h &= h(u - o), \quad h' < 0 \\
\eta_h &= (-h')(u - o)/h
\end{aligned}
\tag{7.24}
$$

where u is per capita income and o is the local currency value of the poverty line.

An elasticity of 0.2 is used here for illustrative purposes based on a regression run on a sample of countries, which related the head-count ratio to the period change in real per capita income.[17] The regression did not take explicit account of varying inflation rates, but it may be expected that the higher the degree of inflation in the observed movement in nominal GNP, the lower this elasticity, as the poor are likely to be less effective in indexing their incomes.

To determine the poverty gap it is necessary to estimate the average per capita income of the poor $\bar{m}$. This could be done by first using the L distribution to determine the proportion of total GNP that accrues to the percentage of the population that was earlier found to lie below the poverty line, i.e. the head-count ratio. On taking account of the population size, the relevant proportion of total GNP is converted into per capita magnitudes. Insofar as incomes of the poor are supplemented by government subsidies and transfers G_{po}, the per capita income estimate for the poor will need to be adjusted to include this amount.[18] It is reasonable to hypothesize that an increase in the average per capita income, relative to the poverty line, will also exert an upward pull on average per capita income of the poor. Two effects are involved here: the first concerns the reduction in the head-count ratio and the associated absolute increase in the amount of income accruing to the remaining poor, while the second concerns the increase in the incomes of some of the poor as a consequence of the general rise in incomes. Once again, the strength of these effects depends on the underlying distribution of income. These effects are conveniently summarized by an elasticity as follows:

$$\bar{m} = f(u - o), \quad f' > 0$$
$$\eta_{\bar{m}} = (f')(u - o)/f.^{19} \tag{7.25}$$

The value of S, which ranges in the bounded interval 0 to 1, with a state of no poverty represented by the lower bound and complete poverty by the upper bound, can now be fully determined on the basis of the preceding hypotheses. The information set needed for a basic analysis comprises the level of the exchange rate, movements in nominal GDP, the size of the population and its rate of growth, the L of the economy, and the amount of government expenditures devoted to the poor, and an estimate of the GI_p.[20]

A simulation

Suppose that the economy were initially in equilibrium, growing at, say, 4.5 percent annually (its underlying secular rate of growth), with inflation at 10 percent and the balance of payments (under conditions of a liberalized external sector) in equilibrium. The equilibrium profile is depicted in column 1 of Table 7.1.

Suppose next the economy is subjected to an external shock – export prices decline by 20 percent. If the economy were to exhibit a pattern of response that has been frequently observed in many countries, there might initially be relatively little policy reaction. Pressures on the budget mount for providing relief in a variety of ways to ameliorate the recessionary effects of the decline in export prices, with the consequence that government expenditures may rise. If so, the balance of payments is likely to become even worse and international reserves will fall. Eventually, declining reserves will force the government either to devalue or, if this is resisted (usually on the grounds that it unnecessarily impoverishes the country), to introduce external controls and taxes on imports. However, the restraint on imports reduces the aggregate supply of goods to the economy, whereas aggregate demand is being

Table 7.1 Simulation results (in units except where otherwise noted)

	Initial equilibrium *t*	*Shock/ nonadjustment* *t + 1*	*'Additive' adjustment approach (basic model)* *t + 2*			*'Integrated' adjustment approach* *t + 2*
	(1)	*(2)*	*(3a) prediction*	*(3b) outcome*	*(3c) add on*	*(4)*
Macro indicators:						
Nominal GDP growth (in percent)	15.0	33.7	15.0	2.0	2.0	24.1
Balance of payments (in foreign currency)	–	–3.6	–1.0	–2.7	–2.7	–1.0
Fiscal balance (percent of GDP)	–3.2	–8.3	–3.1	–3.1	–3.1	–3.8
Sen poverty index (*S*)	0.119	0.075	0.122	0.146	0.118	0.118
(head-count ratio)	(0.30)	(0.23)	(0.30)	(0.33)	(0.30)	(0.29)
Instruments:						
Credit expansion	2.5	10.0	4.9	4.9	4.9	7.0
Of which: to budget	1.0	7.5	1.0	1.0	1.0	3.0
(incremental demand for money)	(2.5)	(5.6)	(3.3)	(0.5)	(0.5)	(5.4)
Official external borrowing	2.0	3.0	2.0	2.0	2.0	2.0
Real exchange rate	1.0	0.83	1.20	1.20	1.20	1.25
External liberalization	Full	Restrictions	Full	Full	Full	Partial
Tax ratio (percent of GDP)	15.0	15.0	17.0	17.0	17.0	17.0
Government expenditure	17.1	30.0	28.8	26.0	26.0	32.9
(percent of GDP)	(17.1)	(22.4)	(18.7)	(18.9)	(18.9)	(19.8)
Outlay on poor	0.6	0.7	1.0	1.0	5.6	1.1
(percent of GDP)	(0.6)	(0.5)	(0.7)	(0.7)	(4.1)	(0.7)
Memorandum items:						
Velocity v	6.0	6.0	6.0	6.0	6.0	6.0
Import ratio z	0.2	0.15	0.22	0.22	0.22	0.18
Propensity to consume c	0.9	0.9	0.9	0.9	0.9	0.9
Export price index	1.0	0.8	0.8	0.8	0.8	0.8
Private net foreign transfers and capital inflows	2.0	–2.0	2.0	2.0	2.0	2.0
Nominal GNP	100	133.7	153.8	137.4	137.4	165.9

stimulated by the growing fiscal deficit. Insofar as the latter is financed by the domestic banking system, domestic credit expands and the rate of inflation takes off. If the fiscal situation is not stabilized, the underlying imbalances become entrenched and the economy will increasingly be characterized by the extensive application of controls, accompanied by a growing shift of private activity to less formal channels. It is also likely that the economy will suffer from an outflow of private capital, ending up with stagnation and endemic inflation. Column 2 shows some of these outcomes.

The stimulative fiscal policy pursued in the nonadjustment phase is indicated in the table both by an increase in the government expenditure ratio from 17 percent to over 22 percent and in the increase in the amount of domestic credit expansion to finance the budget from 1 unit to 7.5 (the fiscal deficit jumps from 3.2 percent of GDP to over 8 percent). The effect is to increase sharply the nominal rate of growth in GDP, which jumps to some 34 percent. As the underlying real growth rate was initially assumed to be around its trend path, virtually all of the increase in nominal GDP can be attributed to a surge in the inflation rate. Assuming that the exchange rate is not adjusted generates a substantial real appreciation of the exchange rate. This development, together with the stimulative fiscal policy, causes the balance of payments to deteriorate from an initial state of equilibrium to –3.6. The simulation assumes that the authorities responded in the nonadjustment phase by introducing some controls on imports; otherwise, the balance of payments deterioration would have been worse.

Interestingly, for the nonadjustment case under the assumed structure, *S* registers a significant decline, indicating that the stimulative policies pursued have exerted a favorable anti-poverty effect. This is not surprising given that the overvaluation of the exchange rate has increased the purchasing power of residents, while the stimulative fiscal and monetary policies, together with the controls on imports, have increased domestic nominal per capita incomes. Such developments will reduce the head-count ratio, and the poverty gap is also likely to decline. Although inflation will probably worsen the situation for the poor, there are less of them. It is no wonder that such policies may be more attractive to the poor and to populist governments than those of austerity and adjustment. However, any improvement in *S* is purely temporary, as the policies underlying it are not sustainable.

Suppose next a traditional adjustment strategy is implemented involving tighter monetary and fiscal policy, external sector liberalization, and exchange rate correction. Column 3a of Table 7.1 indicates the profile that is expected to result if the new fiscal target is set at the level that prevailed before the shock; a real devaluation of 20 percent is undertaken; full external liberalization restored; the tax ratio increased by 2 percentage points to 17 percent; and the amount of domestic credit expansion sharply curtailed to a level consistent with the basic financial programming model's solution, including a short-term target for the balance of payments of –1.[21] This expected profile would have resulted if the resources released by the policy package are fully absorbed in higher exports so that domestic production is maintained. Had this basic model's predictions been sustained, the Sen index shows that the outcome for the poor would involve a significant deterioration, but not as extreme as in the case considered next.

Simulating the effects of the above policies in the more general model shows instead a severely contractionary outcome for the economy (column 3b). This is because initially the contractionary effects of the policies are assumed not to be fully compensated by higher exports, while the beneficial supply-side effects are assumed to take longer. Given limited export growth, the simulation results in nominal GDP growth declining to 2 percent (column 3b) indicating, in the face of underlying inertial inflation, that the real growth rate must be significantly negative. (It is possible that the inflation rate will also have been sharply reduced, but this is not explicitly solved here.) Although the fiscal balance target of –3.2 is attained, the balance of payments only improves a little and its outcome (–2.7) is substantially worse than targeted (–1). Owing to the sharp fall in nominal GDP growth, the incremental demand for money is much lower (0.5) which explains the result.

S deteriorates further to 0.146, indicating that the poverty situation has become more aggravated. The elimination of the exchange rate overvaluation pushes the poverty line out, which is not offset by the very small increase in nominal income. As a consequence, both the head-count ratio and the poverty gap index rise. Up to this point, it has been assumed that poverty-related government outlays have grown moderately. However, if there is concern for the severe consequences for poverty under the scenario depicted by the basic model's outcomes, an additive approach could be pursued: increase poverty-related outlays, assumed to be means tested and restricted only to those falling below the poverty line, but do not relax the overall fiscal goals and other policies. The simulation shows that in order to attain the *S* count of the 'integrated' alternative presented next, there will need to be a big increase in poor-related outlays to 5.6 units (column 3c). This sharply compresses available outlays for other purposes, given the requirement of meeting the fiscal deficit target. The welfare and resource allocation costs of this redirection of government expenditure is not evaluated but could be substantial.

Column 4 presents the alternative 'integrated' approach. On taking account of the trade-offs, less emphasis is placed in the short run on the inflation target and achieving both the ambitious fiscal consolidation target and immediate full external liberalization of the addictive approach. Instead, the emphasis is on meeting the balance of payments target, and on ensuring that the initial equilibrium *S* count is attained. (Even so, the fiscal deficit is substantially reduced to 3.8 percent of GDP from the nonadjustment level of 8.3 percent of GDP and is not much bigger than the target level of 3.2 percent of GDP.) The policy instrument settings involve a more moderate reduction in the amount of credit expansion, but a bigger devaluation; less complete liberalization of the external sector, which is assumed to be phased over a longer time horizon; an increase in the tax ratio to 0.17, as in the additive case, but with more emphasis on underlying trade-related taxes (reflected in the simulation by a smaller rise in the import ratio); and outlays for the poor that are in line with assumed historical averages.

The results shown in column 4 are instructive. The nominal GDP growth rate is higher than in the additive case, but less than in the nonadjustment shock case, indicating that inflation is probably being brought down, but not as quickly as in the additive approach. However, unlike with the latter, the balance of payments target is met, while the decline in real output growth will have been restrained. Despite the bigger devaluation, the more favorable per capita income developments have led to smaller deteriorations in the head-count ratio and in the poverty gap measure.[22] Other trade-offs are possible and could be explored.

CONCLUDING REMARKS

The chapter set out to reformulate the financial programming model so as to have the alleviation of poverty as an explicit and central objective of policy. The framework was set up to make relatively limited additional data demands. These are mainly the poverty line (o), the size of the population below the poverty line (n), the mean income of the poor ($\overline{m}$), government outlays to the poor (G_{po}), and an estimate of the Gini coefficient of the poor (GI_{po}). Knowing how the last responds to macroeconomic developments would make the analysis more sophisticated but is not altogether essential.

Integrating these poverty-related concepts in the form of a poverty index as an explicit constraint into a suitably structured financial programming model enables the systematic exploration of alternative policy options. This facilitates choosing that combination of policies that would promote adjustment to desired stabilization and poverty objectives.

Interestingly, the simulation that was carried out, tracing the impact of an external shock on a stylized financial programming model, indicates that the integrated approach that incorporates the poverty constraint can also better achieve the balance of payments target than can the traditional approach, although at the cost, temporarily, of a higher fiscal deficit and more inflation.

However, despite the higher inflation than in the additive case, note that the poverty index is lower reflecting an underlying better output performance. Nevertheless, compared to the shock case, the poverty index does rise whether in the additive, or the integrated, approach. To overcome this adverse shorter-term result, there is no alternative but to ensure a satisfactory achievement of suitable growth and export promotion objectives in the medium term which alone could probably result in a decline in the poverty index to its earlier levels and beyond.

APPENDIX: SUMMARY OF SYMBOLS

M	= money stock
D	= credit stock
F	= net foreign asset position
P	= domestic price level
P_f	= price of imports in foreign currency
P_x	= price of exports in domestic currency
Y	= real gross domestic product
v	= income velocity of circulation of money
u	= average income
E	= domestic currency price of a unit of foreign exchange
X	= real exports
Z	= real imports
Tr	= net foreign transfers from abroad
ΔK	= net foreign capital inflow
A	= real domestic absorption
b	= share of imports in real absorption
z	= share of domestic currency value of imports to nominal absorption
$\bar{m}$	= average income of poor
h	= head-count ratio
e	= real exchange rate (ratio of E to P)
y	= real growth rate or $\Delta Y/Y_{-1}$
p	= inflation rate or $\Delta P/P_{-1}$
GI	= Gini coefficient
GI_{po}	= Gini coefficient for the poor
G_{po}	= Government transfers to the poor
L	= Lorenz curve
PC_p	= nominal private consumption
PI_p	= gross private nominal investment or capital formation
c	= average propensity to consume
PT	= nominal tax revenue
PG	= nominal government expenditure
t	= ratio of taxes net of subsidies to nominal GDP
D_g	= credit extension to government
ΔD_p	= credit extension to private sector
S	= Sen poverty index
*	= target value
η	= elasticity
m_i	= income of the ith household under the poverty line o

Superscript s, d = supply and demand, respectively

Subscript f, d = foreign and disposable, respectively

subscript g, p = government and

private, respectively
subscript po = poor

k = poverty gap

o = local-currency-denominated poverty line

Δ = first difference

n = size of population below poverty line

NOTES

1 The authors are indebted to Anthony B. Atkinson, Ke-young Chu, and Nicholas Stern for helpful comments.
2 Fund staff have also attempted to study directly the effect of adjustment programs on the poor (see, for example, Liuksila, 1991; Gotur, 1991).
3 Atkinson (1993) argues for an integrated approach that explicitly takes account of the trade-offs between poverty alleviation and various macroeconomic objectives. He observes that this is generally not done and finds it 'alarming ... that undue faith is placed on the efficiency of social policy to solve the distributional problems generated by macroeconomic policy' (p. 11).
4 In addition to the preceding macroeconomic factors, structural reforms such as removing price subsidies on commodities predominantly consumed by the poor could also worsen the plight of the poor.
5 This assumes, of course, that such programs could be quickly designed, financed, and implemented, a matter that comes increasingly under doubt from actual experience.
6 The more general version is needed because the basic or standard model assumes that nominal income growth and its output and inflation components are exogenously given.
7 The terminology is defined in the Appendix.
8 For specific country applications, the model will, of course, have to be tailored to country conditions both with regard to behavioral and market specifications.
9 Export and import price indexes are assumed to be exogenously determined.
10 Having exports as the sole equilibrating variable in the basic model eliminates the possibility of trade-offs involving nominal income, as this is constant.
11 Note that the intention in incorporating poverty as a criterion in the financial program of a particular country is not to attempt an international comparison, which would be a more difficult task.
12 The denominator in *GI* is half the area of the square diagram.
13 Similar estimates of *GI* for the entire population would enable comparisons for the population as a whole.
14 Note that while the head count by itself does not satisfy this property, the poverty gap satisfies it.
15 See Table 3.7 of the WDR for several country instances of short-run recession (Colombia, Costa Rica, Côte d'Ivoire, Malaysia, Poland, Venezuela, Yugoslavia). Note, however, that even with positive economic growth and a commensurate rise in per capita incomes, it is not impossible to imagine a worsening of income distribution and additions to the ranks of the poor. See, for example, the cases of China, Brazil, and Thailand in the same table that indicate a worsening head-count ratio in the face of a positive growth in mean incomes. This latter case is not examined here.
16 The informational requirements for measuring changes in the Gini coefficient for

the poor as a result of macroeconomic shocks or policy shifts are potentially formidable. For the simulation that follows GI_{po} is set at 0.2.

17 The regression related the proportional change in the head-count ratio to the proportional increase in real per capita income over periods ranging from 10–24 years for a sample of 11 developing economies reported in Table 3.7 of the World Bank Report (1990):

$$\Delta h/h = -33.2 - \underset{(2.3)}{0.16}\Delta u/u, \quad R^2 = 0.35.$$

18 In a fuller analysis, the total effect of government's redistributive actions should be taken into account, including taxation and quasi-fiscal transactions.

19 For purposes of the simulation an elasticity of 0.3 is assumed.

20 For the simulation this is set at 0.2.

21 Because of the limited structure of the basic model, the effects of these policies cannot be adequately simulated using it. Viewed individually or as part of a package, the preceding set of policies appear appropriate. However, to establish properly the dosage and sequencing of such policies requires that account be taken of their impact on welfare affecting variables such as GDP, which the basic model does not allow to change endogenously.

22 The strategy underlying the simulation of the integrated case is to ensure that while observing the balance of payments constraint, the poverty index is kept within acceptable bounds. This is done by manipulating policy instruments in such a way that some progress is also made in reducing nominal output and, by implication, inflation; liberalizing the external sector; and achieving the fiscal consolidation target. Traditional targets with regard to the last are thus phased over a somewhat longer period of time.

REFERENCES

Anand, Sudhir, and Martin Ravallion (1993) 'Human Development in Poor Countries: On the Role of Private Incomes and Public Services', *Journal of Economic Perspectives*, Vol. 7, No. 1 (Winter), pp. 133–50.

Atkinson, A.B. (1993) 'The Institution of an Official Poverty Line and Economic Policy', Welfare State Programme, Discussion Paper WSP/98, London School of Economics.

Blackwood, D.L., and R.G. Lynch (1994) 'The Measurement of Inequality and Poverty: A Policy Maker's Guide to the Literature', *World Development*, Vol. 22, No. 4, pp. 567–78.

Chand, Sheetal K. (1989) 'Toward a Growth-Oriented Model of Financial Programming', *World Development*, Vol. 17, No. 4, pp. 473–90.

Chu, Ke-Young, and Sanjeev Gupta (1993) 'Protecting the Poor: Social Safety Nets During Transition', *Finance and Development*, Vol. 30, No. 2 (June), pp. 24–7.

Cornia, Giovanni Andrea, and Frances Stewart (1993) 'The Fiscal System, Adjustment and the Poor', in *Fiscal Issues in Adjustment in Developing Countries*, ed. Riccardo Faini and Jaime de Melo, New York: St Martin's Press, pp. 197–226.

European Institute for South and South-East Asian Studies (EISSEAS) (1994) *Proceedings*, Conference on The Social Dimension of Economic Development in Asia, Brussels (November).

Gotur, Padma (1991) 'Bangladesh: Economic Reform Measures and the Poor', International Monetary Fund Working Paper 91/39 (April).

Gupta, Sanjeev, and Karim Nashashibi (1990) 'Poverty Concerns in Fund-Supported Programs', *Finance and Development*, Vol. 27, No. 3 (September), pp. 12–14.

Heller, Peter S., A. Lans Bovenberg, Thanos Catsambas, Ke-young Chu, and Parthasarathi Shome (1988) 'The Implications of Fund-Supported Adjustment Programs for Poverty: Experiences in Selected Countries', IMF Occasional Paper No. 58, Washington, DC: International Monetary Fund, May.

IMF 'Theoretical Aspects of the Design of Fund-Supported Adjustment Programs', Occcasional Paper No. 55, Washington, DC: International Monetary Fund.

IMF Development Committee (1990) *Development Issues*, Washington, DC.

Liuksila, Claire (1991) 'Colombia: Economic Adjustment and the Poor', International Monetary Fund Working Paper 91/81 (August).

Nashashibi, Karim, Sanjeev Gupta, Claire Liuksila, Henri Lorie, and Walter Mahler (1992) 'The Fiscal Dimensions of Adjustment in Low-Income Countries', IMF Occasional Paper No. 95, Washington, DC: International Monetary Fund, April.

Shorrocks, A.F. (1983) 'The Class of Additively Decomposable Inequality Measures', *Econometrica*, Vol. 48, pp. 613–25.

Tanzi, Vito, and Ke-Young Chu (1989) 'Fiscal Policy for Stable and Equitable Growth in Latin America', International Monetary Fund Working Paper 89/93 (November 2).

World Bank (1990) *World Development Report 1990*, June.

8

ECONOMIC REFORMS, SOCIAL SAFETY NETS, AND THE BUDGET IN TRANSITION ECONOMIES

*Ke-young Chu and Sanjeev Gupta**

INTRODUCTION

The economic transformation of former centrally planned economies has been accompanied by large declines in output, significant changes in relative prices, and, at least initially, rapid increases in inflation and declines in living standards. While much of the decline in living standards is attributable to the economic dislocations resulting from the breakdown of the CMEA trading regime, the breakup of the FSU, and loose national financial policies, a significant part of it has stemmed from reform policies, which, in the short run, have increased the prices of essential commodities and reduced employment opportunities.

The transition economies will have to persist with reform policies to achieve sustained and broad-based growth, as this alone can raise the living standards over the long term. In the meantime, to sustain the reform process, specific policy measures will have to be adopted, and resources allocated, to mitigate the short-term adverse effects of reform policies on vulnerable groups.

The transition economies have sought to deal with these adverse effects of reform policies in a variety of ways. While economic transformation is still underway, some common elements of these efforts can be identified. A critical issue is the budgetary implications of social protection measures. This chapter reviews social protection experiences of different transition economies and, with the help of a stylized model, illustrates interactions between the measures adopted and the budget. Some lessons for the future are also drawn.

SOCIAL PROTECTION AND TRANSITION ECONOMIES

Social safety nets in transition economies

'Social safety nets' in this chapter are defined as the measures adopted to mitigate short-term adverse effects of economic reforms on the poor. These effects stem from price increases of essential goods and services and reductions in employment opportunities. Both effects are unavoidable in the course of economic transformation. Correcting relative prices is necessary for improving the allocation of resources which reduces real incomes for some, while increasing them for others; strengthening of the macroeconomic position requires a reduction in budgetary transfers and/or tightening of bank credit, which causes inefficient state enterprises to shed labor.

Many economies in transition inherited extensive consumer subsidies for essential goods and services and other social protection arrangements (or social insurance and social assistance systems) that had been maintained to address normal life cycle contingencies such as old age, sickness, and disability; they have only recently established unemployment benefits aimed at 'normal' unemployment. However, in many instances, the reform-induced income changes can – and do – dominate normal life cycle and other income changes. Under the circumstances, the existing social protection instruments may not be adequate, and it may become necessary to integrate transitory social safety nets into reform programs. To this end, existing social protection instruments may have to be adapted or modified; in addition, new measures may have to be introduced specifically to mitigate the reform-induced reductions in the incomes of the more vulnerable members of society. The nature and the cost of social safety nets depend very much on living standards, demographic profiles, and the mix and sequence of reform policies in each country.

The following depiction of the prereform conditions, in most cases, is still valid, while the reform efforts are ongoing.

As regards overall income levels, some were extremely low-income countries (Albania, Ethiopia, Lao People's Democratic Republic), while others were middle-income countries (Hungary, Poland, and many FSU states) (Table 8.1). The poor in the former group of countries had relatively low incomes and had little room to withstand reform-induced income losses. In comparison with the middle-income countries, the low-income countries had a relatively large number of vulnerable people to protect, but weak social policy institutions. This suggests that the low-income countries required a relatively large amount of resources for social safety nets, but had little scope for adapting existing social programs for this purpose.

The demographic profile also influenced the nature of social safety nets and their financing. In some countries, a large proportion of the population was

Table 8.1 Demographic structure and living standards in selected transition economies, 1992

			Population			
	Population (millions)	*GNP per capita (US dollars)*[1]	*Percent aged 14 and under*	*Percent aged 65 and over*	*Life expectancy at birth (years)*	*Infant mortality rate per 1,000 births*
Lower-income countries:						
Many elderly						
Georgia	5.5	850	24	12	73	17
Many children						
Albania	3.4	415	32	5	73	28
Armenia	3.5	780	30	7	72	21
Azerbaijan	7.4	870	33	6	71	32
Ethiopia	52.5	110	47	3	49	128
Kyrgyz Republic	4.5	810	38	6	66	40
Lao P.D.R.	4.5	250	45	3	51	97
Tajikistan	5.7	480	45	4	69	49
Uzbekistan	21.8	860	42	4	69	44
Higher-income countries:						
Many elderly						
Belarus	10.3	2,910	22	13	71	15
Bulgaria	8.9	1,330	20	14	71	17
Estonia	1.6	2,750	22	12	70	13
Hungary	10.4	3,010	19	14	70	16
Latvia	2.7	1,930	22	13	69	16
Lithuania	3.7	1,310	22	12	70	14
Poland	38.4	1,960	24	10	71	15
Romania	23.2	1,090	22	11	70	27
Russian Federation	148.3	2,680	23	12	69	20
Ukraine	51.9	1,670	21	14	70	18
Many children	17.0	1,680	31	7	69	31
Kazakhstan						
Macedonia, FYR of	2.1	1,452[2]	25	8	72	29
Moldova	4.4	1,260	31	9	68	23
Turkmenistan	3.9	1,270	41	4	66	55

Sources: World Bank: Socioeconomic Time Series System, World Population, Population Structure and Vital Statistics; The World Bank Atlas 1994; and IMF staff estimates.
[1] Estimates for the FSU states are preliminary and have changed substantially since 1992.
[2] Gross social product, which excludes value of many services.

elderly (Belarus, Bulgaria, Hungary, and Ukraine), while in others the young tended to dominate the population (the Kyrgyz Republic, Lao People's Democratic Republic, Tajikistan, Turkmenistan, and Uzbekistan). While the proportion of the working population that supported the financing of benefits to the elderly and the young was low in both country groups, protecting the old became a major issue in the former group of countries, whereas ensuring adequate protection for children was a principal concern in the latter.

The reform policy mix has also dictated the characteristics of social safety net instruments. A change in relative prices has required cash transfers (e.g. supplements to existing cash benefits) to the poor who were adversely affected by the higher prices. Consequently, whether or not some subsidies should be retained as a social safety net has been a major issue. Large cuts in transfers to loss-making enterprises, which have followed the price liberalization, inevitably reduced demand for labor. At the same time, an increase in unemployment has required transfers to the new poor (e.g. through unemployment benefits or public works programs). East European countries have shown tolerance for higher open unemployment, as evidenced by average unemployment rates that in 1993 ranged between 10.2 percent in Romania and 17.5 percent in Albania. However, most FSU states other than those in the Baltic area have suppressed open unemployment, resulting in an average registered unemployment rate of less than 1 percent.[1] The Baltic area countries lie somewhere in between.

Targeting social safety nets to intended beneficiaries has not been easy, since it has been difficult to identify society's poor members and those whose welfare is adversely affected by reform measures. The administrative requirements to track all household incomes and assets has been formidable, particularly as informal sector activities have been growing. Furthermore, it has not been possible to establish new administrative structures during the transition period to deliver means-tested benefits. Targeting benefits on the basis of income has also been difficult because household incomes have been typically clustered around the poverty line – the income level that is often used to distinguish the poor from the nonpoor.

Existing social protection institutions in transition economies

Except for low-income African and Asian transition economies, most transition economies started with an extensive system of social protection, comprising general budgetary consumer and producer subsidies, provided through unrealistically low administered consumer prices, and cash benefits, including pensions, sickness, and maternity benefits, and child allowances (Table 8.2). These benefits had universal coverage, regardless of the incomes of the beneficiaries. At the outset of the reform, most Central European and FSU states formally abandoned the long-established system of guaranteed employment and instituted unemployment benefits. In African and Asian

Table 8.2 Pre- and post-reform subsidies and cash transfers in selected transition economies (as percent of GDP)

	Total government expenditure		*Subsidies*[1]		*Cash benefits*		*Pensions*		*Unemployment benefits*		*Child allowances*		*Other*[2]	
	1990 or 1991[3]	*1993*[4]	*1990 or 1991*[3]	*1993*[4]	*1990 or 1991*[3]	*1993*[4]	*1990 or 1991*[3]	*1993*[4]	*1990 or 1991*[3]	*1993*[4]	*1990 or 1991*[3]	*1993*[4]	*1990 or 1991*[3]	*1993*[4]
Average	42.1	40.3	7.0	5.4	9.5	8.3	5.9	5.7	–	0.6	1.4	0.7	2.5	1.3
Lower-income countries:														
Many elderly	33.0	46.3	...	33.3	6.0	0.6	3.9	0.5	–	–	1.7	0.1	0.4	–
Georgia														
Many children	62.1	44.2	15.6[5]	2.6[6]	8.6	11.9	8.6	6.5	–	4.2	–	...	–	1.2
Albania														
Armenia	28.0	68.6	1.5	8.4	...	7.0	...	7.0[7]	...	–	...	–	...	–
Azerbaijan	40.7	52.0	7.2	4.4	15.3	11.5	6.5	7.6	–	–	7.2	3.8	1.6	–
Ethiopia	46.9	34.3	0.7	–	3.0	4.7	1.3	1.3	...	–	...	–	1.7	3.4
Kyrgyz Republic	...	25.4	...	3.3	...	3.7	...	2.4	...	–	...	1.0	...	0.3
Lao PDR	23.4	17.8	–	–	0.8	1.3	0.8	1.3	–	–	–	–	–	–
Uzbekistan	52.3	60.5	6.5	7.3	7.6	3.7	1.0	2.6	–	0.4	6.1	0.7	0.5	–
Higher-income countries:														
Many elderly														
Belarus	...	51.9	...	14.3	...	9.8	...	6.3	...	0.9	...	0.3	...	2.3
Bulgaria	64.3	41.7	14.9	3.9	12.0	12.9	8.8	9.4	–	0.8	...	–	3.2	2.7
Estonia	31.8	33.9	2.5	1.3	10.4	8.8	2.6	5.6	–	0.2	0.3	1.8	7.5	1.1
Hungary	57.4	60.4	9.6	4.8	14.9	18.2	9.7	10.4	–	1.4	...	–	5.1	6.4
Latvia	31.0	26.7	1.3	1.2[8]	9.2	12.7	7.8	6.0	–	1.8	0.7	2.4	0.6	2.5
Lithuania	49.2	25.0	14.2	1.4	8.5	5.3	7.0	4.1	...	0.3	–	0.5	1.5	0.4
Poland	39.8	48.6	7.3	2.3	10.6	18.8	8.1	14.9	0.2	1.2	...	2.7	2.3	...
Romania	38.7	33.3	7.9	5.8	10.6	8.9	7.9	6.5	–	1.7	...	0.7	2.7	–
Russian Federation	...	34.8	...	0.7	...	6.4	...	5.5	...	0.1	...	0.6	...	0.7
Ukraine	53.9	73.4	13.0	12.1	9.7	8.2	9.7	8.0	–	0.2	–	–	–	–
FSU	50.9	...	15.0	...	20.1	...	6.3	...	...	...	...	...	13.8	...
Many children														
Kazakhstan	31.4	22.9	...	2.3	3.9	0.7	3.9	0.3	–	–	–	0.2	–	0.2
FYR of Macedonia	40.4	43.9	–	3.2	17.5	18.4	10.0	11.7	0.5	0.6	–	0.5	6.9	5.6
Moldova	25.3	25.9	5.1	3.0	7.9	4.8	4.9	3.9	–	–	2.4	0.4	0.6	0.5
Turkmenistan	42.3	15.2	4.3	3.1	3.0	3.6	3.0	2.9	–	–	–	–	–	0.7

Source: IMF staff estimates

[1]Producer and consumer subsidies for goods and services. [2]Includes maternity and sickness benefits and social assistance programs. [3]1991 for Armenia, Azerbaijan, Estonia, Georgia, Latvia, FYR of Macedonia, Moldova, Ukraine, and Uzbekistan. 1988 for FSU and 1990 for all other countries. [4]Estimates for Bulgaria, Hungary, Kazakhstan, Lao People's Democratic Republic, Poland, Romania, and Uzbekistan. Preliminary actuals for Azerbaijan, Ethiopia, and Moldova. Budget figures for Latvia. [5]Includes payments to idle workers of state enterprises amounting to 12.4 percent of GDP. [6]Includes bread compensation for state enterprises. [7]Includes child allowances. [8]Heating allowance.

countries (Ethiopia and Lao People's Democratic Republic), reliance has been more on subsidies and informal social protection arrangements based on extended family ties.

Budgetary outlays on benefits provided by the government have varied across countries. Before reform measures were initiated in Central European countries and FSU states, subsidies ranged between 1.3 percent of GDP in Latvia and 15.6 percent of GDP in Albania.[2] Outlays on cash benefits ranged between 8.6 percent of GDP in Albania and 20.1 percent of GDP in the FSU. The major cash benefit provided was pensions, the cost of which ranged between 6.3 percent of GDP in the FSU and 10 percent of GDP in the FYR of Macedonia. Since no unemployment was officially recognized, there were no unemployment benefits. Two low-income countries (Ethiopia and Lao People's Democratic Republic) incurred relatively small expenditures on subsidies and cash benefits; the latter was confined to formal sector employees only.

Expenditures on social protection in most transition economies have been financed through the government budget (subsidies and some child allowances) and payroll taxes, paid by both employers and employees (pensions, unemployment benefits, and sickness and maternity benefits). In most countries, extrabudgetary funds collect payroll taxes and disburse pensions, unemployment compensation, and sickness and maternity benefits. The combined payroll tax burden has averaged 40 percent of the wage bill and has exceeded 50 percent in one country (Ukraine).

SOCIAL SAFETY NETS AND THE BUDGET

A stylized model

The main features of the social protection arrangements and their financing in many of the transition countries can be captured in a simple stylized model that incorporates key aspects of the economies, demography, and social protection arrangements. This model can then be used to illustrate the budgetary implications of social safety net options.

First, the population, labor force, and employment have the following relationships:

$$N_t = (1 - u_t)L_t \qquad (8.1)^3$$

$$\begin{aligned} POP_t &= N_t + BU_t + BY_t + BO_t \\ &= L_t[(1 - u_t) + u_t + by_t + bo_t] \end{aligned} \qquad (8.2)$$

$$\begin{aligned} W_t &= w_t N_t \\ &= w_t(1 - u_t)L_t \end{aligned} \qquad (8.3)$$

where

L_t = labor force;
l_t = labor force participation rate;
POP_t = population;
N_t = employment;
BU_t, BY_t, BO_t = the number of unemployed, children, and elderly who are receiving unemployment benefits, child allowances, and pensions, respectively;
u_t, by_t, bo_t = the number of unemployed, children, and elderly as ratios of the labor force (the last two are equivalent to child and old-age dependency ratios);
W_t = wage bill of the economy; and
w_t = average wage of the economy.

Different cash benefits may be expressed as follows:

$$CBO_t = cb_t BO_t \tag{8.4}$$

$$CBY_t = cb_t BY_t \tag{8.5}$$

$$CBU_t = cb_t BU_t \tag{8.6}$$

where

CBO_t, CBY_t, CBU_t = the total amounts of pensions, child allowances, and unemployment benefits; and
cb_t = average cash benefit (assumed to be equal for pensions, child allowances, and unemployment benefits).

Second, the nonpoor and poor households consume two commodities – one is subsidized and the other is not. For simplicity, we assume that each employed worker earns an income above a minimum subsistence level for him- or herself and a spouse; this income, when he or she has children, may reduce the average household income to below the minimum subsistence level. The child allowances are aimed at preventing the household from falling into poverty. We also assume initially that pensions and unemployment benefits are the only sources of income, respectively, for the elderly and the unemployed. For the purposes of our model, the worker and his or her spouse are considered to be nonpoor; others are poor.[4] The quantities consumed, prices, and production costs are denoted as follows:

q_{11_t}, q_{12_t}= average consumption quantities of the subsidized commodity by the nonpoor and the poor;

q_{21_t}, q_{22_t} = average consumption quantities of the unsubsidized commodity by the nonpoor and the poor;
p_{1t}, p_{2t} = consumer prices of the subsidized and unsubsidized goods, respectively;
c_{1t}, c_{2t} = production costs including normal profits of the subsidized and unsubsidized goods, respectively;
$c_{1t} > p_{1t}$; and
$c_{2t} = p_{2t}$.

The government subsidizes consumption of the first good by maintaining a below-cost sale price. The amount of subsidy may be expressed as follows:

$$\begin{aligned} SUBS_t &= c_{1t}[1-(p_{1t}/c_{1t})][N_t q_{11t} + (BO_t + BY_t + BU_t)q_{12t}] \\ &= c_{1t}[1-(p_{1t}/c_{1t})]L_t[(1-u_t)q_{11t} + (bo_t + by_t \\ &\quad + u_t)q_{12t}]. \end{aligned} \tag{8.7}$$

The extrabudgetary fund, financed through a payroll tax, provides pension and unemployment benefits.[5] The extrabudgetary fund's revenues and expenditures may be expressed as follows:

$$\begin{aligned} REV_t &= tw_t(1-u_t)L_t \\ &= [T/(1+\pi_t)^2]w_t[1-u_t]L_t \end{aligned} \tag{8.8}$$

$$\begin{aligned} EXP_t &= CBO_t + CBU_t \\ &= cb_t(bo_t + u_t)L_t \end{aligned} \tag{8.9}$$

where

REV_t, EXP_t = revenues and expenditures of the extrabudgetary fund;
T, t = statutory and effective payroll tax rates, in percent of the wage bill; it is assumed that there is a *two-month* lag in tax collection,[6] and
π_t = monthly inflation rate.

Total spending on social protection of the consolidated general government may be expressed as follows:[7]

$$\begin{aligned} L_t\{&c_{1t}[1-(p_{1t}/c_{1t})][(1-u_t)q_{11t} + (bo_t + by_t + u_t)q_{12t}] \\ &+ cb_t(bo_t + u_t) - [T/(1+\pi_t)^2]w_t(1-u_t)\} \end{aligned} \tag{8.10}$$

with the first and the second lines in braces, { }, in (8.10) indicating, respectively, the amount of subsidy expenditures and the deficit of the extrabudgetary fund per person in the labor force.

The subsidy part of equation (8.10) illustrates two aspects of budgetary subsidies: their budgetary costs and their effects on household consumption.

The unit subsidy, $c_{1t} - p_{1t}$ (i.e. per kg), of the subsidized commodity, is determined by the cost, c_{1t}, and the rate of cost recovery, p_{1t}/c_{1t}, which is determined by government policy. In our simplified model, q_{11} and q_{12}, the average consumption of the subsidized commodity by the nonpoor and the poor partly determines the extent of subsidy benefits provided to the nonpoor. The former (q_{11}) is greater than the latter (q_{12}); thus, the nonpoor benefit more than the poor from generalized subsidies administered through price controls.

The deficit of the extrabudgetary fund per person in the labor force is the difference between total expenditure and revenue per person, the former being the product of the average benefit and the number of beneficiaries, and the latter the product of the effective payroll tax rate and the wage bill. The deficit of the extrabudgetary fund gives rise either to central government transfers to the fund or the fund's resort to bank borrowing.

Equation (8.10) shows the first-round fiscal effects of various exogenous and policy changes.

An increase in unemployment would affect the fiscal balance through the following channels: it would reduce subsidy expenditures for employed (nonpoor) workers, but increases those for unemployed (poor) workers; at the same time, it would increase unemployment benefits and reduce the wage bill and, thus, the revenue for the extrabudgetary fund. These effects per person in the labor force can be shown as follows:

$$\{(c_{1t} - p_{1t})(-q_{11t} + q_{12t}) + cb_t + [Tw_t/(1 + \pi_t)^2]\}\Delta u_t$$

where Δ denotes 'an increase'.

An increase in the average cash benefit would have the following fiscal effect:

$$(by_t + bo_t + u_t)\Delta cb_t.$$

Equation (8.10) also indicates what the government can do to reduce subsidies, while maintaining cash benefits for the poor. The government could eliminate subsidies by increasing the cost recovery rate to 1; this measure, however, would reduce the real incomes of the net consumers, including some of the poor, of the subsidized commodity.[8] Alternatively, the government could liberalize prices and establish a free market for the subsidized commodity and provide certain poor groups with limited cash transfers. The government could also maintain limited subsidies for the commodity targeted to certain groups. In this latter case, the amount of subsidies would still be determined by equation (8.10), but the government could limit subsidies by increasing the cost recovery rate and limiting subsidized quantities and the number of beneficiaries.

The net fiscal effect of reforming the social protection arrangements by eliminating subsidies and replacing them with cash benefits of an equal amount for pensioners, children, and unemployed workers would be

$$-\Delta p_{1t}(1-u_t)q_{11t}L_t \quad \text{or} \quad -(c_{1t}-p_{1t})(1-u_t)q_{11t}L_t. \tag{8.11}$$

The savings would be large when the increase in the official price is large (i.e. when the prereform cost recovery rate was low) or the prereform subsidized quantity for the nonpoor is large.

The financial balance of the extrabudgetary fund – that is, the negative of the second part of equation (8.10) – is defined as

$$REV_t - EXP_t = w_t\{[T/(1+\pi_t)^2](1-u_t) - (cb_t/w_t)(bo_t + u_t)\}L_t \tag{8.12}$$

For a balanced extrabudgetary fund, the following condition must be satisfied:

$$[T/(1+\pi_t)^2](1-u_t) = (cb_t/w_t)(bo_t + u_t). \tag{8.13}$$

In the absence of unemployment and inflation, this is simplified to

$$T = (cb_t/w_t)bo_t \tag{8.14}$$

which defines the statutory payroll tax rate needed to ensure balanced extrabudgetary operations as the product of the replacement rate (cb_t/w_t) and the old-age dependency ratio (bo_t). In the presence of inflation and lags in the collection of the payroll tax, the statutory tax rate must be high enough to offset the negative effect of collection lags on revenue. Then, in the presence of unemployment, inflation, and a collection lag of two months, the statutory tax rate to ensure balanced operations of the extrabudgetary fund would be

$$T = [(cb_t/w_t)(bo_t + u_t)(1+\pi_t)^2]/(1-u_t). \tag{8.15}$$

In this case, the statutory tax rate should be high enough to offset not only the negative effect of collection lags on revenue, but also the negative effects of unemployment on both revenue (reduced tax base) and expenditure (increased benefits to the unemployed).

Equation (8.15) shows key factors that would raise the payroll tax burden: an increase in unemployment (through a reduction in the wage bill and an increase in unemployment benefits), an increase in the old-age dependency ratio (through an increase in pension payments), an increase in the average unemployment benefit or the average pension, a decline in the average wage (through a reduction in the wage bill), a lengthening of collection lags, and an increase in inflation (through a further erosion of revenue).

Numerical illustration

The relative importance of different variables in the model developed above can be assessed with the help of the following numerical illustration. The advantage of this illustration is that it gives a flavor of social safety net measures that impact the most on the budget, particularly in the short term.

Personal expenditures

Table 8.3 displays expenditures of hypothetical nonpoor and poor persons on basic food and nonfood items. For the purpose of analysis, the following assumptions are made initially: (a) a 'nonpoor' person is a worker, while a 'poor' person is a pensioner or a child;[9] (b) there are 100 persons in the country: 50 workers, 30 pensioners, and 20 children; and (c) there is no unemployment.[10]

Whether a given household is poor or not would depend on the number of poor persons in each household (pensioners and children) and whether the average family income falls below the subsistence level. The nonpoor individual, on average, earns Rub 100, and spends Rub 40 on food items (i.e. Rub 10 per year each on bread, milk, meat, and other food items) and the remaining Rub 60 on nonfood items.[11] In contrast, the poor person, on average, has an income of Rub 40, of which Rub 28, or 70 percent of income, is spent on food.[12] For simplicity, it is assumed that neither individual saves. Table 8.3 also shows quantities consumed by the members of two income groups. In absolute terms, the nonpoor person consumes larger quantities of food items than the poor.

Subsidies and their financing

Table 8.4 shows budgetary subsidies on food and nonfood items that benefit both poor and nonpoor persons. These subsidies arise because the retail prices of bread, milk, and meat shown in Table 8.3 cover only 50 percent of their production costs. Budgetary subsidies of Rub 30 are provided to every nonpoor individual and Rub 21 to every poor individual. Total budgetary subsidies amount to Rub 2,550 per year, with the aggregate benefit equaling Rub 1,500 and Rub 1,050 for nonpoor and poor population groups, respectively.[13]

Cash benefits and their financing

Pensions are financed through payroll contributions, and child allowances through the budget. The annual average wage is assumed to be Rub 100, and the average pension Rub 40, with the average child allowance equal to the average pension. The wage bill for the economy is thus equal to Rub 5,000.

Table 8.3 A hypothetical country: annual expenditures of an average individual in nonpoor and poor households

	Total food and nonfood	*Bread*	*Milk*	*Meat*	*Other food items*	*Total food*	*Total nonfood*
Nonpoor:							
Expenditure composition (percent)	100.0	10.0	10.0	10.0	10.0	40.0	60.0
Quantity (kg)		10.0	10.0	10.0	10.0	40.0	60.0
Price (rubles per kg)		1.0	1.0	1.0	1.0		
Total expenditure (rubles)	100.0	10.0	10.0	10.0	10.0	40.0	60.0
Income (rubles)	100.0						
Savings (rubles)							
Poor:							
Expenditure composition (percent)	100.0	20.0	20.0	12.5	17.5	70.0	30.0
Quantity (kg)		8.0	8.0	5.0	7.0		12.0
Price (rubles per kg)		1.0	1.0	1.0	1.0		
Total expenditure (rubles)	40.0	8.0	8.0	5.0	7.0	28.0	12.0
Income (rubles)	40.0						
Savings (rubles)							

Table 8.4 A hypothetical country: budgetary cost of subsidies

	Total food and nonfood	*Bread*	*Milk*	*Meat*	*Other food items*	*Total food*	*Total nonfood*
				(Rubles per kg)			
Budgetary cost:							
Retail price		1	1	1	1		1
Production cost		2	2	2	1		1
Subsidies	3	1	1	1	–	3	–
				(Rubles)			
Average per capita subsidy benefit:							
Nonpoor	30	10	10	10	–	30	–
Poor	21	8	8	5	–	21	–
Total budgetary cost of subsidies:							
Nonpoor	1,500						
Poor	1,050						
Memorandum items							
Population:	100						
Nonpoor persons:							
working population	50						
Poor persons:							
pensioners	30						
children	20						
unemployed	–						

Pension and child allowance outlays amount to Rub 1,200 and Rub 800, respectively.[14]

The national economy, the budget, and extrabudgetary fund

It is assumed that annual nominal GDP amounts to Rub 25,000. The annual inflation rate is 1,000 percent, or 22.1 percent per month. Total budgetary revenues and expenditures amount to 30 percent and 40 percent of GDP, respectively.[15] Table 8.5 summarizes the overall fiscal position of this stylized economy.

The economy spends 10.2 percent of GDP on subsidies, 5 percent of GDP on pensions, and 3.2 percent of GDP on child allowances.[16] The budgetary deficit is assumed to amount to 10 percent of GDP, while the extrabudgetary pension fund has a deficit of 0.5 percent of GDP.

Social protection options, social safety nets, and the budget

As stressed earlier in the chapter, parameters of the stylized economy are representative of transition economies. Nevertheless, Table 8.6 displays the impact of variations in selected underlying parameters on the general government balance.[17] For instance, a change in shares of pensioners and children to the total population from 30 percent and 20 percent, respectively,

Table 8.5 The overall budgetary position and the extrabudgetary fund

	Rubles	*As a percentage of GDP*
Budget:		
Revenue	7,500	30.0
Expenditure	10,000	40.0
Of which:		
subsidy	2,550	10.2
child allowance	800	3.2
Overall deficit	2,500	10.0
Extrabudgetary fund		
Revenue[1]	1,114	4.5
Expenditure	1,200	4.8
Deficit	86	0.3
Memorandum items:		
Average pension/average wage (percent)	40.0	
Statutory payroll tax (percent)	33.2	
Effective payroll tax (percent)	22.3	

[1] Assuming a collection lag of two months and monthly inflation rate of 22.1 percent.

Table 8.6 Summary of budgetary impact of policy and other exogenous developments in a stylized economy

Factors	*Effects on fiscal balance*	
	(rubles)	*(percent of GDP)*
Prereform social protection expenditures:		
Budgetary subsidies	2,550	10.2
Child allowances	800	3.2
Extrabudgetary fund revenue	1,114	4.5
Pension expenditure	1,200	4.8
Effects on the general government fiscal balance of:		
10 percent increase in the poor's consumption of bread, milk, and meat on subsidies	+105	+0.4
Change in shares of pensioners and children from 30 and 20 percent to 20 and 30 percent on:		
subsidies	–	–
child allowance expenditures	–400	–1.6
pension expenditures	+400	+1.6
Increase in unemployment from zero to 10 percent (or a Rub 500 reduction in the economy's wage bill) on:[1]		
extrabudgetary fund revenue	–112	–0.4
unemployment benefits	–200	–0.8
Effects on extrabudgetary fund revenue of:		
20 percent reduction in the statutory payroll tax rate from 33.2 percent to 26.6 percent	–891	–3.6
One-month longer collection lag	–202	–0.8
20 percent reduction in inflation rate from 22.1 to 17.7 percent per month	+84	+0.3

[1] If unemployed workers receive wages without any contribution to output (not an unlikely situation in some transition economies), there would be a positive effect of Rub 500 on the fiscal balance, if this leads to reduced budgetary transfers to state enterprises.

to 20 percent and 30 percent would not have any fiscal impact.

The stylized model assumes no *unemployment*. So far, transition economies in the FSU have witnessed low open unemployment. However, since unemployment in these economies is expected to increase in the near term, the stylized model could be adapted to illustrate how the safety net for the unemployed would interact with budgetary policy.

Let us assume five of the 50 workers become jobless, implying an unemployment rate of 10 percent. If no change in the average wage were assumed, the wage bill would be reduced from Rub 5,000 to 4,500. The payroll contributions to the extrabudgetary fund for pension payments would be reduced by Rub 112 (0.5 percent of GDP). Moreover, unemployment benefits, replacing 40 percent of the average wage, would cost Rub 200 (0.8 percent of GDP). This alone would require the introduction of a 6 percent payroll tax, if this benefit were to be financed wholly from an extrabudgetary fund.

Subsidies

If retail prices were increased to cover the costs of food items for which there are explicit budgetary subsidies, the immediate impact would be to raise the cost of living for the nonpoor by 30 percent, on average, while raising it for the poor by 52.5 percent (Table 8.7). As a means of mitigating the effects on the poor, three policy options could be considered:

- Categorically targeted cash transfers equaling the amount of explicit subsidy – Rub 21 – could be given to pensioners and children in lieu of the subsidy.[18] This option would enable the poor to maintain their standards of living. The cash transfer could be delivered through the existing channels as supplements to pensions and child allowances. The budgetary cost of these transfers would be Rub 1,050 (4.2 percent of GDP) and would only partly offset the reduction in the budgetary cost of subsidies. Therefore, there would be a net budgetary savings of Rub 1,500 (6 percent of GDP).

  In the absence of other policy measures, the deficit of the extra-budgetary fund would widen by Rub 630 (2.5 percent of GDP) because of higher pension payments necessitating increased budgetary transfers. However, the consolidated general government (central government and extrabudgetary fund) deficit would be lower than before. The central government could use part of the savings from the subsidy reform to

Table 8.7 Effect on the cost of living of the nonpoor and the poor

	Retail price		*CPI for the nonpoor*			*CPI for the poor*		
	Old[1]	*New*[2]	*Weight*	*Old*[1]	*New*[2]	*Weight*	*Old*[1]	*New*[2]
Total	1.000		1.000	1.000	1.300	1.000	1.000	1.525
Food:			0.400			0.700		
Bread	1.000	2.000	0.100	0.100	0.200	0.200	0.200	0.400
Milk	1.000	2.000	0.100	0.100	0.200	0.200	0.200	0.400
Meat	1.000	2.000	0.100	0.100	0.200	0.125	0.125	0.250
Other	1.000	1.000	0.100	0.100	0.100	0.175	0.175	0.175
Nonfood	1.000	1.000	0.600	0.600	0.600	0.300	0.300	0.300

[1] Before subsidy removal.
[2] After subsidy removal.

finance the categorically targeted cash transfers and still achieve an improvement of the fiscal position. The composition of budgetary expenditure would also change; part of the savings from the subsidy reform would be offset by increased outlays of Rub 420 (1.7 percent of GDP) on child allowances.

- When relative prices change – as would be the case with the subsidy reform – the consumption pattern could be affected depending on price elasticities. In this case, to achieve even greater savings, the value of cash transfers to the poor could be reduced, say, to Rub 15, that is less than full compensation for the price increase.[19] The budgetary savings would amount to Rub 1,800 (7.2 percent of GDP).[20] However, the demand for basic commodities could be expected to be relatively price inelastic, and consequently, their consumption would not change significantly immediately following relative price changes.
- The 30 percent increase in the cost of living of the nonpoor (i.e. wage earners in this model) could be too drastic. Wages might have to be raised. However, wage increases fully compensating removal of the subsidy would achieve no improvement in the fiscal position if all workers were employed in the budgetary sector, although the removal of subsidies accompanied by price liberalization would improve the allocative efficiency. A drastic reduction in the subsidy might not be politically feasible. In the circumstances, subsidies could be phased out over a longer time period – say, two years – or a partial compensation could be given to wage earners. This would mean, however, that the budgetary savings would be smaller.[21]

Cash benefits

As noted earlier, the stylized country has a permanent social security institution – the extrabudgetary fund – which is responsible for making *pension* payments. As also noted earlier, the subsidy reform could increase the extrabudgetary fund's deficit if pensioners were compensated for the cut in subsidies. The fund's widening deficit would require new revenue and expenditure measures, especially if the central government were unable to cover fully the deficit through transfers. At the same time, it would also be necessary to ensure that pensioners earning minimum pensions were paid an adequate amount to subsist.

Initially, all pensioners were assumed to be poor. In reality, however, this may not be the case. Some pensions may exceed the subsistence income level, and some pensioners may be working – supplementing their pensions with wages. When reform-induced changes in real incomes become dominant, the link between social insurance contributions and benefits may have to be broken to place a substantially higher weight on the redistributive aspects of existing social protection arrangements.[22] It also becomes imperative to seek other measures that make the fund's existing expenditures more cost effective and strengthen its revenue position. Various possibilities can be considered to restructure pension benefits while ensuring adequate protection for minimum pensioners.

First, the pension amount for working pensioners could be reduced. If some 25 percent of the 30 pensioners receiving an average pension worked, a 25 percent reduction in their pensions could save about Rub 75.[23]

Second, the replacement rate (i.e. the ratio between the average pension and the average wage) could be reduced, while the minimum pension is being maintained constant in real terms. This outcome could be secured by an indexation policy which would provide full compensation for price increases to lower pension earners but not to those receiving the higher pensions. Another possibility would be to reduce explicitly the differential between the minimum and the maximum pension through a two-tiered pension system, the lower tier providing a minimum pension and a higher tier catering to those with relatively high wages and longer work history. At the extreme, a flat pension close to a subsistence income level could be provided. Such a system would have the advantage of ensuring a minimum pension to all pensioners at sustainable financial and administrative costs. The main drawback would be that it would decouple social insurance contributions from pension payments. In the stylized economy, a reduction in the average replacement ratio from 40 percent to 35 percent would reduce pension expenditures by Rub 150, or 0.6 percent of GDP.

Third, as both statutory and actual retirement ages in most of these countries are low by international standards – generally 55 for women and 60 for men with extensive provisions for early retirement – the possibility of gradually raising the retirement age could also be considered. Increasing the retirement age would be consistent with the current practice in almost all transition economies of permitting retired persons to work – usually on the same job as prior to reaching statutory retirement age.[24,25]

On the revenue side, the following possibilities can be considered. First, the two-month lag in revenue collection could be eliminated or shortened. If the lag were shortened by a month, the revenue position would improve by Rub 246 (or 1 percent of GDP). The impact of this measure on revenue would tend to be greater if the prevailing inflation rate were high.

Second, some transition countries apply lower rates of payroll tax to certain sectors (e.g. agriculture, self-employed) or enterprises with certain types of employees (e.g. the disabled). Further, some payments (e.g. vacation pay) may not be included in the base used for levying payroll taxes. If the payroll tax base were expanded to include all payments to employees and the tax base as a result expanded by 5 percent, additional revenue collected would amount to Rub 56.

Third, the effective yield from payroll taxes is also affected by weak enforcement procedures resulting in widespread evasion of payroll tax liabilities. A system of more frequent audits with increased and stringent penalties (in the form of interest payments on the amount due at real positive interest rates) would further enhance the extrabudgetary fund's revenue position.

In the stylized economy, there are 20 children receiving an *allowance* of Rub 40 each. Although categorically targeted, across-the-board payments to all children extend the benefit to both the poor and the nonpoor. A more appropriate option would be to increase the child allowance amount and limit its award to families who are genuinely poor. However, as noted earlier, it is not always administratively feasible to target benefits based on family incomes. Some imperfect method would, therefore, have to be found to provide adequate income support to families with children.

Since poverty is frequently correlated with the number of children, one possibility would be to eliminate the allowance for the first child, except for the single-parent family. The drawback would be that it would fail to capture working poor families with one child. This would not be a problem if a second-tier safety net existed to fill the gap between the earned income and the minimum subsistence income. The other option would be to eliminate the allowance for relatively older children – say, above the age of 14 – on the assumption that caregivers are better placed in their life cycles and that they do not have to withdraw from the labor force to care for the children.

Average unemployment compensation of Rub 40 is high. A reduction in the replacement rate to 30 percent would reduce the cost of unemployment benefits by Rub 50. Income-support programs for the long-term unemployed – in the form of public works – would further add to budgetary expenditures.[26] As unemployment rises, the need for financing unemployment benefits would also rise.

An increase in unemployment could be a result of cuts in either subsidized credits (quasi-fiscal expenditures) or direct budgetary transfers to loss-making enterprises. In these cases, the short-run budgetary analysis should take into account the savings resulting from cuts in credits and transfers; any long-run analysis should take into account the budgetary implications of possible efficiency gains for the economy and the concomitant effects on revenues and expenditures.

Table 8.8 summarizes the short-term budgetary impact of reform options enumerated above. It shows that the maximum budgetary savings arise when generalized consumer subsidies are replaced by targeted cash transfers.

RECENT SOCIAL PROTECTION REFORM EXPERIENCE

As noted earlier, transition economies began reforming under diverse economic, demographic, and institutional settings. Those considerations, together with the speed of price reform and tolerance of open unemployment,

Table 8.8 Summary of budgetary impact of social protection reform options in a stylized economy

Reform options	*Effects on fiscal balance*	
	(rubles)	*(percent of GDP)*
Consumer subsidies:		
Replace generalized subsidies with cash transfers targeted to pensioners and children	+1,500	6.0
Subsidies	+2,550	
Cash benefits	–1,050	
Pensioners[1]	(–630)	
Children	(–420)	
Extrabudgetary fund operations		
Benefit measures:		
Reduce pensions to working pensioners by 25 percent[2]	+75	0.3
Reduce the replacement rate from 40 percent to 35 percent	+150	0.6
Revenue measures:		
Broaden the payroll tax base by 5 percent	+56	0.2
Reduce the collection lag by one month	+246	1.0

[1] This would increase the extrabudgetary fund expenditures by the same amount, which could be financed through budgetary transfers. No unemployment is assumed.
[2] 25 percent of the pensioners are assumed to be working for wages.

influenced the nature and the financing of social safety nets in the reforming countries.

Many transition economies have reduced generalized subsidies and replaced them with different types of cash transfers, resulting in real food price increases. The other measures, introduced with a lag, often included cuts in transfers to public enterprises, which have forced the particularly inefficient ones to reduce production and employment. The restructuring and reform of state-owned enterprises has also contributed to unemployment. East European transition economies have already experienced large increases in open unemployment – to more than 10 percent of the labor force. Others, however, have pursued policies to keep unemployment hidden; at end-1993, the average rate of registered unemployment in most FSU states was less than 2–3 percent.

Two major factors have been responsible for low open unemployment in the FSU states. Budgetary transfers and subsidized central bank credits have facilitated labor hoarding by enterprises. Moreover, inadequate unemployment benefits have made it difficult for an employee to give up a job that provides not only a wage but crucial nonwage benefits (e.g. health services). As a result, there has been large-scale underemployment, with a rising proportion of workers on short working days or on unpaid leave. In the presence of declining output, this phenomenon has reduced average labor productivity. In some countries (e.g. Romania), attempts have been made to reduce unemployment through early retirement schemes, with questionable fiscal and labor market consequences.

In many transition economies, exogenous shocks and loose economic policies have accompanied pricing reforms, aggravating the decline in living standards. These exogenous shocks ranged from increases in the prices of imported oil (Armenia, Belarus, and Ukraine) to natural disasters (the Kyrgyz Republic), civil strife (Georgia), imposition of trade embargoes (Hungary, FYR of Macedonia, Romania), and the disruption of interstate trade (all countries of the COMECON, FSU, and former Yugoslavia). Loose financial policies – reflected in large fiscal deficits and high rates of credit expansion – caused prices to rise rapidly in many countries.

Reform measures, together with a worsening macroeconomic position, have had significant effects on the living standards of various population groups. It is not easy, however, to estimate these effects and assess social safety net needs, particularly since formal sector activities have been declining, and informal sector activities have been increasing. Recent household expenditure surveys (in the Kyrgyz Republic, Poland, and the Russian Federation) have indicated that, despite cuts in officially reported real incomes, the consumption of basic food items has not declined significantly or even increased, either because households have reduced nonfood expenditures drastically or because increases in informal sector incomes have offset the decline in formal sector incomes.[27]

Overall mix of subsidies and cash benefits

During 1990–3, most countries other than the FSU and Baltic states listed in Table 8.2 reduced subsidies as a percentage of GDP, with the cuts ranging between 1.2 percent of GDP (Estonia) and 13 percent of GDP (Albania), and increased outlays on cash benefits, with the increases ranging from 0.9 percent of GDP (Bulgaria, FYR of Macedonia) to 8.2 percent of GDP (Poland). In many countries in this group, there was a reduction in the overall spending on social protection. There were, however, two exceptions: Romania, which has reduced both subsidies and cash benefits as a proportion of GDP, and Poland, which has increased overall social protection expenditures in relation to GDP.

The FSU states have pursued a variety of strategies. While most have reduced subsidies to below the 10 percent of GDP level that the FSU registered in 1988, some have maintained persistently high levels of subsidies. For example, in 1993, subsidy expenditures were 8.4 percent of GDP in Armenia, 14.3 percent of GDP in Belarus, 33.3 percent of GDP in Georgia, 12.1 percent of GDP in Ukraine, and 7.3 percent of GDP in Uzbekistan.

Subsidies

As noted earlier, the initial reform measures included freeing prices of essential goods and services. For example, in early 1992, a number of FSU states raised the prices of many essential goods and services (e.g. bread, sugar, electricity, and gas) by a factor of between 3 and 6 (Kazakhstan, the Russian Federation, and Ukraine). Non-FSU European and Asian transition economies had also freed prices at the outset of the reform process (Poland, the Czech and Slovak Republics, Romania and Lao People's Democratic Republic). Some countries were quicker in initiating liberalization of prices (Albania and Lithuania), while others retained some consumer subsidies (Armenia, Georgia, Romania, Ukraine).

Some countries totally eliminated consumer subsidies (Estonia, Latvia, and FYR of Macedonia) or succeeded in containing these subsidies in a relatively short period of time (Albania, Bulgaria, and Poland), mitigating any adverse social consequences by increasing wages and various cash benefits for pensioners, children, and the unemployed. Others have replaced generalized subsidies with limited cash transfers to certain population groups (Albania, the Kyrgyz Republic, Kazakhstan, and Moldova). Some have introduced coupon schemes for a few essential commodities (milk, sugar, vegetable oil) other than bread to provide limited quantities of these goods at subsidized prices to the population (Uzbekistan). While most transition economies have kept subsidy expenditures under the control of the central government, countries with decentralized systems of decision making have shifted subsidy costs to local governments (Poland and the Russian Federation).

The constraints on phasing out subsidies have been both political and administrative. Replacing generalized subsidies with subsidies targeted to vulnerable groups was difficult as a large number of politically influential middle-class and upper-class income groups faced income losses. The bread subsidy was a particularly sensitive issue, especially in Central Asian FSU states. Even in countries which reduced nonbread subsidies substantially, significant bread subsidies remained until recently (Armenia in 1994). The administrative requirements for targeting, for example through coupon schemes, have also posed a substantial problem. Countries have experienced leakages of the subsidized goods distributed through the coupon schemes. Even those countries who had introduced coupons for nonbread commodities appeared reluctant to expand the system to bread.

Replacing generalized subsidies with limited cash transfers to vulnerable groups appears to be a promising approach to phasing out subsidies. However, even in this case, there are a number of problems. For example, the pressure for a general wage increase to replace the lost income transfer can be intense. In many FSU economies, wages and various cash benefits are often determined as multiples of the minimum wage. Therefore, an increase in the minimum wage, following the removal of subsidies and the consequent increase in prices, could imply no change in real wages and cash benefits – and a limited improvement in the fiscal position.

Even countries that have completely eliminated food subsidies have generally retained limited subsidies for selected services (e.g. transportation in Estonia, at a cost of 1.2 percent of GDP in 1993; and a heating allowance for nonworking pensioners in Latvia, at a cost of 1.2 percent of GDP in 1993, which was borne by the Social Insurance Fund).

Although declining in most transition economies, producer subsidies to industrial enterprises and to agriculture still continue to be provided (FYR of Macedonia, Romania, and the Russian Federation), often in an implicit form (Uzbekistan), with adverse effects on the production efficiency and consumption decisions, and on the environment (increased use of subsidized fertilizers).

Cash benefits

As subsidies for major goods and services consumed are phased out, cash benefits (mainly pensions, child allowances, and unemployment benefits) are becoming increasingly important instruments of social safety nets. At the same time, the increasing outlays on cash benefits have strained the financial positions of the budget and extrabudgetary funds, requiring a high rate of payroll contributions. Therefore, the reform of cash benefits itself has become an important issue. A major dilemma in this context has been the extent to which the provision of pensions and unemployment benefits should be based on social insurance principles.

In general, countries have continued an explicit link between work history and pension payments, although the dispersion between the highest and the lowest pension has narrowed as a result of the indexation mechanism (Armenia, the Russian Federation, Ukraine). Only a few countries have adopted flat-rate pensions in the first years of transition (for nonworking pensioners), but have now decided to link pensions to the work history of the beneficiary and the average wage growth in the economy (Latvia). Most countries, as yet, do not tax or reduce pension income of working pensioners. In a few countries, working pensioners have not been given cash compensation when prices of basic goods (e.g. bread) were freed (Azerbaijan and Georgia). Some countries have moved to raise the statutory retirement ages for both men and women (FYR of Macedonia and Romania), although these still remain below western standards. Many have also tightened early retirement provisions (Albania, FYR of Macedonia, and Poland).

Some tightening of eligibility for unemployment compensation has also taken place to prevent misuse of the benefit (Estonia, where in addition to the requirement of a six-month work history, the applicant has to participate in public relief works for 10 days over a one-month period). Similarly, the duration of unemployment benefits has been shortened to obviate job search disincentives (Albania, FYR of Macedonia, Poland, and Romania). This has been accompanied by a financial and administrative strengthening of social assistance programs (Albania and Macedonia FYR). However, the average unemployment benefit in relation to the prevailing wage remains low in many countries, creating disincentives for the unemployed to register (Armenia, the Russian Federation, and Estonia).

Child allowances have been maintained because families with children are considered to be vulnerable. In this respect, child allowances are considered targeted transfers. Child allowances are a particularly important element of the social safety net in many central Asian FSU states with a high child dependency ratio. However, there is widespread recognition that not all families with children are vulnerable. Therefore, means testing of child allowances is also being attempted, though notionally, to reduce the cost to the budget (the Kyrgyz Republic and FYR of Macedonia). However, these countries face the usual difficulties of measuring with accuracy the income and assets of targeted families. Countries with a very young population and with a high birth rate (Uzbekistan) face the conflicting pressures between child allowances as a safety net and as an incentive to have large families.

Attempts are under way in some countries to institute income support programs for individuals who fall below the poverty threshold (the Russian Federation). Other countries are either running this type of program relatively successfully (FYR of Macedonia) or are planning to implement one soon (Estonia). Some countries (Albania, Latvia, and Poland) are also using the social assistance program to provide income support also to the long-term unemployed.

SUMMARY AND CONCLUSIONS

In the short term, social safety nets are meant to protect the vulnerable from the negative effects of reform measures. In this way, they enhance the sustainability and acceptability of reform programs. Using a stylized model and drawing on experiences of economies currently undergoing transition, this chapter highlighted the interaction between social safety nets and the budget. One message that emerged is that enhancing the cost-effectiveness of social safety net expenditures is not only a social policy issue but also an important consideration for macroeconomic stability and sustainability.

The other important message that emerges from the numerical example is that, in the short term, improved targeting of subsidies provides the maximum budgetary savings. For instance, in the stylized economy, the bulk of the estimated expenditure savings are from the improved targeting of the generalized subsidies. The numerical example also shows that significant financial savings are feasible from reforming pensions while improving their adequacy. Although the short-term impact of some measures (such as the raising of retirement ages) is relatively small, it can be quite significant over a period of time.

There has been some discussion that a strengthening of social safety nets in transition economies would require new foreign financing. The above analysis shows that this is not necessarily true, since possibilities exist for reducing the cost of ongoing programs and raising additional revenues without increasing the payroll tax.

This chapter enumerated various options for reforming social safety net expenditures. Unfortunately, the survey of country experiences showed that, with the exception of limited rationalization of commodity subsidies, the success to date in improving the cost-effectiveness of other elements of safety nets has been rather limited. This could partly be because many countries, particularly in the FSU, are still in the initial stages of transition. Political considerations, too, have played a role; the individuals likely to lose benefits have prevented reforms from taking place.

What lessons can be drawn from the preceding analysis to ensure that the twin objectives of shielding the poor and ensuring fiscal sustainability are met in transition economies continuing with the reform process?

First, generalized commodity subsidies would have to be replaced with subsidies or cash transfers that are narrowly targeted to the truly needy. This would not only increase the efficiency of resource use but also improve the overall fiscal position. This chapter discussed various options in this regard, and depending on administrative and other considerations, either of these could be adopted. It appears that countries that reformed subsidies quickly have also succeeded in restraining their fiscal deficits.

Second, the rationalization of existing social protection mechanisms is critical. In the initial stages of reform, it is important to provide social protection to population groups considered most vulnerable. This means that in many cases the minimum benefit should be maintained at a subsistence level, while ensuring that the average benefit is financially sustainable. The net result could be a compressed or flat benefit structure, which – at least in the short term – breaks the link between contributions and benefits.

Third, structural reforms of cash benefits would also have to be implemented quickly to improve their financial viability. Unless retirement ages were raised and early pensions considerably tightened, the pressure on cash benefit expenditures would persist.

Fourth, much of the focus of policymakers in many transition economies has been on tailoring expenditures to available revenues. This concentration on the benefit side can lead to a neglect of possibilities of increasing revenue without raising the statutory payroll tax rates. Steps to increase payroll tax compliance (and, therefore, the effective payroll tax rate), including, for example, reducing or eliminating exemptions and instituting real positive interest rates on unpaid obligations, would yield increased revenue receipts while removing distortions. Some institutional improvements, such as reducing or eliminating the lags in transfer of payroll tax to accounts of the benefit-disbursing agency and holding surplus funds in interest-bearing accounts, would also strengthen the financial position of extrabudgetary funds providing these benefits.

Finally, open unemployment in the majority of transition economies has thus far been relatively low. As economic reforms gather momentum, the number of individuals who become openly unemployed – in contrast with disguised unemployed – would be expected to rise. This would be a necessary condition for restructuring the enterprise sector in these countries. But a major consequence of increased unemployment is that the short-term need for social safety net expenditures would increase. Under conditions of a tight fiscal position, it would be necessary to improve the cost-effectiveness of existing social safety net expenditures to meet the contingency of higher unemployment.

APPENDIX

Table A8.1 Average consumption per person in selected transition economies

	Lowest two income deciles	*Overall population*
Composition of household expenditures		
	(percent of total)	
Lao PDR[1]		
Food	42.9	42.2
Own produce	29.8	14.6
Clothing	3.1	3.6
Other	24.2	39.6
Romania[2]		
Food	31.0	32.6
Own produce	37.8	24.9
Clothing	10.4	12.2
Other	20.8	30.3
Russian Federation[3]		
Food	79.3[4]	50.2
Nonfood	17.5	46.8
Alcoholic beverages	3.2	3.0
Per capita household food consumption[5]		
	(kg per month)	
Romania		
Bread and bread products	10.3	11.4
Corn flour	2.8	1.9
Meat and meat products	3.3	4.7
Beans	0.5	0.5
Potatoes	3.2	3.9

Table A8.1 continued

	Lowest two income deciles	*Overall population*
Russian Federation		
Bread products	10.1[6]	9.2
Potatoes	9.3	9.7
Meat and meat products	3.2	5.1
Milk	23.2	26.5

Sources: Authors' estimates based on data provided by the authorities
[1]Data are for urban households based on 1992–3 household expenditure survey.
[2]1992 data.
[3]1993 data.
[4]Household headed by a pensioner.
[5]Data on per capita food consumption are not available for Lao People's Democratic Republic.
[6]Lowest decile of the population.

NOTES

*We wish to thank our colleagues in the Expenditure Policy Division, Robert Hagemann, and an anonymous referee for helpful comments, and Mrs Tarja Papavassiliou for computational assistance.

1 The phenomenon of disguised unemployment in transition economies is reflected in the enterprise tendency to hoard labor, which has meant a cut in real wages for all workers. In a way, this shows the 'flexibility' of labor markets to allow for an across-the-board real wage cut. The main difficulty is that this situation is not sustainable.
2 In Albania, this estimate includes large payments made to idle workers which, in some countries, are shown under other expenditure headings.
3 For modeling purposes, no distinction is made between the number unemployed and those actually registered to receive unemployment benefits. In other words, all unemployed are assumed to be registered with official agencies.
4 In transition economies, women's labor force participation is high. The model can easily be extended to include the working poor.
5 Typically, in most transition economies, there are separate extrabudgetary funds for providing unemployment benefits and sickness and maternity benefits.
6 t is the rate 'effectively' faced by the payroll tax payers in the current time period. Because of the collection lag, t is lower than the statutory rate, T.
7 In the formulation presented here, only the *deficit* of the extrabudgetary fund is considered to be a part of the general government expenditure.
8 The net consumers are those who consume more than they produce.
9 This means that even the lowest wage exceeds the subsistence income level, while many pensions fall short of it.
10 The ratios of 30 percent and 20 percent for the number of pensioners and children to the total population, respectively, are indicative of the actual situation in many transition economies. For example, in 1992, the ratios of the number of pensioners to the population were, respectively, 23 and 21 percent in Poland and Russia because of low retirement ages and proliferation of special pensioners.

The ratios of the number of children to the population were 24 and 22 percent, respectively, for these two countries.

11 The currency unit, ruble (Rub), is used throughout for illustration.

12 In 1993, the estimated share of food consumption in the household budget for the two lowest income deciles in the Russian Federation was approximately 80 percent; the share for the average household was 50 percent. (See Appendix Table A8.1.)

13 Many transition economies maintain unrealistically low agricultural producer prices and an overvalued exchange rate, giving rise to implicit subsidies. If the implicit subsidy is also rub 1 per kg for the three items listed in Table 8.3 (i.e. bread, milk, and meat), the total benefit of the implicit subsidy and its distribution across income classes will be the same as for explicit budgetary subsidies. The major difference is that the cost of the implicit subsidy is borne by producers and not by the budget. The total annual cost of subsidies to the economy would then be Rub 1,500.

14 In 1993, the ratio of the average pension to the average wage ranged between 30 and 60 percent. For example, the ratio was 36 percent in both Belarus and Russia. While the incidence of poverty is greatest among families with a large number of children, the amount of child allowance in most transition economies was less than 15 percent of the average wage in 1993 (e.g. Armenia, the former Yugoslav Republic of Macedonia, the Russian Federation). The wage bill as a ratio of GDP is assumed to be 25 percent in this model and lower than the labor share of GDP in many transition economies. The wage bill in this model, however, is shown net of payroll taxes and does not include in-kind or other wages that do not form the payroll tax base.

15 Expenditures in relation to GDP assumed in the numerical illustration are close to the average of 42 percent of GDP prior to the initiation of reforms in transition economies (see Table 8.2).

16 In selected transition economies, the average spending on subsidies and child allowances was 7.0 percent of GDP and 1.4 percent of GDP in 1990 or 1991, respectively (see Table 8.2). Two countries spent 6 percent of GDP or more on child allowances.

17 The following methodology assumes that the parameters underlying the hypothetical economy do not change significantly with the onset of economic reforms. Should these parameters (e.g. consumption pattern) alter, the policy response would also have to be different from that enumerated here. However, the analysis presented in this chapter is essentially of a short-term nature. Most model assumptions are thus expected to hold, even when the economy has begun to reform.

18 It can be argued that in-kind transfers are superior to cash transfers, since the former assure a minimum provision of essential consumption items to the poor. This argument assumes that an effective administrative mechanism is in place to deliver in-kind goods, which is not always the case. Furthermore, experience has shown that commodities mainly consumed by the poor are difficult to identify. By contrast, the principal advantage of cash transfers is that they can be easily added to the existing benefit amounts without significant additional administrative costs.

19 The assumption here is that the base period consumption levels were distorted by subsidies and that a correction in relative prices would reduce consumption of subsidized items.

20 If implicit subsidies are to be eliminated by either raising the producer prices and/or adjusting the exchange rate to a realistic level, the increase in budgetary expenditure would be larger. If the first option of compensating the poor is

adopted, the cash transfers would amount to Rub 1,050 (4.2 percent of GDP). The advantage would be that the relative price structure in the economy would reflect more accurately relative scarcities with a favorable impact on resource allocation.

21 There are other ways to target benefits. For instance, the food subsidy could be targeted to the population in food deficit regions, or it could be targeted to elderly or disabled workers, unemployed workers, and families with a large number of children.

22 The link between contributions and benefits is already weak in many countries since payroll taxes are typically not paid by employees.

23 Pensioners being denied a full pension might decide to stop working. This would reduce the wage bill and the payroll tax revenue to the pension fund, unless the vacated positions were filled by unemployed workers.

24 In transition economies, low retirement ages took pressure off the labor market as jobs were guaranteed for everyone. Since these guarantees have been eliminated, there seems little rationale for keeping retirement age low.

25 This did not hold for the former Yugoslav Republic of Macedonia in 1993–4.

26 Public works are not part of social insurance systems and, therefore, should not be financed out of the extrabudgetary fund's revenue.

27 Recent reports from the Statistical Committee of the Russian Federation note that the official estimates of output may be understated by as much as 40 percent because of informal sector activity.

REFERENCES

Ahmad, Ehtisham, and Ke-young Chu (1993) 'Russian Federation – Economic Reform and Policy Options for Social Protection', in *Transition to the Market: Studies in Fiscal Reform*, ed. Vito Tanzi, Washington, DC: International Monetary Fund.

———, Jean Dreze, John Hills, and Amartya Sen (eds) (1991) *Social Security in Developing Countries*, Oxford: Clarendon Press.

Atkinson, A. B. (1992) 'The Western Experience with Social Safety Nets', Suntory-Toyota International Economic and Related Disciplines, Number WSP/80, London: London School of Economics.

Chu, Ke-young, and Sanjeev Gupta (1986) 'Protecting the Poor: Social Safety Nets During the Transition', *Finance and Development*, Washington, DC: International Monetary Fund and the World Bank, June.

Fiscal Affairs Department (1986) *Fund-Supported Programs, Fiscal Policy, and Income Distribution*, IMF Occasional Paper 46, Washington, DC: International Monetary Fund.

Grosh, M. E. (1992) 'Towards Quantifying the Trade-Off: Administrative Costs and Targeting Accuracy', draft, Washington, DC: World Bank.

Gupta, Sanjeev, and Robert Hagemann (1994) 'Social Protection During Russia's Economic Transformation', *Finance and Development*, Washington, DC: International Monetary Fund and the World Bank, December.

Halter, William A., and Richard Hemming (1987) 'The Impact of Demographic Change on Social Security Financing', *Staff Papers*, Washington, DC: International Monetary Fund, September.

Heller, Peter, A., and Lans Bovenberg, Thanos Catsambas, Ke-young Chu, and Parthasarathi Shome (1988) *The Implications of Fund-Supported Adjustment Programs for Poverty: Experiences in Selected Countries*, IMF Occasional Paper 58, Washington, DC: International Monetary Fund.

Kopits, George (1991) 'Social Security', in *Fiscal Policies in Economies in Transition*, ed. Vito Tanzi, Washington, DC: International Monetary Fund.

Mackenzie, G. A. (1988) 'Social Security Issues in Developing Countries: The Latin American Experience', *Staff Papers*, Washington, DC: International Monetary Fund, September.

Milanovic, B. (1992) 'Distributional Impact of Cash and In-Kind Transfers in Eastern Europe and Russia', draft, Washington, DC: World Bank.

Tanzi, Vito (1978) 'Inflation, Real Tax Revenue, and the Case for Inflationary Finance: The Theory with Application to Argentina', *IMF Staff Papers*, Washington, DC: International Monetary Fund.

——(1987) 'Quantitative Characteristics of the Tax Systems of Developing Countries', Chapter 8 in *The Theory of Taxation for Developing Countries*, ed. D. Newbery and N. Stern, New York: Oxford University Press.

——(ed.) (1992) *Fiscal Policies in Economies in Transition*, Washington, DC: International Monetary Fund.

——(ed.) (1993) *Transition to the Market: Studies in Fiscal Reform*, Washington, DC: International Monetary Fund.

9

CONSUMER PRICE REFORMS AND THE SAFETY NET IN TRANSITION ECONOMIES

Ehtisham Ahmad and Liam Halligan[1]

INTRODUCTION

The reform of administered consumer prices in the formerly centrally planned economies is a key to the successful transition to a market-based system. The sequencing of consumer price adjustment has implications for the effective use of market signals to guide production decisions, particularly though not exclusively in agricultural activities. However, the transition may falter if effective measures are not put in place to 'protect' the most vulnerable groups of the population. Vito Tanzi (1992) has stressed the importance of assessing the applicability of policies in relation to institutional constraints. 'Apparent' first-best options may fail if such constraints are not explicitly considered.

Many transition economies have size distributions of income characterized by a concentration of individuals at a relatively low level of income, with increasing inequality as the market opens up an income generation potential for some.[2] This leaves many of those at the lower end of the income scale particularly vulnerable to unforeseen changes in consumer prices, which may be more marked in some regions than others. Thus the provision of a basic 'safety net' would be needed to ensure that individuals and families do not fall below (an austere) minimum standard of living – an important ingredient in ensuring equity and political acceptability of the reforms. At the same time, a basic 'safety net' would be better targeted and considerably less costly than a system of generalized subsidies, which may obtain through subsidized inputs, even if consumer prices are freed. Such a basic 'safety net' could be denominated in cash, once prices have stabilized, or in kind, which would provide better insurance to consumers despite some possible administrative complexity, given the incomplete markets and uncertainty which characterize the second- or third-best world of the transition.

The cost implications of a 'basic social safety net' are critical in the transition. As Tanzi (1992, 1993) has argued, the transition is a period of revenue decline, where mandatory profit transfers and administrative controls are replaced by modern tax instruments. There is often a time lag associated with the establishment of an efficient tax administrative machinery, that would presage improvements in revenue collections in the medium term. Thus, in the initial periods of the transition, there is a fairly limited financial ability of the state to provide for additional expenditures on social protection.

Indeed, during the transition, there is a tendency for explicit social expenditures to increase. Price reforms turn implicit subsidies (e.g. on essential food and consumptions items) into explicit budgetary liabilities. The elimination of lifetime employment guarantees in state-owned enterprises is not generally feasible without measures to support newly unemployed workers. Inefficient state-owned enterprises need to be restructured or closed, and many of the formal social functions of the state (such as housing, payments mechanisms and the provision of family benefits, health and education facilities), which were carried out by such enterprises, have to be devolved to central or lower levels of government. All these essential structural reform measures place additional pressures on the limited public finances, as well as scarce administrative resources. This puts a premium on measures that are simple to specify and implement.

ADJUSTMENT SPEED AND ONE-OFF CASH COMPENSATION

A rapid, or 'cold turkey', approach to price reform is often recommended, to encourage supply responses, and reduce incentives for hoarding (see van Wijnbergen, 1992). Typically, this involves a freeing, or drastic adjustments, of administered prices, accompanied by a one-time cash compensation to protect those affected by the price change. The argument is predicated on the assumption that institutional mechanisms exist that would (a) permit the supply response to occur, and (b) enable the cash payments to be made in a timely manner to those affected by the price change.

Arguably, Poland is an example of a 'big bang', where the price reforms followed the pattern described in the previous paragraph – generating the desired supply response (Ebrill *et al.*, 1994). It was then possible to institute formal social protection instruments, to take care of standard life cycle and unemployment contingencies – although benefits and eligibility criteria have had to be readjusted to match financing constraints (see Maret and Schwartz, 1993).[3]

In some of the states of the former Soviet Union, the 'big bang' has produced less tangible results. While it is undoubtedly true that the price adjustments carried out in early 1992 led to the elimination of queues, the supply response has not materialized (see e.g. the discussion in Goldman (1994)). Continuing inflation has devalued the one-off cash compensation – and the institutions and mechanisms that might make means-tested social assistance feasible are likely to take a considerable amount of time to establish. While the initial price shock led to a concentration of incomes at relatively low levels, inequality has subsequently increased.[4] With an increasing difficulty in administering transfers through enterprises, or sub-national levels of government, or to those outside the formal sector, it is not surprising that agricultural input subsidies have reappeared, turning the price reform process full circle.

While China is typically characterized as having followed a gradualist approach to reforms, it actually adopted some key features of the 'big-bang' approach. In China during the late 1970s/early 1980s, there was a rapid adjustment in producer prices (especially of agricultural goods) to engender an agricultural supply response – with spectacular success. However, urban consumers were protected by a limited ration (akin to the classic model of rationing, see Pudney and Limin (1991) and the next section below) – limited quantities of essential goods were made available at a fixed price, with additional purchases available in the 'free market'. With gradual adjustments in ration prices, the ration system was withdrawn during 1993 without the need for additional compensation.

A MODIFIED RATIONING MECHANISM

In this section, we review a model illustrating the effects of modified rations, along with market-based transactions including the possible resale of goods through market channels. This should be distinguished from the traditional type of rationing that has existed in former transition economies – with no legitimate free markets, or resale possibilities. Thus, with a modified rationing mechanism, quantity-constrained markets for a few commodities are deemed to co-exist with market-clearing prices for the same commodities. A twin-market structure results in a system of dual pricing, as seen in the Chinese example.

The theory of rationing developed as a result of wartime rationing in Britain, and has been surveyed in a classic paper by Tobin (1952). A subsequent literature has utilized the notion of virtual pricing and duality to examine the phenomenon of rationing in a disequilibrium framework. Neary and Roberts (1980) provide an authoritative exposition. We argue that traditional rationing schemes could fail to guarantee the availability of essential commodities, largely as a result of administrative and institutional difficulties, and could thus aggravate the fiscal implications of 'cold turkey' price liberalization.

In this chapter we illustrate some of the key features of rationing systems with a mainly diagrammatic exposition (Tobin's 1952 paper provides an early typology of rationing). This approach should be treated as purely illustrative, focussing on features of a modified rationing arrangement relevant for the formulation of an effective safety net.

The basic model

It is possible to illustrate the effect of a specific ration on commodity demand, plotting the rationed good against money, deemed to represent the demand for all other goods.[5] In Figure 9.1, the ration level is *R* and money income is 0*E*; welfare assessments of rationing may be made, as usual, by evaluating the income changes associated with the move from *I* to *I′*. This simple treatment is essentially an indication of the detrimental effect of a ration on the individual consumer due to the departure from optimality.

In the presence of a ration, we may think of a utility-maximizing consumer under rationing as being subjected to a non-linear budget constraint – since if an individual's supply of ration coupons is fixed, the individual may be described as being subject to multiple constraints, which may be represented by a single *non-linear* budget line. The non-linearity is due to the administrative setting of some prices. When rations are bought and sold for cash, there is no reason why the individual consumption constraint implied by the ration will bind. Once ration entitlements can be resold and purchased on the market, the ration serves to generate income effects, and rationing will serve only to change the effective price of goods, and a linear budget constraint applies. Underlying a linear budget constraint are assumptions that markets

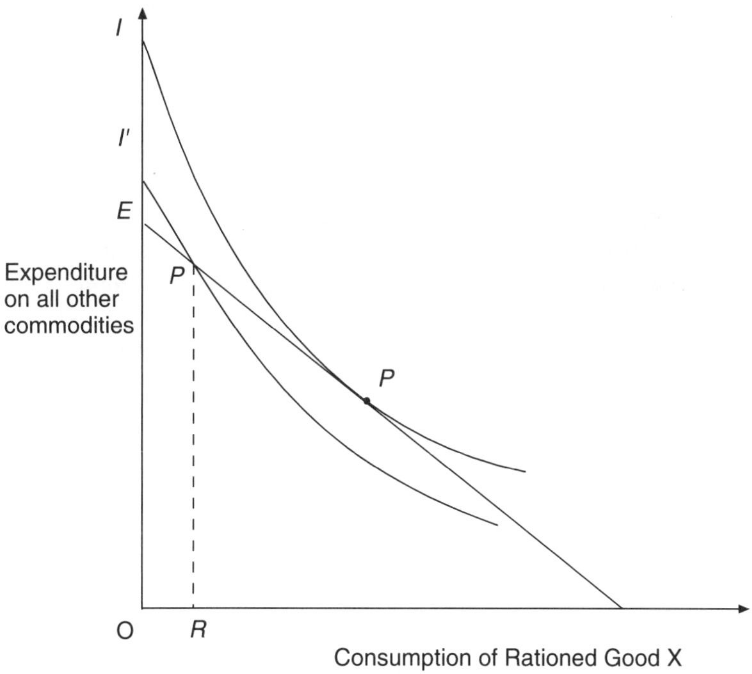

Figure 9.1 A simple representation of rationing

work to set prices efficiently and with minimal transactions costs. This may be expressed more formally as follows.

Let the rationed good be q_0 and $q = q_i$ ($i = 1, \ldots, n$) be a vector of unrationed goods subject to the administered price p_0 and the vector of free market prices $p = p_i$, respectively. The level of consumption of q_0 is limited to z by the rationing regime. Assuming a standard utility function, the consumer will choose the consumption levels of goods to

$$\text{maximize } U = V(q_0, q) \tag{9.1}$$

$$\text{s.t. } p_0 q_0 + p.q = M \quad \text{and} \quad q_0 = z \tag{9.2}$$

where M represents an income constraint. If preferences are weakly separable, the ration level only has income effects. Given such weak separability, and assuming that the ration binds, we can think of the consumption problem as

$$\text{maximize } U = V(z, \phi(q)) \tag{9.3}$$

$$\text{s.t. } p.q = M - p_0.z. \tag{9.4}$$

We may think of dual prices giving rise, in the absence of resale (and arbitrage), to the kinked budget line.[6] We assume that consumers have identical preferences and are differentiated only by their respective income levels. An efficient market for rationed goods will sufficiently reduce such a non-linearity. With weak separability, as in the case where coupon resale takes place, the ration level will operate the basic relationships between income levels, ration quotas, and such on demand solely through income effects. Provided that these are incorporated into the budget constraint, standard consumer theory can be used to analyze the effect of the ration.[7]

We can illustrate the arbitrage possibilities that exist between co-existing markets for the rationed good, using a diagrammatic treatment of the multi-dimensional approach. In Figure 9.2, good 1 is rationed and *AB* is its price line in the rationed market; *CD* represents its higher price in the free market. The consumer characterized by these given budget constraints will purchase the rationed good until, if desired, the quota bites at point *R*, with a budget line *ARC*. For given preferences, consumption will be at *P*. If arbitrage or entitlement resale was to take place, however, 0*S* of the rationed commodity could be consumed and *ST* sold in the free market, with a constraint *DC* and a welfare increase of *RAD*. The consumer in Figure 9.2 purchases good 1 exclusively in the rationed market (O*Q*) and buys less than the existing quota (O*T*); a relaxation of the quota (i.e. an increase in the per capita purchasing allocation) would not affect the consumption pattern. The consumer will be more concerned with the possibilities of selling between the rationed market

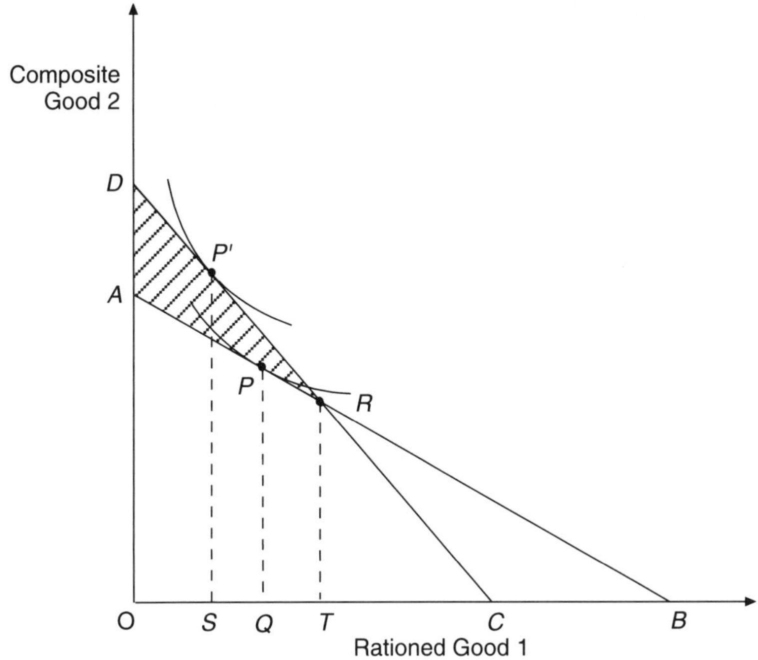

Figure 9.2 Kinked budget constraint in the absence of arbitrage

and the free market as arbitrage represents a positive welfare effect for those on low incomes.[8]

More affluent consumers may wish to consume in excess of point *R* and this case is shown in Figure 9.3. A consumer with an income endowment underlying the budget lines shown will purchase the entire ration quota O*T* and will buy *TN* on the open market. The consumer in Figure 9.3 will be conscious of the level of the ration quota. If the quota is relaxed to *T′*, the superior optimum *P′* could be attained at the same level of expenditure.[9] In this case, the consumer modifies behavior by now consuming solely in the administered market, but being aware of the possibilities of arbitrage at *P″*.

Raising ration quotas, given homogeneous preferences, will affect consumers differently according to their level of income. Lower-income consumers will seek rents from enhanced arbitrage possibilities, whilst the relatively more affluent will consume less of the rationed good in the free market. This analysis demonstrates the varying effects of rationing on consumers differentiated by income and hence the need for targeting.

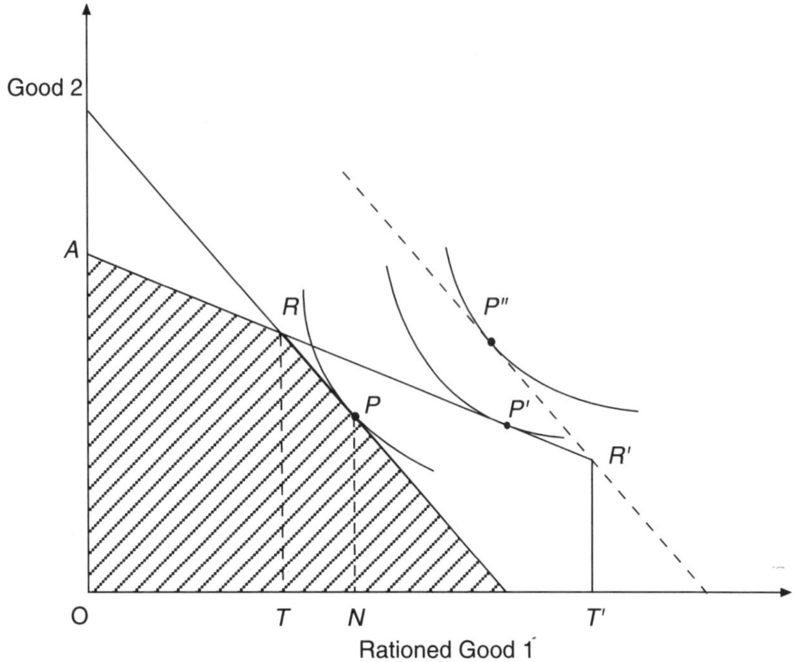

Figure 9.3 Quota relaxation and arbitrage possibilities

Convertibility

At the core of the ration resale debate is the issue of the relative importance of collective, as opposed to individual, welfare. Non-convertible rationing is motivated not only by a resolve of *specific egalitarianism*,[10] but also by a desire to influence directly the consumption of the vulnerable. The debate in economics between specific and *general* egalitarianism is very relevant here, and addresses the question of intervention and non-intervention

Ration resale is a crucial issue *vis-à-vis* a mechanism of distribution. Should ration resale be permitted, or strongly resisted? Analytically, we may see arbitrage by the consumer and ration resale as synonymous; a glance at Figure 9.2 suggests that ration resale enhances welfare, and increasingly so the lower the income level of the consumer. Attempted prevention of resale will be expensive and may well misdirect precious resources and administrative capacity during the transition.

While convertible rationing could be potentially welfare enhancing, its practice may work to undermine desired targeting. If rationing is motivated by an attempt to influence consumer tastes or enhance public health this could be undermined by resale. A commonly observed difficulty with rationing schemes is the misappropriation of rationed commodities by the retailers for sale at the free market price or use as inputs into goods which are later sold at a profit. This leakage element, though, may be partially offset by secondary income effects of ration resale for the poor – but these are not likely to be significant.

Initially, we assume non-convertible rationing, that individual demand in the absence of rationing is linear, and that prices are constant. We also assume conditions of genuine shortage, so that supply is fixed in the short run, there being no recourse to the free market. Figure 9.4 considers the relationship between individual and collective average consumption of a rationed good and the level of a consumer's income. When the ration level is set at *Z*, consumers of income status above Y_0 will feel the ration. The individual and collective demands will be given by *ABD* and *AD* respectively. Now assume that rations can be sold for cash. Given that there are consumers on the line *BD*, a positive price for coupons will emerge. This will increase the effective income of individuals holding rations.

The effect of ration resale is to shift individual consumption to *A′C′* and collective consumption to *ABD*. Individuals below the mean level of income $\bar{Y}$, though able to consume at *Z*, will sell their rations. The increasing curve O*E* traces a probable consumption path for the poor. Rich individuals, with incomes above $\bar{Y}$, will be able to buy additional quantities and achieve a consumption level of *EC′*. From a collective standpoint, the prevalence of

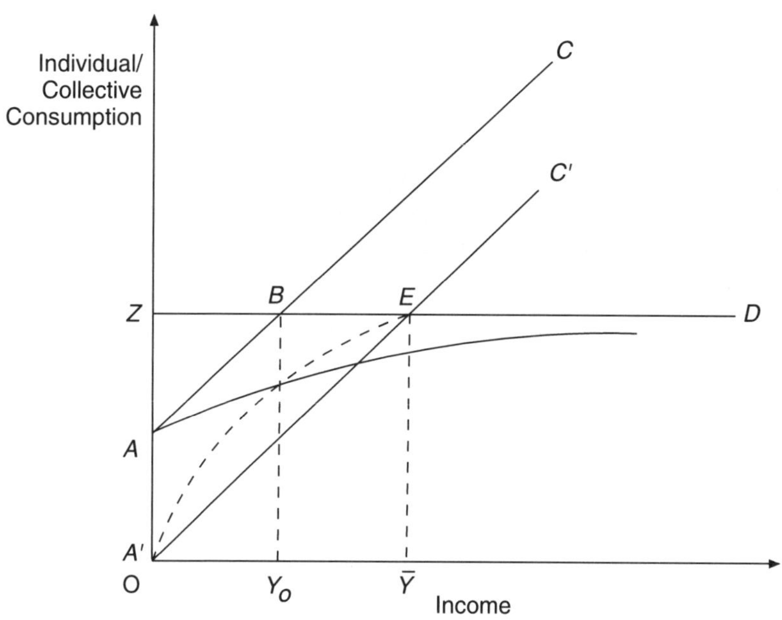

Figure 9.4 Ration resale and effective demand for a rationed good

convertible rations allows a welfare gain of the area *ABD*, but this is due to a reduction in the consumption of the good by poorer individuals, given that supply is fixed. Individuals, though, will be presented with an opportunity to fall through, for instance, a nutritional minimum standard, if this is incorporated in the safety net. In the early stages of a transition economy, supply will be inelastic in the short run, so the aggregate welfare-enhancing benefits of ration resale may prevail.

Transferable rations would encourage participation in the rationing scheme and, given that supply will initially be constrained, would not damage incentives. The appeal of rationing as a short-term measure only, part of a temporary social safety net rather than a permanent social security system, is reinforced if we presume that supply elasticities will rise in the longer term. As supply becomes more responsive, the benefits of rationing, and convertible rationing in particular, are increasingly offset by detrimental effects on production incentives. Given the administrative difficulties in preventing ration resale, its inevitable occurrence is another reason why a rationing scheme must be seen as a temporary measure of a transition economy rather than a permanent feature.

Income distribution

> The distribution of incomes is altered by rationing so that some consumers may be made better off even though rationing entails a departure from the conditions of optimal equilibrium.
>
> (Tobin, 1952, p. 545)

Whilst rationing is often seen as a crude device, it does guarantee the delivery of certain basic commodities to those severely displaced by transition, provided that subsidized prices are not prohibitive from a budgetary perspective, and that the government is stable. Weitzman (1977, p. 517), makes an obvious point:

> If a market clearing price is used, this may mean only that it will be driven up until those with more money end up with more of the deficit commodity.

Weitzman assumes that demand for a commodity in shortage is linear in real prices, allows for tastes, and derives an expression for the relative effectiveness of a rationing system in 'getting a commodity to those who need it most' *vis-à-vis* the price mechanism. Weitzman's analysis suggests that rationing, from a theoretical standpoint, rather than an ethical or administrative one, is more suitable than the price mechanism in distributing goods which display a low variance in demand patterns, and in situations of income inequality. However, if the aggregate deviation in demand is only marginally greater then the mean deviation for income, the price mechanism becomes relatively more desirable than a scheme employing rations.

In a pre-transition economy, demand patterns for essential goods may not differ greatly across income classes. However, inequality increases in most cases, as has been seen in Russia. The Weitzman arguments could be taken to apply in such conditions, leading to the rationing of an essential good during a transition period. However, while a traditional rationing mechanism would probably be unworkable in most transition economies, we argue below that a *modified* form of rationing, based on limited-quantity-denominated food-stamps, would be consistent with the operation of the market mechanism, and could provide an important step in protecting vulnerable consumers during the transition.

Budgetary implications

The budgetary implications of a new ration-type mechanism should be determined in relation to the status quo – typically including the situation where generalized subsidies are being provided, either explicitly, or implicitly (e.g. through combinations of an overvalued exchange rate, or through subsidized provision of inputs to the agricultural sector). The precise budgetary savings in replacing a general subsidy for a good by a ration would be a function of the pattern of consumption and the level at which the ration quota is set. As observed in IMF *et al.* (1991), typically the poorest two deciles in most countries of the FSU consumed around 40 percent of the average consumption of basic food items such as meat and edible oils. Thus a universal ration set at the consumption level of the second decile would reduce the subsidy cost to 40 percent of the pre-ration outlay.

In principle, it should be easy to restrict the ration still further, as was the case in China, to, say, the urban areas. This would further reduce the amount of the subsidy, and may also be acceptable if the 'supply response' in rural areas actually lifts agricultural incomes so that the effects of the price shock are reduced.

The poorest two deciles would be fully protected from the effects of the food price adjustment, and those with higher consumption levels would be correspondingly less protected. The ration thus acts like an *indexation mechanism*, where compensation on average is less than fully indexed on prices, with the level of indexation being greater for the poorer income groups.

Institutions and administration

It is evident that, where distribution channels do not exist, it would be administratively cumbersome to create these to facilitate a traditional rationing scheme. However, traditional state distribution networks could be used if they exist, as was the case in China, provided that this is for a limited period to absorb the effects of the agricultural price shock.

In some cases, even when state distribution networks exist, there is a possibility of hoarding and arbitrage by the managers of the ration outlets, leading to contrived shortages and queues – all features that were visible in the dying days of the Soviet Union. Thus the administrative costs of a traditional rationing mechanism may be quite significant. Further, there may be political advantages in eliminating the remaining vestiges of a command economy, as well as the inconvenience to consumers caused by hoarding and diversion of 'rationed' goods to the free market by retailers. But does this imply the disappearance of the 'safety net' and an inevitable reliance on ineffective and expensive implicit subsidization? We examine the institutional arrangements for an alternative in the following section.

FOOD-STAMPS AS AN ALTERNATIVE TO RATIONS

Fiscally prudent schemes can be designed, however, which maintain a uniform price for producers and a safety net for consumers in the midst of price reform. A possibility is to institute a system of convertible food-stamps, which would *not* be means tested during the transition period, to avoid the administrative difficulties that would be involved in this procedure. A similar scheme was proposed as one of the possible safety net options by the Joint Study on the Soviet Economy (IMF *et al.*, 1991). The food-stamps could be issued through post offices or banks, and could be geographically restricted, as in the traditional rationing case, for example to urban areas.

In order to provide *instantaneous* protection to the consumers during the early phase of the transition, or in developing countries following a major devaluation or price shock (essentially while price stability is still to be achieved), it may be preferable to denominate the food-stamps in kind, permitting the recipient to quantities, say, equivalent to the consumption of essential commodities by the poorest deciles.

A number of administrative arrangements are possible, and some of the permutations are outlined here. The food-stamps could be issued free of charge, and then used as payment for the specified items. Alternatively, the food-stamps could be sold to consumers by the distributing agency through, for example, post offices, entitling them to specified supplies by retailers. There would not have to be a special distribution network, and the food-stamps could be redeemed by private retailers as easily as by public distribution outlets. Again there are a number of possibilities – but the underlying principle is to eliminate the price wedge for the retailers, so that they would be indifferent between open market and food-stamp sales. One option is for redemption by monthly in-kind reimbursement for the retailer, plus a *handling fee*. This would eliminate information requirements on free market sales, but would require a state distribution network. The alternative is for a cash reimbursement (or redemption of food-stamps) based on average prices during the relevant period – with greater information requirements. It is to be stressed that the information requirements in the second case are considerably lower than would be needed if means testing were also to be incorporated.

But there are key differences from the pure ration model. The principal difference amongst these is that the kink (Figure 9.2) disappears with the introduction of the convertible food-stamps – which operate like partially indexed cash transfers to consumers. Also for the retailers, there is a single price (or approximately so, where there is cash redemption based on average prices) for the food-stamp items, with little or no incentive to discriminate against holders of food-stamps, or to divert supplies into other channels. This option also eliminates queues, and should be politically feasible. An advantage in not targeting too finely (e.g. on the basis of income and assets – which are also difficult to identify) is that the system could be used to engender a feeling of solidarity in the population (also one of the major aims of a ration system (Tobin, 1952)).

The main advantage of the safety net based on in-kind food-stamps is the reduction in uncertainty faced by consumers during the initial phases of the transition, when the price level is yet to stabilize, and there could be considerable spatial price variation. Once prices have stabilized, it should be possible to move to a food-stamp denominated in cash – this would considerably reduce any administrative complexity associated with redemption of in-kind food-stamps. As with all such schemes there are possibilities of abuse, but these could be minimized with additional features in the design, such as an expiry date on each food-stamp. However, this last feature could only be introduced if the regular availability of the specified good could be guaranteed.

The potential budgetary savings would depend, as in the pure ration model, on average consumption patterns and the level of protection that is desired. In time, both the quantity and the price at which the food-stamp is determined could be adjusted, so as to eliminate the subsidy (as with the ration system in China). The food-stamps could subsequently be used, as in the United States, to provide assistance to particular groups of the population, and would then be subject to different and more stringent eligibility criteria.

CONCLUDING REMARKS

Essentially the simple model outlined in this chapter characterizes the behavior of consumers, individual and in the aggregate, in the presence of a multiple (non-linear) budget constraint. Economic behavior is examined in an institutional structure significantly different from that of the free market. We argue that there are parallels in the policies needed to ensure the functioning of a market economy in disequilibrium, and those required for the transition from a planned economy to a market mechanism. Underlying the analysis are 'second-best' considerations that a degree of intervention should not be seen as necessarily detrimental to a broad reform process ostensibly designed to introduce the benefits of the free market.[11]

Traditional rationing mechanisms are open to considerable administrative complexity, and are subject to arbitrage and abuse by retailers – thus vitiating their usefulness as a safety net in many countries where administrative resources are at a premium. Thus, in general, when there is considerable administrative disruption during a transition, it is unlikely that a traditional rationing scheme will be suitable as an effective safety net.

But there are alternatives, which should be administratively more attractive, without the arbitrage temptations associated with traditional rationing, would avoid production disincentives, and could also continue to provide as much social protection as a well-designed and effectively functioning ration mechanism. As stressed by Tanzi, the entire debate needs to be set in the context of the 'administrative feasibility of various options' as well as the 'revenue crisis' during the early stages of transition.

NOTES

1 At the present time Ahmad is at the Fiscal Affairs Department, IMF, and Halligan is at the Centre for Economic Performance of the LSE, based in Moscow. The views expressed in this chapter are personal and do not implicate the institutions with which the authors are associated.

2 See e.g. Ahmad (1993) on the concentration of incomes at low levels in transition economies, and Atkinson and Micklewright (1992). In the Russian Federation, the Gini coefficient for income inequality for individuals increased from 0.24 at the beginning of 1992 to 0.41 during the fourth quarter of 1994 (*Russian Economic Trends*, 1994, Vol. 3).

3 In Poland, inflation accelerated from about 250 percent in 1989 to 585 percent in 1990, before slowing down to 70.3 percent in 1991 and 49 percent in 1992. Cuts in subsidies from 12.1 percent of GDP in 1989 to 1.8 percent in 1992 were broadly offset by increases in social spending, with pension expenditures rising from 7.1 percent in 1988 to 14.9 percent in 1992 (Kolodko, 1992). Budgetary transfers to the public pension system over the same period increased from 1.4 percent of GDP to 6.5 percent (Maret and Schwartz, 1993). These numbers illustrate the potential for large changes in the financial position of pension funds in economies in transition which, if not offset (as they were in Poland) by cuts in subsidies, could lead to continued unsustainable fiscal deficits.

4 See IMF *et al.* (1991) for a description before the breakup of the Former Soviet Union, and Atkinson and Micklewright (1992) for a detailed description of the patterns of income distribution and consumption in the transition economies.

5 Whilst this technique can only illustrate the rationing of a single good, it is possible to think of a selection of rationed goods as a Hicksian 'composite commodity', given that rationed prices will be administered and may often move in parallel.

6 When arbitrage is possible, of course, the budget line may be seen as linear. Resale of ration coupons and arbitrage can be seen as analytically identical in this case. They differ in that one involves trading a part entitlement to a good, while the other is a trading of the good itself.

7 The issue of coupon resale in China has received attention in work by Pudney and Limin (1991).

8 That said, arbitrage will temper the effectiveness of the rationing scheme in targeting consumption. We meet this trade-off again when considering coupon resale more fully.

9 Note that the relaxation in the quota is assumed not to change the free market price.

10 This is the view that specific commodities are of such importance that they should not be distributed as unevenly as the ability to pay for them would predict.

11 'Market mechanisms alone cannot succeed in transforming economies in which large clusters of the population are essentially immobile and initially dependent on large industrial enterprises that could not survive in a *laissez faire* environment' (Dooley and Isard, 1991).

REFERENCES

Ahmad, E. (1992) 'Poverty, Inequality and Public Policy in Transition Economies', in P. Pestieu (ed.) *Public Finance in a World of Transition*, *Public Finance*, Vol. 47, pp. 94–106.

Ahmad, E. (1993) 'Poverty, Demography and Public Policy in CIS Countries', in B. Wolfe (ed.) *On the Role of Budgetary Policy during Demographic Changes*, *Public Finance*, Vol. 48, pp. 366–379.

Atkinson, A.B., and J. Micklewright (1992) *Economic Transformation in Eastern Europe and the Distribution of Income*, Cambridge University Press.

Dooley, M.P., and P. Isard (1991) 'Establishing Incentive Structures and Planning Agencies that Support Market-Orientated Transformations', *IMF Working Paper*, WP/91/113.

Ebrill, L.P., A. Chopra, C. Christofides, P. Mylonas, I. Otker, and G. Schwartz (1994) 'Poland – the Path to a Market Economy', *Occasional Paper 113*, Washington, DC: International Monetary Fund.

Goldman, M.I. (1994) *Lost Opportunity – Why Economic Reforms in Russia have not Worked*, New York: Norton.

International Monetary Fund, World Bank, Organization for Economic Cooperation and Development, and European Bank for Reconstruction and Development (1991) *A Study of the Soviet Economy*, Vols I, II, III, Washington, DC: IMF.

Kolodko, G. (1992) 'From Output Collapse to Sustainable Growth in Transition Economies: The Fiscal Implications', *Mimeo*, Washington, DC.

Maret, X., and G. Schwartz (1993) 'Poland: The Social Safety-net During the Transition', Working Paper, Fiscal Affairs Department, International Monetary Fund.

Neary, J.P., and K. Roberts (1980) 'The Theory of Household Behavior under Rationing', *European Economic Review*, No.13, pp. 25–42.

Pudney, S., and Limin Wang (1991) 'Rationing and Consumer Demand in China: Simulating the Effects of Reform in the Urban Food Pricing System', *London School of Economics*, DERP – CP No. 15.

Tanzi, V. (ed.) (1992) *Fiscal Policies in Economies in Transition*, Washington, DC: IMF.

Tanzi, V. (1993) 'Fiscal Policy and the Economic Restructuring of Economies in Transition, *IMF Working Paper*, WP/93/22.

Tobin, J. (1952) 'A Survey of the Theory of Rationing', *Econometrica*, Vol. 20, pp. 521–533.

Van Wijnbergen, S. (1992) 'Intertemporal Speculation, Shortages and the Political

Economy of Price Reform', *Economic Journal*, Vol. 102, pp. 1395–1406.
Weitzman, M.L. (1977) 'Is the Price System or Rationing more Effective in Getting a Commodity to Those Who Need it Most?', *Bell Journal of Economics*, pp. 517–524.

Part V

FISCAL POLICY REFORMS AND THE TRANSITION FROM CENTRAL PLANNING

10

EXCESS WAGES TAX

Alan A. Tait and S. Nuri Erbas[1]

SUMMARY

Excess wages tax (EWT) is a tax-based incomes policy instrument used in some FSU and East European countries in transition. Under EWT, the government taxes the excess of the wage bill above the norm, calculated typically on the basis of inflation and some multiple of the prevailing minimum wage. The main goal of EWT is to curb inflationary pressures by penalizing through taxation the 'excessive' wage awards granted by enterprises in the course of wage and price liberalization. This chapter examines the effect of EWT on enterprise behavior, wages, profits, and its possible impact on inflation.

First, EWT's impact on the profit-maximizing enterprise under monopsony is examined as a benchmark. It is shown that EWT increases the marginal cost of labor. Consequently, although EWT serves to lower the wage award, this is achieved at the cost of lower output and employment, and smaller profits. Also, EWT penalizes more productive enterprises. The impact of EWT on total tax revenue (standard corporate tax revenue plus EWT revenue) is ambiguous because even though the statutory tax base with EWT is broader, taxable profit is lower. Furthermore, although EWT can curb the enterprises' wage awards in the face of inflation, EWT can be pro-inflationary and even result in stagflation, depending on the government's minimum wage policy.

A more realistic model for enterprise behavior in the economies in transition is provided by the labor-dominated enterprise. In this case, with homogeneous labor, it is shown that EWT results in a decline in wages. With heterogeneous labor (managers and workers), wages will also decline, regardless of whether labor shedding is feasible. However, it is argued that the impact of EWT on wages is moot and the main determinant of wage awards is the degree of fiscal discipline imposed by the government or the extent to which the government subsidizes the enterprise. It is further argued that EWT does not necessarily serve to curb asset stripping by the employees to pay for higher wage awards.

The experience with EWT in some FSU and East European countries is reviewed briefly. Notably, the evidence from Poland suggests that while EWT has reduced wage awards, it has penalized more productive enterprises, is likely to be highly distortionary, and is not directly correlated with asset stripping. The evidence concerning the impact of EWT on inflation is inconclusive.

The chapter suggests that the only role for an EWT might be as a temporary measure implemented on the way to privatization and competition. However, even in that role, the distortions introduced would be likely to slow the pace of transition, discourage rapid adaptation, and penalize efficiency and innovation. It is better to control credit expansion, impose credible budget constraints and performance requirements on state-owned enterprises, permit bankruptcy when necessary, and expose the protected enterprises to competition and privatization.

INTRODUCTION

Tax-based incomes policies (TIPs) were debated in the economic literature in the late 1970s and early 1980s when the industrial countries went through a highly inflationary period.[2] A TIP was introduced in France (see below) briefly in 1975 but their serious application was in the socialist centrally planned economies of Central and Eastern Europe. The dissolution of the centrally planned economies of the former Soviet Union (FSU) and Eastern Europe and the structural adjustment efforts that followed resulted in inflationary pressures in those countries and a rejuvenated interest in TIPs. A policy instrument under the general umbrella of TIPs, called the excess wages tax (EWT), has been adopted in one form or another in almost all the FSU and East European countries. An assessment of the theory and practice of the EWT may help inform any future policy makers who may be tempted to experiment.

The application of EWT in the FSU and East European countries is summarized in Table 10.1. The government sets a 'norm' on a quarterly or annual basis that takes into account the projected rate of inflation, often with reference to some multiple of the prevailing minimum wage. Then, the excess of the enterprise's wage bill over and above the norm is taxed at the standard corporate income tax rate; that is, the excess wage bill is not allowed to be deducted as a cost of production. In some countries, the excess wage bill is taxed at special progressive rates (Bulgaria, Estonia, Latvia, Poland).

In most countries, the tax is applied as explained in the following example which is representative of the general practice.[3] Suppose that the minimum wage, as stipulated by law or as chosen by the government, in units of domestic currency (DC), is DC 800 per month, and a given enterprise employs 100 workers. The workers of the enterprise are paid according to a given wage scale under which many employees are paid wages which exceed the minimum wage. However, by imputing the minimum wage to the existing number of workers, a hypothetical 'enterprise minimum monthly wage bill' is calculated as DC 80,000 per month. The law specifies that EWT is applicable when the actual monthly wage bill for all employees (paid at different pay scales at or above the minimum wage) exceeds a certain predetermined multiple of the minimum monthly wage bill. If the predetermined multiple is 6, then the relevant threshold is DC 480,000 per month. So, if the actual monthly wage bill of the enterprise is DC 500,000 per month, the difference of DC 20,000 is added to the reported profit of the enterprise to be taxed at the standard enterprise profits tax rate. For example, if the monthly reported profit of the enterprise were DC 100,000, then its taxable profit including the EWT base would be calculated at DC 120,000. Thus, if the tax rate were 40 percent, the enterprise's tax liability would be increased from DC 40,000 to DC 48,000.

The main macroeconomic goal of EWT is to curb inflationary pressures in the economy by penalizing through taxation the 'excessive' wage awards granted by the managers of state-owned enterprises (SOEs) during the course of wage and price liberalization. An EWT can be seen as a sort of bridge between completely planned and executed wage norms and awards by SOEs and full market determination of wages. In practice, in most countries, the emphasis is on modifying the willingness of SOE managers to pay larger wage increases. With relaxed or no price constraints enforced through a national plan, enterprise managers can buy industrial peace and possibly reap personal gain by increased wage awards. The presumption is that SOE managers, often in a protected dominant market position, once price control is lifted, can pass on cost increases to the consumer. So, although SOEs are allowed to determine wages, EWT penalizes and, supposedly, helps restrain excessive wage awards. Similarly, worker behavior in demanding higher wages also is supposed to be modified in consideration of EWT. Thus, if EWT can be expected to lower wages, it might be intended to serve as an indirect policy tool to lower unemployment and restrain cost-push inflation.

Additionally, EWT may serve as a temporary tool in the course of the transition to a full market economy. The SOEs in the FSU and East European countries are huge employers and the breakdown of COMECON has shattered their markets and abruptly reduced the demand for their products. If, in addition, SOEs had to face international competition, the unemployment consequences might be deemed unacceptable. Therefore, it may be argued that, during the transition, SOEs must be allowed to continue operating in a protected market, which allows them to pass forward costs. Consequently, 'unreasonable' costs or 'excessive' wage awards must be controlled to curb inflationary pressures – hence EWT. Nevertheless, this line of reasoning begs the question of how the government will force SOEs to become more competitive and profitable and whether EWT can be instrumental in this process. The real problem is the lack of competition in wage and price determination and the main issue is the determination and success of the government in encouraging competition through implementing a hard budget constraint on SOEs. If governments were prepared to allow SOEs to operate

Table 10.1 Some examples of EWTs, 1992–4

	Base	*Coverage*	*Norm*	*Rates*	*Notes*
Armenia	Wage bill	All enterprises	Five times the minimum wage	Taxed at the corporate rate	
Azerbaijan	Wages bill in excess of four times the minimum wage	All enterprises	Four times the minimum wage	Not treated as costs and hence taxed at full corporate rate (35–70 percent)	
Belarus	Wage bill	SOE	Four times the minimum wage	Taxed at the corporate rate	Abolished the EWT Nov./Dec. 1992
Bulgaria	Wage bill quarterly	Enterprises with 50 percent and state participation	Excess of quarterly ceiling based on projected inflation and seasonal factors	Progressive rates up to 800 percent	See Appendix IV
Estonia	Average employee compensation	Government sector	Full compensation for targeted inflation (maintained real wage)	Rates for wages in excess of norm 1–3 percent 200 percent > 3 percent 400 percent	Special allowances for price increases in some goods, e.g., bread, gas, etc. Abolished June 1993
Hungary	Wages bill increases	Government enterprises	Exceeding the value added of the firm	Not treated as costs and hence taxed at full corporate rate	Abolished EWT Jan. 1992
Kazakhstan	Wages in excess of four times the minimum wage	All enterprises	Four times the minimum wage	Not treated as costs and hence taxed at full corporate rate (35–70 percent)	Parliamentary approval sought in May 1992 but rejected
Kyrgyzstan	Wages in excess of six times the minimum wage	All enterprises	Six times the minimum wage	Not treated as costs and hence taxed at full corporate rate (35 percent)	

Table 10.1 continued

Latvia	Wage bill	SOE	Government-determined norm for each quarter	1–2 percent 150 percent > 2 percent 350 percent	If actual inflation exceeds projections by over 10 percent the target for the following quarter is adjusted. An allowance for productivity is made
Moldova	Wages bill in excess of four times the minimum wage	All enterprises	Four times the minimum wage	Not treated as costs and hence taxed at full corporate rate (32–80 percent)	
Poland	Average wage	SOE	Average wages set by Council of Ministers	Rates for wages in excess of norm: 0–3 percent 100 percent 3–6 percent 200 percent > 6 percent 300 percent	(a) Exemptions can be negotiated; (b) SOE *reducing* average employment can increase wage norm by half wage norm lost due to employment reduction
Russia	Quarterly wage bill		Six times the monthly minimum wage	Taxed at corporate rate 32 percent	
Turkmenistan	Wages bill in excess of four times the minimum wage	All enterprises	Four times the minimum wage	Not treated as costs and hence taxed at full corporate rate (32–60 percent)	

in truly competitive markets for goods and factors, then the successful enterprises could reward labor and management as they wished. However, it appears that EWT by itself does nothing to encourage competition and greater efficiency. In contrast, it may be argued that EWT appears to trap SOEs like the fly in amber in a semi-permanent non-competitive state without imposing an appreciable constraint on their inefficiency. Therefore, the underlying and unstated intent of EWT might be allowing SOEs to continue operating in an inefficient manner.

Although not necessarily and specifically designed to do so, EWT can also be seen as a tool to encourage private sector growth. In many countries, in particular in Eastern Europe (Bulgaria, Estonia, Latvia, Poland), EWT applies only to the state-owned sector. The underlying assumption behind this practice seems to be that, in an economy dominated by non-competitive public enterprises, the private sector, in its infancy, needs incentives for growth and the profit-maximization motive should be allowed to take root in that sector.

It has also been argued that EWT may have a preventive impact on malfeasance by the SOE managers and workers through asset stripping. During the course of privatization, the property rights are rather ambiguous and the SOE managers may be tempted to sell the assets of SOEs to pay large wage increases to the workers – or at least the favored workers. EWT may help reduce the incentive for such asset stripping by penalizing excess wage awards.

Finally, EWT may be instrumental in generating additional tax revenue by indirectly serving, in essence, as a surtax on corporations over and above the standard corporate income tax. However, although relatively significant revenues are collected from EWT in some countries, the revenue that can be generated by EWT appears to be limited.[4] A relatively small increase in the standard corporate income tax rate would be sufficient to generate additional revenue to more than match the revenue potential of most EWT.

Conceptually, EWT may achieve one or more of its explicit or implicit goals. There are two main drawbacks. First, in the second-best context in which EWT should be evaluated, its superiority (lower excess burden) over an alternative TIP scheme has to be argued on highly theoretical grounds and is therefore difficult to demonstrate in an empirically measurable way. For example, if the goal is to curb 'excessive' wage awards by affecting management and labor behavior, instead of EWT, a portion of the wages may be paid under a profit-sharing agreement. Then, if the enterprise is making losses, the workers participate in the enterprise's losses by taking proportionate wage cuts.[5] Further, it is not immediately apparent why the use of a conventional tax tool would create greater distortions and therefore be inferior to EWT or any other TIP scheme. If the goal is increasing output and employment levels and encouraging the private sector, this may be achieved by providing a conventional set of tax incentives to the more productive enterprises and sectors in the economy. If the goal is to increase government revenue, this may be achieved by means of resorting to a more familiar menu of conventional taxes. Then, with sufficient expenditure restraint, higher government revenue may reduce recourse to inflationary finance and help lower inflation. The second drawback of EWT is the administrative difficulties it may pose in application. For example, it is difficult to discern how much of the workers' wages above the minimum wage or the norm is to be deemed 'excessive' and how much should be attributable to inflation adjustment or increases in productivity.

This chapter analyzes the impact on enterprise behavior of a simplified version of EWT and examines whether such a tax can actually contribute toward some of its apparent general goals. A model of the impact of EWT on the behavior of the profit-maximizing enterprise is presented in the next section along with an analysis of the incidence of EWT and its possible impact on inflation. While the profit-maximization motive may be unrealistic in the case of SOEs, this model provides a benchmark for the analysis of the more realistic case of the labor-dominated enterprise. Under an alternative specification that the enterprise maximizes workers' income, the effects of EWT on enterprise behavior are examined and some observations on the impact of EWT on managerial behavior are presented in the third section. The experience with EWT in some FSU and East European countries is discussed in the section after that, and concluding remarks are presented in the final section. Some technical proofs are presented in Appendices I, II, and III. In addition, in Appendix IV the text of the Bulgarian decree on the 'Increment and Formation of Wage Funds in 1994' is presented as an example of legislation and regulations.

THE PROFIT-MAXIMIZING ENTERPRISE

The model

This model assumes that the profit-maximization motive dominates corporate behavior. This assumption may not be very suitable to examine the behavior of SOEs in the transition economies. Nevertheless, it provides a framework for a first-order analysis of the impact of EWT and is pertinent owing to the ongoing reform efforts to restructure and privatize SOEs in the process of transition to a competitive market system in which the profit motive is dominant.

Let us assume that the representative enterprise employs ℓ types of labor, n_i, $i = 1, 2, \ldots, \ell$, and each type of labor is paid the nominal wage, W_i. Let us further assume that capital, k, is homogeneous, the return to capital accrues to the enterprise,[6] and the enterprise produces a single good which it sells in a competitive market at price p. Let the production function be

$$f(k, n_1, n_2, \ldots, n_\ell)$$
$$f_k > 0; \quad f_{n_i} > 0, \quad i = 1, 2, \ldots, \ell. \tag{10.1}$$

The total (real) wage bill of the enterprise can be expressed as

$$\sum_{i=1}^{\ell} w_i n_i \tag{10.2}$$

where $w_i = W_i/p$. Assuming that the corporate income tax is levied at a single rate, $0 < \tau < 1$, the enterprise profit, π, is

$$\pi = (1-\tau)[f(\;) - \sum_{i=1}^{\ell} w_i n_i]. \tag{10.3}$$

Suppose the economy-wide minimum wage is determined by the government at $\bar{W}$.[7] Hypothetically, if all types of labor were paid the minimum wage, the enterprise's total wage bill would be

$$\bar{w} \sum_{i=1}^{\ell} n_i \tag{10.4}$$

where $\bar{w} = \bar{W}/p$. EWT is triggered if the total wage bill, as expressed in (10.2), exceeds a predetermined multiple, $\alpha \geq 1$, of the hypothetical wage bill calculated at the minimum wage, as expressed in (10.4). Therefore, the EWT base is

$$(\sum_{i=1}^{\ell} w_i n_i - \alpha \bar{w} \sum_{i=1}^{\ell} n_i) \tag{10.5}$$

to be taxed at the standard corporate income tax rate, τ.[8] Then, the enterprise after-tax profit with EWT, π^*, is

$$\begin{aligned} \pi^* &= (1-\tau)[f(\;) - \sum_{i=1}^{\ell} w_i n_i] - \tau(\sum_{i=1}^{\ell} w_i n_i - \alpha \bar{w} \sum_{i=1}^{\ell} n_i) \\ &= (1-\tau) f(\;) - (\sum_{i=1}^{\ell} w_i n_i - \tau \alpha \bar{w} \sum_{i=1}^{\ell} n_i). \end{aligned} \tag{10.6}$$

The analysis can be simplified if we assume k is constant, labor is homogeneous ($\ell = 1$), and $\alpha = 1$.[9] Under these assumptions, (10.3) and (10.6) simplify to, respectively,

$$\pi = (1-\tau)[f(n) - wn] \tag{10.7}$$

$$\begin{aligned} \pi^* &= (1-\tau)[f(n) - wn] - \tau(w - \bar{w})n \\ &= (1-\tau) f(n) - (w - \tau \bar{w})n \end{aligned} \tag{10.8}$$

where k is suppressed.

Competitive labor market

If the profit-maximizing enterprise were facing a perfectly competitive labor market, with or without EWT, the enterprise would take w as given and maximize profit by choosing n. Then, from (10.7) and (10.8), the equilibria without and with EWT are

$$f_n = w \tag{10.9}$$

$$f_n^* = (w - \tau\bar{w})/(1-\tau) \tag{10.10}$$

where f_n and f_n^* are respectively the marginal product of labor without and with EWT. Notice that if $w \leq \bar{w}$, the minimum wage becomes the wage floor which the enterprise takes as given to maximize profit by choosing n. Then, as is clear from (10.9) and (10.10), with $w = \bar{w}$, $f_n = f_n^*$; hence $\pi = \pi^*$, that is EWT has no impact on enterprise behavior. If $w > \bar{w}$, the comparison of the right-hand side of (10.9) and (10.10) shows that marginal cost with EWT is higher than without EWT; then, as is generally true, $f_n < f_n^*$; hence $n > n^*$, and $f(n) > f(n^*)$. Therefore, although in a competitive labor market EWT has no impact on the wage level, it reduces the amount of labor employed by the enterprise and output. It is also interesting to note that the closer $\bar{w}$ is to the market wage, w, the closer the output level with EWT will be to the output level without EWT, and conversely (see below).

Monopsonist enterprise

Since the main purpose of imposing EWT is presumably to discourage 'excessive' wage awards by the enterprise, in order to conjecture that the enterprise has the leeway to affect the wage rate, we need to assume that the enterprise has monopsony power. We assume that the enterprise takes $\bar{w}$ as given and may not pay a wage below it; however, as a monopsonist, the enterprise may choose to pay a wage exceeding $\bar{w}$ and bear the implied EWT liability. This assumption implies that labor supply is less than perfectly elastic. Accordingly, let us further assume that labor supply is a function of w as in

$$n^s = n(w) \tag{10.11}$$

where $\partial n/\partial w = n' > 0$. Suppose the enterprise pays an excess over and above $\bar{w}$ such that

$$w = \bar{w} + b; \quad w^* = \bar{w} + b^*, \quad b, b^* \geq 0 \tag{10.12}$$

where, respectively, w and w^* are the wages and b and b^* are the excesses over the minimum wage paid without and with EWT.

Maximizing (10.7) with respect to w and making use of (10.11) and (10.12), the profit-maximizing levels of w and b without EWT are

$$w = \frac{\theta}{1 + \theta} f_n; \quad b = \frac{\theta}{1 + \theta} f_n - \bar{w} \tag{10.13}$$

where $\theta = (w/n)n'$, which is the elasticity of supply of labor. Similarly, maximizing (10.8) with respect to w and making use of (10.11) and (10.12), we can show that the profit-maximizing levels of w and b with EWT are

$$\begin{gathered} w^* = \frac{\theta}{1 + \theta}[(1 - \tau)f_n + \tau\bar{w}] \\ b^* = \frac{\theta}{1 + \theta}(1 - \tau)f_n - \frac{\bar{w}}{1 + \theta}[1 + \theta(1 - \tau)]. \end{gathered} \tag{10.14}$$

In order to focus on EWT's impact on the wage award by the enterprise, we shall restrict the analysis in the rest of this section to the monopsonist enterprise case which allows for greater scope in examining the impact of EWT on 'excessive' wage awards.[10]

The incidence of EWT

Let us first examine the case where $\theta = 0$ or labor supply is perfectly inelastic. In this case, (10.13) and (10.14) imply that $b = b^* = 0$ since $b, b^* \geq 0$ by assumption; hence $w = w^* = \bar{w}$, that is the monopsonist enterprise pays the lowest wage possible. Therefore, $\pi = \pi^*$ and the equilibrium wage and employment levels are not affected by EWT.

To examine the intermediate case when $0 < \theta < \infty$, let us first note from (10.7) that the total (effective) cost of production without EWT is $C = (1 - \tau)wn$; hence the marginal cost is

$$g = (1 - \tau)(n + wn'). \tag{10.15}$$

Similarly, (10.8) indicates that the total (effective) cost of production with EWT is $C^* = (w - \tau\bar{w})n$; hence the marginal cost is

$$g^* = (n + wn') - \tau\bar{w}n'. \tag{10.16}$$

Comparison of g and g^* shows that, as in the competitive labor market case,

$$g < g^* \tag{10.17}$$

for all $w > \bar{w}$. The enterprise maximizes profit by equating marginal cost to marginal revenue. Notice that, with or without EWT, the net marginal product is plotted by $(1-\tau)f_n n'$ for all $w \geq \bar{w}$. Therefore, in equilibrium,

$$w^* < w; \quad b^* < b; \quad n^* < n \tag{10.18}$$

where n^* is the equilibrium level of employment with EWT corresponding to w^* and n is the equilibrium level of employment corresponding to w.[11] Hence the output level with EWT is less than the output level without EWT.

As regards the profit level, comparison of (10.7) and (10.8) in equilibrium shows that maximum profit with EWT, $\pi^*_{\max}$, is less than maximum profit without EWT, $\pi_{\max}$, that is

$$\pi^*_{\max} = (1-\tau)[f(n^*) - w^*n^*] - \tau(w^* - \bar{w})n^*;$$

$$\pi_{\max} = (1-\tau)[f(n) - wn]; \tag{10.19}$$

$$\pi^*_{\max} < \pi_{\max}$$

unambiguously; (10.19) holds since $w > w^*$ or the wage level at which (10.7) is maximized is not the same as w^*.[12]

It may also be noted that EWT penalizes more productive enterprises. From (10.13), we can show that, without EWT, for the enterprise to pay $w > \bar{w}$, the marginal product of labor needs to be such that $f_n > \bar{w}(1+\theta)/\theta$. But with EWT, for $w^* > \bar{w}$, (10.14) indicates that it is necessary to have $f_n > \bar{w}[1+\theta(1-\tau)]/\theta(1-\tau)$, and, for constant θ, $[1+\theta(1-\tau)]/\theta(1-\tau) > (1+\theta)/\theta$.

First suppose the enterprise's (labor) productivity without EWT is such that it pays the minimum wage; then, the enterprise is unaffected by the imposition of EWT. Now suppose that the enterprise productivity without EWT is such that $(1+\theta)/\theta < f_n < \bar{w}[1+\theta(1-\tau)]/\theta(1-\tau)$; then, with EWT, the enterprise pays the minimum wage. Only if the enterprise productivity is high enough such that $f_n > \bar{w}[1+\theta(1-\tau)]/\theta(1-\tau)$, is it profitable for the enterprise to pay a wage exceeding the minimum and bear the burden of EWT. It follows that the more productive enterprises are the ones to pay wages exceeding the minimum wage under EWT.

To recapitulate, the incidence of EWT is both on labor and the enterprise; with EWT, wage and profit are lower than they would be without EWT.

If the enterprise profit is totally or partially transferred to the government, then the government revenue also suffers from the decline in profits resulting from the imposition of EWT, which may or may not be wholly compensated by EWT revenue, because tax revenue with EWT is not necessarily greater than revenue without EWT. Tax revenue collected from the enterprise without and with EWT can be expressed as, respectively,

$$T = \tau[f(n) - wn] \tag{10.20}$$

$$\begin{aligned} T^* &= \tau[f(n^*) - w^*n^*] + \tau(w^* - \bar{w})n^* \\ &= \tau[f(n^*) - \bar{w}n^*]. \end{aligned} \tag{10.21}$$

Comparison of (10.20) and (10.21) shows that $T^* \geq T$ if

$$[f(n^*) - \bar{w}n^*] \geq [f(n) - wn]. \tag{10.22}$$

Since the condition in (10.22) need not hold in general, the imposition of EWT may well result in a net loss of tax revenue to the government. This is because even though the statutory tax base with EWT is broader, taxable profit is lower.[13]

The incentive to avoid EWT

The enterprise may have the leeway to remunerate workers in ways that do not trigger EWT (see the Russian example below). For example, certain types of bonuses or overtime pay may not be included in the statutory EWT base and the excess of the wage bill over the hypothetical wage bill for EWT purposes may thus be lowered. Let us assume that all payments in excess of the minimum wage may be deducted as cost under the corporate income tax but only the portion $0 < \beta < 1$ of such payments is entered in the EWT base. Under these assumptions, the enterprise profit under EWT, denoted as $\pi^*(\beta)$, can be expressed as

$$\begin{aligned} \pi^*(\beta) &= (1-\tau)f(n) - (1-\tau)(\bar{w} + b^*)n - \tau(\bar{w} + \beta b^* - \bar{w})n \\ &= (1-\tau)[f(n) - \bar{w}n] - [(1-\tau) + \tau\beta]b^*n. \end{aligned} \tag{10.23}$$

If $\beta = 0$, all EWT liability is avoided; if $\beta = 1$, the EWT liability is paid in full. From (10.23), it can be shown that

$$\partial\pi^*(\beta)/\partial\beta < 0 \tag{10.24}$$

for any $b^* > 0$. Therefore, the greater the leeway to avoid EWT, the higher the profit and w^*; hence both the enterprise and the workers have an incentive to collude in order to avoid EWT.

The incidence of EWT with two types of labor

Now suppose that the enterprise employs two types of labor, skilled and unskilled, denoted respectively by n_1 and n_2. Further assume that n_2 is paid the minimum wage whereas n_1 may be paid a wage, w_1, exceeding the minimum wage; that is, the enterprise takes $\bar{w}$ as given and chooses the level of w_1 and n_2. Then, from (10.3), the enterprise profit without EWT is

$$\pi = (1 - \tau)[f(n_1, n_2) - (w_1 n_1 + \bar{w} n_2)]. \tag{10.25}$$

Maximizing (10.25) with respect to w_1 and n_2, we obtain

$$w_1 = \frac{\theta_1}{1 + \theta_1} f_1, \quad b_1 = \frac{\theta_1}{1 + \theta_1} f_1 - \bar{w};$$
$$f_2 = \bar{w}, \quad b_2 = 0 \tag{10.26}$$

where f_1 and f_2 refer respectively to the marginal product of n_1 and n_2 and b_1 and b_2 to the increments exceeding the minimum wage paid to n_1 and n_2, and θ_1 refers to the elasticity of supply of n_1.

However, with EWT, and $\alpha = 1$ as before, the enterprise profit from (10.6) is

$$\pi^* = (1 - \tau) f(n_1, n_2) - (w_1 - \tau \bar{w}) n_1 - (1 - \tau) \bar{w} n_2. \tag{10.27}$$

Maximization of (10.27) yields

$$w_1^* = \frac{\theta_1}{1 + \theta_1} [(1 - \tau) f_1 + \tau \bar{w}]$$

$$b_1^* = \frac{\theta_1}{1 + \theta_1} (1 - \tau) f_1 - \frac{\bar{w}}{1 + \theta_1} [1 + \theta_1 (1 - \tau)]; \tag{10.28}$$

$$f_2 = \bar{w}, \quad b_2^* = 0.$$

Under the assumption that θ_1 is constant, it is shown in Appendix I that

$$w_1^* < w_1, \quad n_1^* < n_1; \tag{10.29}$$

that is, the wage and employment levels of skilled labor with EWT are lower than they would be without EWT. If the two types of labor are complementary

($f_{12} > 0$), this result implies that the level of employment of n_2 is lower with EWT than it would be without EWT; therefore, output with EWT also is lower. Along with the results obtained earlier, it can also be shown that the enterprise profit is lower; hence the incidence of EWT is on both the (skilled and unskilled) workers and the enterprise. Thus, if the skilled workers can be viewed as the managers, the managers also bear the burden of EWT along with the unskilled workers. Finally, the impact of EWT on tax revenue remains ambiguous as before.

The impact of EWT on inflation

The discussion in this section will be restricted to the homogeneous labor case discussed earlier where the analysis has been conducted under the assumption of constant prices. The same results hold with perfectly anticipated inflation since, given the inflation rate and the real minimum wage, the profit-maximizing enterprise will adjust the nominal wage such that (10.13) and (10.14) hold. It is shown in Appendix II that, in the absence of EWT, adjustment of the minimum wage with respect to inflation does not affect the equilibrium because $\partial w/\partial \bar{w} = 0$; however, the government's minimum wage policy with respect to inflation affects the wage level under EWT because

$$\partial w^*/\partial \bar{w} > 0. \qquad (10.30)$$

This result is due to the fact that when $\bar{w}$ is increased the EWT base declines for any $w^* > \bar{w}$ and the tax penalty for paying a wage exceeding the minimum wage is diminished at the margin. The result in (10.30) implies that, with EWT, the government has the leeway to lower the wage award granted by the enterprise by means of lowering the minimum wage. In an inflationary environment, this policy would amount to adjusting the nominal minimum wage, $\bar{W}$, at a rate less than the rate of inflation which would result in a lower real minimum wage and therefore a lower real wage paid by the enterprise exceeding the real minimum wage.[14] Therefore, even though EWT affords the government the facility to lower the wage award granted by the enterprise in the face of inflation, this happens at the cost of lower output since in this model lower w^* implies a lower level of employment.[15]

Against the background provided by the foregoing observations, the relevant question is: can EWT result in a lower rate of inflation given the rate of increase in money supply? The following heuristic arguments indicate that the answer is negative.[16] For simplicity, let us assume that all the enterprises in the economy are identical so that aggregate output of the economy, Y, is the sum of the outputs of z individual firms. Let us further suppose that capital stock is constant and the trend growth rate of the economy is zero. Then, the relationship in (10.30) indicates that aggregate output can be expressed as a function of the minimum wage as

$$Y = zf\{n[w(\overline{w})]\} = zh(\overline{w});$$
$$\partial Y/\partial \overline{w} = z(\partial h/\partial \overline{w}) > 0. \tag{10.31}$$

At a point in time, suppose the equilibrium in the economy is determined by the quantity equation, $MV = PY$, where V is velocity, which is assumed to be constant, M is the money stock, and P is the price level.[17] Substituting (10.31) into the quantity equation, we obtain

$$P = VM/Y = (VM/z)[1/h(\overline{w})]$$
$$\partial P/\partial \overline{w} < 0. \tag{10.32}$$

First, let us assume that M is constant. Given the minimum wage, when EWT is imposed, then the equilibrium real wage and aggregate employment level decline ($w^* < w$, $zn^* < zn$) and therefore aggregate output declines ($Y^* < Y$). It follows that, given M, the price level jumps.[18]

Price dynamics under EWT can be evaluated by taking the logarithm of (10.32) and differentiating with respect to time. Thus, it can be shown that the dynamic relationship between the price level and the minimum wage is

$$\rho = \mu - \varepsilon\omega;$$
$$\rho = \frac{1}{P}\frac{\mathrm{d}P}{\mathrm{d}t}; \quad \mu = \frac{1}{M}\frac{\mathrm{d}M}{\mathrm{d}t}; \quad \omega = \frac{1}{\overline{w}}\frac{\mathrm{d}\overline{w}}{\mathrm{d}t}; \quad \varepsilon = \frac{\overline{w}}{h(\overline{w})}\frac{\partial h}{\partial \overline{w}} > 0. \tag{10.33}$$

Of course, (10.33) does not represent a steady-state equilibrium since the minimum wage cannot decrease or increase indefinitely. However, it is possible to imagine that, for a period of time, the inflation adjustment in the minimum wage is such that the government allows the minimum wage to decrease (see the case of Poland below) or increase. As long as the minimum wage is adjusted with respect to inflation ($\omega = 0$), the inflation rate is equal to the rate of money creation and (10.33) describes a steady-state equilibrium. If the minimum wage is allowed to decrease over a period ($\omega < 0$), then output declines and the inflation rate exceeds the rate of money creation ($\rho > \mu$). The reverse arguments hold if the minimum wage is adjusted such that for a period of time it increases and output rises and inflation rate declines.

The foregoing arguments indicate that, although instrumental in curbing the wage award by the enterprise in the face of inflation, depending on the government's minimum wage policy, EWT can actually be pro-inflationary and even result in stagflation.

THE LABOR-DOMINATED ENTERPRISE

Homogeneous labor

Throughout the previous section we assumed that the enterprise's objective was profit maximization. However, this assumption may not be representative of the behavior of the state-owned enterprises. Such enterprises are often controlled by labor unions or, at least, unions exert decisive influence on management decisions.[19] Therefore, alternatively, we may conjecture that the enterprise's objective is to maximize its workers' income subject to a profit constraint as determined by the government which owns the enterprise. In other words, we assume that the enterprise is under obligation to pay tax out of its gross profit and transfer a fixed net profit to the government. The profit constraint set by the government essentially corresponds to the extent to which the government is willing to support the enterprise. For example, if the profit target is set at a negative level, this would imply that the government is subsidizing the enterprise. Such a subsidy would likely be in the form of easy credit extended to the enterprise either directly by the government or through the state-controlled banking system. In this sense, the profit target can be interpreted as the parameter that establishes the extent to which the government is willing to impose a hard budget constraint on the enterprise.

As regards the wage and employment policy of the labor-dominated enterprise, two simple cases are considered. In the first case, we assume that the enterprise takes the present level of employment as given and does not lay off workers and, at the same time, the workers supply labor inelastically; that is, the number of workers employed by the enterprise is given. This conjecture appears to be roughly representative of the employment policy of the state-owned enterprises in the FSU which are either unable to or unwilling to effect lay-offs and alternative employment opportunities for the workers of the enterprise are very limited. In the second case, we assume that the enterprise has the leeway to set the wage level and, as the wage level is adjusted, either the workers choose to work fewer (more) hours or some workers choose to quit (enter) the work force. The second conjecture is given impetus by the presence of early retirement options, retraining possibilities, unemployment and welfare benefits.[20] The decline in labor supply can also be interpreted as a decline in work effort, and conversely. We maintain the assumption that labor supply is less than perfectly elastic, as assumed in the previous section.

In the first case, suppose the government sets the profit target at π^g, a constant. Then, without EWT, from (10.7) w can be expressed as

$$w = \frac{f(n)}{n} - \frac{\pi^g}{(1 - \tau)n}$$
$$= \bar{w} + \frac{(1 - \tau)[f(n) - \bar{w}n] - \pi^g}{(1 - \tau)n} \tag{10.34}$$

and, with EWT, from (10.8) w^* can be expressed as

$$w^* = \frac{(1 - \tau)f(n)}{n} + \tau\bar{w} - \frac{\pi^g}{n}$$
$$= \bar{w} + \frac{(1 - \tau)[f(n) - \bar{w}n] - \pi^g}{n}. \tag{10.35}$$

Comparison of (10.34) and (10.35) (given the same n, $\bar{w}$, π^g, and τ) shows that

$$w^* < w; \tag{10.36}$$

that is, EWT serves to lower the wage level.[21] This result obtains for the simple reason that the government increases the tax base without lowering its profit share and the additional tax is paid by the workers.[22] In either case, the government has the leeway to choose π^g such that $w = \bar{w}$ or $w^* = \bar{w}$; therefore, the effect of EWT on wages is moot. Further, it is clear that the lower the profit target set by the government, the higher the wage with or without EWT. It is therefore in the interest of the workers to understate the profit of the enterprise to increase their wages. This opens up the possibility of a wage bargain between the enterprise and the government in the process of deciding the level of π^g. If the government does not have the capacity to monitor the enterprise profits adequately and may therefore be inclined to settle for a lower profit transfer than targeted (or if the government lacks the political will to lower subsidies to the enterprise), the enterprise may attempt to 'negotiate' a lower profit transfer (or a higher subsidy level) to maximize the workers' wages.[23] While the effect of EWT in this case is moot, it nevertheless affords the government an additional bargaining chip; for example, with EWT, the government might settle for a lower π^g than it would without EWT and attempt to make up the difference indirectly with additional revenue from EWT.

In the second case, the enterprise maximizes the workers' income (wn without EWT or w^*n^* with EWT) by choosing the wage level. Elastic labor supply implies that the level set for π^g by the government cannot exceed the maximum profit levels implied by the maximization of (10.7) and (10.8), that is π_{max} without EWT, and π^*_{max} with EWT. If the government chose $\pi^g = \pi_{max}$ without EWT or $\pi^g = \pi^*_{max}$ with EWT, the enterprise would choose w and w^* exactly at the levels found earlier; therefore, $w^* < w$ and hence $w^*n^* < wn$. If the government chose $\pi^g < \pi_{max}$ or $\pi^g < \pi^*_{max}$, then w and w^* would be higher than before with $w^* < w$; hence the workers' income would also be higher. However, if the government chose $\pi^g > \pi_{max}$ or $\pi^g > \pi^*_{max}$, then the enterprise would be unable to achieve the profit target set by the government.[24] Therefore, in this case also, the effect of EWT on the wage level is moot and the wage, output, and employment levels depend on the profit target (or the subsidy level) chosen by the government.

Self-seeking managers

The model in the preceding section can be extended to the heterogeneous labor case to shed light on the behavior of self-seeking SOE managers. It has been argued that EWT provides an incentive to managers to avoid the tax by averaging in a few high salaries – those of the managers – with many low salaries – those of the workers. Let us assume that the enterprise now employs two types of labor, skilled labor or the managers, n_1, and unskilled labor or the workers, n_2. Then, the managers' wages without and with EWT, w_1 and w_1^* can be expressed as, respectively,

$$w_1 = \frac{f(n_1, n_2)}{n_1} - \frac{w_2 n_2}{n_1} - \frac{\pi^g}{(1 - \tau)n_1} \tag{10.37}$$

$$w_1^* = (1 - \tau)\frac{f(n_1, n_2)}{n_1} - \frac{(w_2 - \tau\bar{w})n_2}{n_1} + \tau\bar{w} - \frac{\pi^g}{n_1} \tag{10.38}$$

where π^g is the profit level required by the government. Suppose that n_1 is given, that is the managers are ensconced in their positions and have the collective power to maximize their wages, w_1 or w_1^*, by choosing the level of w_2.

If labor shedding is not possible, that is if the level of n_2 is given, then it is clear from (10.37) and (10.38) that the managers will prefer to pay as small a wage as possible to the workers, which is the minimum wage.[25] Perhaps in this sense, it would be possible to argue that EWT would result in a few managers surrounding themselves with many low-wage workers in order to avoid the tax. In this case, by substituting $\bar{w}$ for w_2 in (10.37) and (10.38), it is possible to show that

$$\bar{w} < w_1^* < w_1 \quad \text{if } \pi^g < (1-\tau)[f(n_1, n_2) - \bar{w}n_1 - \bar{w}n_2]; \tag{10.39}$$

that is, for the same π^g, EWT lowers the managers' wages. However, the impact of EWT on the managers' wages is moot because the government has the leeway to choose π^g such that the managers' wage obtains at a desired level ($w_1, w_1^* \geq \bar{w}$).

If labor shedding is possible, then the managers can choose the level of w_2. Assuming, as before, that the supply elasticity of n_2, θ_2, is between zero and infinity, maximization of (10.37) and (10.38) with respect to w_2 yields, respectively,

$$w_2 = \frac{\theta_2}{1 + \theta_2} f_2 \tag{10.40}$$

$$w_2^* = \frac{\theta_2}{1 + \theta_2} [(1-\tau)f_2 + \tau\bar{w}]. \tag{10.41}$$

Along the lines of the arguments leading to the result in (10.18) in the case of the profit-maximizing enterprise, it can be shown from (10.40) and (10.41) that

$$w_2^* < w_2; \quad n_2^* < n_2. \tag{10.42}$$

This result holds because now the managers are behaving as 'profit' maximizers by maximizing their wage and they pay the workers lower wages because with EWT the marginal cost of n_2 is higher. So, when labor shedding is possible, the analysis indicates that self-seeking managers would shed labor to maximize their own income. In this case, we can also show that $w_1^* < w_1$.[26] However, again, the impact of EWT on the managers' wages is moot since the level of such wages can be manipulated by the government through choosing the level of π^g.[27] In practice, management and workers are likely to connive to subvert the EWT (see the Russian example below).

Whether or not labor shedding is possible, the incidence of EWT is unambiguously on both the workers and the managers. The government has the leeway to choose the level of π^g in order to control the managers' wages; the lower π^g the higher is the managers' wages. Hence the managers have an incentive to conceal the level of profits and 'bargain' for lower profit targets or higher subsidies. Therefore, the relevant question is one of fiscal discipline or the 'hardness' of the budget constraint imposed on the enterprise by the government as the ultimate owner of the enterprise.

Another related issue concerns possible preventive impact of EWT on malfeasance by the managers in stripping the assets of the enterprise. Asset stripping can be accomplished by means of excess wage payments during the course of privatization when property rights are rather ambiguous. One possibility is that the managers foresee that the government cannot or will not subsidize the enterprise indefinitely (i.e. the government will not settle for low or negative levels of π^g). Then, an option may be gradually to sell the enterprise assets and pay the proceeds to the workers (or at least to the favored workers) in the form of excessive wages.[28] Since EWT discourages wage payments in excess of the norm, it may be instrumental in preventing asset stripping by the managers. For the managers to prefer a bankruptcy bonanza, they would have to figure that the present value of the proceeds in the process of bankruptcy (plus the present value of the wages they expect to make from alternative employment) is somehow larger than the present value of the wages they expect to make in their current positions if they did not bankrupt the enterprise. The present value calculations may well favor bankruptcy and, in some fashion, the managers can become 'corporate raiders'. However, this does not appear feasible or realistic in the context of the transition economies because, first, by and large, the market institutions and political will to facilitate bankruptcy of SOEs do not exist; second, the process is too conspicuous; and third, alternative employment opportunities for an overwhelming majority of workers, including the managers, may be limited. Therefore, the preventive impact of EWT on asset stripping appears to be at best marginal (see the evidence and discussion below on the experience of Poland).

EXPERIENCE WITH EWT IN FSU AND EASTERN EUROPE

Poland

The experience of Poland is a good example and the most recently documented. To contain the growth of wages, a tax on 'inflationary' or 'excessive' wage growth was in force until the end of 1988.[29] This was levied on the profit of enterprises in which the total wage bill exceeded a certain norm. The tax equalled 100 to 500 percent of the excess over the permitted growth of wages, and 200 to 400 percent for awards and premia paid from after-tax profits. In 1989, this tax was abolished in favor of a regulation that wages exceeding a ceiling fixed by the Council of Ministers by executive order were subject to an 'income tax increased by 200 percent' (Fiszer, 1991). In January 1990 a new law was introduced. Excessive wage growth was taxed at progressive rates from 200 to 500 percent, while above-ceiling premia paid out of after-tax profits were taxed at 500 percent. In January 1991, another new law on taxing inflationary wage growth was introduced. The principles were similar to the law that existed before 1989, with the difference that tax payments were tied to progress on privatization, and that the average wage rather than the total wage bill was made the reference point.

The law only applied to state-owned enterprises. The excess of the average wage of a state enterprise in any month over a norm set by the Council of Ministers with reference to the development of average wages in the economy was subjected to a progressive tax with rates between 100 percent (for exceeding the norm by up to 3 percent) and 500 percent (for exceeding the norm by more than 5 percent). On the face of it, this system was quite restrictive as the inflation indexation coefficient on the norm was 0.6 during 1991–2. In fact, however, the policy was not particularly restrictive as the actual implementation of the EWT allowed for special exemptions, adjustments, and non-index-linked modifications to the norm. This, together with the apparent willingness of many enterprises to pay the tax, led to significant increases in nominal wages. For example, in 1990, the average wage typically exceeded the norm, particularly towards the end of the year.[30]

Although EWT revenue represented some 1.5 percent of GDP in 1992, state enterprises accumulated large EWT arrears. In 1991 accrued EWT liabilities amounted to Zl 39 trillion, but actual collections amounted to only Zl 27 trillion; about 50 percent of all outstanding tax arrears were EWT arrears. It was clear that some large SOEs simply refused to pay the full EWT due. The arrears were concentrated in a few large SOEs, such as the State Railroad Company (PKP) and the State Airlines (LOT), which, incidentally, were the same companies that also received large amounts of subsidies. By the end of 1993, 'Popiwek' arrears amounted to over 1 percent of GDP (Schwartz, 1994, p. 9).

As regards the incidence of PPWW in Poland, evidence provided by Pinto (1992a) is illustrative. Three sets of SOEs during January to June 1992 have been analyzed: those having a positive net profit; those with a positive gross profit but negative net profit; and those with a negative net profit. Table 10.2 shows that tax arrears as a percentage of taxes due have been most substantial and have grown fastest for those firms that are the least profitable.

Further, Table 10.3 shows that average wages were larger and increased faster in the more profitable firms.

The PPWW per worker accrued (but not necessarily paid – see Table 10.2) shown in Table 10.4 suggests that the most profitable firms have paid the highest EWT. This is consistent with the earlier analysis and indicates that EWT penalizes the more productive enterprises and that EWT in Poland did not prevent the profitable companies from paying wages exceeding the norm.

Table 10.2 Tax arrears relative to taxes due (in percent)

Profits	*1990*	*1991*	*1992*[1]
Positive net	1.8	3.3	3.7
Positive gross, negative net	0.2	17.4	26.8
Negative net	5.0	42.7	50.8

[1] First six months.

Table 10.3 Average wages for selected months (thousands of zlotys per worker)

Profits	*Dec. 1989*	*June 1990*	*Dec. 1990*	*June 1991*	*Dec. 1991*	*June 1991*
Positive net	658	918	1,568	1,573	2,178	2,169
Positive gross, negative net	765	1,014	1,763	1,334	1,885	2,017
Negative net	603	852	1,395	1,440	1,737	1,858

Table 10.4 PPWW per worker (thousands of zlotys)

Profits	*1990*	*1991*	*1992*[1]
Positive net	3,665	6,500	1,635
Positive gross, negative net	5,675	4,740	219
Negative net	1,319	1,518	256

[1] First six months.

EWT's cost was borne by successful SOEs while those with lower average wage payments and decapitalization coped with their PPWW liabilities by running up arrears.

Further evidence suggests there is no direct connection between PPWW liability and running down the capital stock of a company. Although the least profitable firms were running down their capital, this could not be ascribed to PPWW payments, as the most profitable firms had the highest PPWW liabilities and almost zero arrears.

There is also evidence that, as predicted by our model, real wages and employment (although no doubt influenced by many more prominent factors such as credit and interest rate policies) declined after PPWW was introduced, especially in the high-productivity industries.[31]

In view of the decline in the wage norm, our model would also predict a decline in output–employment level and hence a rise in the inflation rate, given the rate of money creation. However, the evidence on the impact of EWT on inflation is inconclusive. Pinto (1992b) argues that the effectiveness of the wage policies under EWT in controlling inflation is suspect. In contrast, Blanchard and Layard (1992) argue that, in the absence of the incomes policy effected through EWT, there would be an increase in the inflation rate.

A disadvantage of the Polish EWT has been the tendency of the government to fine-tune the PPWW by introducing narrow exemptions from EWT. A 100 percent exporter can be exempted from PPWW; this led, for instance, to a rush to export semi-processed steel, cutting domestic supplies and also hurting finished-steel producers. Again, in 1993 enterprises were allowed to negotiate exemptions with local tax chambers for exemption from the PPWW in light of their individual wages policies. An overwhelming criticism of the PPWW was the relative and partial way it was administered. Numerous examples of discrimination could be cited.[32] SOE managers had a strong preference (59 out of 63 sampled) for a wage bill formula rather than the average wage norm. If the PPWW was to be retained, managers wanted uniform enforcement, no forgiveness for arrears, and no exceptions. Managers proposed that PPWW should be simplified and a maximum rate of 100 percent should be used. On this issue, the IBRD study concludes:

> A more positive way of inducing firms to focus on profits and long-run health is to simplify the PPWW . . . and link managerial compensation to profits, at the same time clarifying the position and rewards for management following privatization so that the maximization of the firms' value becomes paramount.
>
> (Pinto, 1992a, p. 29)

Of course, this begs the question of why, if managers are to be driven by a focus on profits, they should need any artificial excess tax on wages. Presumably, given a credible timetable for privatization, the SOEs will pay those wages that will maximize profits in the medium term?

It has been proposed to move away from the PPWW system in 1994 to a form of trilateral wage bargaining (government, workers, employers).[33] Given the long history of such arrangements (e.g. the Netherlands in the 1950s and 1960s), this may be wishful thinking as a solution to wage-cost control. A better solution would be to face up to the lack of financial discipline in some 50 SOEs and impose stringent financial controls, including the potential for ultimate bankruptcy.

Azerbaijan

As shown in Table 10.1, the Azerbaijan EWT norm is four times the minimum wage and levied at the corporate profit tax rate of 35 percent. Because the corporate tax rate structure is progressive in Azerbaijan, the marginal rate at which excess wages can be taxed can be as high as 70 percent. So the rate at which EWT is levied varies not only according to the size of the wage bill, but also according to the size of profits and hence is further distorted between different enterprises at different times. It was reckoned that about a quarter of the profits tax revenue was attributable to EWT (some 3 to 4 billion rubles in 1992). Arguably, an EWT that generates substantial revenue is not working well to discourage wage awards. The reasons for this apparent failure in Azerbaijan are threefold. First, SOEs in a monopoly position regard EWT as a cost and pass it forward in price increases. Second, lack of financial discipline and generous credit expansion allow full pass-through of costs. Finally, rapidly accelerating inflation means that calculations based on a minimum wage that is quickly out of date are mostly irrelevant to the wages paid to skilled workers.

Belarus

In Belarus, both SOE managers and the government viewed EWT as a badly focussed tax; that is, distortionary, widely evaded, and difficult to administer fairly. The most potent criticism of EWT in Belarus is that the authorities abolished the tax in late 1992. This reflects a widespread view of EWT in countries that have had to use them for many years (Hungary).

Bulgaria

The table presented in Appendix IV is a good illustration of how the tax operates in Bulgaria. The regulations under the Bulgarian EWT show that this is no simple tax to administer, suggesting that compliance costs must be considerable. Under Article 3 of the regulations, there are six ways of establishing the basic reference amount of the wages depending on whether the volume of sales has increased or decreased, whether debts and arrears have changed, and a choice of appropriate coefficients.

In contrast to Azerbaijan, if low revenue indicates EWT is working to restrain wage awards, then Bulgaria has a success story on its hands. In 1991 the revenue collected from EWT was equal to about 0.4 percent of GDP, equivalent to about 5 percent of the revenues from social security contributions; the figures were similar for 1992. However, perhaps the greater competition and better credit control explain more of the wage restraint than the impact of EWT.

Estonia

The intent of the Estonian EWT is to allow real wages to be maintained but to penalize any increase above the expected inflation guidelines. Average employee compensation is defined as gross incomes per employee. Gross incomes include salaries, premia, cash and in-kind support, interest subsidies, distributed profits, and incomes from company shares. Revenue has been negligible. Once again, the Estonian economy has been more open to competition and wages appear to have been restrained not so much by EWT as by the extremely tight credit availability enforced through the Estonian Currency Board.

Hungary

Hungary has a long history of using EWT, based on both the wages bill and the average wage.[34] Again, like Belarus, the most convincing commentary may be that the government abolished EWT as of January 1992. The tax was more sophisticated than in many countries including allowances for performance indicators limiting the permissible wage increase to gross value added and profitability. Separate schemes, at times, allowed for wage increases for enterprises subject to competitive pricing rules and for agriculture. Most recently, wage increases exceeding the increase in the value added of the firm were not treated as costs and were taxed at the corporate rate. Boote and Somogyi argue that 'wage regulation schemes largely prevented sizable wage overruns associated with loose financial discipline' (pp. 18–19). Increasing competition from the private sector (not liable to EWT) required the SOEs to pay wages differentiated according to productivity and efficiency; the EWT had become a constraint on remodelling the public sector industries. Moreover, it was clear that the administration of this tax was difficult and it was resented by managers, especially thrusting and modernizing managers. Increasingly, the EWT had become irrelevant in containing wage growth in public enterprises.

Kazakhstan

Parliament rejected the EWT sought by the administration in May 1992. They did so for at least three reasons: widespread recognition that other countries' experience with EWT had been disappointing; intensive lobbying by enterprises against the new tax; and strong doubts about the ability of the tax administration to apply and monitor EWT.

Kyrgyzstan

If small revenues are to be a measure of EWT's success, the Kyrgyzstan tax is working well. In 1991 it is reckoned that revenue from EWT was about 1.7 percent of total revenue from the enterprise profits tax. Of course, this could also be an indication that the tax administration was simply failing to assess and collect the tax.

Latvia

The revenue from EWT in 1992 seems to have been small (0.4 percent of total central government revenue). The success in controlling wage increases is probably due more to a tight monetary policy and to extremely depressed demand. Most recently, the authorities introduced an amendment so that increases in productivity (defined as the change in real output divided by the change in employment) would not be subject to EWT. It was also suspected that if trade started to expand, firms would start to evade EWT.

Russia

The Russian authorities agree that EWT's objective is not to raise revenue but to encourage enterprises to use profits for investment rather than excessive wage payments.[35] The enterprises' profits tax for the quarter is paid in advance. In principle the enterprise should incorporate an estimate of its EWT to be taxed under the enterprise profits tax. It is unclear whether this is, in fact, calculated. However, in the month following each quarter the enterprise profits tax and EWT are computed based on actual profits, wages, and the norm for the previous quarter. An immediate settlement is made by the enterprise. It is thought that EWT is less than it might be as enterprises increase non-wage compensation to labor in the form of payments to pensions funds, vacation funds, and other employer-provided benefits.

SUMMARY AND CONCLUSIONS

In the case of the profit-maximizing enterprise, the main conclusion of our model is that, even though EWT has the potential to curb wage awards, this is achieved at the cost of a decline in the output and employment level because EWT increases the marginal cost of labor. In the extreme cases of perfectly elastic or perfectly inelastic labor supply, EWT amounts to a wage floor. The effect of EWT on total tax (standard corporate income tax plus EWT) paid by the enterprise is ambiguous. Moreover, depending on the degree of inflation adjustment of the minimum wage or the wage norm effected by the government, EWT may well be pro-inflationary and even result in stagflation. In the case of the labor-dominated enterprise seeking to maximize the workers' or the managers' income, the impact of EWT on the enterprise behavior is moot. At best, EWT might serve as an indirect bargaining chip for the government in the process of guiding the wage award to be made by the enterprise. Further, EWT does not appear to have a significant effect on asset stripping. As the revenue potential of EWT appears weak, the conventional taxes are likely to perform much better in generating additional revenue. The foregoing observations indicate that, if effective to a significant degree, EWT is likely to have deleterious consequences for enterprise efficiency and for output and inflation levels.

Have the recent EWTs modified wage claims or SOE behavior to restrain inflation? Those countries where the revenue from the tax has been low (Bulgaria, Estonia, Kyrgyzstan, and Latvia) ascribe the moderation of wage increases not to EWT but to tighter control over credit and to an inability to pass forward cost increases owing to depressed demand. Where SOE managers are not subject to tight credit control (Azerbaijan, Belarus), EWT has not been effective in holding down wage awards. If it is successful and SOEs find themselves squeezed, immediately bargains are struck to avoid paying EWT (Poland, Hungary) or ways are found to get around the tax (Russia).

Applied to the wage rate, EWT is skewed against capital-intensive industries with high-productivity workers. Applied at the corporate rate (excess wages not allowed as a cost) it starts to become a value-added tax but a highly discriminatory and distortionary one, somewhat like the confused (and startlingly distortionary) example in France in 1975.[36]

The EWT may not be too difficult to administer except that the incentive for collusion to evade the tax between the managers and the employees is great. The definition of wages has to be all embracing to prevent circumvention using special bonuses, pension fund payments, contribution to vacation funds, rent payments, free meals, transport costs, and so on, as observed in Russia. As noted by Dildine and Sunley (1978), '(e)xperience with wage measurement problems of the income tax suggests that opportunities for substituting forms of compensation that understate the true increase in labor cost cannot be completely eliminated (p. 389). If EWT is to operate for anything but the shortest time, allowances have to be made for promotions, new machinery skills, and productivity.[37] The experience of economies in transition suggests that arrears can build up in firms that are so politically sensitive that tax collection is almost impossible, exemptions are made, and efficient administration starts to collapse as those paying the EWT resent those avoiding it and compliance is eroded (Poland).

For a given policy of financial restraint and a given pace of change to privatization and competition, proponents argue that an EWT will enable inflation to fall faster with less loss of output than would simply relying on financial policies. Conclusive empirical testing is probably not possible with the limited data currently available for economies in transition. However, experience in both western and eastern economies suggests EWTs are usually unsuccessful in controlling wage awards and, if successful, they are distortionary. It is much better to control credit expansion, impose credible hard budget constraints and performance requirements on SOEs, permit bankruptcy when necessary, and, gradually, open the protected SOEs to competition and privatization. The only role for an EWT might be as a temporary transitional measure on the way to privatization and competition but, even in that role, the distortions introduced would likely slow the pace of transition, discourage rapid adaptation, and penalize efficiency and innovation.

APPENDIX I

The profit-maximizing enterprise: comparison of wages and employment without and with EWT with two types of (skilled and unskilled) labor

The proof presented here serves to generalize the heterogeneous labor model in the second section. In that section, we assumed that $\alpha = 1$; hence n_2 may not be paid a wage less than $\bar{w}$. However, if $\alpha > 1$, then it is possible that the n_2 class of workers are paid a wage less than $\alpha\bar{w}$.[38] Then, how does EWT affect $w_2 < \alpha\bar{w}$ along with $w_1 > \alpha\bar{w}$ under monopsony? This case is interesting because it sheds light on whether EWT creates an incentive for the firm to surround a few high-wage employees (managers), n_1, with many low-wage employees (workers), n_2. With $\alpha > 1$, from (10.3) and (10.6), the enterprise profit without and with EWT are, respectively,[39]

$$\pi = (1-\tau)[f(n_1, n_2) - w_1 n_1 - w_2 n_2] \tag{10.43}$$

$$\begin{gathered}\pi^* = (1-\tau)[f(n_1, n_2) - (w_1 - \alpha\tau\bar{w})n_1 - (1-\tau)w_2 n_2; \\ w_1 > \alpha\bar{w}; \quad w_2 < \alpha\bar{w}.\end{gathered} \tag{10.44}$$

As explained in the second section, using (10.43) and (10.44) we can show that the (effective) marginal cost of n_1 with EWT is unambiguously greater than the marginal cost without EWT since

$$n_1 > -(w_1 - \alpha\bar{w})n_1' \quad \text{for all } w_1 > \alpha\bar{w}; \quad n_1 > 0; \quad n_1' > 0; \quad w_2 > 0. \tag{10.45}$$

We are interested in the impact of the increase in the marginal cost of n_1 under EWT on the amount of both types of labor employed by the firm, and hence on the wages paid; that is, we wish to compare (n_1^*, w_1^*) and (n_2^*, w_2^*) with (n_1, w_1) and (n_2, w_2).

The first- and second-order conditions which follow from (10.43) are[40]

$$\begin{gathered}f_1 = (n_1 + w_1 n_1')/n_1' = g_1(w_1); \quad f_2 = (n_2 + w_2 n_2')/n_2' = g_2(w_2); \\ \pi_{11} < 0; \quad \pi_{22} < 0; \quad \Delta = (1-\tau)^2(\pi_{11}\pi_{22} - \pi_{12}) > 0 \\ \text{where} \\ \pi_{11} = (1-\tau)[f_{11}(n_1')^2 - 2n_1' + (f_1 - w_1)n_2'']; \\ \pi_{22} = (1-\tau)[f_{22}(n_2')^2 - 2n_2' + (f_2 - w_2)n_2'']; \\ \pi_{12} = (1-\tau)(f_{12}n_1'n_2').\end{gathered} \tag{10.46}$$

Totally differentiating the first-order conditions in (10.46) and making the relevant substitutions, we can show that

$$\mathrm{d}w_1/\mathrm{d}w_2 = -f_{12}n_1'n_2'/\pi_{11}; \quad \mathrm{d}w_2/\mathrm{d}w_1 = -f_{12}n_1'n_2'/\pi_{22}. \tag{10.47}$$

Therefore, $\mathrm{d}w_1/\mathrm{d}w_2 > 0$ and $\mathrm{d}w_2/\mathrm{d}w_1 > 0$, provided that $f_{12} > 0$ and n_1', n_2' > 0. Since it is also clear from (10.46) that $\mathrm{d}g_1 = g_1'\mathrm{d}w_1$ and $\mathrm{d}g_2 = g_2'\mathrm{d}w_2$, it follows that $\mathrm{d}g_1/\mathrm{d}g_2 > 0$.[41]

Further, totally differentiating the first-order conditions in (10.46), we can show that

$$f_{11}\mathrm{d}n_1 + f_{12}\mathrm{d}n_2 = \mathrm{d}g_1;$$

$$f_{12}\mathrm{d}n_1 + f_{22}\mathrm{d}n_2 = \mathrm{d}g_2;$$

hence

$$\mathrm{d}n_1/\mathrm{d}g_1 = (1/\hat{\Delta})(f_{22} - f_{12}\mathrm{d}g_2/\mathrm{d}g_1); \qquad (10.48)$$

$$\mathrm{d}n_2/\mathrm{d}g_1 = (1/\hat{\Delta})(f_{11}\mathrm{d}g_2/\mathrm{d}g_1 - f_{12});$$

$$\hat{\Delta} = f_{11}f_{22} - f_{12}^2.$$

Since $\mathrm{d}g_1/\mathrm{d}g_2 > 0$, the signs of $\mathrm{d}n_1/\mathrm{d}g_1$ and $\mathrm{d}n_2/\mathrm{d}g_1$ would be negative provided that

$$f_{11} < 0; \quad f_{22} < 0; \quad f_{12} > 0; \quad \hat{\Delta} > 0.$$

The foregoing conditions correspond to the first- and second-order conditions in the perfectly competitive labor market case.[42] While these conditions are neither sufficient nor necessary for profit maximization under monopsony, they are adequately general. They indicate that with decreasing marginal product for both types of labor and $f_{12} > 0$, $\mathrm{d}n_1/\mathrm{d}g_1 < 0$ and $\mathrm{d}n_2/\mathrm{d}g_1 < 0$ under monopsony.

Therefore, under adequately general assumptions for the production function, it follows that, since $g_1^* > g_1$, $n_1^* < n_1$ because $\mathrm{d}n_1/\mathrm{d}g_1 < 0$, and $n_2^* < n_2$ since $\mathrm{d}n_2/\mathrm{d}g_1 < 0$. But n_1', $n_2' > 0$; hence $w_1^* < w_1$ and $w_2^* < w_2$. Therefore, the output and employment levels with EWT are less than they are without EWT, or $f^*(n_1^*, n_2^*) < f(n_1, n_2)$.

The foregoing results can be easily extended to the case discussed in the second section with $\alpha = 1$, $w_2 = \bar{w}$ by simply noting that, in that case, $\mathrm{d}g_2 = \mathrm{d}\bar{w} = 0$; hence $w_1^* < w_1$, $n_1^* < n_1$, $w_2^* = w_2 = \bar{w}$, $n_2^* < n_2$.[43] Similarly, the same results are valid in the case of the perfectly competitive labor market if the second-order conditions for profit maximization hold and $f_{12} > 0$, since, in that case, $\mathrm{d}g_2 = \mathrm{d}w_2 = 0$ also. We can similarly show that if both n_1 and n_2 are paid wages exceeding the norm, the marginal costs of both types of labor are increased ($g_1^* > g_1$; $g_2^* > g_2$); hence the same results obtain.

Thus, under an adequately general set of assumptions, when n_1 and n_2 are interpreted to be the managers and workers, we can conclude that the incidence of EWT is on both the managers and the workers. Under EWT, the profit-maximizing enterprise does not surround a few high-wage employees with many low-wage employees in order to reduce the tax burden.[44] With heterogeneous labor, irrespective of whether some classes of labor are paid wages below the norm ($\alpha\bar{w}$), as long as some workers are paid wages exceeding the norm, EWT results in a decline in the wages and employment of all classes of labor, and hence a decline in output.

APPENDIX II

Behavior of w and w^* with respect to $\bar{w}$

From (10.7), the first- and second-order conditions for maximum profit without EWT can be found respectively as

$$\partial\pi/\partial w = (1-\tau)\,[f_n n' - (n + wn')] = 0 \tag{10.49}$$

$$\partial^2\pi/\partial w^2 = (1-\tau)\,[f_{nn}(n')^2 + f_n n'' - 2n' - wn''] < 0 \tag{10.50}$$

where $n'' = (\partial^2 n/\partial w^2)$. Differentiating (10.49) with respect to $\bar{w}$ and using (10.50), we can show that

$$(\partial^2\pi/\partial w^2)^{\cdot}(\partial w/\partial\bar{w}) = 0; \tag{10.51}$$

hence $(\partial w/\partial\bar{w}) = 0$.

However, from (10.8), the first- and second-order conditions for maximum profit with EWT can be found respectively as

$$\partial\pi^*/\partial w^* = (1-\tau)f_n\partial n/\partial w^* - [n + (w^* - \tau\bar{w})\,\partial n/\partial w^*] = 0 \tag{10.52}$$

$$\partial^2\pi^*/\partial w^{*2} = (1-\tau)\,[f_{nn}\,(\partial n/\partial w^*)^2 + f_n\,(\partial^2 n/\partial w^{*2})] \tag{10.53}$$

$$- [2(\partial n/\partial w^*) + (w^* - \tau\bar{w})\,(\partial^2 n/\partial w^{*2})] < 0.$$

Differentiating (10.52) with respect to $\bar{w}$ and using (10.53), we can show that

$$\partial w^*/\partial\bar{w} = -\tau[(\partial n/\partial w^*)/(\partial^2\pi^*/\partial w^{*2})]; \tag{10.54}$$

hence $(\partial w^*/\partial\bar{w}) > 0$.

For a sufficiently high minimum wage, $\bar{w}_{max}$, $w^* = \bar{w}_{max}$; and, for all $\bar{w} < \bar{w}_{max}$, $\bar{w} \le w^* < \bar{w}_{max}$. As $\bar{w}$ rises, w^* rises and, finally, $w^* = \bar{w}_{max}$; that is, $f_n = \bar{w}_{max}$. Then, the monopsonist enterprise behaves like a competitive enterprise; that is, given $\bar{w} \ge \bar{w}_{max}$, the enterprise chooses n to maximize π.

APPENDIX III

Self-seeking managers: comparison of the managers' wages without and with EWT

From (10.37) and (10.38), the managers' share without and with EWT can be shown as, respectively,

$$w_1n_1 = f(n_1, n_2) - w_2n_2 - \frac{\pi^g}{(1-\tau)} \tag{10.55}$$

$$w_1{}^*n_1 = (1-\tau)f(n_1, n_2{}^*) - (w_2{}^* - \tau\bar{w})n_2{}^* + \tau\bar{w}n_1 - \pi^g. \tag{10.56}$$

Since n_1 is assumed to be the same in both cases, $w_1{}^* < w_1$ if $w_1{}^*n_1 < w_1n_1$. From (10.56), $w_1{}^*n_1$ can be expressed as

$$w_1{}^*n_1 = \left(f(n_1, n_2{}^*) - w_2{}^*n_2{}^* - \frac{\pi^g}{(1-\tau)}\right) + \frac{\tau}{(1-\tau)}\{\pi^g - (1-\tau)\,[f(n_1, n_2{}^*) - \bar{w}n_1 - \bar{w}n_2{}^*]\}. \tag{10.57}$$

Also notice from (10.56) that, for $w_1{}^*n_1 > \bar{w}n_1$ $(w_1{}^* > \bar{w})$, as assumed, it is necessary to have

$$\pi^g < (1-\tau)\,[f(n_1, n_2{}^*) - \bar{w}n_1 - \bar{w}n_2{}^*] - (w_2{}^* - \bar{w})n_2{}^*; \quad w_2{}^* \geq \bar{w} \tag{10.58}$$

which indicates that the second term on the right-hand-side of (10.57) is negative. Since $w_2{}^* < w_2$, it is clear from (10.55) and (10.58) that

$$\left(f(n_1, n_2{}^*) - w_2{}^*n_2{}^* - \frac{\pi^g}{(1-\tau)}\right) < \left(f(n_1, n_2) - w_2\,n_2 - \frac{\pi^g}{(1-\tau)}\right) \tag{10.59}$$

because the value of w_2 for which (10.55) is maximum is different from the value of w_2 for which (10.56) is maximum. Therefore, in view of (10.58) and (10.59), $w_1{}^*n_1 < w_1n_1$ and hence $w_1{}^* < w_1$.

APPENDIX IV

REPUBLIC OF BULGARIA
Council of Ministers
Decree No. 28 of 9 February 1994
on Adopting the Regulations
on the Increment and Formation of Wage Funds in 1994

Article 1

(1) These Regulations shall establish the way of regulating the increment and formation of wage funds in companies or other enterprises and organizations with more than 50 percent state and/or municipal participation

(including joint ventures with foreign participation).

(2) These Regulations shall determine also the terms and procedure of raising wage funds in companies or other enterprises and organizations engaged in business activities which receive subsidies from the state or municipal budgets or funds from extra-budgetary accounts of the Ministry of Finance.

Article 2

(1) The increment of wage funds in companies, enterprises and organizations under Art. 1, para 1 for each quarter of 1994 compared to the basic reference amount of wage funds established in these Regulations shall be taxed in accordance with the following rates:

	Tax rate depending on the average monthly gross wage for the respective quarter of 1994 (percent)			
Percentage increment of wage funds compared to the basic reference amount	*Up to two minimal wages*	*Up to three minimal wages*	*Up to four minimal wages*	*More than four minimal wages*
Up to 2	–	–	–	–
More than 2 up to 3	10	50	75	100
More than 3 up to 4	20	75	100	200
More than 4 up to 5	50	100	200	600
More than 5	100	200	600	800

Note: Tax rates are distributed in four groups (columns) depending on the minimal wage established in the country for the respective quarter or 1994.

(2) Tax rates under the table in the preceding paragraph shall apply separately to the amount of the wage funds increment which comes under the specific range. When the wage fund increment is more than 2 percent, the amount already taxed shall be deducted from the taxable amount under the next range. In this case, only the balance between the two amounts shall be subject to taxation.

(3) The tax due shall be paid pursuant to the provisions of Art. 75 of the Regulations on the Enforcement of Decree No. 56 on Economic Activities.

(4) When the average monthly gross wages in companies, enterprises and organizations from the financial and lending system or the system of foreign trade exceed six-fold the minimal wage established in the country for the respective quarter of 1994, tax rates determined for the respective quarter of 1994 under para 1 shall be doubled.

Article 3

(1) The basic reference amount of wages fund used to determine the increment under Art. 2, para 2 shall be established by adjusting the funds for the respective quarter of the preceding year:

1. For companies, enterprises and organizations where the volume of sales of goods and services per person in comparable prices during the respective quarter of 1994 has increased in comparison to the respective quarter of the preceding year, without any debts in arrears to the state and/or municipal budgets, the State Social Security, the Training and Unemployment Fund or to commercial banks and the result during the relevant period is profit:
   (a) by a coefficient equal to the quarterly estimate of the consumer price index for the country during the current quarter of 1994 compared to the respective quarter of the preceding year;
   (b) by a coefficient obtained through a 0.6 adjustment of the percentage increment of the volume of sales of goods and services per person in comparable prices during the 1994 quarter compared to the respective quarter of the preceding year;
2. For companies, enterprises and organizations where the volume of sales of goods and services per person in comparable prices during the respective quarter of 1994 has decreased in comparison to the respective quarter of the preceding year, without any debts in arrears to the state and/or municipal budgets, the State Social Security, the Training and Unemployment Fund or to commercial banks and the result during the relevant period is profit:
   (a) by the coefficient under section 1, subsection (a);
   (b) by a coefficient obtained through a 0.3 adjustment of the percentage reduction of the volume of sales of goods and services per person in comparable prices during the 1994 quarter compared to the respective quarter of the preceding year;
3. For companies, enterprises and organizations where the volume of sales of goods and services per person in comparable prices during the respective quarter of 1994 has increased or decreased in comparison to the respective quarter of the preceding year, with debts in arrears to the state and/or municipal budgets, the State Social Security, the Training and Unemployment Fund or to commercial banks and the result during the relevant period is profit:
   (a) by the coefficient under section 1, subsection (a);
   (b) by a coefficient obtained through a 0.3 adjustment of the percentage increment or reduction of the volume of sales of goods and services per person in comparable prices during the 1994 quarter compared to the respective quarter of the preceding year, the percentage increment of the volume of sales per person used to calculate the coefficient being restricted to 40 percent;

4. For companies, enterprises and organizations where the volume of sales of goods and services per person in comparable prices during the respective quarter of 1994 has increased or decreased in comparison to the respective quarter of the preceding year, without any debts in arrears to the state and/or municipal budgets, the State Social Security, the Training and Unemployment Fund or to commercial banks and the result during the relevant period is loss:
   (a) by the coefficient under section 1, subsection (a);
   (b) by a coefficient obtained through a 0.3 adjustment of the percentage increment or reduction of the volume of sales of goods and services per person in comparable prices during the 1994 quarter compared to the respective quarter of the preceding year, the percentage increment of the volume of sales per person used to calculate the coefficient being restricted to 40 percent;
5. For companies, enterprises and organizations where the volume of sales of goods and services per person in comparable prices during the respective quarter of 1994 has increased in comparison to the respective quarter of the preceding year, with debts in arrears to the state and/or municipal budgets, the State Social Security, the Training and Unemployment Fund or to commercial banks and the result during the relevant period is loss:
   (a) by the coefficient under section 1, subsection (a);
   (b) by a coefficient obtained through a 0.2 adjustment of the percentage increment of the volume of sales of goods and services per person in comparable prices during the 1994 quarter compared to the respective quarter of the preceding year, the percentage increment of the volume of sales per person used to calculate the coefficient being restricted to 30 percent;
6. For companies, enterprises and organizations where the volume of sales of goods and services per person in comparable prices during the respective quarter of 1994 has decreased in comparison to the respective quarter of the preceding year, with debts in arrears to the state and/or municipal budgets, the State Social Security, the Training and Unemployment Fund or to commercial banks and the result during the relevant period is loss:
   (a) by the coefficient under section 1, subsection (a);
   (b) by a coefficient obtained through a 0.6 adjustment of the percentage reduction of the volume of sales of goods and services per person in comparable prices during the 1994 quarter compared to the respective quarter of the preceding year, the amount of the coefficient being not less than 0.7.

(2) Companies, enterprises and organizations shall apply the relevant section of para 1 for the respective quarters of 1994 depending on their specific financial and economic condition. When one or more debts are in arrears,

the existence of debts in arrears shall be presumed.

(3) The percentage increment or reduction of the volume of sales of goods and services per person in comparable prices by industries and activities shall be calculated through the methodology of the National Statistical Office.

(4) The result during the relevant period – profit or loss within the meaning of para 1, sections 1–6 shall be established on the basis of the Income Statement in the Annex to Art. 40, para 1, section 2 of the Accountancy Act less the unspecified tax on the wage funds increment during the current quarter.

(5) When the actual accrued level of the consumer price index for the respective quarter of 1994 exceeds the estimates by more than 6.2 percentage points compared to the fourth quarter of 1993, the estimate index shall increase by 70 percent of the balance for the subsequent quarters.

(6) Companies, enterprises and organizations from the financial and lending system as well as those whose objects of activity include water supply and sewerage and those maintaining and operating students' hostels and canteens shall not apply the coefficient reflecting the increment or reduction of sales per person.

(7) Companies engaged in shipbuilding or ship repair as well as companies, enterprises and organizations with the following objects of activity: mechanized services in arable farming, livestock breeding and erosion control; agrochemical services; land reclamation and irrigation; crop raising and livestock production; greenhouses; production of seeds and saplings shall either apply or not apply the coefficient for the volume of sales per person in accordance with the specificities of their operations, starting from the first quarter of 1994 and the approach adopted is not subject to alteration during the subsequent quarters.

Article 4

(1) The tax on the wage funds increment shall be calculated and paid irrespective of the final financial results of companies, enterprises and organizations, i.e. profit or loss. Their amount shall be specified in Chapter Four of the Income Statement, Annex to Art. 40, para 1, section 2 of the Accountancy Act.

(2) The loss reported in the annual financial statements of companies, enterprises and organizations with more than 50 percent state and/or municipal participation as a result of the tax on the wage funds increment calculated and paid in the course of the year shall not be covered during the subsequent year or at the expense of the state budget.

Article 5

(1) Wage funds of companies, enterprises and organizations under Art. 1, para 2 shall be formed through adjusting the funds for the respective

quarter of the preceding year or the preceding quarter of the current year by:

1. A coefficient equal to the quarterly estimate of the consumer price index for the country during the current quarter of 1994 compared to the respective quarter of the preceding year or the preceding quarter of the current year;
2. A coefficient obtained through a 0.2 adjustment of the percentage increment or 0.3 adjustment of the percentage reduction of the volume of sales of goods and services per person in comparable prices during the 1994 quarter compared to the respective quarter of the preceding year or the preceding quarter of the current year, the calculation in comparable prices being based on the methodology of the National Statistical Office by industries and activities.

(2) Companies, enterprises and organizations under Art. 1, para 2 which receive subsidies from the state or municipal budgets or funds from the extra-budgetary accounts of the Ministry of Finance shall choose any of the two ways of forming wage funds under para 1 with respect to the basic reference quarter in accordance with the specificities of their operations, starting from the first quarter of 1994. The approach adopted shall not be subject to alterations during the subsequent quarters.

(3) When the actual accrued level of the consumer price index for the respective quarter of 1994 exceeds the estimates by more than 6.2 percentage points compared to the fourth quarter of 1993, the estimate index shall increase by 70 percent of the balance for the subsequent quarters.

(4) When wage funds of the respective quarter of 1994 exceed the funds established under paras 1 and 2, the full amount of the surplus shall be deducted from the subsidies or funds received from extra-budgetary accounts of the Ministry of Finance. The surplus shall not be included in the basic reference amount used to calculate the wage funds during the subsequent quarters of 1994.

(5) The average monthly gross wage for the respective quarter of 1994 in companies, enterprises and organizations receiving subsidies for the state and/or municipal budgets or funds from extra-budgetary accounts of the Ministry of Finance shall not exceed the six-fold amount of the minimal monthly wage established in the country for the same period.

Article 6

Companies, enterprises and organizations subject to full liquidation shall raise wage funds on a quarterly basis for 1994 as of the date of the announcement of the liquidation on the basis of the average gross wage for the preceding quarter and the actual number of the remaining staff (less persons on maternity leave), adjusted by the applicable coefficient when the reference basis is the preceding quarter.

Article 7

(1) When the amount of wage funds in companies, enterprises or organizations cannot be established of the respective quarter of the preceding year (the preceding quarter), it shall be determined through multiplying the actual number of staff during the 1994 quarter by the average wage for the respective activity during the respective quarter of 1993 (the preceding quarter) in accordance with the statistical reports, adjusted pursuant to the provisions of Art. 3 or 5. The information about the average wage for the respective activity shall be provided by the National Statistical Office.

(2) Paragraph 1 shall not apply to new joint ventures with foreign participation established in 1994. They are free to determine the average gross wage used to calculate the basic reference amount of wage funds during the subsequent quarters of 1994. It cannot exceed the six-fold amount of the minimal wage established in the country for the respective quarter of 1994.

Article 8

(1) The wage funds for the respective quarter of 1993 shall be subject to readjustment when the average number of staff (less persons on maternity leave) in the company, enterprise or organization has increased or decreased in the course of the current quarter of 1994 compared to the reference quarter as a result of:

1. Establishment or closing down of subdivisions (structural units);
2. Expansion of operations and increase or reduction of shifts;
3. Shift of subdivisions (structural units) from or to the corporate structure of the company, enterprise or organization;
4. Leasing of facilities;
5. Started liquidation of operations or activities.

(2) The readjustment under para 1 shall be calculated through increasing or reducing the wage funds of the respective quarter of 1993 by an amount obtained as the production of the difference in the average number of staff (less persons on maternity leave) and the average gross wage in the company, enterprise or organization as a whole during the respective period of the preceding year.

Article 9

(1) The provisions of Art. 8, para 1 shall apply also to the wage funds for the preceding quarter used as the reference basis under Art. 5, para 2 in companies, enterprises and organizations receiving subsidies from the state or municipal budgets or funds from extra-budgetary accounts of the Ministry of Finance.

(2) The readjustment under para 1 shall be calculated through increasing or reducing the wage funds for the respective quarter of 1993 by an amount obtained as the product of the difference in the average number of staff

(less persons on maternity leave) between the current and the preceding quarter and the average gross wage in the company, enterprise or organization as a whole during the preceding quarter.

Article 10

The application of these Regulations to the wage funds during the quarters of 1993 and 1994 shall exclude the amounts actually paid during the respective quarters for compensations under Arts. 22 and 224, para 1 of the Labor Code, the remuneration paid to members of Supervisory Boards, Boards of Directors, Chief Executive Officers, Managers and Comptrollers of companies, enterprises and organizations with more than 50 percent state or municipal participation as well as the remuneration paid pursuant to the provisions of Section 6 of Order No. 7 of 1991 of the Council of Ministers on the Development and Safety of Nuclear Power Generation (Not promulgated).

Article 11

The Ministry of Labor and Social Affairs shall provide clarifications as to the enforcement of these Regulations.

NOTES

1 Mr Tait is Special Trade Representative and Director, Office in Geneva, and Mr Erbas is a Senior Economist in the Middle East Department. The views expressed in this chapter are the personal views of the authors and do not reflect the official position of the International Monetary Fund. The authors wish to thank Sheetal Chand, Professor Gerald Dwyer, James Gordon, Daniel Hewitt, Zubair Iqbal, Malcolm Knight, Professor Chera Sayers, Victor Thuronyi, Jean-Philippe Vincent, an anonymous referee, and the participants of a seminar at the Department of Economics, Clemson University, for their input and helpful comments. The authors are responsible for any remaining errors.

2 For an overview of references and collected articles, see Walker (1982), Colander (1986), Fender (1990, Chapter V).

3 In this example, the minimum wage may also be viewed as the norm against which 'excessive' wage awards are compared, triggering the EWT. Thus, the inflation adjustment of the minimum wage would correspond to the inflation adjustment of the norm. The choice of a one-month tax period for the purposes of this example is arbitrary; in reality, the relevant period is the statutory tax period.

4 For example, in Russia such revenue amounted to about 5.0 percent of budget revenue in 1993/4 (or 30 percent of the corporate tax yield). In contrast, in Kyrgyzstan revenue from EWT made up less than 2 percent of enterprise profits tax revenue in 1991.

5 This arrangement would be similar to wage indexation; see Gray (1976). For a discussion of profit-sharing arrangements and their macroeconomic impact, see Weitzman (1984, 1985); on the same subject, also see Nordhaus (1988) and Weitzman's (1988) rejoinder.

6 The state-owned enterprise may totally or partially transfer the returns to capital to the government. In this case, if EWT affects profit, total government receipts

(the government's share of profits plus taxes) are also affected.

7 For simplicity, the minimum wage can be viewed as the norm or inflation-adjusted average wage, as determined by the government.

8 Modeling a progressive corporate income tax (Azerbaijan, Kazakhstan, Moldova) or progressive taxation of the excess wage bill (Poland, Estonia, Latvia) would not affect the general analytical results below.

9 The heterogeneous labor case which allows for a distinction between managers and workers is discussed below; for the case of $\alpha > 1$, see Appendix I.

10 We shall not attempt to compare the monopsony case to the competitive labor market case since it is well known that the equilibrium with monopsony is inferior to that which obtains with a competitive labor market. However, the main conclusions that are derived for the monopsony case can be readily extended to the competitive labor market case.

11 Comparing g and g^* at the same values for the wage rate, we can show that $g < g^*$ if $n + (w - \bar{w})n' > 0$, which holds if $w > \bar{w}$ as assumed. We also assume that the second-order condition for profit maximization holds in both cases; that is, in equilibrium, $\partial[(1 - \tau)(n')f_n]/\partial w$ is less than $\partial g/\partial w$ and $\partial g^*/\partial w$. Thus, the marginal product curve intersects g and g^* from above on the plane where the vertical axis measures the marginal product and marginal cost and the horizontal axis measures labor (n). Therefore, since $g < g^*$, the value of n at $(1 - \tau)f_n n' = g^*$ is less than the value of n at $(1 - \tau)f_n n' = g$; that is, the amount of labor demanded with g^* is less than the amount of labor demanded with g, or $n^* < n$. Since $n > 0$, on the (w, n) plane, $n^* < n$ indicates $w^* < w$.

12 That is, $(1 - \tau)[f(n) - wn]$, evaluated at w^*, is smaller in value than when it is evaluated at w; hence $(1 - \tau)[f(n^*) - w^*n^*] < (1 - \tau)[f(n) - wn]$ and $\pi^*_{max} < \pi_{max}$. The same result holds with competitive labor market as can be seen by comparing π^*_{max} and π_{max} at the same wage rate, $w = w^* > \bar{w}$.

13 As shown above, the effectiveness of EWT depends on f_n and θ. Given those parameters, if EWT is effective then w^* does not exceed the minimum wage by a wide margin; then, as indicated by (10.21), EWT revenue is lower. Therefore, it may be argued that the more effective is EWT the lower is the revenue from EWT.

14 The opposite results would hold if the rate of increase in the nominal minimum wage exceeded the rate of inflation. Here, we focus on the policy aim of containing 'excessive' wage awards by the enterprise in the face of inflation.

15 Similar arguments are valid in the case of the competitive labor market. As shown earlier, in that case, although EWT does not affect the wage level, it affects the firms's output–employment level. Thus, if the minimum wage declines, then, as indicated by (10.10), marginal cost rises, which implies a lower aggregate output–employment level.

16 We define a formal analysis of inflationary adjustment over time in response to the government's minimum wage policy under EWT as outside the scope of this chapter.

17 Thus, $Y = V(M/P)$ is assumed to represent the aggregate demand function.

18 For the stability of the new path of the price level, we may assume that at the time when the price level jumps upward, the government adjusts the nominal minimum wage so as to keep the real minimum wage at its initial level. The lack of such adjustment, as it is likely to present itself in reality, implies interesting inflationary dynamics under EWT. If the nominal minimum wage is not adjusted in response to the jump in the price level, then the real minimum wage declines, which sets in motion a further decline in the equilibrium real wage, and hence a decline in output, and hence a further jump in the price level.

19 In this chapter, we do not attempt to provide a comparative analysis of the effects

of EWT on the competitive enterprise versus the labor-dominated enterprise and limit the analysis in this section to the impact of EWT on the labor-dominated enterprise. Nevertheless, such a comparative analysis would be illuminating in explaining the aggregate wage and employment behavior in the former socialist countries during structural transition from a system characterized by labor-dominated enterprises to a system characterized by competitive privatized enterprises; a study related to this issue has been done by Stewart (1984).

20 In the FSU, the common practice for the enterprises is to make significant contributions toward such benefits.

21 We can show that $w^* < w$ if $\pi^g < (1 - \tau)[f(n) - wn]$, which holds if w and w^* are both greater than $\bar{w}$ as assumed.

22 In this case, since output level is not affected by EWT and τ is given, the increase in the tax base would unambiguously lead to an increase in tax revenue with EWT. To the extent the increase in revenue results in a lower recourse to inflationary finance, the rate of money creation may decline and hence the inflation rate may decline.

23 This phenomenon has been observed in most transition economies.

24 Arguably, the government is not likely to have enough information to choose $\pi^g = \pi_{max}$ or $\pi^g = \pi^*_{max}$. Therefore, similar to the first case discussed above, the enterprise has the leeway to negotiate the level of profit transfer to the government.

25 Both $\partial w_1/\partial w_2$ and $\partial w_1^*/\partial w_2$ are negative.

26 See Appendix III. Akin to the result in the case of a profit-maximizing enterprise in (10.19), the 'profit' or the rent reaped by the managers through maximizing their own wages is lower with EWT.

27 In this case, since n_1 is constant, lower n_2 would generally imply a lower output level; therefore, given constant money supply and velocity, price level would jump when EWT is imposed.

28 This point invokes a question which is similar to the familiar one that may be posed in market economies: would the tax authority allow the enterprise to declare losses by making excessive wage payments to the managers or to shareholders who are disguised as workers? At least in the case of the United States, the Internal Revenue Service's answer is patently no. In the case of FSU and East European countries, the existing EWT legislation does not address the question.

29 This went by the delightful name of the 'POPIWEK' or PPWW.

30 In 1990, the excess of actual wages above the norm toward the end of the year has been partly attributed to consuming the unutilized margin between the actual wages and the norm from the first half of the year, which could be carried out without triggering PPWW; see Pinto (1992b, p. 107, and Figures 2–6, pp. 118–22).

31 For evidence on wage and output–employment developments in 1990, see Pinto (1992b) in Coricelli and Revenga (1992); the inflation adjustment of the wage norm (minimum wage in our model) being only partial (the inflation adjustment coefficient was typically less than unity), from December 1990 to March 1991, the real wage norm and actual real wages declined (Table 4, p. 107). For further evidence on the negative impact of PPWW on wages, see Pinto and van Wijnbergen (1994).

32 A shipyard paying about 30 percent above the average wage, in arrears on PPWW, received a one-third reduction of debts (including accounts payable). Mining companies also were exempted.

33 In fact, further shuffling to and fro occurred. The 'Popiwek' lapsed as of March 31, 1994, but a further revised version re-emerged in August 1, 1994 (Schwartz, 1994, p. 21).

34 See Boote and Somogyi (1991, Section VI).

35 This exemplifies a problem in many reforming socialist economies regarding the ownership of capital. Since capital used to be allocated through the plan, enterprise managers had little obligation or incentive to pay a return on capital; instead managers paid as much of enterprise revenue as they could in wages or in other forms of compensation to labor.

36 This extremely controversial tax, applied to wages and profits, was suspended in September of the year it was introduced, forgiven for the first two quarterly payments, reintroduced in 1976 but not applied, introduced again in 1977, and again not applied, and finally, like the Cheshire cat's grin, faded from view for ever; see de Wulf (1976) and Chand (1981, 1986) for descriptions. This emphasizes the difficulty, experienced in most countries reviewed in this chapter, of administering this tax in the face of intransigent non-compliance.

37 See the Belgian example in 1976 in Chand (1981).

38 The authors are grateful to the participants of a seminar at the Department of Economics, Clemson University, for pointing out this possibility, which had been omitted in the previous version of the chapter.

39 Notice from (10.44) that, trivially, EWT does not apply in the reverse; that is, the enterprise does not receive a subsidy for paying $w_2 < \alpha\bar{w}$.

40 Notice that (10.44) can be written as $\pi^* = (1 - \tau)[f(n_1, n_2) - \hat{w}_1 n_1 - w_2 n_2]$ where $\hat{w}_1 = (w_1 - \alpha\tau\bar{w})/(1 - \tau)$. Therefore, the first- and second-order conditions for maximizing π^* and π can be evaluated by using the modified expression above for π^* or by using (10.43).

41 As in (10.13), we can show that $f_1 = g_1 = (1 + \theta_1)w_1/\theta_1$ and $f_2 = g_2 = (1 + \theta_2)w_2/\theta_2$. If θ_1 and θ_2 are constant, as assumed, we have $\mathrm{d}g_1/\mathrm{d}g_2 = \gamma(\mathrm{d}w_1/\mathrm{d}w_2) > 0$, where $\gamma = [(1 + \theta_1)\theta_1]/[(1 + \theta_2)\theta_2] > 0$.

42 Notice that in the competitive labor market case, the first-order conditions are $f_1 = g_1(w_1) = w_1$ and $f_2 = g_2(w_2) = w_2$, where w_1 and w_2 are constants.

43 Further notice that the model in the second section is useful in determining the impact of EWT on the level of capital employed by the firm. In that model, if we treat n_2 as capital, k, and assume that the rental on capital is given as r, by substituting k for n_2 and r for $\bar{w}$ in (10.27), we can see that the foregoing proof that $n_2^* < n_2$ also indicates that, with $f_{12} = f_{nk} > 0$, we have $k^* < k$, where k^* and k are respectively the levels of capital employed with and without EWT. That is, with variable capital, EWT results in a decline in the level of capital employed by the firm.

44 In contrast, see the case of self-seeking managers facing an inelastic labor supply, presented in the third section.

REFERENCES

Blanchard, Olivier J., and Richard Layard (1992) 'Post-Stabilization in Inflation in Poland', in F. Coricelli and A. Revenga (eds), 'Wage Policy during the Transition to a Market Economy', World Bank Discussion Papers, No. 158, Washington, DC pp. 51–72.

Boote, A.R. and Somogyi, J. (1991) 'Economic Reform in Hungary since 1968', Occasional Paper No. 83, International Monetary Fund, Washington, DC, July.

Chand, Sheetal K. (1981) 'Some Tax Based and Other Incomes Policies', Working Paper DM/81/40 International Monetary Fund, Washington, DC.

——(1986) 'European Experiences with Tax-Based Income Policies', in David C. Colander (ed.) *Incentive-Based Incomes Policies*, Cambridge, MA: Ballinger.

Colander, David C. (ed.) (1986) *Incentive-Based Incomes Policies, Advances in*

TIP and MAP, Cambridge, MA: Ballinger.

Commander, Simon (1992) 'Inflation and Transition to a Market Economy: An Overview', *The World Bank Economic Review*, Vol. 6, No. 1, Washington, DC, January.

Coricelli, F. and A. Revenga (eds) (1992) 'Wage Policy during the Transition to a Market Economy', World Bank Discussion Papers, No. 158, Washington, DC.

de Wulf, Luc (1976) 'The Taxe Conjonturelle: Can it Work?', *Bulletin for International Fiscal Documentation*, Vol. XXX, March, pp. 112–21.

Dildine, L., and E.M. Sunley (1978) 'Administrative Problems of Tax Based Incomes Incomes Policies', *Brookings Papers on Economic Activity* 2, Special Issue, Innovative Policies to Slow Inflation, pp. 363–89, Washington, DC.

Fender, John. (1990) *Inflation, Welfare Costs, Positive Theory, and Policy Options*, Ann Arbor: The University of Michigan Press.

Fiszer, Janusz (1991) 'Tax Reform in Poland' Friedrich Ebat Foundation, Warsaw, June.

Gray, Joanna (1976) 'Wage Indexation: A Macroeconomic Approach', *Journal of Monetary Economics*, Vol. 2, pp. 221–35.

Marresse, M. (1994) 'An Incomes Policy for Russia?', International Monetary Fund PPAA/94/3, Washington, DC, February.

Nordhaus, W. (1988) 'Can the Share Economy Conquer Stagflation?', *Quarterly Journal of Economics*, February, pp. 201–17.

Pinto, B. (1992a) 'Transforming State Enterprises in Poland: Microeconomic Evidence in Adjustment', Mimeo, World Bank, Washington, DC, 12/21/92.

———(1992b) 'Incomes Policy and Wage Setting Behavior: Evidence from Polish SOEs during the Economic Transformation Program', in F. Coricelli and A. Revenga (eds), Wage Policy during the Transition to a Market Economy, World Bank Discussion Papers, No. 158, Washington, DC, pp. 99–122.

Pinto, B. and S. van Wijnbergen (1994) 'Ownership and Corporate Control in Poland: Why the State Firms Defied the Odds', IFC Seminar paper, April.

Pinto, B., M. Belka, and S. Krajewski (1993) 'Transforming State Enterprises in Poland: Evidence on Adjustment by Manufacturing Firms', *Brookings Papers on Economic Activity* 1, pp. 213–70, Washington, DC.

Schwartz, G. (1994) 'Public Finances', in L.P. Ebrill *et al.* (eds) *Poland: The Path to a Market Economy*, International Monetary Fund Occasional Paper No. 113, Chapter 2, pp. 7–22, Washington, DC, October.

Shome, P. and J. Escolano (1994) 'The State of Tax Policy in the Central Asian and Transcaucasian Newly Independent States', *Bulletin*, International Bureau of Fiscal Documentation, pp. 159–66, April.

Stewart, G. (1984) 'Labor-Managed Firms and Monopsony Power', *International Journal of Industrial Organization*, Vol. 2, pp. 63–74.

Tanzi, V. (1991) 'Tax Reform in Economies in Transition: A Brief Introduction to the Main Issues', International Monetary Fund WP/91/23, Washington DC, March.

Walker, M. (ed.) (1982) *Tax-Based Incomes Policies, A Cure for Inflation?*, Toronto, The Fraser Institute.

Weitzman, Martin (1984) *The Share Economy*, Cambridge, MA: Harvard University Press.

———(1985) 'Simple Macroeconomics of Profit Sharing', *American Economic Review*, Vol. 75, December.

———(1988) 'Comment on "Can the Share Economy Conquer Stagflation?"', *Quarterly Journal of Economics*, February, pp. 221–3.

11

THE FISCAL COMPONENT OF THE FIRST RUSSIAN STABILIZATION EFFORT, 1992–3

Piroska M. Nagy[1]

INTRODUCTION

The year 1992 was a watershed in the economic history of the Russian Federation. Immediately following the political dissolution of the Soviet Union at the end of December 1991, Russia launched its initial comprehensive reform effort, involving price, foreign exchange market, and trade liberalization, privatization, and implemented the first in a series of attempts aimed at macroeconomic stabilization. The record so far has been rather uneven: while financial stabilization has not yet been achieved, progress on the structural front has been pronounced, with price liberalization almost completed, and commercialization and privatization advancing at a rapid pace.

This chapter focusses on the transformations in the functions of government and on the roles of the budget and of fiscal policies in the first years of the Russian reform process. It deals with the initial public sector conditions prevailing in the Russian economy and analyzes the record of financial policy implementation in 1992–3. In the first section the public policy conditions and the economic background against which Russia started its reform process in 1992 are briefly discussed. The next section provides a record of financial policies in 1992–3, with special focus on fiscal policies. The following section derives several general lessons from the 1992–3 macroeconomic developments, and discusses some conclusions.

INITIAL CONDITIONS FOR RUSSIA'S ECONOMIC TRANSFORMATION

In order to understand the conception and the results of the reform strategy of the Russian Federation since 1992, it is useful to analyze the initial conditions of the post-Soviet economic–political system. There were three distinct characteristics of the economic–political system of the newly established Russia that conditioned the outcome of the reform program of the Gaidar government that took office in October 1991. First, the economic struggles of 1991 that ended with the dissolution of the Soviet Union left the government sector weakened and the enterprise sector strengthened, relative to each other. Second, although the need for reform was generally recognized, there was no clear political consensus as to which reform strategy was to be followed. Moreover, unlike the East European reformists, the Russian reformers did not have the support of major interest groups. Third, the economic space was not well defined: the boundaries of the ruble zone were not set, and the nature and extent of economic disintegration of the former Soviet Union was obscure. These factors are examined in more detail below.

The combination of weak government/strong enterprise sector

Reforms were launched against the background of a weak government apparatus which merged some remains of the previous Soviet administration with the already-existing, but not well-functioning, Russian state apparatus. The outcome of the merger was a feeble state. The previous Soviet government administration had been discredited, and the Russian apparatus was coming from the second line of state administration, having been in the past only the executor of the decisions of the Soviet Union government. The enterprise sector, however, remained relatively well organized and powerful: enterprise managers survived intact the collapse of the old political regime, and became proficient in bargaining with the weak state for economic privileges.

This combination of weak government and strong enterprises resulted from the manner in which the former Soviet Union – including its administrative apparatus – was dismantled. It is often overlooked that the undermining of the Soviet state was the product not only of a political battle but also, to a large extent, of an economic war between the Soviet Union government and the major constituent republics of the former USSR. Since this internal economic struggle has been hardly discussed and because of its direct relevance to the Russian economic transformation, it is important to describe the nature of the economic war between the Soviet Union and the republics.[2]

The economic war between the republics and the Union was fought on two fronts. The first was a purely fiscal front, related to the revenue-sharing arrangements between the republics and the central government of the Soviet Union (to be referred to in what follows as 'the Union'). In the second half of 1991, the republics, led by Russia, decided to withhold the transfer of taxes to the Union budget, although they continued to draw resources from this budget and from its extrabudgetary funds. Republican administrative bodies ordered banks to withhold tax payments to the Union; and regions were encouraged not to pay taxes. Indeed, it was at this time that Boris

Yeltsin, then Russian President, developed his strategy designed to win the support of the regions over the central state apparatus, by exempting them from tax payments to central funds. Regions learned quickly how to optimize their financial position by taking advantage of the power struggle in Moscow.

The second front took the form of a fierce competition between the Soviet Union government and the Russian republican government for ownership of state enterprises. Until 1991, enterprises 'belonged', as a matter of jurisdiction, either to the Union government or to the lower-level republican governments. Since the ownership situation was quite chaotic, it was feasible for enterprises to decide to whom they belong. Tax payments and receipts of state transfers, including government provision of social benefits channeled through enterprises, depended on the ownership of the enterprises. In 1991, the Russian government launched an aggressive campaign to extend its ownership over those enterprises owned by the Union. A central element of that campaign was the 'tax war': the Russian government offered lower profit taxation to enterprises under its jurisdiction, compared with those paid by Union-owned enterprises. In order to make the move for enterprises more attractive, the Russian government also provided higher compensation and better family support to workers of firms under Russian government ownership. It also increased the level of subsidization of firms, in excess of what already was provided by the Union government.[3]

These developments largely discredited and undermined the existing state structure, financially strengthened the enterprise sector, and, in general, taught enterprises the necessary skills needed to bargain with weak administrations for subsidies and other forms of financial support. Moreover, in the wake of the disintegration and ultimate outlawing of the communist party, enterprise managers succeeded in acquiring the political clout and power of the former party. An additional element in the enterprise sector muscle-gaining arose from the fact that many enterprises formed associations within their sector (or subsector), effectively taking over the economic power from the soon-to-be-dismantled branch (or sectoral) ministries. Thus, still under the old leadership, and on the eve of launching the first comprehensive reform effort, the enterprise sector possessed much larger political and economic powers than ever before and much more than the emerging government structure.

Lack of consensus on reform strategy

At the end of 1991, there was no political consensus in Russia on the type of economic policies that should be adopted. While there may have been, at best, a consensus on doing away with central planning,[4] there was no defined positive strategy for implementing the reform process.[5] On the one hand, there was disagreement on the extent and speed of reforms and of macroeconomic adjustment, and on the other hand, there was disagreement on the type of fiscal federalism that Russia should choose for the future.

In this apparent policy vacuum, President Yeltsin handpicked one elite reformist group, led by Igor Gaidar, head of a reformist research institute. This group's only source of power was the President; and it was isolated from other power groups, in particular, the industrialists – who were strengthened, as discussed above – and the military complex and the agricultural lobby, whose representatives were sitting in the parliament and in the government. The lack of an actual power base distinguished the situation of Russian reformers from that of their East European counterparts, who, at least at the beginning of their reform, enjoyed the support of major interest groups and of the population. The apparent dependence of reformers on President Yeltsin made the operation of the group vulnerable and its reform strategy less credible to the extent that the President could – and often did – interfere with their policy actions.

To make things more difficult, the new government was also deeply divided, particularly regarding the role of fiscal adjustment and the type of budgetary spending that should be eliminated. The first independent Russian government comprised not only researcher–reformers, but also representatives of the less reform-minded groups (notably industrialists and old-time bureaucrats). As a result, the government's stated objectives were ambiguous: the Gaidar group emphasized radical liberalization and strict fiscal and monetary adjustment to combat inflation, while the more conservative group argued for giving priority to 'stabilizing production' through subsidization and cheap credits.

Lack of definition of economic boundaries

Although the political disintegration of the Soviet Union was well advanced at the outset of 1992, the economic disintegration was a chaotic process, where the nature of future economic ties remained undetermined and has been ever evolving. Even though separate fiscal budgets were immediately put in place in each of the new fifteen republics, there was no clear definition of the monetary sphere since the 'ruble zone/area' remained, with continuously changing boundaries, effective. Some former republics (i.e. the Baltic states) introduced their own currency early on, while others kept the Russian ruble as the only or main form of their currency through 1992 and much of 1993. In these circumstances, financial stabilization in Russia was an almost impossible task. The Russian Government's decision to 'seal off' all the leakages in the ruble's sphere came as late as mid-1993.

In sum, the economic arena in which stabilization was supposed to set in was ill defined; the government that came to power had virtually no experience, no political alliances other than the President, and no strong state apparatus to rely on. Moreover, it inherited an aggressive and powerful enterprise sector and lower-level regional apparatus that planted its representatives in the government, and the highest legislative forum, the Supreme Soviet.

MAIN ECONOMIC PERFORMANCE IN 1992–3: FISCALLY LED MACROECONOMIC CYCLES

In light of the above, the initial conditions for the first reform package of the Gaidar government were clearly complicated and difficult. Moreover, they were conducive to the initiation of largely fiscally led, stop–go cycles that have since become a key characteristic of macroeconomic policies. There are as many as seven distinguishable economic cycles between January 1992 and December 1993:

1 **STOP**:	January–March 1992
2 **GO**:	April–August 1992
3 **STOP**:	September–October 1992
4 **GO**:	November–December 1992
5 **BREAKS** and STOP:	January–June 1993
6 **GO**:	July–September 1993
7 **BREAKS**:	October–December 1993

STOP phase: January–March 1992

The main philosophy of the first Gaidar government was to introduce a bold package of structural changes that would make reforms irreversible in Russia. From the viewpoint of structural policies, the government's package had all the necessary ingredients of a radical reform package: price reforms, fiscal reforms, and foreign exchange and trade sector reforms on the macro side, and privatization/commercialization on the micro (enterprise-level) side.

Probably the most important element of the macro structural package, one that in addition to its efficiency effects had major budgetary implications, was price and wage liberalization. Price liberalization had two main objectives: to realign the distorted relative price structure inherited from central planning, and to absorb the existing monetary overhang.[6] Price setting was liberalized for the majority of goods and services at the beginning of January 1992.[7] The state also withdrew from interfering with the wage-setting mechanism.[8]

The main elements of the fiscal reform were tax reforms and cuts in subsidies and defense spending. Tax reforms centered around the streamlining of the tax system. A unified value-added tax (VAT) at 28 percent was introduced, replacing a turnover and a sales tax,[9] and the profit tax rate was reduced from the (Russian) level of 35 percent to 32 percent. On the spending side, producer and consumer subsidies were reduced in the aftermath of price liberalization, and defense spending was halved.[10] In addition, to ameliorate the budgeting process and to break with past procedures, the Government decided to set up a Treasury.[11]

The exchange rate was devalued and partially liberalized (although the government maintained, for its own transactions, an exchange rate of about one-half the market price in the first half of 1992). The trade system was also partially liberalized: while exports remained restricted by quotas and licensing, imports were completely free of quantitative restrictions, and in the first half of 1992, were also free of any import tariffs.

Micro-reforms focussed primarily on transforming the ownership of enterprises. The privatization strategy contained a two-tier approach. Under the first tier, small-scale enterprises were privatized, typically in the services sector. This process started simultaneously with the launching of the reforms in January 1992. The second tier, involving corporatization and commercialization, and the start-up of the voucher-based mass privatization process, started about mid-1992, but the necessary preparatory work had begun earlier.

While action on the structural front was decisive and quick, action on the macrostabilization front was incoherent. The Gaidar government simply did not have a consistent macroeconomic framework within which the structural transformation described above was to work. The government, however, did have a set of general financial objectives. Fearing hyperinflation after price liberalization, tight fiscal policies (a balanced budget) and a relatively restrictive credit allocation to the enterprise sector were targeted, with a monthly ceiling on total credit growth of 15 percent, or a quarterly growth of 52 percent. It was not clear, however, that such ambitious objectives were feasible. This would have required Russia, in a matter of three months, to reduce its fiscal deficit from its estimated level of 16 percent of GDP in 1991 (see Table 11.1).[12] In addition, notwithstanding the feasibility issue of the fiscal objective, the government did not have a package of measures to underpin the objectives. Both the necessary fiscal and monetary measures were lacking, the latter involving the government's failure to increase interest rates according to the announced and expected inflation rate, resulting in a rapid flight from the ruble into hard currencies. To make things worse, the macro objectives that were announced appeared to be inconsistent with the publicly proclaimed, and thus generally expected, outcome of the liberalization package. In December 1991, President Yeltsin, together with various senior government officials, reiterated that price liberalization should lead to an increase in the average price level of about '3 to 5 times' (200–400 percent). While the accuracy of such a projection may be questioned, there can be little doubt that expectations in the economy were formed on that basis, undermining, from the outset, the credibility and feasibility of tight financial policies.

In the event, consumer price inflation in January alone reached 296 percent (382 percent for producer goods), and 486 percent in the first quarter over

Table 11.1 Russian Federation: summary of main economic indicators, 1991–3 (percent change, unless indicated otherwise)

	1991	*1992*	*1993*
Real GDP growth	–13	–19	–12
Consumer price increase (within period)	144	2,322	842
Fiscal indicators (percent of GDP)			
General government balance:[1]	–16.0	–6.9	–5.7
Revenues	–	29.0	28.5
Expenditures	–	38.3	35.2
Extrabudgetary funds	–	2.5	0.6
Enlarged government balance:[2]	–	–18.8	–8.4
Subsidized credit via the central bank	–	15.5	5.0
Monetary indicators			
Base money[3]	–	1,066	645
Ruble broad money	77	545	422

Sources: Various publications by the Central Bank of Russia, and the IMF, Economic Review 1993/8 and 1994/16.

1 Consolidated balances of the federal and local government budgets, and extrabudgetary funds. Data in 1991 refer to the notional budget balance (see text).

2 The balance of the general government plus unbudgeted import subsidies.

3 Sum of currency issued and required reserves.

the preceding quarter. Credit growth to the economy, including that to the government, was restricted to 11 percent in January 1992, and only 46 percent in the first quarter as a whole. Broad money expanded at a mere 36 percent (although, clearly, the existence of the monetary overhang played a role there).

Such tight monetary policies were accompanied by tight fiscal policies. Because of the weak and discredited state apparatus that resulted from the dismantling of the Union, and the difficulties associated with the introduction of the tax reform, revenue collection reached an all-time low of 16 percent of GDP in the first quarter, down from an already-reduced estimated level of 28 percent in 1991.[13] Despite falling revenues, the government sought to adhere to the balanced budget target, therefore cutting expenditures to a virtually similar level. This meant a drastic cut in real expenditures from an estimated 45 percent of GDP in 1991 to 18 percent of GDP in the first quarter of 1992. Such a sudden reduction in government demand hit the enterprise sector severely, which was already subjected to tight credit policy.

This drastic tightening of financial policies became a factor behind the rapid increases in interenterprise arrears. Interenterprise debt increased during the first four months of 1992, by over 60 percent of GDP. While creating liquidity through the accumulation of interenterprise debt was not an uncommon reaction of enterprises to tightening financial policy in Eastern Europe,[14] in Russia it was, to some extent, explained by the tightness of financial policies. To be sure, the powerful enterprise sector, which had been accustomed to soft budget constraints, used this to attempt a justification for a reversal of reforms, and to loosen the newly established financial constraints.

The financial record of the first quarter of 1992 was mixed. The drastic tightening did yield immediate results, as inflation dropped from 486 percent in January to 27 percent in February, and to 16 percent in March. These results, however, proved short-lived, as the underlying financial situation was unsustainable.

GO phase: April–August 1992

Under the circumstances described above, the powerful enterprise sector (the industrial–military lobby, and the agricultural lobby) increased pressures on the Gaidar government to loosen financial policies. Moreover, although generally supportive of reforms, the President often undermined his government's tight policy by granting *ad hoc* exemptions to certain enterprises from export taxes, and ordering social expenditures in excess of what was budgeted (e.g. presidential decrees provided for discretionary increases in pensions, and payments by the budget of wage arrears in the enterprise sector if these were due to cash shortages, etc.). By May, the government gave in to forces pressing to increase expenditure, particularly defense spending (which almost doubled as a share of GDP in the second quarter), and outlays for producer subsidies. Spending became practically uncontrollable in the third quarter – which is seasonally also the most expenditure-intensive period of the year – owing to increases in wages and subsidies, including interest subsidies associated with the 'directed credits' to agriculture and the Northern territories, and to the provision of working capital through the budget (see below). Although revenues rose rapidly in the wake of government efforts to increase taxes (see below), these were insufficient to cover the rapidly rising expenses. The result was a general government deficit of 7 percent of GDP in the second quarter and almost 13 percent of GDP in the third quarter. Almost the whole deficit was financed by money creation (Table 11.2).

These deficits did not, however, fully reflect the impact of government operations on domestic demand. Outside the official (and more conventional) fiscal accounts, the government heavily subsidized imported commodities that were tied to foreign credits. These were the 'unbudgeted import subsidies', which were associated with foreign financing provided to Russia by western creditors. Since the breakup of the Soviet Union, virtually all foreign credit to the former non-Baltic states came in the form of tied credits, that is in the form of various commodities (food, spare parts, and machinery). The government decided to pass these commodities to economic agents at prices well below the existing market exchange rate. The difference between the real market price and the price charged for imports represented an

Table 11.2 Russian Federation: summary of fiscal indicators, 1992–3 (percent of GDP)

	1992					*1993*				
	First quarter	*Second quarter*	*Third quarter*	*Fourth quarter*	*Year*	*First quarter*	*Second quarter*	*Third quarter*	*Fourth quarter*	*Year*
I Revenue	16.1	19.3	26.6	38.4	29.0	34.2	33.9	24.7	28.0	28.5
of which:										
VAT	4.6	5.4	9.8	16.2	11.1	10.1	8.2	6.4	6.2	6.9
Domestic energy tax	0.0	0.0	0.0	1.1	0.5	1.0	0.5	0.2	0.1	0.3
Profit tax	4.6	8.5	8.4	10.1	8.7	12.1	12.9	9.5	9.6	10.3
Household income tax	1.5	1.8	2.3	3.0	2.4	2.4	2.6	2.4	3.0	2.7
Export tax	0.9	0.8	1.4	2.6	1.7	3.3	4.2	2.3	2.2	2.7
Import tariffs	0.0	0.0	0.8	0.1	0.3	0.8	0.8	0.4	0.5	0.6
II Expenditure[1,2]	17.5	27.1	41.8	47.3	38.3	37.0	34.1	37.4	33.9	35.2
of which:										
Wage bill[3]	3.8	4.5	6.2	7.2	6.0	8.8	10.1	9.2	8.0	8.1
Producer and consumer subsidies[4]	2.7	3.8	7.8	10.7	7.7	–	–	–	–	5.7
Operation and maintenance	–	–	–	–	6.9	–	–	–	–	4.0
Investment	0.9	1.8	3.0	3.5	2.7	–	–	–	–	5.0
Foreign expenditure	3.3	3.3	2.4	3.9	2.9	4.3	4.3	4.0	2.7	3.9
Defence (including wages)	2.6	4.6	5.9	4.7	4.7	6.3	3.8	4.5	2.8	4.4
Net lending for working capital[5]	0.0	0.0	6.4	3.9	3.3	1.7	1.8	3.9	–0.1	1.6

Table 11.2 continued

III Extrabudgetary funds, net[6]	2.1	1.3	2.1	3.2	2.5	2.1	0.5	0.1	0.6	0.6
IV General government balance	0.8	–6.5	–13.1	–5.6	–6.8	–0.7	0.3	–12.6	–5.3	–6.1
V Unbudgeted import subsidies	22.4	10.6	6.3	12.9	11.9	3.9	4.4	0.8	2.3	2.3
VI Enlarged government balance	–21.6	–17.2	–19.2	–18.5	–18.8	–4.6	–4.1	–13.4	–7.6	–8.4
VII Total financing[7]	21.5	17.2	19.2	18.5	18.8	–3.8	–1.9	11.6	11.7	8.1
1 Net foreign financing	22.5	11.0	6.5	13.0	12.1	3.7	4.2	1.3	2.7	2.6
2 Net domestic financing	–1.0	6.2	12.7	5.5	6.7	–7.5	–6.1	10.3	9.0	5.5
of which: domestic bank financing	–2.0	5.4	11.0	3.6	5.6	–4.3	–5.9	9.1	8.0	5.0

Sources: Ministry of Finance of the Russian Federation, and IMF Economic Reviews, 1993/8 and 1994/16.

1 Payment order basis, as reported by the Ministry of Finance.

2 The economic classification of expenditures is based on estimates made by the MOF and the IMF staff.

3 Includes an estimate for wage bill in the military sector, and social security contributions.

4 Includes estimated subsidies in outlays on national economy, and interest subsidies recorded under investment.

5 Includes partial repayment of on-lending, and new allocation to agriculture in 1993.

6 Includes the balances of the Pension Fund, Employment Fund, Social Support Fund of the Population, Social Insurance Fund, and the Road Fund.

7 Total financing data may differ from the balance of the enlarged government, due to statistical discrepancy between data by the Ministry of Finance and the Central Bank of Russia.

exchange rate subsidy that, following the unification of the exchange rate, became an import subsidy. Such unbudgeted import subsidies differed widely throughout the year (peaking at 22 percent of GDP in the first quarter of 1992, and reaching a bottom of 2 percent of GDP in the third quarter of 1993), depending chiefly on the available foreign tied credits.[15] This part of government expenditures was, by definition, fully foreign financed, and the corresponding demand fully matched by imported commodities.

The IMF staff incorporated these off-budget operations into the fiscal accounts, developing the concept of the 'enlarged government', covering the operations of the general government, and the unbudgeted import subsidies described above. It is important, however, to distinguish clearly these two components because their short-term inflationary impact is very different. The enlarged government fiscal deficit measures the total aggregate demand impact of the government in the economy, which is ultimately reflected either in inflationary pressures or in a worsening of the current account. The unbudgeted import subsidy part of fiscal expenditures is fully financed by foreign resources and matched simultaneously by increased supply from imported goods. While these subsidies increase government foreign debt, they do not have a direct inflationary impact.[16] Meanwhile, the rest of the government deficit was almost fully financed by domestic bank credit, with clear pressures on prices. Measured by the enlarged government concept, state intervention was very high throughout 1992 with the deficit oscillating around 20 percent of GDP.

Moreover, direct government involvement was not limited to the strictly defined enlarged government activities. The government determined most of the amount and direction of credit to the economy (non-budget sector). This was done through the mechanism of allocating the directed credits of the Central Bank of Russia to enterprises, channeled through the commercial banking system, most of them at highly subsidized interest rates. In this process, commercial banks were only passive instruments of government credit policy, which was based on sectoral considerations, without attention to profitability and creditworthiness. The main recipients of such subsidized credits were agriculture, the Northern territories, and the energy industry. The amount of these quasi-fiscal subsidized directed credits was estimated at some 15½ percent of GDP in 1992 (see Table 11.1).[17]

In the process, the difference between monetary and fiscal policy became rather blurred – a point that has been emphasized by Vito Tanzi.[18] One aspect of this interlocking of fiscal and monetary policy has been the high interchangeability between government expenditures (subsidies) and bank credit to enterprises – a characteristic of the central planning model. As the government revitalized the old system of enterprise funding, the difference between state allocation of subsidies and subsidized credits all but disappeared.[19]

In this particular GO phase, government expenditures (excluding unbudgeted import subsidies) rose from 18 percent of GDP in the first quarter to 27 percent of GDP in the second quarter, and to 42 percent of GDP in the third quarter. This temporarily eased pressures for (subsidized) credit for the enterprise sector, and enterprise credit growth in the second quarter was limited to the level of the first quarter. Another aspect of interlocking fiscal and monetary policy was the trade-off between fiscal and credit aggregates. As discussed below, there were occasions when enterprise credit was earmarked for tax payments to the budget, that is the fiscal deficit was reduced at the expense of higher credit to the enterprise sector. Because most enterprise credit was government-allocated subsidized credit, credit policy as such ceased to exist, and basically all financial policy was government-determined fiscal policy.

The record of this phase was disastrous. Inflation accelerated to almost 30 percent monthly by October, bringing the economy to the verge of hyper-inflation; meanwhile, after July, the ruble started its 'free fall'. The exchange rate depreciated from 125 rubles to the dollar in June to 225 rubles to the dollar in September.

STOP phase: September–October 1992

Rational elements within the government made a renewed effort to avert hyperinflation. Their reaction to the emerging large fiscal deficit, however, was to resort to 'stabilizing' instruments that 'used to work' in the past Soviet system.[20] Through this effort, a number of reform steps previously adopted were, at least partially, reversed. The VAT was modified so that it became a hybrid of a VAT and a sales tax.[21] This amendment was introduced in mid-1992, but was made retroactive to the beginning of the year. To facilitate payment of retroactive taxes, the Central Bank of Russia allocated additional credit to enterprises, part of which was *de facto* earmarked for the budget.[22]

The government also started to siphon off increasing resources from enterprises in the form of higher profit taxes. Profit taxes, based on a statutory rate of 32 percent, raised as much revenues in Russia in the first half of 1993 (12.2 percent of GDP) as was raised during the USSR era (12.3 percent of GDP in 1989, see Table 11.3), when a *de facto* profit transfer (confiscation) was in place. The reasons for this very high collection related to the manipulation of profit tax calculation in favor of the state. The main element was a cost–deductibility scheme that kept cost deductions below actual cost levels, producing an artificially high tax base on which the tax was levied. The most important constraint on cost deduction was the limitation of deductible wage costs to only four times the minimum wage. Because the average wage in the economy was systematically much higher than four times the minimum wage, the budget received additional profit taxes worth about 2 to 3 percent of GDP each quarter.[23] In addition, between the beginning of 1992 and November 1993, depreciation allowances were only revalued once (in June 1992) to take account of inflation; artificially low depreciations also increased

Table 11.3 Comparison of structure of revenues between the Russian Federation and the USSR

	1989 (USSR)	*1992*	*1993*
Total revenue[1] (percent of total)	100	100	100
of which:			
VAT/turnover tax	31.5	35.8	24.2
Profit tax/transfer from enterprises	32.8	30.0	36.1
Household income tax	11.7	8.3	9.5
Revenue from foreign activity[2]	16.8	8.6	11.9
Tax on natural resources[3]	1.1	1.7	1.1
Total revenue[1] (percent of GDP)	37.5	29.0	28.5
of which:			
VAT/turnover tax	11.8	11.1	6.9
Profit tax/transfer from enterprises	12.3	8.7	10.3
Household income tax	4.4	2.4	2.7
Revenue from foreign activity[2]	6.3	2.5	3.4
Tax on natural resources[3]	0.4	0.5	0.3

Sources: Joint Study of the Soviet Economy (IMF *et al.*, 1991), Ministry of Finance of Russia

1 Excludes privatization receipts and social security contributions.

2 Includes export taxes (in 1993 net profits from the centralized exports scheme), import tariffs, and ruble collection for budgeted hard currency allocation.

3 Includes natural resources taxes, contributions to the Price Regulation Fund, and excise tax on oil.

the profit tax base. The overall result was an effective profit tax rate that was by far higher than the statutory rate (35 percent in 1992, and 55 percent in the first half of 1993), and profit transfers were returning to levels similar to those under central planning (Table 11.3). These 'revenue-raising' methods proved to be effective, at least in the short run, and revenues started to soar, reaching 27 percent of GDP in the third quarter and 38 percent of GDP in the fourth quarter.

Central planning methods were not limited to tax policies: expenditure policies also showed signs of returning to former approaches. Subsidization of the enterprise sector reached astronomic levels, with total budgeted and unbudgeted subsidies amounting to 23 percent of GDP in 1992 as a whole (Table 11.4). Moreover, starting in July 1992, the government allocated, through the budget, about 5 percent of GDP worth of credit to the enterprise sector for the 'indexation of working capital of enterprises'.[24] As already mentioned, under the central planning system, the budget automatically financed the working capital needs of enterprises (instead of having them borrow from the banking system), and this scheme was revived in July 1992.

This resulted in a self-feeding process whereby state spending rose rapidly, and in turn was partly financed by expanding tax transfers from the enterprise sector. Higher taxes then increased pressure on the state to provide additional

Table 11.4 Subsidization in the USSR and Russia

	1989 (USSR)	*1992 (Russia)*
Total subsidy:[1] (percent of total)	100	100
Coal industry	5	4
Agriculture	79	8
For military conversion	–	3
Subsidy for foreign trade	9	66
of which:		
Total import subsidies[1]	4	66
Interest rate subsidies[2]	–	3
Estimated subsidies from local budgets	–	14
Total subsidy:[1] (percent of GDP)	13.5	22.7
Coal industry	0.7	1.0
Agriculture	10.7	1.9
For military conversion	–	0.7
Subsidy for foreign trade	1.2	15.0
of which:		
Total import subsidies[1]	0.5	15.0
Interest rate subsidies[2]	–	0.6
Estimated subsidies from local budgets	–	3.2

Sources: Joint Study of the Soviet Economy (IMF *et al.*, 1991), Ministry of Finance of Russia, and IMF staff calculations
[1]Total of budgeted and unbudgeted import subsidies.
[2]Explicit cash subsidies.

budgetary outlays to the enterprise sector. The evolving government intervention started to resemble that under the old Soviet system.

The aforementioned 'revenue-raising measures' were supplemented by a sequestration of expenditures, following the Central Bank of Russia's refusal to grant additional credit to the government (the latter, by the end of August, had used up all its annual credit lines with the Central Bank of Russia).[25] Increasing revenues and moderation in spending forced the budget into balance in September and October.

The impact of the fiscal restraint, however, was to some extent moderated by loose credit policies (which, as seen, had directly contributed to the improvement of fiscal accounts). Credits to enterprises – often at highly subsidized rates – as well as to former Soviet republics in the ruble zone rose unchecked, by over 100 percent in the third quarter (28 percent in September and 32 percent in October, when fiscal restraint already prevailed). Within this, quasi-fiscal subsidized credits reached an estimated 14 percent of GDP. Loose financial policies and general mistrust fueled further depreciations in the exchange rate. Overall, this halfhearted fiscal tightening did not make a lasting dent in the inflation process.

GO phase: November–December 1992

The revenue boom, spearheaded by the retroactively modified and partly enterprise credit-financed VAT, peaked in the fourth quarter of 1992.[26] The increase in revenue (12 percent of GDP) more than offset the further rise in expenditures (6½ percent of GDP), and hence a reduction in the general government deficit to 6 percent of GDP in the last quarter.[27] However, because the reduction in the fiscal imbalance occurred with a contemporaneous expansion in government outlays (and in overall government intervention), this period should be regarded as a 'moderate' but still expansionary (GO) phase.

The reasons behind the continued expansion in expenditures in this period differed from those behind previous slippages, and related to the lack of fiscal coordination among various government levels in Russia. In the fourth quarter, both federal and local revenues jumped. The federal government, recognizing the need to reduce the fiscal imbalance, used the additional revenue to reduce the deficit, while the local governments continued their spending uninterruptedly. Had the local governments not had this 'spending spree', the overall fiscal deficit could have been much lower.

The reason why local spending, albeit within its revenue limits, leads to macrodestabilization in Russia needs to be explained. There is a perception that because local budgets cannot borrow from the banking system, they are bound to have a balanced budget.[28] Therefore, logically, from the viewpoint of macrostabilization, it should be sufficient to let local governments pursue their own fiscal policies of balanced budgets. This misconception originates from the wrong assumption that Russian local budgets have a hard budget constraint. Although local budgets may not borrow from the banking system – except for a short term – their budget constraint can be softened through a number of mechanisms. In particular, they can lobby for (a) higher revenue sharing with the federal government; (b) higher transfers from the federal government; (c) tax exemptions; and (d) loans from the federal budget. Local governments frequently resort to all these mechanisms, leading to improvements in their financial position, often at the expense of the federal government. As local governments spend virtually all the resources they acquire through these mechanisms, despite the 'balanced' budget, their spending effectively contributes to macroinstability. This highlights another troublesome area of fiscal policies in Russia, that is problems of fiscal federalism and fiscal coordination at various government levels. At a time when fiscal tightening is clearly necessary, financial adjustment may be unsuccessful unless local governments are brought on board, and/or rules governing inter-governmental relations are reformed.

Credit policy during this phase continued to be accommodating (albeit at a moderated rate, with the growth in enterprise credit reaching 66 percent in the fourth quarter). The size of the quasi-fiscal subsidized credits exploded, however, reaching 18 percent of GDP. By the beginning of 1993, inflation surged to its highest level since the liberalization-induced price jump in January 1992 (close to 30 percent). The ruble exchange rate depreciated further and reached 415 rubles to the dollar by the end of the year. Macrostabilization failed in 1992.[29]

BREAKS and STOP phase: January–June 1993

By the end of the year, Gaidar, the main architect of the first Russian reform package, and some of his associates, were out of office. Prime Minister Chernomyrdin succeeded Gaidar and reinforced the ongoing return to the highest policymaking arena of former Soviet apparatniks.[30,31] The President's new, handpicked reformist in the Government was Finance Minister Fedorov.

Fiscal policies became tighter during the first months of 1993. This tightening was not only due to the usual beginning-of-the-year fiscal squeeze,[32] but also to Finance Minister Fedorov's recognition that without fiscal restraint, inflation could not be reduced. The burden of adjustment fell more on fiscal policy because the Central Bank of Russia at that time had not fully recognized its instrumental role in the inflationary process.

Unfortunately, the key instruments of fiscal restraint were those of central planning. The budget continued to benefit from very high profit transfers, which were further boosted by taxing unrealized capital gains on foreign exchange deposits.[33] Moreover, the government extended the use of central planning instruments to foreign trade as well, through the introduction of the centralized exports scheme. The aim of the centralized exports scheme was to increase export tax collection (which was very low owing to widespread tax exemptions), and to avoid capital flight. To this end, the government elected itself major foreign trade dealer. It purchased goods (mainly oil and gas) at a low domestic price, and sold them at the higher world market price, netting the difference as profit to the government. This scheme was started in the last months of 1992, but became fully operative in 1993.

Finally, fiscal restraint was helped significantly by the lack of budget approval through 1993; thus, the Ministry of Finance was able to resist pressures for higher spending on legal grounds.[34] Moreover, the government deliberately decided to accumulate arrears rather than resort to inflationary bank financing.[35] This led to a gradual but significant reduction in real expenditure levels: government spending dropped from a peak 47 percent of GDP in the fourth quarter of 1992 to 37 percent of GDP in the first quarter of 1993, and further to 34 percent of GDP in the second quarter of 1993.

All this was reflected in a moderate cash deficit of the general government in the first two quarters of 1993 (about 4½ percent of GDP). Although credit policy was also tightened (with an estimated credit growth of 46 percent in the first quarter and 53 percent in the second quarter, following increases in interest rates), inflation remained persistently high, oscillating at about 20 percent a month. By May 1993, the ruble exchange rate had reached 1,100 rubles to the dollar.

GO phase: July–September 1993

Demands for higher expenditures escalated by mid-year. At the same time, revenues virtually collapsed after July, contracting by 8 percent of GDP from the second quarter to the third quarter. Although the Ministry of Finance managed to contain the increase in real expenditures to 1½ percent of GDP (mainly through the accumulation of arrears, as discussed below), the revenue collapse triggered a deficit of 13 percent of GDP in the third quarter.

The drastic revenue decline can be only partially explained by the lagged impact of the VAT rate reduction from 28 to 20 percent at the beginning of the year. Other factors included VAT and profit tax deferrals that the government granted to enterprises allegedly hit by the re-emergence of interenterprise arrears (including interstate arrears), and the reduction in foreign trade taxes attributed to the real appreciation of the ruble. Furthermore, a vicious circle developed, in which efforts to contain the deficit in the context of falling revenues produced an accumulation of government payment arrears to enterprises as well as to households (in the form of wage arrears). In turn, economic agents started to withhold tax payments to the budget, expecting 'netting arrangements'.[36] Finally, economic agents started to get accustomed to the high-inflation environment, with the 'Tanzi effect' kicking in.

As mentioned, the Ministry of Finance had to weather intensifying attacks for higher spending. These attacks actually came from the traditionally populist Supreme Soviet, various parts of the government,[37] and the President.[38] Notwithstanding all the pressures, under the strong leadership of Minister Fedorov, who was backed by the muscle-gaining new Treasury, the Ministry of Finance managed to maintain expenditures in the range of 34–37 percent of GDP for the rest of the year.

The main instrument of expenditure restraint was, however, sequestration. This meant keeping, based on a frequently updated priority list, government spending within the limits of its own revenues and approved bank financing, resulting in non-payments of certain commitments. While sequestration is, in general, not a desirable (or feasible) way of achieving fiscal adjustment, it can be useful in the short run, pending the introduction of more orderly and transparent measures. Sequestration in Russia was also justified for another reason. In Russia, promises on budgetary allocations as well as on tax privileges were made by a number of bodies: the Supreme Soviet, the President, and government ministers. This made the concept of 'government commitment' very vague and, therefore, the turning down of many demands by using sequestration was a meaningful and often justified procedure.

Toward the end of 1993, the second reform year, however, sequestration had become Russia's sole instrument of fiscal adjustment. In this effort, non-payments were not only neglected promises made by non-Ministry of Finance commitments, but also true arrears, that is non-payment of approved wage and social safety-net-related expense increases, utility bills, and domestic debt obligations. This undermined the public's credibility in fiscal policies.

In addition to non-payment of 'true' (Ministry of Finance) commitments, the structure of expenditures suffered several other blows. Working capital allocations from the budget were revived again (under the heading of 'budget loans to enterprises'). Moreover, although not fully paid, budgetary wages appeared to have added to the fiscal strain, because real budgetary wages rose throughout 1993. Hence, there was an undesirable shift in the composition of expenditures, which added to the unsustainability of Russia's fiscal position at the end of 1993.

During this period, credit policy was accommodating. In addition to substantial credit to the government, credit to the economy grew by as much as 55 percent, and the rate of inflation was 90 percent during this quarter. A positive element was that within credit to the economy, the share of quasi-fiscal subsidized credits was reduced from its average level of 15½ percent of GDP in 1992 to only 3 percent of GDP in the third quarter of 1993.

BREAKS phase: October–December 1993

Despite the upcoming elections in the middle of December, the government decided to tackle the renewed upsurge in inflation by tightening financial policies starting November 1993. The key element in the policy mix was reduced credit to enterprises supported by increases in real interest rates.[39] Fiscal policy was also tightened in the fourth quarter, mainly through expenditure cuts/postponements (part of the resulting arrears was paid in early 1994). As a result, inflation declined to 12 percent in December, the lowest level since mid-1992, but still very high. Macrostabilization was still not within reach at the end of the second year of economic reforms.

On the structural front, however, success was measurable. Privatization, which in 1992 was largely limited to small-scale enterprises, mainly in the service sector, was extended to medium- and large-scale enterprises in 1993.

According to the State Committee for the Management of State Property (GKI), at the beginning of 1992, there were about 250,000 state enterprises in Russia. By the end of 1992, about 19 percent of these enterprises were privatized; this number increased to nearly 40 percent by the end of 1993. According to the Center of Economic Reforms, private employment in industry rose from 2.6 percent of the labor force in 1991 to 14 percent in 1992, and to 39 percent in 1993.[40]

Privatization has progressed well in the area of housing, where giveaways were frequent. In the area of agricultural reforms, progress was less spectacular, although the number of private farms more than quadrupled in

1992 to exceed 183,000, and by December 1993, exceeded 270,000.

As in other East European countries, it is difficult to measure the extent of private activities. Existing evidence suggests, however, that private activities grew sharply. The share of private activities in the retail trade, for example, rose from a mere 1½ percent in 1991 to 69 percent in December 1993. Other data that indicate important structural changes were those on the rapidly shrinking share of military-oriented output in total industrial output. This share decreased from 50 percent in 1988 to 29 percent in 1992 (data for 1993 were not available).

LESSONS AND CONCLUSION

The above brief review of events should indicate the richness and complexity of Russia's experience with transformation efforts. From the many possible lessons that could be drawn, five will be offered here, which are likely to have a bearing on how future reform policies might work.

1 There is a general belief that the Gaidar government failed to stabilize the economy at the outset of reforms because of anti-reform forces. This failure, however, was very much rooted in the apparent inconsistency and inadequacy of the government's macroeconomic stabilization program. The government's fiscal and credit policies were inconsistent with announced price increases, and fiscal measures were lacking to underpin the desired fiscal adjustment. The extent of the announced fiscal adjustment – 16 percent of GDP – was not credible either. All this provided major industrial and agricultural interest groups with ammunition to launch a joint attack on reforms. By September 1992, this pushed the country into a situation of chronic inflation.

2 After the initial failure of macroeconomic stabilization in early 1992, the policy mix shifted toward more emphasis on fiscal policies. Subsequently, when fiscal restraint was exercised, credit policy was – often simultaneously – loosened; and this pattern continued throughout 1992 and 1993. In fact, independent monetary and credit policy ceased to exist, with the government determining a large part of credit allocation through the commercial banking system, clearly not on the basis of creditworthiness or profitability. Moreover, the government entered the business of providing additional liquidity via the budget (allocating working capital to enterprises in 1992, and to agriculture and the Northern territories in 1993). Thus, during the first two years of reform, the government was involved in credit policy decisions, as if under a central planning system.

3 To reverse loose financial policies, the government reverted to the use of instruments characteristic of central planning. Owing to various cost limitation schemes, the profit tax was retransformed into confiscation-type profit transfers, with the effective profit tax rate reaching about 55

percent in the first half of 1993. Some reversal also took place with the VAT, which became a mixture of a sales and a genuine VAT. Moreover, the centralized exports scheme, while it helped to increase export tax collection as well as hard currency receipts of the government, re-established the government's role in foreign trade activities.

These elements, together with the government's instrumental role in credit allocation, led to an increase in the state's powers to allocate resources. This had at least two negative consequences. First, stabilization and adjustment based partly on central planning instruments could not be sustainable. Increasing state intervention was at variance with plans to shift toward a market-based economy. Second, such instruments also created perverse incentives for the government, and interfered with the government's capability to conduct appropriate macroeconomic policies. A good example of this interference was the government's involvement in export operations. Because the government became one of the most important oil and gas exporters, it acquired the interest of an exporter, which interfered with its judgment in determining the country's exchange rate policy.

Moreover, the only new 'non-central-planning' instrument that the government increasingly applied during 1992–3 was sequestration. While sequestration in Russia, where a number of legislative and administrative bodies claim the right to make expenditure decisions and promises, was a more justified instrument than in most other countries, its prolonged and virtual sole use led to an unsustainable fiscal structure and position that in its form was unable to underpin a stabilization process.

4 One startling characteristic of the Russian stop–go cycles has been the magnitude of shifts in government revenues, expenditures, and the fiscal balance from one cycle to another. Fiscal revenues and outlays can shift up and down by 8 to 10 percentage points of GDP within quarters. This may perhaps imply that an extreme shift in one direction is bound to trigger quickly another one in a wild and opposite direction. This could be an argument for not using extreme fiscal measures, and that, instead, fiscal restraint should be based, as has been argued, on more permanent and lasting adjustment steps.

5 Although it is perhaps perplexing at first glance, the described macroeconomic chaos did not hamper substantial progress in structural issues. Price liberalization was almost completed and exchange rate liberalization was completed.[41] Progress in privatization was fast and irreversible.[42] In the midst of high inflation, privatization and structural transformation made headway. While this may be counterintuitive, the following factors may shed some light as to the reasons why. First, high inflation may have helped to destroy the existing economic structure by allowing wild and rapid changes in relative prices. Second, owing to the lack of wage indexation in the non-budget sector, enterprise profits may

not have been squeezed excessively.[43] (The reason for the lack of serious attempts to establish a formal indexation was probably that employees preferred to suffer real wage cuts to maintain their jobs.) All together, it appears that macroeconomic instability did not hamper structural transformation in Russia and, most likely, this microstructural transformation will eventually help macroeconomic stabilization to succeed.

NOTES AND REFERENCES

1 Staff member of the International Monetary Fund. The views expressed here are not necessarily those of the IMF. The author is grateful for comments from Mario I. Blejer, Julian Berengaut, Daniel Citrin, Leonid Grigoriev, and Henri Lorie.

2 An exception is a recent book by A Åslund which, despite its misleading title, provides a good summary of such events: A. Åslund, *How Russia became a Market Economy*, Washington, DC: The Brookings Institution, 1995. In contrast, the political events of 1991 leading to the disintegration of the Soviet Union have been extensively analyzed, including the August military coup, and the subsequent removal, in a matter of a few months, of President Gorbachev. For an excellent record of events, see John B. Bunlop, *The Rise of Russia and the Fall of the Soviet Empire*, 1993, Princeton University Press.

3 For details, see International Monetary Fund, 'The Economy of the Former U.S.S.R. in 1991', *Economic Review*, April 1992.

4 This was *de facto* still in place, despite limited reforms under the Gorbachev era.

5 For details, see *Russian Economy in 1992: Trends and Prospects*, Institute of Economic Problems in Transitional Period (Moscow), 1992.

6 For an excellent analysis of the monetary overhang problem, see C. Cottarelli and M. I. Blejer, *Forced Savings and Repressed Inflation in the Soviet Union, 1989–90*, IMF Staff Papers, June 1992.

7 Some crucial prices were not immediately liberalized, however; most importantly energy prices (oil, gas, coal, and electricity), and some agricultural producer prices. For details of price liberalization, see V. Koen and S. Phillips, *Price Liberalization in Russia*, IMF Occasional Papers, No. 104, June 1993.

8 Notwithstanding the introduction of an excess wage tax, built into the profit tax (see later).

9 A lower rate of 15 percent was introduced for foodstuffs and children's clothing at the end of February 1992.

10 The cut in official military spending following 1992 was indeed dramatic, and can perhaps be explained, among other things, by the Russian President seeking to reduce the army's influence, which was inherently a Union institution.

11 In the Soviet model in which planned expenditures are virtually automatically financed through the banking system, there was no need for a Treasury controlled by the Ministry of Finance.

12 Measured by the notional deficit. The notional budget concept was developed for Russia to measure the impact of total government activities in Russia in 1991. It combined the actual outcome of fiscal operations of the Russian government, including the takeover of Soviet Union responsibilities after November 1991, with the imputed revenues and expenditures that would have been affected by the Russian government had the takeover functions agreed for November–December 1991 actually covered all of 1991. The figure cited here excludes the impact of the frozen part of deposit compensation and debt write-offs; taking these into account, the overall deficit reached 27 percent of GDP. For details, see

International Monetary Fund, 'Russian Federation', *Economic Review*, April 1992.

13 Comparable revenue (excluding social security contributions) in the Soviet Union was 37.5 percent of GDP in 1989. See International Monetary Fund *et al.*, *The Study of the Soviet Union*, February 1991.

14 This was the case in Romania (see, for example, M. Khan and E. Clifton, *Inter-Enterprise Arrears in Transforming Economies: The Case of Romania*, IMF, PPAA/92/1) and, to a lesser extent, in Poland, Hungary, and Bulgaria.

15 Until mid-1993, the rate of subsidization, that is the per dollar ruble subsidy, remained virtually unchanged, at about 90 percent on average.

16 It could be claimed that in fact they temporarily alleviate domestic demand pressures.

17 The estimates for the size of the quasi-fiscal subsidized credits channeled via commercial banks are based on information from the Central Bank of Russia.

18 See Vito Tanzi, *Fiscal Policy and Economic Restructuring in Economies in Transition*, IMF Working Paper, No. 22, March 1993.

19 It was not unusual to hear from representatives of the Ministry of Finance that 'decisions have not yet been made if we give additional resources to this sector through subsidies or through bank credit'.

20 It has to be highlighted that Russian experts within the Ministry of Finance – even in the higher positions – were fully aware that they were using old, central planning methods. They regarded this as a 'necessary price for acting quickly to reduce the deficit'.

21 Enterprises were forbidden to credit VAT on inputs that were going into stockbuilding rather than production. At a time of general expectations of high inflation, and very negative real interest rates, stockbuilding became an important way of storing value.

22 These were enterprise credits to clear interenterprise arrears. The budget's outstanding tax claims were satisfied as enterprises received credit to clear arrears to each other.

23 Initially, this 'excess wage tax' was intended to be used as an income policy device. This 'tax', buried in the profits tax, however, proved to be rather buoyant, implying that it was ineffective to curb wage increases.

24 This amount was in addition to the already-discussed directed credit, which was determined and managed by the government, but formally channeled through the banking system.

25 Sequestration in Russia is provided for by law for situations in which budgetary resources are not adequate to cover expenditures. This also became a device for the Ministry of Finance to turn down claims for expenditures that were imposed on the government by various bodies, most importantly, the Supreme Soviet (see later).

26 VAT collection (with statutory rates of 28 percent and 15 percent) reached a world record level of 16 percent of GDP in this period.

27 Extrabudgetary funds also tended to reduce the overall fiscal imbalance. Information on their operation has been very limited. It appears that their surplus (2½ percent of GDP in 1992) was the joint result of their expanding tax base (wages), and the lack of formal indexation of the benefits they pay in the context of high inflation.

28 However, the legal prohibition of borrowing from the banking system was relaxed in the latter part of 1993.

29 For further details of financial policies in 1992, see International Monetary Fund, 'Russian Federation', *Economic Review* No. 8, June 1993.

30 Another such appointment was that of former Gosbank Governor Mr Ger-

aschenko to the post of President of the Central Bank of Russia in mid-1992.

31 During the 1980s, Chernomyrdin was head of Gasprom, the omnipotent gas industry firm. In April 1992, he was brought back to the government as Energy Minister.

32 Indeed, for years, the fiscal accounts showed a clear seasonality. Prompted by the desire to 'balance the budget' after excess spending during the last months of the previous year, the new fiscal year usually started with severe expenditure restraint, only to loosen later.

33 There was a 32 percent profit tax on valuation gains made on foreign exchange deposits, irrespective of whether the gain was realized or not.

34 At the end of March 1993, a budget was formally approved by the Supreme Soviet, but because it was built on admittedly unrealistic assumptions, it was sent back to the Ministry of Finance for recalculation. This was finalized by the end of June, and submitted to the Supreme Soviet. The Supreme Soviet approved a budget that contained twice the amount of expenditures and deficit than that of the government. The President vetoed the inflated budget subsequently; similarly, the government refused to execute it, declaring adherence to its June draft budget. In the end, the dissolution of the Supreme Soviet in early October opened the way for the execution of the government's own budget.

35 Government expenditure arrears reached at least 2½ percent of GDP in the first half of 1993, and an additional 3 to 7 percent of GDP in the second half of 1993.

36 Indeed, rumors were circulating that the government had made a series of netting arrangements with enterprises in the first quarter of 1994, under which enterprise tax liabilities were netted against their claims on the government.

37 Concretely, the defense, energy, and agricultural ministries.

38 The President continued to issue decrees authorizing expenditures outside the budget, and without consulting the Ministry of Finance; for example, to 'index' the savings deposits in Sberbank.

39 Since the start of reforms in 1992, interest rates became positive in real terms for the first time in November 1993.

40 Center of Economic Reforms, 'Government of the Russian Federation', *Information Bulletin*, March 1993 and March 1994.

41 In mid-1992, the exchange rate was unified.

42 For an account of the Gaidar era, see M.I. Blejer, 'Gaidar's Economic Reforms Were Not a Failure', Mimeo, 1993.

43 Notwithstanding the high tax burden, however, to which the enterprise sector has started to react with tax avoidance.

12

TAXATION AND FOREIGN DIRECT INVESTMENT

The experience of the economies in transition

*David Holland and Jeffrey Owens**

INTRODUCTION

Foreign direct investment, FDI, has been identified by countries in transition towards market economies as an important element of that transition. This has led these countries to seek ways to attract FDI. In particular, a number of countries in the region have introduced tax incentives directed at attracting FDI. The use and effectiveness of such incentives in the context of the countries in transition have been the subject of a number of conferences sponsored by the OECD and others. This chapter draws upon these discussions. Experience among OECD countries has suggested that tax incentives are not an effective way to promote or direct economic activity. This experience has led most observers from OECD countries to advise that the use of such incentives be avoided. In the context of advising the economies in transition, a number of questions and observations can be made.

The first question arises from the concern that the experience of OECD countries with developed product and capital markets may not be relevant to countries whose economies are in the first phase of the development of efficient markets. Therefore it is appropriate to ask: is there anything in the actual experience of those countries in the region which have used incentives to cause a reconsideration of the standard advice?

The second question is: what are the risks and potential benefits of different forms of incentives, if policy makers of the economies in transition decide to use incentives to accelerate the adjustments of their economies? In particular, if incentives are to be used, are there provisions to minimize the risks and enhance the achievement of the objectives?

In order to provide some insight into these questions, the OECD conducted a series of consultations with government officials, both tax policy makers and tax administrators, and private sector representatives in a sample of countries in the region. The countries chosen had experience with the use of incentives which, it was hoped, could be usefully shared with other countries in the region. These consultations examined the more general factors that influence the decision to invest, the role of the tax system in the investment decisions of firms, the role of tax incentives in those decisions and the practical implications of the incentives on the functioning of the tax system. This chapter is based upon the report resulting from these consultations.[1] It builds upon the experience from OECD countries and draws conclusions based on the experiences of the countries in the region as revealed by the consultations. It generalizes from the experiences of specific countries to provide information which will be useful for policy makers throughout the region. It concentrates on the following issues: what are the important general features of the tax regimes from the point of view of potential foreign investors; what has been the experience of those countries that have provided special tax incentives to attract foreign investment; and, what are the practical consequences of the incentives on the administration of the tax system?

THE IMPORTANCE OF FOREIGN DIRECT INVESTMENT

Countries have identified a number of reasons for wishing to attract FDI. In general FDI is seen to be a way of compensating for existing deficiencies in the local markets and accelerating the transformation of the economies. The objectives of attracting FDI are:

Attraction of incremental investment capital Local capital markets are often not well developed. They thus cannot meet the capital requirements for large investment projects. Moreover, access to the hard currency needed to purchase investment goods not available locally can be difficult. FDI solves both of these problems at once as it is a direct source of external capital. Foreign investors have access to foreign sources of capital and so are not constrained by the relative underdevelopment of domestic capital markets or by the ability of the country to generate foreign cash flow from the export of domestic production.

Access to advanced technology Relative to OECD production techniques, many firms in the region use outdated equipment and techniques that can reduce the productivity of workers and lead to the production of goods of a lower standard. This reduces the ability of the firms to compete abroad for export markets and contributes to the difficulty of the countries in the region to earn hard currencies. FDI is seen to address this problem as the investment goods are expected to embody advanced technology and the firms would bring in advanced know-how and production techniques. The alternative of purchasing the rights to the technology uses expensive foreign currency. It is also hoped that there would be spin-offs from the innovation process which would enhance the productivity of the local workforce and stimulate innovation among domestic firms.

Access to advanced management techniques Foreign firms bring western management techniques with them when establishing operations. This provides an opportunity for locally engaged staff to acquire new techniques of operation. This transfer is of particular importance when existing firms are taken over and reorganized by foreign investors or when joint ventures are established with foreign investors. In the latter case, the foreign firm can benefit from the local knowledge and contacts of the domestic firm, and the domestic firm can benefit from new productivity-enhancing management techniques.

Enhanced access to western markets Western firms bring with them existing distribution channels and knowledge of the possibilities for sales to the global marketplace. The possibility for significant gains from trade would be opened up in a relatively costless manner. This would further the goal of export promotion as a source of foreign currency.

Facilitate privatization and restructuring Certain types of privatization require large pools of capital and the ability to analyze the economic potential of an enterprise. Foreign firms can contribute in both of these areas. This can enhance the access to external sources of funds as a source of capital when the assets are originally sold and when further investments are required to reorganize production and change product lines. The participation of foreign firms may also make the process more efficient by increasing the likelihood that the newly privatized enterprises would be able to realize their full potential.

Questions have been raised on the effectiveness of FDI in promoting a number of the above goals, for example technology transfer. Certainly not all FDI can be said to contribute to their achievement. Many of the projects attracted by the incentives offered have been short-term ventures that have been of little lasting benefit to the country and have been a drain on hard currency rather than a source. This suggests that, if the attraction of FDI is to be pursued for the above reasons, the instruments chosen must be critically evaluated to see if they are well targeted to the task.

NON-TAX FACTORS AFFECTING FDI

There are many factors other than the tax system that are relevant in the decision to invest in a country. Some of these factors are outside of the control of the government and establish the base for determining the comparative advantages of the country. These can be important in the policy process as the consultations have shown that the perception of relative disadvantages, say of location, is often used by policy makers to justify the provision of incentives to compensate for the disadvantages. Such policies are likely to be ineffective in improving the competitiveness of a country. The tax system can alter the private comparative advantages of firms on an after-tax basis and so has the potential to alter their behaviour. However, it cannot change the relative advantages and disadvantages from a social point of view, that is on a before-tax basis. It is merely dividing the pie differently between the private sector and the government.

Other factors are within the control of, or at least can be influenced by, government policies. In many cases, these factors are seen by the private sector to be more important than the tax system, suggesting that these should be areas of concentration by the government.

It is not possible to assess the relative importance of the different factors in a quantitative manner. Certainly the ordering would be different for different sectors and circumstances. Some investors base their investment decisions on the economic opportunities and risks, with the tax consequences being worked out afterwards. Naturally, an attempt is made to minimize the amount of taxes paid and so any incentives available were used. While this extreme view would certainly not hold in many cases, it underlines the fact that the tax system is probably not the most important factor in the FDI decision process.

Investment decisions are fundamentally driven by a comparison of the potential returns from an investment as compared to its risks. A number of non-tax factors are important in either contributing to the potential return or, often more importantly, reinforcing a perception of potential risk. These include:

Size of the market The larger countries in the region provide substantial potential markets where the consumer demand for certain goods has been largely unfilled to date. This potential has been a draw for many of the initial foreign-owned operations in the region. In some cases these operations do not entail many, if any, of the benefits attributed to FDI. This is especially the case with short-term importation operations established to capture the rents available from satisfying the pent-up demand for goods not previously available. In other cases, the establishment of a low-cost marketing operation represents the first step by a multinational into the market of the country. This establishes a presence in the market and provides important insights into the ways of doing business and possible opportunities in the country.

Uncertainty One of the greatest negative factors inhibiting FDI is the uncertainty that surrounds doing business in the region. To some extent, the uncertainty results from the fact that these markets have been closed to western businesses in the past. It is for this reason that companies may establish small operations initially, in order to gather the necessary information for a full assessment of the risks and opportunities of doing business. In many countries the institutions of government are still evolving and there are unsettled political questions. This uncertainty is one of the major factors causing the somewhat disappointing FDI performance in the region. Companies are unwilling to contribute large amounts of capital into an environment where some of the basic political questions have not been resolved. Unfortunately, even countries that are relatively stable within themselves suffer from the serious problems that are occurring in other parts of the region.

Legal and regulatory framework The transition towards a market economy entails the establishment of a legal and regulatory framework that is compatible with private sector activities and the operation of foreign-owned companies. Much progress has been made in this area in many of the countries of the region. Areas of importance, such as protection of property rights, the ability to repatriate profits, and a free market for currency exchange, have been established in many of the countries. For some, progress has been slower in some of these areas and this may inhibit FDI. It is important that these rules and their related administrative procedures be as transparent as possible. The drafting and enacting of legislation in these areas is a difficult process. In many cases, substantial changes were required from existing practice in the country. Thus the concepts were unfamiliar. In some cases the laws that have been drafted have been unclear. This has led to the need for substantial revisions to the initial laws and regulations. Frequent changes lead to uncertainty and make business planning difficult. The new rules also pose a challenge to the administrators in the country. This can lead to inconsistency of application which contributes to the sense of uncertainty.

Macro-economic environment Instability in the level of prices and the exchange rate makes business planning difficult and increases the level of uncertainty. This increases the perceived risk of making investments and so reduces FDI. Macro-economic instability can also exacerbate other problems in the regulatory environment. For example, exchange rate fluctuations increase the costs to investors in situations where either the foreign exchange market is not totally free or there are delays in receiving payments from the government that are not indexed to changes in currency values.

Access to basic inputs FDI can be attracted to the region by the availability of factors of production. Most countries in the region have highly educated and skilled labour forces that are of low cost compared to the wages paid in OECD countries. This provides an opportunity for foreign firms to make investments in the countries to supply the export market. In fact, there appears to have been relatively little of this investment. This may reflect the absence of some of the other basic features described here. It may also reflect the barriers to which such exports may be subject in overseas markets. Firms will also make investments to have access to raw materials such as oil and gas, minerals and forestry products. In some cases, even when the overall FDI performance has been low, there have been substantial investments in these sectors. In these circumstances a challenge for the countries has been to ensure that they receive an adequate return from the exploitation of their resources.

GENERAL TAX FACTORS AFFECTING FDI

While the tax system is not the only, or even the most important, factor affecting the FDI decision, it clearly has an influence on investment decisions. However, tax incentives directed at attracting FDI are often secondary to the more general features of the tax law. In most cases, firms are concerned to have impediments to investment in the law or administration removed, rather than have incentive measures. Moreover, the concerns of firms often extended beyond the income tax to other taxes not related to the profits of the firm.

Level of tax

The overall level of the tax burden clearly has an impact on the attractiveness of a country for foreign investors. This includes all forms of taxes, not only the income tax. However, it is not appropriate simply to compare the burdens of taxation across different countries to determine their attractiveness (and in practice, such data are still not available). First, tax revenues are the ultimate source of funds for most government expenditures and have an obvious and crucial role in bringing expenditures and revenues into line. Thus, lower taxes, if they lead to a budget deficit that reduces the macro-economic stability of the economy, can be counterproductive in achieving the goal of attracting investment, and this is a policy that few of the economies in transition have followed. Second, if the revenues are spent on purposes which reduce costs and enhance income-generating activities, the expenditures effectively offset the negative impact of the taxation. Expenditures on health can reduce private health care costs and so be reflected in lower wage demands or reduced costs to business of employer-based health plans. Expenditures which enhance the transportation and public utility infrastructure of the country can reduce costs to companies and increase their profit-making potential. For these reasons, the overall level of taxation in the economy has not been a good indicator of relative economic performance among OECD countries.

Transparency of tax system

The concern raised most frequently by the private sector was its ability to predict the tax consequences of its investment and other decisions. This issue is particularly important for the long-term, capital-intensive investments that most governments in the regions are attempting to attract. In most countries, it is difficult for firms to predict the tax outcome of their actions. The first problem stemmed from the law. In many instances it was seen as imprecise and vague. Even professional advisors find it difficult to provide confident interpretations of the law. Many of the provisions which are accepted as normal in the tax laws of OECD countries are not present in the laws in the region. Thus, for more complicated transactions such as reorganizations of corporations or thin capitalization, the law does not directly address the situation facing the taxpayer and so the tax outcome is unclear.

This situation is exacerbated by the frequent, significant changes to the laws and regulations. While fine-tuning is inevitable in a statute as complex as a tax law, many of the changes have had a material impact on the amount of taxes to be paid on particular transactions. This reflects the constant evolution of the policy and legislation which is natural during a transition process. A number of countries have tried to ameliorate this situation by providing protection to investments made before the change. In some cases the authorities modified the change on the basis of consultations with the private sector. While this dealt with the particular problem of the taxpayers affected, it further adds to the feeling of uncertainty. The reaction on the part of business parallels that expressed by businesses operating in OECD countries where the frequency of change contributes more to a sense that the tax system is complex, and difficult to plan and comply with, than do the provisions themselves.

The problems of the lack of transparency and stability of the law are often worsened by difficulties in the administration of the law. Tax administrators were subject to the same difficulties as private sector advisors in keeping up with the rapidly changing legislative environment. In addition, the tax administrations needed to cope with changes occurring in the tax-paying population. Previously there were a relatively limited number of taxpayers who were large state-owned companies. The relationship between the authorities and the taxpayers was close by western standards. In enforcing compliance, the tax authorities could rely on the budgeting cycle to which the firms were subject. The change towards a more market-oriented economy has added to the number of taxpayers. At the same time, the relationship of taxpayers to the government is changing: there is less information provided to the government and taxpayers have a greater incentive to attempt to minimize taxes payable. The effect of these stresses has been to reduce the ability of the tax authorities to provide timely interpretations of the law. Many private representatives voiced frustration that they were unable to receive the material on interpretation of the law and the advance rulings that are available in OECD countries. In addition, it is more difficult to maintain a consistency of interpretation both over time and across different tax offices. In some cases, sublevels of government have authority in setting the rules or an influence over the administration of taxes. In these circumstances taxpayers can be unsure where to turn to find the answers to their questions. These issues of the administration of the law are raised as often as the rules themselves in discussions with the private sector. In many cases, deficient rules can be planned around. However, arbitrary or inconsistent administration can impose significant unanticipated costs on taxpayers. This situation increases the perception of risk for companies contemplating investments and emphasizes the need to develop tax laws that are easily administrable and so do not increase the pressures on the administrators during the difficult period of transition.

The general features of the tax system are important. They are important not only in determining the tax burden of the company, but also for their effect on how the company organizes its operations. These latter effects are often more important than the overall tax burden and were often cited during the private sector discussions.

Statutory tax rate

The statutory tax rate is clearly important in establishing the overall tax liability of an enterprise. However, the statutory tax rate does not, in itself, establish the ultimate tax burden on the activity. Equally important are the effects of the provisions which determine the tax base and the actions taken by firms to minimize their tax burden. Experience in OECD countries has shown that the statutory tax rate can be important in establishing the financial and tax planning strategies of a company. Corporations will generally respond to significant differences in statutory tax rates by streaming income towards the low tax jurisdiction and costs towards the higher tax rate jurisdiction. For example, other things being equal, a company would rather make its borrowings in a manner which places its interest deductions in the subsidiary which faces the highest statutory tax rate. As a result of such tax planning, a higher statutory tax rate does not always result in higher tax revenues, at least from those firms with operations in a number of countries. These concerns are particularly important for countries in the region which are still developing their capacity to respond to tax avoidance activity. In most cases the countries lack the provisions in the law which could be used; have limited access to data, both domestically and through exchange of information provisions in tax treaties; and do not have personnel who are trained and experienced in the more complicated areas of tax auditing. The statutory tax rate can also influence certain marginal production decisions of firms and could have an influence in shutdown situations where the treatment of capital costs is no longer relevant to the decision. On the other hand, lowering the rate reduces profit tax revenues from domestic activity. Profit taxes are often a more important source of government revenues in countries in the region than in OECD countries. This puts a limit on the extent of any rate reduction, at least in so far as it is not matched by an offsetting widening of the tax base. This suggests that the statutory tax rate should remain within international norms of about 30 to 40 percent. This is the range of tax rates for most of the countries in the region.

The tax base

The calculation of taxable income is as important as the statutory tax rate in determining the burden of taxation. The features of its calculation can have a significant impact on the pattern of taxation across different companies. The treatment of different revenues and expenses can also have an influence on how a company arranges its affairs. In particular, the structure of the business, joint-stock company, partnership, joint venture, etc., will be influenced by the relative treatment of these forms of business operations. Financing decisions are also heavily influenced by the way the payments made with respect to the various financing instruments are treated for tax purposes. Finally, it is in the calculation of the tax base that many of the provisions that are the most complex for administration and compliance are found. For these reasons, most of the discussion with the private sector about the income tax revolved around questions that were either directly or indirectly linked to the calculation of taxable income.

In some countries in the region, a number of the features of the tax systems remain different from those of western economies. These differences generally are found in provisions that are holdovers from the taxation regimes that existed under socialist economies. In the past, where the state was both the taxing authority and the owner of the enterprise, many of the issues which arise in determining the tax base where the taxpayer is privately owned do not arise. Therefore the tax system was often used as one of the means to control and influence the behaviour of enterprises. This led to a fundamentally different treatment of most of the important expenditures that are made by corporations. Countries in the region have made important changes to their regimes to bring them more into line with the appropriate treatment of private sector transactions. However, in some countries, problems do remain.

In other cases, the tax systems are distinguished by what they lack. Western firms have evolved a very flexible array of arrangements and methods of organization. These methods of operation have necessitated the development of sophisticated and complicated provisions in the tax systems of OECD countries. For the most part, these provisions are not found in the laws of countries in the region. This can, at times, restrict the ability of firms to arrange their affairs in the most efficient manner. In other circumstances, it leaves the treatment of certain transactions ambiguous and impedes the tax and business planning of corporations. The lack of clear guidance in the law is also a problem for the tax administrations who, at the same time, are dealing with complicated business arrangements that are unfamiliar to them. The resulting lack of clarity increases the likelihood of disputes between taxpayers and the tax services of the countries.

A number of specific elements of the tax system are the focus of particular attention:

Depreciation regime In many of the countries in the region the depreciation system is a holdover from the former taxation system. As compared to the depreciation systems offered in most OECD countries, it is detailed in its differentiation among different assets and industrial sectors and has low rates of depreciation. Such features reflect the different use for depreciation as part of the budgetary control mechanism under the former regime. This comment needs to be qualified in two important respects. First the persistence of significant inflation rates in a number of countries in the region makes simple comparisons of depreciation rates meaningless. Depreciation based upon historic cost is undervalued during inflationary times as the real cost of the depreciation of today's assets is underestimated when the asset base is measured in nominal dollars. A number of countries have allowed *ad hoc* adjustments to the asset cost bases to compensate for the underestimate of true depreciation in the face of inflation. However, such adjustments are not necessarily tied to the underlying changes in the value of the asset and their discretionary nature makes it difficult for firms to take them properly into account in their planning. The second qualification works in the opposite direction of the first. A number of countries allow general investment allowances to the extent that the amounts invested exceed accumulated depreciation. With stable prices, this effectively means that additional deductions, over and above depreciation, are allowed whenever the size of the total investment is increased. The value of this concession increases under inflationary conditions, where today's investments are compared to prior investments measured in nominal, not real dollars. Therefore, a benefit can be received even though there is no real growth in the size of the investment. This compensates to some extent for the underestimation of the depreciation.

Treatment of expenses A number of countries have restrictions on deductions for certain expenditures. In some cases these appear to be intended to improve the fairness of the tax system. In other cases, they are intended to control the activities of state-owned enterprises. Some are implicit restrictions since expenses are generally not allowed unless explicitly noted. In this case, the list of expenses may simply have not kept up with the different ways of doing business under the evolving market economy. An important point is that the companies are often able to arrange their affairs to avoid the burden of the restriction. However, this requires using arrangements that are not efficient from a business point of view or that are somewhat artificial and potentially subject to audit examination.

The restrictions that are most subject to criticism are the restrictions on the deductibility of wages and the limited deductions available for interest expenses in some jurisdictions. Deductions for wages are denied when the aggregate wage and salary bill exceeds some multiple of the minimum wage times the number of employees. In some jurisdictions, this was in effect accomplished by a payroll tax on the excess wages. These restrictions are used for two purposes. They are intended to reduce wage increases as part of an anti-inflation programme and to control the tendency of state-owned enterprises to grant excess wage increases rather than return funds to the state budget. While such restrictions may be appropriate for state-owned enterprises, they are not appropriate in the private sector where companies already have a significant incentive to keep wages to a minimum. The situation is potentially very damaging for foreign investors with expatriate staff who earned wages far in excess of the limits implied by the legislation, although in certain countries non-resident investors are excluded from this form of wage control. In fact, while these restrictions are annoying to foreign taxpayers, they are simple to plan around. Wages can be paid offshore and services provided by a service company or fringe benefits could be paid rather than wages and salaries. Stopping these mechanisms would be complicated legislatively and would put further pressure on the administrations.

Restrictions also historically existed for the deduction of interest. In some cases only bank interest could be deducted for tax purposes. This effectively denied the use of other financing instruments. This forces companies either to stream loans through conduit banks or to use more tax-efficient lending mechanisms such as leasing. Again the result is that the restriction could be avoided at some cost in terms of flexibility. Effectively counteracting the tax planning would be complicated and counterproductive.

Other features Most of the countries in the region are still in the process of developing their tax systems and so they naturally do not have many of the more sophisticated provisions found in OECD tax systems that have been evolving over many decades. Features absent included rules to deal with reorganizations of businesses and rules to allow some form of consolidation of income and losses from companies that belonged to a commonly owned group of companies. In some cases, the relatively unsophisticated approach to accounting effectively deals with the problem as transfers are made at book rather than fair market value. There is one area that is troubling to firms. In some countries loss carryovers are either for a very short period by OECD standards or restricted in some other way. These restrictions are holdovers from the previous regime where the state's role in funding the losses of corporations reduced the need for loss carryforwards. However, for private sector companies the ability to carry forward losses is critical in arriving at an accurate picture of income earned over a period of time. The restrictions are most harmful to companies looking to make long-term, capital-intensive investments. Such firms are likely to experience losses in the start-up phase of the investment. Naturally the firms would at least like to cover these losses with income before beginning to pay tax. Restrictions on loss carryforwards can result in firms paying tax even when they are in a cumulative loss position.

Taxation of expatriates

Companies establishing operations will often wish to use foreign management personnel or technical experts. This is a principal way to transfer such expertise to the country. In some cases, the tax spent in the host country can significantly raise the cost of such expatriate personnel and so discourage FDI. The two areas where this occurs are the social security tax and the personal income tax.

When looked at domestically, social security taxes are payments that are more or less directly reflected in benefits received by the employee. Thus, even though the taxes are for the most part levied on the employer, they are assumed to be reflected in the wages paid to the employee. The move by a number of countries to develop fully funded social security systems should enhance this connection. The existence of state pensions, medical care and unemployment insurance reduces the need for wages that are high enough to self-finance these costs. The taxes applied to domestic workers are not seen as a problem given the low level of wages in the region when compared to wages and salaries in OECD countries.

However, the application of the social security contributions to expatriate service providers in foreign-owned companies can lead to problems. In such cases, the wages paid to the expatriates are at western rates and certainly do not take into account the benefit side of the social security system. Moreover, the expatriates do not qualify for benefits under the system. In this case the taxes simply increased the cost of using the service providers. This is effectively a disincentive for the importation of know-how from the developed market economies that is one of the principal perceived benefits of FDI. In response to this, a number of countries in the region have explicitly removed expatriate employees from either the contribution or benefit side of the domestic social security system. In other cases, companies have found ways of avoiding the payment of the contributions in such circumstances through devices similar to those employed to avoid the restricted deductions for wages and salaries under the profit taxes. Nevertheless, the potential liability for such charges remains a concern to foreign investors (e.g. paying part of the salary offshore).

The personal income tax systems of the countries in the region have rate schedules linked to the level of wages in their country. As expatriate employees generally have higher levels of wages, they may face levels of tax much in excess of what they would pay in their home country. In addition their costs of living could likely exceed those of domestic taxpayers.

Customs duties on imported investment goods

Non-income taxes are also of concern to firms. They are concerned that the taxes are payable even when the firm was not profit making and that they usually had the effect of increasing the cost of basic inputs. These taxes either result in an increased upfront risk of the investment or increased the operating cost of the company. The most prominent taxes are customs duties, or general taxes on goods, that are applied to investment goods.

The application of duties on investment goods has some appeal to countries in need of enhanced revenue sources. Customs duties provide a direct and easy to administer source of revenue for the government. However, such taxes raise the cost of capital investments. This increases the risk of investing in a country and raises the required rate of return to make an investment profitable. Experience in countries in Asia suggests that the most important tax relief for firms examining potential investments is relief from customs duties on imported capital equipment. Customs duties on capital equipment act directly counter to the goals that are generally behind incentives to attract FDI. First, such taxes are most onerous on the long-term, capital-intensive projects that are required to modernize the industrial base in the region. Second, it is through the importation of modern equipment that much of the benefit of introducing advanced production technologies will be realized. For these reasons, most countries in the region provide at least partial exemptions from customs duties for own-use production equipment. However, these exemptions are sometimes linked to the initial capital contribution associated with the establishment of a new foreign-owned business and so may be of limited use for a company which makes its investment in stages. In other cases, a VAT is charged on the importation of the capital item, the normal treatment, but a delayed or incomplete refund is given. This effectively levies a tax on the capital item which would be inconsistent with any investment incentives that might be provided.

Tax treaties

Tax treaties provide a framework within which companies which operate across borders can plan their affairs. Their principal purpose is to coordinate the application of the tax systems of the home and host countries. Both countries have a legitimate claim to tax the revenues derived from cross-border operations. The purpose of the tax treaties is to provide the rules under which the tax pie is divided up to ensure that there is not double taxation of the income. They also provide a framework under which administrative issues that arise in the determination of the allocation of income between the two jurisdictions can be resolved.

Anti-avoidance rules

One final observation is important to put the foregoing discussion in context. It is not always disadvantageous to foreign firms that some of the features typical to the tax systems of OECD countries are missing or that the tax administrations in the region are not yet fully experienced in dealing with the market-oriented business arrangements. A number of typical provisions to protect the tax base are often not in the tax systems of the countries in transition. For example, arm's length pricing rules and thin capitalization rules are generally missing. These are tools used by tax authorities to constrain the ability of firms to arrange their affairs to avoid taxation. Even with these rules, tax authorities have a substantial challenge in identifying and reversing tax avoidance. This is particularly challenging for the taxation authorities in the region who lack experience in dealing with market-based transactions and the methods of tax minimization routinely used by taxpayers in OECD countries. Therefore, foreign-owned firms can often arrange their affairs to eliminate their tax liability in the country. In such cases, tax incentives may be redundant.

COSTS AND BENEFITS OF TAX INCENTIVES

The classic argument raised against the use of incentives is that they distort economic activity. Incentives cause the after-tax pattern of returns to diverge from the before-tax pattern and therefore lead to an allocation of resources that differs from the efficient equilibrium the market is assumed to generate. These results are generally valid for a developed market economy and are one of a number of powerful arguments that have led most OECD countries to curtail their use of incentives. However, clearly the conditions that are required for an efficient market have not yet developed in most of the countries of the region. Many firms remain under state control. Capital markets are rudimentary by the standards of developed market economies. Basic information on market possibilities and the way of doing business is imperfect, particularly from the perspective of foreign firms looking to invest in a country. The commercial and legal infrastructure that epitomizes market economies is still being developed. Many of the actors in the economy, managers and workers, are not yet familiar with the basic concepts of how markets work and so may not operate in an efficient manner. In these circumstances, there is an argument that, for the reasons noted in the Introduction, FDI has benefits above and beyond the private return to the investment in creating markets and training domestic agents how to operate in a market environment. Under this argument, incentives could play a transitional role in creating a critical mass of market activity until capital markets in particular have been developed. In fact, one of the reasons for special tax treatment of foreign firms under the old system was that the tax system applied to the domestic state-owned sector was not appropriate to foreign firms and so they needed a special regime to be able to operate. This reason could also apply during the transitional period of a country, before it has brought its tax system into line with the norm for a market economy.

Thus, there is an argument that some form of incentive could be justified in the situation in which the countries in the region find themselves. However, it is important in evaluating whether incentives, and in particular tax incentives, are justified to consider their costs relative to the assumed benefits arising from the incentives.

Revenue cost

The most obvious cost to the government of a tax incentive is the resulting forgone tax revenues. The hope would be that a tax incentive would have a small revenue cost relative to the investment induced. That is, a small contribution of public money would induce a substantial increase in private sector funds for investment. Moreover, the investment being private would hopefully be more efficient than an investment by the government. However valid the latter point might be, there is little in the experience of OECD countries to suggest that the government would be the beneficiary of such a significant response to its forgone revenue.

In most econometric studies on the question, the forgone tax revenue has exceeded the increase in the desired investment. The reason is that the incentives are not targeted to incremental investment. Therefore, a substantial amount of the incentive is earned by investments that would have occurred in any event. From the point of view of the government, this is wasteful as it does not result in an increase in the desired activity. In the case of the economies in transition, there is the possibility that the investment, particularly of footloose industries, would not have occurred without the incentive. In this case, it could be argued that there is no forgone revenue as the revenue would have been zero if the incentive had not induced the investment. There are a number of observations that can be made on this statement. First, if there are good investment opportunities, it is unlikely that no investments would be made without the incentives. If no investments, in fact, are being made, it is probably because some of the critical problems outlined above are present. As the experience to date in the region demonstrates, tax incentives alone cannot in themselves induce investment in such circumstances. Moreover, even if the type of investment receiving the incentive would not have occurred without the incentive, there is always some indirect substitution among investments. This substitution can occur in a number of ways. For example, the importation of capital for one project will increase the rate of exchange from what it would have been. This will act to depress economic activity by causing a shift away from domestically produced goods in the domestic market or making it harder to export goods.

The data do not yet exist to perform econometric studies on the effectiveness of the tax incentives provided by the countries surveyed. Still, the lack of substantial investments in many of the countries with incentives suggests that the incentives have not been effective in attracting investment to the region. Moreover, for the most part the types of activities that have been attracted have not been the long-term projects envisioned by policy makers when they provided the incentive. Rather they have been short-term, quick-profit ventures that would have occurred in any case. The tax incentives have merely succeeded in making a profitable venture more profitable.

Complexity of the tax system

One of the most serious problems with incentives is the complexity they introduce into the tax system. This complexity is manifested in a number of ways and imposes a variety of costs on the country. These costs must be taken into account in assessing the desirability of tax incentives.

Incentives require definitions of the eligible activities. This in itself complicates the tax legislation. The legislation must be sufficiently precise to allow taxpayers to predict accurately whether or not they qualify for the provision. If it is not, then taxpayers cannot plan their affairs on the assumption that they will receive the incentive. Its receipt is simply a windfall to them, with no positive impact on their behaviour. Moreover, rules are often required to deal with special situations, such as loss years or corporate reorganizations, in order for firms that undertake the desired activity actually to be able to make use of the incentives earned.

It is difficult to ensure that the firms which are intended to use the incentive are able to do so with a degree of confidence. But it is even more difficult, as many countries in the region have found, to ensure that taxpayers who are not intended to take advantage of the incentive are not able to. Taxpayers naturally try to arrange their affairs to qualify for the incentives. Anti-avoidance rules are often required. These rules are inevitably complicated and frequently work against the certainty that is required if there is to be any incentive effect from the measure.

The tax planning by firms and the attendant reactions by the taxation authorities lead to frequent change in both the legislation and the administration of the provisions. Frequent changes to the tax system have been identified by companies as the greatest single source of the impression that the tax system is complex.

This complexity imposes costs not only on the taxpayers, but also on the taxation authorities. They too must keep up with rule changes and time spent auditing incentive provisions reduces the time that can be spent on auditing other aspects of the income tax. This burden is particularly onerous on tax administrations which must cope with the transition to a market economy. Moreover, the attempt to direct incentives to special classes of activities, such as 'technology transfer', are subjective in nature and very hard to audit in practice as any tax authority in the OECD who has had to administer a tax incentive for research and development (R&D) has discovered.

Unintended results

As noted above the windfall gains to investments that would have occurred in any event make tax incentives relatively cost ineffective in many cases. This ineffectiveness is exacerbated to the extent that taxpayers in other situations are able to plan their affairs to qualify for the benefits. The experience in OECD countries is that this can make the amount of government tax revenues hard to predict. Tax incentives can be used by unintended beneficiaries and this can inflate the revenue costs significantly above predicted levels. This experience has been borne out in the economies in transition. This will be discussed in greater detail in the sections on the individual incentives. In many cases the bulk of the activity that has qualified for the incentives has been the result of tax planning rather than an increase in the desired activity. This experience has shown that it is difficult to target the incentive to the desired activity given the relatively simple tax systems in the region and the difficult circumstances under which the taxation authorities are working during the transition.

Precedent

The provision of even targeted tax incentives establishes the precedent for their wider use. Firms engaged in activities that do not qualify for the incentives will lobby for their extension to their activities or at least the provision of some form of incentive. This is a difficult argument for policy makers to counter as it involves making explicit choices between different activities which are both in some sense deserving. Moreover, whenever incentives are provided to one type of activity there will be other activities which are closely related to the preferred activity that do not qualify for the incentive. They will be able to argue that they are disadvantaged in competing with the firms which are in receipt of the incentive. The experience in OECD countries is that incentives once introduced have a tendency to spread to other activities. Accordingly the establishment of such incentives introduces a dynamic into the policy process that further undermines the revenue base of the government.

There is another aspect. The provision of an incentive often takes on the characteristics of an entitlement. Once given incentives are very hard to eliminate owing to the lobbying by the constituency created by their existence. The recent experience of many OECD countries as they reformed their tax systems is instructive. Despite the fact that incentives were generally recognized to be ineffective, and thus many large incentives were eliminated, many smaller incentives remained which are of questionable economic or social benefit, but which are given to politically vocal groups.

GENERAL TAX INCENTIVES

Tax incentives can be grouped into a number of categories: tax holidays, investment allowances and tax credits, timing differences, or reduced tax rates. Each of these types of incentives raises different design issues which must be resolved.

Tax holidays

This has been the typical form of tax incentive used by countries in the region. It is a tax incentive that is targeted at new firms, and is not available to existing operations. With a tax holiday, new firms are allowed a period of time after some initial point when they are relieved from the burden of income taxation. Sometimes, this initial period has been extended to a subsequent period of taxation at a reduced rate of tax.

One advantage of tax holidays that is sometimes cited is that they provide a simple regime for foreign investors at a time when the tax systems in the region are not yet fully developed since there is no need to calculate taxes in the early years of operation. This is certainly not valid for long-term investors. For them the tax treatment after the holiday has expired will be as important as the treatment during the holiday in determining the after-tax profitability of the investment. In addition, the tax treatment of the initial capital expenditures made before and during the holiday period must be determined so that appropriate records will be available for the calculation of depreciation when the holiday ends.

There are a number of technical issues that are important in determining their impact on the return on investments. The first question is when does the holiday start? It could be when production starts, the first year in which the firm makes a profit or the first year that the firm achieves a positive cumulative profit on its operations. For large projects, in particular, losses are usually generated in the early years of production. These are typically the years of the highest capital costs, there are special costs that are linked to the start-up period, the workforce may need to be trained and there may be costs of developing the local market. For such projects, a tax holiday which starts when production occurs may actually increase the taxes paid over the life of the project and so act as a disincentive for investment. If losses are experienced during the holiday period they may not be allowed to be carried forward out of the holiday period. Thus the holiday may occur when no taxes would have been paid in any event and taxes may be increased following the holiday because no losses are available to offset the profits. A similar situation can occur if the holiday starts when profits are first generated. Income may be sheltered that would have been eliminated in any case by the use of the tax losses. This may result in an overall increase in taxation in circumstances when the loss-carryforward period is short or the use of losses is restricted in some way. The laws in the region usually specify that the holiday commences when profits first occur. However, they are often ambiguous whether this means the first year that is in itself profitable or the first year that cumulative net profits are positive.

A related question is the treatment of depreciation during the holiday period – should it be deducted during the holiday period or can it be deferred until after the holiday has terminated? Depreciation represents a cost in the calculation of income and so its deduction is necessary to measure accurately the amount of income that should be subject to the holiday. Allowing a deferral of the deduction effectively overestimates the costs associated with the post-holiday period and so leads to a further reduction in tax which can lead to a very generous incentive. The issue is more complicated if some form of accelerated depreciation is also offered with respect to the investment. Forcing the use of the accelerated deductions during the holiday period at the least reduces their value and can actually lead to an increase in the level of taxation relative to the situation where no incentives are provided. A complete deferral of the deduction, however, can again lead to a very generous incentive and an effective tax holiday which is much longer than intended.

Another design question is the length of the holiday. Most of the holidays offered in the region have been of short duration. As is discussed below, such holidays are of very little benefit to long-term, capital-intensive projects. Longer holidays would be of greater benefit and there is some evidence in Asia and Hungary that the longer holidays did succeed in attracting some long-term investment. However, the longer is the holiday the higher the revenue cost and the greater the vulnerability to tax planning schemes.

Investment allowances and tax credits

These are tax reliefs based upon the value of expenditures on qualifying investments. They provide tax benefits that are over and above the depreciation allowed for the asset. A tax allowance is used to reduce the taxable income of the firm. A tax credit is used directly to reduce the amount of taxes to be paid.

The major technical issues are the definition of the eligible expenditures, the choice of the rate of the allowance or credit, any restrictions on their use and the treatment of any amounts of incentive that cannot be used in the year that they are earned owing to insufficient taxable income. The major problem with the determination of the eligible expenditures is achieving a precise definition that targets the incentive to the desired activity to minimize revenue leakage and, at the same time, provides the taxpayer with certainty in the application of the incentive to increase the effectiveness of the incentive.

The choice of the rate of incentive is directly linked to the amount of incentive that it is desired to provide and the revenue cost to the government. One problem which arises as the rate of the incentive increases is that the incentive for firms to control costs is decreased, leading to so-called 'gold plating' of investments where the most cost-effective techniques are not employed. A number of tax avoidance possibilities are encountered when the rate of credit and tax allowance is too high. For example, if an investment allowance is provided, firms can flow services through a subsidiary and make money simply by increasing the amounts that the subsidiary charges its parent company for the services rendered. The basic problem is that, because the total amount of tax allowance and depreciation which can be deducted against taxable income exceeds the actual amount spent, the tax benefit to the parent company of spending one dollar exceeds the tax cost to the subsidiary of receiving a dollar of revenue.

The use of the incentives can also be constrained to ensure that they cannot fully eliminate the tax payable by the firm in the year. For example, the allowance could be restricted to some percentage of taxable income or a credit could be limited to some percentage of tax otherwise payable. The calculation of these limits can interact with other provisions in a complicated manner and can cause firms to enter into arrangements of the type discussed below. They do, however, limit the revenue cost to the government and ensure that firms cannot entirely eliminate their tax payable through the use of incentives.

An important design issue is what to do if the firm has insufficient taxable income to use that incentive fully in the year that it is earned. In some cases in the region the incentive is simply lost. This restrictive access to the incentive operates against start-up firms without other income. This is the typical situation for new foreign investors and can effectively eliminate the benefits of the incentive for such firms. It may also lead to unproductive arrangements being devised simply to make use of the incentive. For example, an investment allowance can be transferred from a firm benefiting from a tax holiday to a taxable firm through the use of a lease. In effect the firm obtains both incentives and government revenues fall by more than the tax which would have been paid by the firm in the absence of the holiday.

The chance that the incentive may be effectively lost also increases the uncertainty to the firm in estimating the value of the incentive and so reduces its effectiveness. To avoid this problem, rules need to be provided to allow a carryforward of the incentive and to determine its treatment if there is a reorganization of the business.

A special form of investment allowance is provided by a number of countries in the region. It is a reduced tax rate for reinvested profits. It is not entirely clear why this particular form of incentive is provided and how it operates in practice. Even without special incentives, retained earnings are the major source of capital for investment in OECD countries as they are seen to be cheaper than either debt or new equity. Moreover, there are a number of sources of capital and a number of uses other than dividends and capital investments, such as debt retirement or offshore investments. Tracing the funds from retained earnings to investment would not be simple. Finally, it not clear why one source of capital should be favoured over others. This distorts capital markets and favours established firms. The use of an allowance linked to the amount of investment, perhaps capped by a percentage of profits otherwise calculated, would be a more direct way to achieve the goal. It could also be better targeted to the desired activity.

Timing differences

Timing differences can arise through either the acceleration of deductions or the deferral of the recognition of income. The most common form of accelerated deduction is accelerated depreciation where the cost of an asset acquired may be written off at a rate that is faster than the economic rate of depreciation. This can be in the form of either a shorter period of depreciation or a special deduction in the first year. This has a similar impact to an investment allowance in the first year, but differs since the amount written off reduces the depreciation base for future years and so the total amount written off does not exceed the actual cost of the investment. Rather it allows the deductions to occur sooner than otherwise. This provides a deferral of tax which is effectively an interest-free loan to the company from the government.

Important timing differences can occur in other, more technical areas. For example, incomes may not be realized until there is a sale of the asset while certain costs are recognized immediately. A typical example is the current deduction of interest on an asset which is held for a period of time. A significant net profit can be realized on an asset whose pre-tax return equals the rate of interest on the funds borrowed for its purchase, simply because of the mismatching of the deductions and the taxation of the income. These technical timing differences can often be more important than any explicit investment incentives.

The technical issues with accelerated depreciation are similar to the issues of targeting and carryovers that face investment allowances. However, the problem of deductions exceeding the cost of the investment which occurs with an investment allowance is avoided.

General tax rate reductions

General tax rate reductions can be provided to income from certain sources or to firms satisfying certain criteria. These reductions differ from tax holidays since the tax liability of firms is not entirely eliminated, the benefit is extended beyond new enterprises to include income from existing operations and the benefit is not time limited. Identification of the qualifying income is the major design issue. It may require rules to define eligible taxpayers, if the benefit is to be targeted to specific types of firms, such as small businesses. If only certain types of income are to qualify, then rules must be defined to measure the income. These can rely on separate accounting for different sources of income, which is subject to manipulation and the streaming of costs and income to maximize the benefit. The alternative is to use a formula approach which will be less accurate in targeting the benefit. With either approach the rules tend to be complex and subject to manipulation.

Non-income-tax-based incentives

In many instances taxes other than income taxes are of primary concern to potential investors. In particular, taxes on business inputs constitute a barrier to the importation of the very factors that tax incentives are designed to attract. Examples include border charges, like customs duties or turnover taxes, on imported capital equipment and social security taxes on expatriate wages and salaries. Removal of these tax impediments to FDI would provide an incentive which eliminates distortions rather than creating them. (The treatment of domestic firms in this regard is also important. If revenue considerations allow, importation of business capital inputs should be free from effective border charges for domestic firms as well.)

COMPARISON OF THE DIFFERENT GENERAL INCENTIVES

The various tax incentives can differ markedly from one another in a number of important ways. In particular they can differ in terms of:

- the types of companies and activities which are likely to benefit from them;
- the time profile of the revenue impact on the government for any given level of incentive; and
- the difficulty of administration and the possibility of tax avoidance.

Beneficiaries

By their construction, tax holidays are of greatest value to firms and projects which make substantial profits in the early years of operation. Such enterprises are likely to be engaged in sectors such as trade, short-term construction or the service sector. They are less likely to be of benefit to major capital-intensive projects which do not normally have profits in the early years. This has in fact been the experience of the countries in the region which have introduced tax holidays. Most of the beneficiaries of the tax holidays have been small firms operating in sectors such as real estate, restaurants and short-term market exploitation, such as trade or woodcutting. The tax holidays are open ended in the sense that their value depends upon the amount of profit earned. Arguably, the types of high-profit activities that benefit the most are the least in need of the incentive and would have occurred in the absence of the incentive. Thus the bulk of the revenue forgone is likely to have had no beneficial impact on investment and so the ratio of benefits to costs is likely to be very low.

The experience in Asia with tax holidays targeted at export-oriented industries is relevant. Low-cost assembly plants that are highly mobile can be the most affected by holidays. In a number of instances, plants were established in a country to take advantage of a tax holiday. However, when the holiday expired, the plant was disassembled and moved to an adjacent jurisdiction to take advantage of the holiday offered there. The mobility that made the project responsive to the incentive also acted to limit the benefit to the country from the investment.

Investment allowances, tax credits and accelerated depreciation, on the other hand, are specifically targeted at capital investment. Their revenue cost is constrained by the amount of capital that the firm is willing to put at risk. As such they are of little benefit for the quick-profit types of firms which can take best advantage of tax holidays. Tax allowances are of greatest benefit for firms with income from existing operations. These firms can shelter a portion of such income from tax with the incentives earned on the new investment. Firms with low income or start-up firms cannot begin to take advantage of the incentive until the investment begins to earn income. Provided that a carryforward of the incentive is allowed, an investment allowance can operate in a manner similar to a tax holiday since it can eliminate the tax liability of the firm in the early years of operation. However, the incentive no longer has an unlimited amount of tax benefit; the potential tax benefit to the firm of the incentive is now capped by the amount of its investment.

General tax rate reductions differ from the other incentives in that they are not specifically targeted to new activity. Income from both existing and new operations is eligible for the incentive. Thus, when viewed as a short-term investment incentive they are less likely to be cost effective than, in particular, incentives which are related to the amount of the investment.

Profile of revenue impact

The revenue impact of tax holidays and investment allowances is, in theory, tied to the degree of new activity. Thus the revenue impact is relatively low in the early years of the programme and grows over time as more firms become eligible. A general tax rate reduction, on the other hand, has reasonably significant upfront revenue costs as it applies to income from existing operations as well. Accelerated deductions confer a timing benefit only. Thus to achieve the same incentive effect there will be a higher level of upfront cost to the government. The revenue cost actually falls over time, as in future years the tax benefits from further new investments are in part offset by the reduced deductions resulting from the acceleration of deductions on the old investments.

For investment allowances and accelerated deductions, the carryforward of deductions by firms which cannot fully utilize them can lead to considerable growth in the revenue cost over time. The experience of a number of OECD countries that provided broad-based investment incentives is that over one-half of incentives were earned by firms with no current taxable income. This reduced their cost in the early years of the programme. However, there is a significant build-up over time of unused deductions from previous years. As the firms which had these accumulations began to earn income, the accumulations are used to offset income even though they are no longer making expenditures eligible for the incentives. The claiming of the deductions is merely delayed and there is an increasing impact on tax revenues as the deductions from previous years are added to those being earned and used in the current year.

The build-up of unused deductions and losses also reduced the predictability of the government's revenue stream. Firms that did not expect to be able to use their deductions for a period of time sought out ways of transferring them to firms with current taxable income. This was often done in the form of transactions which traded a lower cost of financing for the tax deductions. Thus the deductions earned in one sector reduced the taxable income of another. Loss trading mechanisms such as leasing are frequently used in this regard.

A number of countries in the region have experienced serious unexpected shortfalls in revenues during the transition period. This has been in part due to reduced economic performance and problems of tax administration in the face of a changing economic structure. Tax incentives, particularly holidays, have contributed to this shortfall as they have provided opportunities for firms to arrange their affairs to avoid paying taxes on income ordinarily subject to taxation.

Administration and tax avoidance

The administration of incentive schemes provides an extra challenge to tax administrators. First, they have to verify that the incentive has been correctly applied. Verification can be difficult if complicated calculations are involved. Second, administrators need to ensure that the activity or firm actually qualifies for the incentive. This can be complicated if concepts and definitions are vague or ambiguous or, as in the case of incentives for foreign-owned firms, the records establishing the eligibility of the firms are in another country. (This problem is compounded by the limited range of tax treaties for most countries in the region which denies them access to the exchange of information facilities usually contained in the treaties.) Third, they must ensure that the amounts eligible for the incentive are correctly reported; for example, that the value that a machine or service has been transferred at is its fair market value. This again can be difficult if the transaction occurs across borders, particularly among related parties. The need to carry out these audits and assessments diverts resources from other administrative tasks, and may have a substantial revenue cost of its own, given the shortages of trained staff that exist in most of the countries of the region. All of these problems have been evident in the countries in the region that have introduced tax incentives.

Avoidance experience with tax holidays

Among the tax incentives, the tax holidays have been most susceptible to tax planning, much of which is especially problematic for taxation authorities. Tax planning can lead to considerable revenue leakage, which can exceed the revenue forgone from incentives earned by legitimate activities. This further reduces the cost-effectiveness of tax incentives. The main tax avoidance strategies employed by firms, which are often used in combination, include:

Fictive foreign investment Tax holidays in a number of countries have been directed at firms with a sufficient percentage of foreign ownership. There would appear to have been considerable leakage of tax revenues arising from the creation of fictive foreign-owned companies which carried on what was in fact a domestically owned business. One method by which this is accomplished is the transfer of funds from a domestic enterprise to a company incorporated offshore which in turn reinvested in the home country, as if it were a foreign-owned company. Thus the investment qualified for the incentive. It depends upon how the law is written whether this type of transaction is tax avoidance or evasion. In either event it is very difficult for tax authorities in the region to detect such activity on audit.

Transfer pricing The existence of a tax holiday introduces the possibility of transferring profits from operations that do not qualify for the holiday to the firm that enjoys it. For example, a domestic firm transfers a small part of its operation to a joint venture with a foreign-owned company. The joint venture qualifies for the incentive. Income is transferred to the joint venture from the original domestic company by manipulating the allocation of costs and the charges made on transactions between the firms. These types of transactions are very difficult for tax authorities to detect, and even harder to challenge successfully.

Rollover of businesses It can be very difficult to establish what is a new operation to qualify for the tax holiday. A new corporation can be established which then purchases the assets of an existing operation in order to qualify for the incentive, even though no new activity is occurring. This has occurred in combination with the above types of tax avoidance. In other cases, such as the construction industry, new firms were established for each new project, thus maintaining perpetual access to the holiday. This occurred in one country in the case of a logging operation that used a new company every time it moved to a new woodlot.

Regional tax avoidance Tax holidays also put the revenues of adjacent jurisdictions at risk. Firms exporting to third countries from the country would ordinarily pay tax on their profit from the sale. In some cases, these firms establish trans-shipment companies in an adjoining state. The sole purpose of the company was to purchase the goods from the exporting company and then sell them to the actual purchaser in the third country. The trans-shipment company qualifies for a tax holiday in the second jurisdiction. Goods are sold at cost to that company and all the profits on the sale are transferred to it through transfer pricing to be sheltered from tax by the tax holiday.

A number of countries in the region have attempted to curtail these abuses by requiring that the foreign investment exceed some threshold, say $50,000, in order to qualify for the incentive. While such restrictions may deter some small problems, they are unlikely to be effective in preventing tax avoidance. Firms may contribute overvalued capital goods as part of their initial capital contribution to achieve the threshold. There are no restrictions on the use of the capital and it is very hard to impose them effectively. Accordingly, firms can effectively repatriate the funds in a number of ways, such as non-recourse loans, offshore deposits and returns of capital. Here the thresholds impose no effective constraint on tax avoidance.

Other incentives

The other forms of incentives are also open to tax planning. However, the scope is somewhat more limited, particularly in the case of investment-related incentives at moderate rates of incentive. The incentive has an upper limit related to the amount of the expenditure and so is not as exposed to the shifting of large amounts of profits as a tax holiday. Problems can occur, especially with assets transferred from related offshore companies. There is a motivation to overvalue the purchase price of the asset to maximize the incentive. Clearly this motivation is increased as the rate of the incentive rises. However, this problem already exists to a certain extent, as firms try to increase their depreciation bases for tax purposes. As noted above, at high rates of incentive this problem can occur even within a country, if the rate of incentive leads to a value of tax deductions that exceeds the value of the expenditure. It is possible to increase the benefits to the enterprise on a transfer of assets or services between related companies simply by increasing the price of the item transferred. The other issue which can arise in these circumstances is the multiple access to the incentive through flipping the asset among a group of companies. Recapture rules and capital gains taxes can deal with this problem in the case of accelerated depreciation as the increased deductions of the purchaser are offset by the reduced write-offs of the seller. For investment allowances and tax credits, the problem can be dealt with through fairly simple anti-avoidance rules, such as providing the incentive only for first use of the asset in the country.

SPECIAL PURPOSE INCENTIVES[2]

A serious disadvantage of offering tax incentives to attract investment is that, to the extent that the incentives are claimed by enterprises that would have invested in any event, there is a loss of tax revenue without any corresponding benefit to the host country. These costs can, in theory, be reduced if means can be found to target the incentives to particular desirable activities or to projects that would not have occurred without the incentive. Countries have employed a number of techniques to achieve this better targeting. These include:

- linking the incentive to specific low-growth regions;
- tying the incentive to particular objectives, such as employment creation, technology transfer or export promotion;
- the use of free trade or export promotion zones; and
- the use of administrative discretion.

Each of these approaches has potential advantages, but is likely to give rise to substantial problems in implementation.

One general problem with special incentives is that their provision inevitably leads to pressure from other deserving sectors for special treatment. This pressure is much more difficult to withstand once some targeted incentives have been given. The experience in a number of countries in the region and in the OECD has been spread over time to other activities and the difficulty of removing the incentives in the future once the reason for them has gone. While any one targeted incentive may not involve a significant revenue cost, the total for all the resulting incentives can sharply erode government revenues from the business sector.

Regional development

Regional development has often been an objective of tax incentives in OECD countries and elsewhere. Typically, investors in designated regions – usually the more remote, economically less-developed regions of a country, or regions with high levels of unemployment – receive tax holidays, investment allowances or accelerated depreciation. Experience demonstrates that relatively little new activity is generated in the targeted region relative to the revenue cost. In so far as the incentives have any effect at all, the chief effect is to divert investment away from its optimum location.

Employment creation

Tax incentives for job creation are frequently linked with regional policies, seeking to attract investment to areas of high unemployment. In other cases, incentives are given to promote the establishment of labour-intensive industries or the employment of particular categories of workers, such as young persons, the disabled, or the long-term unemployed. Many of the issues that arise with investment incentives, such as incentives going to employment that would have occurred in any event, are also associated with employment incentives. Moreover, incentives targeted to particular types of employment or increases in the level of employment are subject to manipulation and administrative complexity.

Technology transfer

Many countries have sought to attract technology-advanced investment, or R&D activities, through the grant of tax incentives, usually with very little success. It is frequently difficult for tax authorities to determine when particular technology should qualify as 'advanced' or 'appropriate', and difficult to define precisely what constitutes 'research'. In most cases it is likely that the investor will be receiving a tax break for doing what it would have done in any event, and it is the experience of many developing countries that technology which is introduced is rarely 'transferred' to the host country. It is due to the generally unsatisfactory experience with tax incentives that a number of Asian countries are turning to non-fiscal inducements, such as the establishment of 'Science Parks'.

Export promotion

There is evidence, especially from developing countries in Asia, to suggest that incentives to attract export-oriented investment tend to be more effective than most other forms of investment incentives. Certain types of export-oriented enterprises, notably those in the textiles and electronics sectors and other labour-intensive assembly industries, are especially sensitive to taxation. Such industries do not rely much on local sources of material supply and do not target sales at the domestic market. Rather, they are attracted to low-cost environments. While the most important local cost for such industries is labour, taxes may form a significant part of costs and so tax reliefs may be especially attractive to such firms. Investment incentives are commonly provided in the form of tax holidays or special investment allowances for firms designated as 'export oriented', by exemption from tax of a proportion of profits corresponding to the proportion that export sales bear to total sales, or by generous deduction provisions for expenditures aimed at export promotion. Undoubtedly, some of these policies have been successful in attracting foreign investment and have, at least in the short term, had relatively little cost in terms of tax forgone, since much of the investment would not have been attracted without tax exemptions. The benefits of such investment, however, are questionable. As noted above, many of the enterprises attracted are 'footloose', and tend to move on as soon as tax holidays expire. There tends to be little in the way of creation of linkages to domestic firms, little transfer of technology, and little sourcing of local raw materials. Moreover, the success of such operations depends to a large extent upon the reaction of the countries which provide the sources of capital and the markets for the exports. Many of the incentives that could be offered to attract export-oriented investment are contrary to the provisions of the GATT; the success of others depends in part upon home countries being prepared to grant 'tax sparing' treatment in their double taxation treaties (see below). With the heightened competition in world markets there is a likelihood that these issues will be more important in the future.

Free trade or export processing zones

Closely related to the issue of promotion of export-oriented investment is the phenomenon of the establishment of export processing zones. These zones, also called customs-free zones, duty-free zones, free trade zones, or special economic zones, have over the past thirty years or so been established in more than fifty countries in all parts of the globe and are now being established in many countries of Central and Eastern Europe.

The principal feature that distinguishes these zones is that they provide a discrete environment in which enterprises (usually both foreign and domestically owned) can import machinery, components and raw materials free of customs duties and other taxes, for assembly, processing or manufacture, with a view to exporting the finished product. Normally, sales of zone products to the domestic market are treated as exports/imports, and are liable at that stage to import duties and taxes.

From the point of view of the country establishing an export processing zone (EPZ) the principal objective is to earn foreign exchange from export sales. Frequently, there are additional objectives, such as the creation of employment, technology transfer, promotion of regional policy.

Incentives to attract foreign investors to the EPZs commonly take a variety of forms:

Exemption from customs duties and other taxes on importation

This is the essential feature of EPZs. Such exemptions apply to materials and components that are imported and re-exported. They are also often extended to capital goods that are used in the production process by the firm. As mentioned above, exemption from such taxes is often one of the more important tax incentives offered to foreign investors since they have an immediate impact upon costs. To the extent that zone products are re-exported, such exemptions appear to be entirely consistent with the provisions of the GATT and, so far as product taxes are concerned, produce essentially the same result as the zero rating of exports under a value-added tax. The chief advantage of the zonal exemptions is in terms of administration and cash flow, as opposed to having to apply for duty and tax refunds where goods are re-exported. Such incentives can be seen as removing impediments rather than providing a special break to encourage exports.

Other tax incentives Much of the investment attracted to EPZs is highly mobile, cost conscious and tax sensitive, and frequently additional tax incentives for investment are offered in the zones. In some cases, special incentives (e.g. tax holidays) apply for investment in the zone; in others, zone enterprises qualify for the same incentives as are provided – notably for export-oriented investment – elsewhere in the country. The concerns raised above in relation to incentives for export-oriented investment apply equally to zonal incentives of this nature.

Regulatory concessions It is normal for a variety of non-fiscal incentives to be provided for investment in EPZs. Such incentives commonly take the form of simplified approval procedures, relaxation of exchange control restrictions, suspension of employee rights under labour legislation, etc.

Subsidized infrastructure In many cases, the host country subsidizes EPZ activities by providing transport and communications infrastructure, low-cost utilities, low rentals for factory sites, etc. All of these, of course, come at a cost to the host country.

It is difficult to evaluate the success, or otherwise, of EPZs. In a few countries they have been successful in generating substantial foreign currency earnings. However, in other countries EPZs have proved a dismal failure, while in between are instances where it is difficult to say whether the enhanced foreign exchange earnings have been worth the costs of establishment.

Real (net) foreign exchange earnings are often but a small proportion of total export sales, since most components and raw materials are imported; textile manufacturers in some zones have even imported such items as thread and buttons. Employment creation has been impressive, but has often had little impact upon local unemployment since the great majority of jobs have been filled by young women who had not previously been part of the workforce. Technology transfer has usually been negligible and in only a very few countries have substantial backward linkages with domestic producers been established. Attempts to use EPZs as an instrument of regional development policy have mostly been total failures. Since tax incentives have been the rule in most EPZs, very little tax revenue has been generated directly, though EPZ investors have undoubtedly contributed to revenues through employment creation, in the form of payroll taxes, income tax on salaries and sales taxes on spending by employees.

It is instructive to note that the countries in which EPZs have tended to be most successful have been those which have concentrated upon generating foreign exchange earnings, without attempting to pursue ancillary objectives such as regional development, and which have emphasized the removal of obstacles to export processing rather than the provision of investment incentives *per se*. They have also tended to be countries in which the general domestic tax climate has been relatively hospitable to investment.

To the extent that tax incentives (other than exemption from taxes and duties on imports) are employed, a potential advantage of EPZs is that they localize access to the incentives and so, in theory, allow a closer monitoring of the operation of firms. However, they certainly do not eliminate the problems already referred to. There are various ways to shift profits from operations outside the zone to firms which are based in the zone through intra-group transactions, and so lead to the effective leakage of zone benefits to ordinary domestic activity.

Finally, the caution recorded in relation to tax incentives for export promotion bears repeating in the context of EPZs. Whilst there would seem to be nothing objectionable in providing exemption from customs duties and taxes on importation, other tax incentives directed specifically at export promotion may run contrary to the GATT and might invite countervailing measures that could negate any advantages obtained from the establishment of the zones.

Administrative discretion

Should the incentives be discretionary and only granted with the pre-approval of the authorities? There are a number of potential advantages to this approach:

- As the policy priorities of the government change, it is possible to tailor the incentives to support them, since fewer firms are affected by the changes and problems of transition can be more easily handled.
- If there appears to be a risk of tax avoidance under the scheme then the authorities can deny access to the incentive.
- Where the extent as well as the availability of the incentive are administratively determined, it may be possible to provide only that degree of incentive which is required to make the investment economic.

This would improve the cost-effectiveness of the programme by improving its targeting towards incremental investment.

In practice, however, there is little evidence that these gains are realized. Approval processes can be time consuming and cumbersome. The authorities can only obtain the detailed information necessary for evaluation from the company which has an incentive to portray it in an advantageous manner. In the real world of politics, it is difficult to deny the incentives to companies which are promising the creation of employment. Finally, the greatest problem is that an approval process undermines the transparency of the tax system which is probably the number one criterion of foreign companies making the investments. For these reasons, the track record of discretionary incentives is not encouraging.

Domestic versus foreign investors

Incentives offered in the region are often tied to foreign investment. These can be in the form of special tax holidays under the income tax or special reliefs from customs duties or turnover taxes. The incentives are sometimes directed at firms that are 100 per cent owned by foreigners and at other times offered to joint ventures, often with as little as 30 per cent foreign ownership. Under the tax systems that formerly existed in the region such special treatment was often appropriate. The tax regimes applied to state-owned firms served a different purpose to tax systems in the OECD countries. Accordingly, compared to OECD practice, they had features, such as restricted deductions for interest or wages or relatively slow rates of depreciation, that were not appropriate for the taxation of the income of foreign enterprises. It was necessary to apply special tax provisions to foreign-owned firms to enable them to do business in the country. It may still be necessary for those countries which have not yet changed their tax systems to provide transitional relief for foreign firms until their tax systems have been brought into line with OECD practice.

Providing tax incentives targeted only to foreign companies raises different issues when the tax system of the country is similar to those of market-oriented countries. The clear attraction for policy makers is that the targeting dramatically reduces the revenue costs of offering the incentives as the bulk of current revenues comes from domestic firms. In addition, many of the domestic firms are still state owned and not operating fully as private sector firms. However, as more firms become privatized and must compete in the market with foreign-owned firms, the question must be asked why it would be government policy to disadvantage domestic firms relative to foreign firms. The discrimination leads to resentment which is likely to reduce voluntary compliance with the tax system, just at the time when the tax administration is most vulnerable. Domestic firms would lobby, with justification, for an extension of the incentives to them. This pressure could be difficult to resist and so the incentives would spread, leading to a deterioration of the domestic tax system. Moreover, as seen above, the restrictions often do not work. Domestic firms are induced to enter into tax avoidance strategies that have proven difficult for tax authorities to counter.

INTERNATIONAL ASPECTS OF TAX INCENTIVES

In looking at the tax treatment of FDI, it is necessary to look beyond the tax treatment in the country where the activity takes place, the source country. It is also necessary to consider the tax treatment in the country of the foreign parent, the residence country. There are often further tax consequences in the residence country on income that is earned and taxed in the source country. This can lead to an interaction between the tax systems of the two jurisdictions that modifies the impact of a tax incentive compared to when looked at only from the point of view of the source country.

There are a number of forms in which an investment can take place. The two basic methods are through a branch and through a subsidiary. A branch is simply a division of the foreign company making the investment. It is not a separate legal entity. Accordingly, the branch's profits are ordinarily taxed as they are earned in the residence country under the principle of worldwide taxation. Any residence-country tax consequences occur immediately.

The other form of investment is through a subsidiary. In this case the subsidiary of the foreign company is a separate legal entity and its income is usually not included in the income of the foreign parent until it is repatriated as a dividend. Any residence-country tax consequences occur at the time. This delay in the residence-country taxation is known as deferral.

As a subsidiary is the normal form of investment for non-financial institutions, the balance of the discussion will focus on the treatment of repatriated dividends. Much of the discussion also applies to income earned in branches, except the residence-country tax consequences occur as the income is earned, rather than being deferred until it is repatriated as a dividend.

Taxation of foreign-source income

There are basically two types of tax treatments that are applied dividends paid to the residence country. These have very different implications for the potential effectiveness of tax incentives provided by the source country.

The first type of tax treatment is the foreign tax credit method. Under this method, the residence country applies its tax regime to the income when it is repatriated, but allows a credit for any foreign taxes paid to the extent that they do not exceed the amount of residence-country tax that would be levied on the income. This effectively says that the source country is allowed the first opportunity to tax the income, but that the residence country will move in to tax the income to the extent that it is not fully taxed in the source country. In the simple case of only one source of foreign income, this has clear negative implications for tax incentives. To the extent that the incentive results in a tax liability that is less than the tax burden that would be applied in the residence country, then the benefit given is taxed back when the income is repatriated to the residence country. There is simply a transfer of tax revenue from the Treasury of the source country to the Treasury of the residence country. A number of OECD countries use the foreign tax credit method, unless modified by treaty, for example the United Kingdom and the United States.

The alternative basic system of taxing foreign-source income is the exemption method, employed by OECD countries such as France and Germany. Under this method there is no further tax on the repatriated profits and so the effective taxing back of the incentive which occurs under the tax crediting method does not occur. In fact, simple categorization of countries is difficult as many countries incorporate aspects of both systems depending upon the type of income and its country of source. A foreign tax credit is applied in some of these countries in certain circumstances, such as if there is no tax treaty or if the source country does not have a 'comparable tax system'. The fact that some exemption systems are structured on the basis of a 'subject to tax' test or a 'comparable tax' test means that the existence of a tax holiday causes the exemption not to be available in the residence country and a credit system applies in its stead. In this event the comments made in relation to credit systems become relevant.

In examining the extent of the reversal of source-country incentives through foreign tax credits there are a number of qualifications that need to be made to the simple case outlined. With deferral, to the extent that the earnings are retained in the source country and reinvested they are not subject to residence-country taxation. Thus any adverse tax consequences can be deferred until the time of repatriation. There is some theoretical discussion about the true impact of deferral in that the tax on the distribution will occur at some point in the future when the income is repatriated and so should be taken into account in the planning of the firm in making its investment decision. However, there is little doubt that firms act as if deferral matters to them. Thus to the extent that the adverse tax consequences can be delayed they are less problematic to the companies. This does have an implication for the design of tax incentives. It suggests that incentives in the income tax of the source country are more likely to be effective than incentives that are provided at the time of repatriation such as withholding tax relief. These latter incentives are more likely to be simply a transfer to the other national Treasury.

The next qualification is that tax crediting systems of most countries are generally limited to the amount of tax that would have been paid on the foreign income in the residence country. The recent tax reforms in OECD countries have the effect in some countries of lowering the overall domestic tax burden on foreign-source income below that of the source-country taxation. This places many firms, particularly in the United States, in what is known as an excess foreign tax credit position. The residence-country taxation has been completely eliminated and a residual source-country burden remains. In such circumstances, relief from source-country taxation does not result in a transfer of tax liability to the residence country and so is of benefit to the firm.

The final qualification is that foreign tax credit regimes are difficult to operate effectively. In particular the use of offshore financing companies can defer the taxation in the residence country indefinitely. Dividends paid from the source country can be routed to a third country that does not tax them. In addition, in some foreign tax systems which pool the income from different countries in making the calculation, it is possible to mix the income from high- and low-tax countries to ensure the efficient use of tax credits. In such circumstances, the transfer of the tax benefit arising from the incentive to the residence-country Treasury can be avoided.

Nevertheless, despite all of these qualifications, many companies do make their plans taking into account the eventual tax consequences in the residence country. Whether they measure the actual impact residence-country taxation will have after all tax planning routes have been exploited or whether it is a simplification used in the evaluation of projects is not clear and certainly varies depending upon the situation of the foreign investor. It does appear to reduce the effectiveness of tax incentives below what they would be when viewed from a purely domestic context.

Tax treaties and tax sparing

One method that is used to avoid this problem is 'tax sparing'. Under tax sparing, the residence country treats the income remitted as if it had been fully taxed and had not benefited from the tax incentive. This ensures that the full benefit of the tax incentive goes to the investor and is not simply transferred to the residence-country Treasury. Tax sparing provisions are usually granted as part of tax treaties. Traditionally, they are given by developed countries, which are most likely to be the residence country in the flow of international investments, to developing countries, which are more likely to be the source countries.

The role of tax sparing provision is to allow the source country to be able to provide tax reliefs without the concern that it is simply transferring money to the Treasury of the more developed country and so can be seen as preserving the sovereignty of the source country. This provides more freedom for the source country in designing its incentive regime. (In order to qualify for tax sparing it is necessary to be able to calculate the extent of the benefit that has been provided. This can be done most readily for simple reliefs in the form of tax holidays, low tax rates and withholding tax reliefs.)

The true tax benefits of other incentives such as tax credits, investment allowances and, in particular, accelerated depreciation are more difficult to calculate. Hence tax sparing provisions in treaties do not usually apply to such incentives. The result can be that the operation of the international tax system ends up increasing total taxation over what would apply without the incentive through a combination of the source and residence taxation of the investor. In particular if the residence country has a credit system without a system of carryback for excess foreign tax credits, the reduced taxation in the source-country in the early years of the investment results in increased taxation over a number of years. The residence country collects tax on the investment in the early years because of the low source-country tax and does not fully credit the higher source-country tax in later years because of the foreign tax credit limit. If the investment is made through a subsidiary, the problem can be overcome by postponing dividend payments until the later years of the investment and so averaging the source-country tax over the low and high years – this would be the natural pattern for the payment of dividends in any event. Other tax planning strategies may be available in the case of a branch to overcome the problem.

Not all countries, however, are willing to provide tax sparing provisions and a number of countries that have offered them in the past are reconsidering their position. The reasons are related to why foreign tax credit regimes are used instead of exemption methods. The use of a foreign tax credit ensures that when profits are repatriated they are taxed at the rate of other income in the country. This may be considered to increase the fairness of the domestic tax regime since it ensures that the recipients of foreign-source income face the same tax rates as do recipients of domestic income. A second reason for a foreign tax credit regime is to improve the integrity of the domestic tax regime. It is very difficult to divide accurately domestic income from foreign income, particularly when companies try to arrange their affairs to maximize the benefits of low tax rates in offshore jurisdictions. The use of a foreign tax credit seeks to ensure that if income is transferred to low-tax jurisdictions it is taxed fully when it is returned to the residence country. So far as there is any discernible trend with respect to tax sparing it is for OECD countries to be more reluctant to include such provisions in tax treaties.

The provision of incentives in one country can have implications for the tax revenues of other countries if income is diverted to the incentive country to be sheltered from taxation. Certain types of incentives, such as tax holidays and low tax rates, are particularly susceptible to this type of tax planning. Certain types of activities, such as offshore finance and insurance companies and foreign sales companies, can also be vehicles for international tax avoidance. Therefore, tax sparing provisions are rarely blanket exemptions and may be provided in a restricted manner. They can be time limited or may be restricted to certain key sectors such as manufacturing. The latter limit is usually achieved by specifying the domestic incentive provisions to which the tax sparing applies. Where there is a time limit for tax sparing relief under a treaty, power to extend the time by mutual agreement or another procedure is often included. Such restrictions may in the end not be effective in practice as income can be changed in form and source through tax planning. It is such concerns that have led a number of countries to conclude that tax sparing provisions pose an unacceptable risk to home-country tax revenues.

Just as the domestic law of one country can impact on taxation in another country, so the tax treaties of one country can affect other countries besides the treaty partner under each treaty. This arises under the practice commonly known as 'treaty shopping'. The basic idea is that intermediary companies are set up in third countries (besides the ultimate residence and source countries) to take advantage of provisions in the tax treaty between that country and the source country that have the effect of lowering source-country taxation (typically a treaty with a narrow definition of permanent establishment or low or zero tax rates on dividends, interest and/or royalties). Part of the planning often consists of recharacterizing business income as royalties or interest. As a result an increasing number of treaties include provisions intended to deny the benefits of tax treaties in treaty shopping situations. Such provisions become particularly important when tax treaties are used within a free trade group of countries to lower taxation on cross-border flows, as each country in the group becomes vulnerable to the tax treaties of the other countries in the group with third countries.

CONCLUSIONS ON THE DESIGN OF THE TAX SYSTEM TO ATTRACT FDI

The foregoing discussion has highlighted the importance of non-tax factors to investors in their determination of whether or not to invest in a country. Every effort should be made to deal with those factors under the government's control which may be inhibiting FDI. It is also important to ensure that the basic tax system does not contain features that themselves deter investment. These areas should be addressed on a priority basis. The clear experience of all the countries in the region that have offered incentives is that they, in themselves, are not sufficient to overcome the other impediments to investment. That having been said it must be recognized that incentives may be justified in some circumstances and, in any event, will certainly be offered. If they are, the experience of the countries in the region offers some clear lessons on the design of such incentives.

Basic income tax law

The most basic concern of businesses is the lack of clarity and stability of the tax laws and their application. A number of actions by governments in the region could help to reduce the resulting uncertainty:

- Governments should move on a priority basis to provide a clear and stable legislative income tax framework. New laws that contain the main features of a tax law in clear legislative language would provide a framework for business planning. It is recognized that all tax laws evolve over time to meet changing circumstances and this is particularly important in the economies in transition. Thus, not all aspects that characterize tax systems in OECD countries need be present. However, the structure of the law should be such that they can be added to as the economy and the capacity of tax administrators evolve.
- Provisions, such as penalties and interest and general rules to curb tax avoidance, should be added, if they are missing from the existing law. These rules provide tax authorities with the tools that they need to attack tax avoidance, thus protecting those incentives that are provided from abuse, and at the same time beginning to establish a habit of tax compliance.
- Clear interpretation guidelines should be developed and made public. The most persistent complaint from tax advisors is their inability to obtain clear indications of the official treatment of certain transactions and for the apparent interpretations to change over time.
- Basic features of the profits tax law should be consistent with international norms. This means:
  - statutory tax rates between 30 and 40 per cent;
  - depreciation rates consistent with OECD practice;
  - loss carryforwards of five to ten years;
  - deductions for costs to earn income, like interest and wages;
  - certain technical rules necessary for business operations, for example tax treatment of reorganizations.

Income tax incentives

The overwhelming experience in the region with tax holidays has been that they are particularly susceptible to tax avoidance and have been ineffective in attracting FDI. Part of the problem in the context of attracting foreign direct *investment* is that a holiday is only indirectly linked to the investment. It is tied to the establishment of a new enterprise and the amount of the incentive depends not upon the size of the investment but on the profits that are made during the initial years of the investment. This is at the heart of both the tendency for holidays to be used by firms making short-term investments and the various tax avoidance schemes that have been observed. These problems are significantly reduced with investment allowances and credits and so these types of incentives are recommended if the goal is the promotion of productive investment.

Investment-based incentives

While investment-linked incentives are to be preferred to tax holidays, experience has shown that they have problems themselves. There are a number of guidelines that should be followed if the incentives are to be as free from abuse as possible:

- As the examples of tax avoidance activities demonstrate, the tax avoidance problems associated with investment allowances and credits are most evident at higher rates of allowance or credit. Therefore, the rates of benefit offered should be moderate.
- Attempts to target the incentives too finely or at vague objectives are counterproductive in that they introduce complexity and uncertainty for both the taxpayer and the tax administrator. If the taxpayer cannot be certain of the eligibility of an expenditure for the incentive, its effect on behaviour is reduced significantly or even eliminated. Therefore, the investments eligible for the incentive should be clearly defined and the rules kept as simple as possible.
- In many cases the principal justification for an incentive will be to help to create a basic amount of market-oriented activity in the country. As the market develops and foreign firms become familiar with a country, the rationale for an incentive will be reduced. This suggests that incentives should be introduced for a set period of time to expire at the end of the period established. This is known as sunsetting and ensures that some review and action on the part of the government is required for the continuation of the incentive.
- Upfront incentives are susceptible to sales and resales of the same asset to produce multiple access to the incentive. Appropriate recapture and capital gains rules reduce the problem and should be in place. However, for an incentive such as an investment tax credit other rules are needed to ensure that an asset only receives the incentive once. One approach is to claw back the incentive if the asset is resold, perhaps within a time limit. This approach requires complex tracking of assets. A simpler approach is to allow the incentive only for the purchase of assets that have not been previously used. To allow the use of second-hand assets from abroad that might embody technology that is unavailable in the country, the rule could be extended to allow the incentive only for the first use of the asset in the country.
- Any asset purchase from abroad from a related person risks being done so at an inflated price to maximize the write-off for depreciation purposes. Adding an investment incentive on top of depreciation increases the incentive to engage in such tax avoidance. Avoiding this problem is not simple, but there are some guidelines that will help. The law should contain a provision that transactions between related parties be done at fair market value. This at least establishes a legal basis for

attacking the transaction and will curb somewhat the aggressiveness of major companies.

- Target the incentive to assets, such as machinery and equipment, that have some external second-hand market transaction for comparison. Intangible expenditures like know-how and business services are typically hard to value.
- The key to auditing any transaction is information. Typically the taxpayer has it and the tax administrator does not. This problem is compounded in the case of foreign taxpayers. This problem is addressed internationally through the exchange of information provisions in tax treaties. Consequently, the conclusion of tax treaties with the major source countries of FDI that contain exchange of information articles is helpful.

Tax holidays

If tax holidays are to be introduced there are a number of ways that the potential for abuse can be curtailed. These also have the effect of reorienting the holidays to an objective that is related to their design. As noted above, holidays are more linked to the establishment of enterprises than to the level of investment. The experience in the countries has documented the extent to which holidays can be used to shelter income from existing domestic operations from taxation through transfer pricing and the transfer of operations from existing firms to new firms that qualify for the holiday. These problems suggest a number of tightening restrictions that eliminate some of the most obvious abuses and direct the holiday incentives towards the creation of new businesses rather than indirectly attempting to attract new investment. The objective may be pursued by a government both in relation to attracting foreign firms and in helping the establishment of new private sector activity domestically.

- A frequently encountered problem was the transference of existing business assets to a new firm to qualify for the holiday. This also occurred with firms whose holidays were expiring to refresh the holiday. This suggests that the holiday should be restricted to firms, the bulk of whose assets have not previously been employed in the country. This ratio of new-to-the-country assets should be quite high, say 90 per cent. The assets so restricted would not include buildings given that existing buildings may be renovated for a new use. This would also deny the holiday to firms that simply change their form, such as through privatization.
- The second restriction would address the problem of transfer pricing and focus the incentive on the objective of the creation of new enterprises. It would deny the incentive to any company that was related to a company operating in the country that did not itself qualify for the holiday.

- Holidays are frequently targeted to industries that are internationally mobile, such as manufacturing, and denied to firms that are engaged in other activities that are more tied to the country, such as distribution and wholesale trade. The question arises as to what happens if a firm is established to manufacture but carries on ancillary activities that do not qualify. A strict targeting to manufacturing could operate in conjunction with the previous restriction to deny the holiday in this situation. Another approach is to allow the holiday provided that over one-half of the assets or revenues of the company are employed in the desired activity.
- If this is done, the holiday benefits should be restricted to income from the targeted activity. Profits for each activity could be separately accounted for. This is complex and subject to manipulation. A simple formula approach should be used to determine the proportion of profits to qualify for the holiday. This proportion could be on the basis of some overall figure such as wages and salaries employed, total revenues or assets.

Non-income taxes

Certain non-income taxes may act as impediments to FDI. These had the common characteristics of being unrelated to profit and an addition to the cost of basic inputs. The taxes most often causing problems are the application of social security taxes to wages and salaries paid to expatriates and the imposition of customs duties or turnover taxes on imports of equipment to be used in a business. In both of these cases the imposition of the tax runs directly counter to any investment incentives that may be provided and its removal should be the first 'incentive' considered.

- In the case of social security taxes wages and salaries paid to expatriates are at levels much higher than local wages and salaries. At the same time, there is little likelihood the expatriate would ever benefit from the services which the social security taxes fund. Therefore, for expatriates with a temporary attachment to work in the country, an option not to participate in the social security plan of the country could be provided. This would provide relief from the social security taxes, but would mean that the expatriate is denied any related benefits. Education, medical coverage, etc., would need to be covered privately.
- A related issue is the imposition of personal income taxes. As the expatriates benefit from the general services of the country, they should pay income taxes if they are resident for tax purposes in the country. Moreover, in many cases such taxes may be creditable in the home country. However, the progressivity of the rate schedule that is linked to the domestic distribution of incomes may result in an excessive burden of tax when applied to the higher level of expatriate salary. Moreover, the

expenses faced by the expatriate are likely to be higher than the local population. Thus, an enhanced tax allowance might be applied to the income of such individuals.

- Customs duties on business inputs raise the cost of capital items and discourage investment. In a number of countries, this is recognized in the foreign investment laws which exempt foreign-owned firms from the payment of customs duties on own-use business imports. However, these benefits are sometimes restricted to contributions of original capital or require 100 per cent ownership of the firm. In other cases, other taxes like the turnover tax impose a charge on such importations. (While a VAT in theory avoids these problems as a refund is given for any taxes on business inputs, certain features of the VAT systems of a number of countries in the region have led to an effective tax being imposed on imports.) As these are a direct impediment to investment, duties and taxes on the import of capital goods for own use should be eliminated.

International design issues

A number of conclusions can also be drawn about the features of the tax system that are related to taxation in an international context. These relate both to the attraction of FDI and ensuring that countries receive their fair share of revenues from profits earned from sources in them. The vulnerability of countries in the region to tax avoidance is especially pronounced in the area of international flows of interest and business services among related parties. Tax treaties and withholding tax policies should be designed to reduce the exposure of the ax base to erosion.

Withholding taxes

Countries in the region are likely to be net capital importers over the foreseeable future. As such they will wish to have a tax treaty policy that ensures that source countries maintain a fair share of profits derived from operations within their borders. Income tax systems in the countries are, and will remain, vulnerable to tax avoidance. Withholding taxes, which tax distributions on a gross basis without deductions, are less vulnerable than income taxes to tax avoidance and in many circumstances would ensure that a country gets some revenues from operations within its border.

- In order to protect revenues, countries in the region should maintain withholding taxes on dividend payments made to non-residents outside the region. Given the reasonable level of income taxes in the region, for the most part these taxes will be creditable against home-country taxes and so will not deter FDI. Moreover, in combination with relatively low statutory tax rates and moderate investment incentives, they provide an incentive for reinvestment of profits which is the primary source of investment capital.

- Tax bases are particularly threatened by payments between related parties, such as interest, lease payments, rents, royalties and management fees that generate deductions against the profit tax of the countries. If there is no withholding tax on these payments then the host country gets no tax on the underlying profits. Therefore, withholding taxes should be maintained on tax-base-reducing payments to related non-residents.
- However, withholding taxes on such payments to unrelated parties are typically passed forward, in the sense that they are added into the price charged. In such cases the withholding tax increases the cost of capital or the service to the domestic company and so reduces its ability to compete. Therefore, consideration should be given to removing withholding taxes on such payments to unrelated parties. It is recognized that this provides an opportunity for flowing what are in fact payments between related parties through unrelated firms to disguise the nature of the true recipient. Rules can be developed to confront such back-to-back transactions, but auditing is very difficult in this area.

Tax treaty network

A tax treaty network is an important ingredient in the mix of tax policies to attract FDI. There are two broad groups of tax treaties that require a different policy perspective. The first are the treaties between countries in the region and those countries outside of the region and which are prospective sources of FDI. From the perspective of the foreign firm a tax treaty establishes the 'rules of the game' for the interaction of the source- and residence-country tax systems. From the perspective of the taxing authority, it provides access to the exchange of information facilities that would allow a better chance to police some of the trans-border tax avoidance schemes that firms might employ. The second group are the treaties among countries in the region. Tax treaties among countries in the region should be designed to facilitate flows of investment and trade within the region, or subregions, reflecting the historic close economic ties. This may often result in provisions on withholding taxes that are less stringent than in treaties with countries from outside the region. They should also be used to allow close administrative cooperation to help to counteract regional tax evasion.

- The two groups of treaties have the potential to interact in ways that can frustrate the objective of protecting the receipt by the country of its fair share of tax revenues. This can occur if withholding tax rates on certain types of distributions between countries in the region and countries outside the region vary between countries. This is most likely to occur if countries in the region operate separate tax treaty negotiation programmes. This suggests that for those countries which have continuing close economic links an attempt should be made to develop a coordinated tax treaty strategy and perhaps negotiate in concert. Consideration should also be given to the problem of treaty shopping in this context and the possible inclusion of provisions to protect the domestic tax base against this practice.

- Countries should endeavour to expand their tax treaty networks. This would facilitate both tax compliance and tax administration. Access to tax sparing is through treaties and many countries with exemption systems for treaty countries apply a foreign tax credit system to non-treaty countries. Thus the existence of treaties makes any incentives which are provided more effective.

Tax competition

Experience with tax incentives, particularly in Asia, suggests that so-called footloose manufacturing plants for export may be influenced by tax incentives when choosing the location for a new plant when they are comparing sites in different countries that are otherwise similar. This situation may also occur where a firm targets a region for a strategic investment, but is indifferent as to which country it operates from. For example, it may view any one national market in the region to be insufficient for efficient production and plans to supply the entire region from one plant. Countries may therefore be tempted to try to attract these footloose export industries.

Another reason that policy makers give for offering tax incentives is that it is necessary to have them to maintain their country's competitive position *vis-à-vis* neighbouring countries. They may view that another country has a natural advantage, such as location or raw materials that make it more attractive as a destination for foreign investment.

This rationale can be criticized on basic principles. All countries face natural advantages and disadvantages in relation to other countries. The provision of a tax incentive merely shifts the private disadvantage from the investor in the particular activity to other economic agents in the country. It does nothing to change the total disadvantage to society as it does not affect the social rate of return which is the sum of the private after-tax return and the taxes collected from the activity. In fact the competitive position of the country might be diminished overall as the production in the economy is less efficiently organized than it would have been without the incentive.

It is not necessary to rely on such economic efficiency arguments, however, to see the potential futility of tax competition. The normal response of a country that views itself as being in competition for foreign investment to the tax incentives of another country is to introduce some form of offsetting incentive. Thus in the end the tax incentives offered by the two countries do nothing to alter the relative incentive to invest between the two countries. The only result of the competition is that both countries receive lower tax revenues. They would both be better off if they could agree not to compete.

The foregoing suggests that countries in the region should attempt to develop fora and processes to reduce the possibility of counterproductive tax competition. The OECD may provide an appropriate forum for such discussions to take place.

Given the inability of OECD countries to develop mechanisms in this area, one cannot be too sanguine about the prospects for reaching binding accords. Nevertheless, there are some reasons for optimism. A number of countries in the region have eliminated incentives in concert in an attempt to avoid tax competition, although there is some pressure on this. Second, among OECD countries, the wave of tax reform that swept the tax world in the latter half of the 1980s had the effect of sweeping away many tax incentives in different countries at the same time. While there was no pre-arrangement for this to happen, the move by a number of influential countries certainly provided an opportunity for other countries to do the same.

NOTES

*The authors wish to thank Alex Easson who co-authored the original report and Richard Vann who made many useful comments. The views expressed are their own and do not commit the OECD or its member governments.

1 A further discussion of these consultations can be found in *The Role of Tax Systems in Encouraging Foreign Direct Investment*, OECD, 1994.

2 This section is substantially based upon contributions by Alex Easson to the original report.

Part VI

LIST OF SELECTED PUBLICATIONS BY VITO TANZI

SELECTED PUBLICATIONS BY VITO TANZI

(Chronologically listed)

BOOKS WRITTEN

Taxation In An Integrating World (Washington, DC: Brookings Institution, 1995).

Public Finance in Developing Countries (Brookfield, Vt: Edward Elgar, 1991). Spanish edition by Instituto de Estudios Fiscales (Madrid: 1995).

Inflation and the Personal Income Tax: An International Perspective (Cambridge University Press, 1980). Spanish edition published by Instituto de Estudios Fiscales (Madrid: 1983). Italian edition published by *Il Mulino*.

The Individual Income Tax and Economic Growth (Baltimore, Md: Johns Hopkins Press, 1969). Published in Japanese by Toyo Keizai Shinposha in 1970.

Taxation: A Radical Approach (with two other authors) (London: Institute of Economic Affairs, 1970).

BOOKS EDITED WITH CONTRIBUTIONS

Transition to Market: Studies in Fiscal Reform, (Washington, DC: IMF, 1993). Chinese and Russian editions also available.

Fiscal Policies in Economies in Transition (Washington, DC: IMF, 1992). Chinese and Russian editions also available.

Public Finance, Trade, and Development, Proceedings of the 44th Congress of the International Institute of Public Finance (Wayne State University Press, 1990).

Fiscal Policy in Open Developing Economies (Washington, DC: IMF, 1990). Chinese edition available.

Taxation, Inflation and Interest Rates (Washington, DC: IMF, 1984).

The Underground Economy in the United States and Abroad (Lexington Books, 1982).

ARTICLES IN BOOKS

'Corruption, Arm's Length, and Markets,' in *The Economics of Crime*, Fiorentini and Peltzman (eds) (Cambridge University Press, 1995).

'Fiscal Deficits and Public Debt in Industrial Countries,' in *The New Fiscal Order*, Stenerle and Kawai (Washington DC: The Hebrew Institute, 1995).

'The Political Economy of Fiscal Deficit Reduction,' in *Public Sector Deficits and Macroeconomic Performance*, W. Easterly, C. Rodriguez, and K. Schmidt-Hebbel (eds) (Oxford University Press, 1994).

'International Systems of Public Expenditure Auditing: Lessons for Italy,' in *Nuovo Sistema di Controlli Sulla Spesa Pubblica* (Rome: Banca d'Italia, 1994).

'Taxation in Developing Countries,' in *Tax Systems in North African and European Countries*, L. Bernardi and J. Owens (eds) (Kluwer, 1994).

'The Consistency Between Long-Term Development Objectives and Short-Term Instruments in Fund Activities,' in *Adjustment and Development in Sub-Saharan Africa*, Cornia and Helleiner (eds) (London: Macmillan, 1994).

'Restrictions to Foreign Investment: A New Form of Protectionism?' (with Isaias Coelho) in *Protectionism and World Welfare*, Dominick Salvatore (ed.) (Cambridge: Cambridge University Press, 1994).

'The IMF and Tax Reform,' in *Tax Policy and Planning in Developing Countries*, A. Bagchi and N. Stern (eds) (Oxford: Oxford University Press, 1994).

'The Fisher Effect and the Term Structure of Interest Rates,' in *Public and International Economics*, Ali M. El-Agraa (ed.) (London: St Martin's Press, 1993).

'Interest Rates and Government Debt: Are the Linkages Global Rather than National?' (with Mark Lutz) in *The Political Economy of Government Debt*, H.A.A. Verbon and F.A.A.M. Van Winden (eds) (Amsterdam: North-Holland, 1993).

'Fiscal Issues in Adjustment Programs,' in *Fiscal Issues in Adjustment in Developing Countries*, Riccardo Faini and Jaime de Melo (eds) (London: St Martin's Press, 1993).

'Structural Factors and Tax Revenue in Developing Countries: A Decade of Evidence,' in *Open Economies: Structural Adjustment and Agriculture*, Ian Goldin and L. Alan Winters (eds) (Cambridge: Cambridge University Press, 1992).

'Fiscal Issues in Economies in Transition,' in *Reforming Central and Eastern European Economies*, V. Corbo, F. Coricelli, and J. Bossak (eds) (Washington, DC: World Bank, 1991).

'International Coordination of Fiscal Policies,' in *The Reality of International Economic Policy Coordination*, H.J. Blommestein (ed.) (Amsterdam: North-Holland, 1991).

'Tax Reform and the Move to a Market Economy: Overview of the Issues,' in *The Role of Tax Reform in Central and Eastern European Economies* (Paris: OECD, 1991).

'Mobilization of Savings in Eastern European Countries: The Role of the State,' in *Economics for the New Europe*, Anthony B. Atkinson and Renato Brunetta (eds) (London: Macmillan, 1991).

'Is There a Need for Harmonizing Capital Income Taxes Within EC Countries?' (with Lans Bovenberg), in *Reforming Capital Income Taxation*, Horst Siebert (ed.) (Tübingen: J.C.B. Molin, 1991).

'The Use of Presumptive Income in Modern Tax Systems,' (with Milka Casanegra), in *Changes in Revenue Structures*, Proceedings of the 42nd Congress of the IIPF: Athens (Wayne State University Press, 1989), pp. 37–51.

'International Coordination of Fiscal Policies: Current and Future Issues,' in *Fiscal Policy, Economic Adjustment, and Financial Markets*, Mario Monti (ed.) (IMF, 1989), pp. 7–37.

'Economic Interdependence and the International Implications of Supply-Side Policies,' (with Lans Bovenberg), in *A Supply-Side Agenda for Germany*, G. Fels and G. M. von Furstenberg (eds) (Heidelberg: Springer-Verlag 1988).

'Public Debt and Fiscal Policy in Developing Countries,' (with Mario Blejer) in *The Economics of Public Debt*, Kenneth J. Arrow and Michael J. Boskin (eds) (Macmillan Press, 1988).

'Quantitative Characteristics of the Tax Systems of Developing Countries,' in *The Theory of Taxation for Developing Countries*, David Newbery and Nicholas Stern (eds) (Oxford University Press, 1987).

'Fiscal Policy, Growth, and Design of Stabilization Programs,' in *External Debt, Savings, and Growth in Latin America*, Ana Maria Martirena-Mantel (ed.) (Washington, DC: IMF 1987), pp. 121–41.

'The European Monetary System and Fiscal Policies,' (with Teresa Ter-Minassian), in *Tax Coordination in the European Community*, Sijbren Cnossen (ed.) (Antwerp: Kluwer 1987).

'Public Expenditure and Public Debt: An International and Historical Perspective,' in *Public Expenditure: The Key Issues*, John Bristow and Declan McDonagh (eds) (Institute of Public Administration: 1986).

'Fiscal Management and External Debt Problems,' in *External Debt Management*, Hassanali Mehran (ed.) (Washington, DC: IMF, 1985), pp. 65–87.

'The Deficit Experience in Industrial Countries,' in *The Economy in Deficit, Essays in Contemporary Economic Problems*, Phillip Cagan (ed.) (Washington, DC: American Enterprise Institute 1985), pp. 81–119.

'Monetary Policy and Control of Public Expenditure,' in *Public Expenditure and Government Growth*, Francesco Forte and Alan Peacock (eds) (Oxford: Basil Blackwell, 1985).

'Is There a Limit to the Size of the Fiscal Deficits in Developing Countries?'

in *Public Finance and Public Debt*, Proceedings of the 40th Congress of the IIPF: Innsbruck (Wayne State University Press, 1984).

'Taxation and Price Stabilization,' in *Comparative Tax Studies: Essays in Honor of Richard Goode*, Sijbren Cnossen (ed.) (Amsterdam: North-Holland, 1983).

'Adjusting Personal Income Taxes for Inflation: The Foreign Experience,' in *Inflation and the Income Tax*, Henry Aaron (ed.) (Washington, DC: Brookings Institution, 1976).

'Theory of Tax Structure Development and the Design of Tax Structure for Industrialization,' in *Fiscal Policy for Industrialization in Latin America*, David Geithman (ed.) (University of Florida Press, 1975).

'Personal Income Taxation in Latin America: Obstacles and Possibilities,' in *Readings on Taxation in Developing Countries*, third edn, R. Bird and O. Oldman (eds) (Baltimore, Md: Johns Hopkins Press, 1975).

'Should We Stop Economic Growth?' in *Political Economy: Radical and Orthodox Approaches*, J.H. Weaver (ed.) (Allyn and Bacon, 1973).

ARTICLES IN PROFESSIONAL JOURNALS

'Fiscal Federalism and Decentralization: A Review of Some Efficiency and Macroeconomic Aspects,' in *Proceedings of the World Bank Annual Conference on Development Economics*, 1995.

'Reforming Public Finances in Economies in Transition,' in *International Tax and Public Finance* Vol. 1, No. 2 (1994).

'A Primer on Tax Evasion,' (with Partho Shome) in IMF *Staff Papers*, Vol. 40, No. 4 (December 1993).

'The Budget Deficit in Transition: A Cautionary Note,' in IMF *Staff Papers*, Vol. 40, No. 4 (December 1993).

'A Tax on Gross Assets of Enterprises as a Form of Presumptive Taxation,' (with Efraim Sadka) in *Bulletin of the International Bureau of Fiscal Documentation*, Vol. 47, No. 2 (February 1993).

'Time Constraints in Consumption and Savings Behavior,' (with Howell Zee) in *Journal of Public Economics*, No. 50 (1993).

'Fiscal Policy for Latin America,' in *World Development*, (May 1992).

'Modernization, Ethics and Public Policy,' (with Ke-young Chu) in *Journal of Regional Policy*, Vol. II (July–December 1991).

'Barriers to Foreign Investment in the United States and Other Nations,' (with Isaias Coelho) in *The Annals of the American Academy of Political and Social Science*, Vol. 516 (July 1991), pp. 154–68.

'Fiscal Issues in Adjustment Programs in Developing Countries,' in *Ricerche Economiche* (November 1990).

'The Impact of Macroeconomic Policies on the Level of Taxation and the Fiscal Balance in Developing Countries,' in IMF *Staff Papers*, Vol. 36, No. 3 (September 1989).

'Inflation and the Measurement of Fiscal Deficits,' (with M. Blejer and M. Teijeiro) in IMF *Staff Papers*, Vol. 34, No. 4 (December 1987).

'The Response of Other Industrial Countries to the U.S. Tax Reform Act,' in *National Tax Journal*, Vol. XL, No. 3 (September 1987), pp. 339–55.

'Fiscal Policy Responses to Exogenous Shocks in Developing Countries,' in *The American Economic Review*, No. 76 (May 1986).

'Fiscal Deficits and Interest Rates in the United States: An Empirical Analysis, 1960-84,' in IMF *Staff Papers*, Vol. 32, No. 4 (December 1985).

'The Underground Economy in the United States: Annual Estimates for 1930–80,' in IMF *Staff Papers*, Vol. 30, No. 2 (June 1983).

'Expected Inflation and Interest Rates: Comment,' in *The American Economic Review*, Vol. 73, No. 3 (June 1983).

'Fiscal Disequilibrium in Developing Countries,' in *World Development*, Vol. 10, No. 12 (December 1982).

'Inflationary Expectations, Economic Activity, Taxes, and Interest Rates: Reply,' in *American Economic Review*, Vol. 72, No. 4 (September 1982).

'Inflation, Interest Rate Policy, and Currency Substitutions in Developing Economies: A Discussion of Some Major Issues,' (with Mario I. Blejer) in *World Development*, Vol. 10, No. 9 (September 1982), pp. 781–89.

'Inflationary Expectations, Taxes, and the Demand for Money in the United States,' in IMF *Staff Papers*, Vol. 29, No. 2 (June 1982).

'The Impact of Taxes on Wages in the United States: An Example of Supply-Side Economics?' (with George Iden) in *Economic Notes*, Vol. 11, No. 3 (1982).

'Underground Economy in the United States: Estimates and Implications,' Banca Nazionale del Lavoro *Quarterly Review* (Rome) No. 135: 427–53 (December 1980).

'Inflationary Expectations, Economic Activity, Taxes, and Interest Rates,' in *American Economic Review* (March 1980).

'Inflation Accounting and the Taxation of Capital Gains of Enterprises,' in *Proceedings of the International Institute of Public Finance*, 1979 Congress, (1980).

'Income Taxes and the Demand for Money: A Quantitative Analysis,' in Banca Nazionale del Lavoro *Quarterly Review* (Rome) No. 128, (March 1979).

'Import Taxes and Economic Development,' in *Economia Internazionale*, Vol. XXXI, Nos. 3–4 (1978).

'Inflation, Real Tax Revenue, and the Case for Inflationary Finance: Theory with an Application to Argentina,' in IMF *Staff Papers*, Vol. 25, No. 4 (1978).

'Inflation and the Incidence of Income Taxes on Interest Income: Some Results for the United States, 1972–74,' in IMF *Staff Papers* (July 1977).

'Inflation, Lags in Collection, and the Real Value of Tax Revenue,' in IMF *Staff Papers*, (March 1977).

'Inflation, Indexation and Interest Income Taxation,' in Banca Nazionale del Lavoro *Quarterly Review* (Rome) (March 1976).

'The Sensitivity of the Yield of the U.S. Individual Income Tax and the Tax Reforms of the Past Decade,' in IMF *Staff Papers* (July 1976).

'Fiscal Policy, Keynesian Economics and the Mobilization of Savings in Developing Countries,' in *World Development* (October 1976).

'Inflation and the Indexation of Personal Income Taxes in Theory and Practice,' in Banca Nazionale del Lavoro *Quarterly Review* (Rome) (September 1976).

'Time Preference: A Psychological Concept in Economics,' in *Journal of Behavioral Economics*, Vol. III (1974).

'Demand for Money, Interest Rates and Income Taxation,' in Banca Nazionale del Lavoro *Quarterly Review* (Rome) (December 1974).

'Redistributing Income through the Budget in Latin America,' in Banca Nazionale del Lavoro *Quarterly Review* (Rome) (March 1974).

'The Effect of the 1964 Tax Reform on the Sensitivity of the U.S. Individual Income Tax,' (with Tom Hart) in *Review of Economics and Statistics*, (August 1972).

'Exclusion, Pure Public Goods, and Pareto Optimality,' in *Public Finance*, Vol. XXVII, No. 1 (1972).

'Natural Resources, Human Capital and the Purchasing Power Parity Doctrine: Some Empirical Results,' (with Chris Clague) in *Economia Internazionale* (February 1972).

'Measuring the Sensitivity of the Federal Income Tax from Cross-Section Data,' in *Review of Economics and Statistics* (May 1969).

'Tax Incentives for Economic Development: The Ecuadorian Case,' in *Finanzarchiv* (March 1969).

'Comparing International Tax Burdens, A Suggested Method,' in *Journal of Political Economy* (October 1968).

'Determinants of Government Revenue Shares Among Less Developed Countries,' in *The Economic Journal* (June 1967).

'National Tax Systems and the Balance of Payments: An Alternative Analysis,' in *National Tax Journal* (March 1967).

'A Proposal for a Dynamically Self-Adjusting Personal Income Tax,' in *Public Finance*, Vol. IV (1966).

INDEX

Note: Tables and figures are indexed separately (page numbers shown in italics) only if they appear on pages where there is no reference to the subject in the text.

Aeroméxico *27*, 28
Albania 135, *136*, 137; social safety nets *138*, 139, 154, 155, 156, 157
Argentina *16*, *17*, 40
Armenia *136*, 154, *183*; social safety nets *138*, 154, 155, 156, 157
asset stripping 181, 186, 199–200
assets: positive or negative value 36; privatization by sale of 33, 42–4
Australia 20, *40*
Azerbaijan *136*, *138*, 156, *183*, 203, 206

Bangladesh *16*, *17*
bankruptcy 182, 200, 207
Belarus *136*, 137, 154; excess wages tax *183*, 204, 206; social safety nets *138*, 154
Blanchard, O.J. and Layard, R. 202
Brazil *16*, *17*, 19, *40*
British Airways 26, *27*
British Telecom (BT) 25–6, *27*
British Thermal Unit (BTU) tax, US 102, 104
budget: balancing 229, 237; hidden 56–7; implications of rationing for 173; 'off-budget' techniques 56, 57–8, 233; and social safety nets 139–52
budget of restrictions on competition 57–60
Bulgaria *136*, 137; excess wages tax 182, *183*, 186, 204, 206, 211–18 (Appendix); privatization 32, 42–3, 48; social safety nets *138*, 154, 155

Canada 20, *40*
capital markets 32, 41, 43, 44, 247
carbon tax *see* taxes
cash benefits: economic reform and 137, *153*, 154, 156–7, 158; in social safety net 140, 142–3, 144–7, 150–2
Central Bank of Russia 233, 236, 238
central planning methods 234–6, 238, 241–2
Chernomyrdin, Viktor 238
child allowances 140, 150, 152, *153*
Chile *16*, *17*, 29; privatization 19, 27–8, 29, *40*
CHILGENER *27*, 28
China 166, 173–4, 175
Colombia *16*, *17*
COMECON breakdown 185
competition: regulation of 54–6; restrictions on 50–1, 53, 54–62; in state-owned enterprises 185–6; *see also* liberalization policies
consumption 35, 37, 38–9
contestable markets theory 56
corporate governance 39
corporate taxes *see* taxes
corporatization 42
Côte d'Ivoire 19
credit: 'directed' 230, 233–4, 242; expansion 127–8; foreign 230–3
credit policy: Russian 228–9, 230–4, 236, 237, 238–9, 240; *see also* monetary policy
crowding out 34, 35, 36
CTC (Chile) 27–8
Czech Republic 20, *40*, 44–5, 46, 155

debt: interenterprise 229–30; *see also* government debt
defense spending 227–8, 230
Denmark: effect of tax reform 79–80, 82,

83, 84; financial deregulation 73; tax system 68–71 *passim*, 77, *78*, 79; *see also* Scandinavia
depreciation 255, 266
Dildine, L. and Sunley, E.M. 207
distribution of income *see* income distribution

East Germany 20, 40–1, 43
Eastern Europe and former Soviet Union (EEFSU): excess wages tax 181–7, 200–6; privatization 20, 41–7; public enterprises in 12; *see also* Russian Federation; Soviet Union
economic growth 83
economic reform: Russian 223–43; and social safety nets 134–59
electricity industry 13–14
employee ownership 38, 39, 43, 45
employment: and environment taxes 104–5; and privatization 43; and social safety nets 139–40; tax incentives for creation of 273; *see also* labor supply; unemployment
energy taxes *see* environment taxes
ENERSIS *27*, 28
environment taxes 93–107; British Thermal Unit (BTU) tax 102, 104; or broad-based taxes 103–4; carbon tax 93, 94, 102, 103–4, 106; 'double dividend' of 97–8, 102, 103–4, 107; earmarking 99, 100; energy taxes 93, 103–4, 105, 106; equity aspects of 93–4, 100–1; fiscal implications 96–100; and government expenditure 93, 98–100; and government revenue 93, 96–8; international aspects 106; macroeconomic aspects 94, 101–6; Pigouvian 93, 94–7, 99; social cost of 102–3, 104, 106–7
Estonia 45–6, *136*; excess wages tax 182, *183*, 186, 204, 206; social safety nets *138*, 154, 155, 156, 157
Ethiopia 135, *136*, *138*, 139; privatization of land 41, 47, 48
European Commission, environment taxes 94, 102, 106–7
excess wages tax 181–207; and asset stripping 181, 186, 199–200; as curb on wage awards 185, 189–94, 198, 206; effect on tax revenue 181, 186, 194; and inflation 185, 194–5, 206–7; and labor supply 190–2, 193–4, 196–8, 199; in labor-dominated enterprise 196–200, 206; and monopsony 189–94, 210 (Appendix); in profit-maximizing enterprises 187–95, 206, 207–9 (Appendix); and self-seeking managers 198–200, 210–11 (Appendix); in state-owned enterprises 185–6, 196–200, 207; and transition to market economy 182, 185–6, 206–7; and wage maximization 197–8, 206
exchange rates: and poverty 122–3, 124, 127, 128–9; Russian 228, 238, 242
excise taxation 60–1
expatriates, taxation of 257, 286–7
expenditure: household *159* (Appendix); personal 144; *see also* government expenditure
expenses, taxation of 255–6
export processing zones 274–6
export promotion 273–4
extrabudgetary funds 139, 141–3, 147, 148–50

Fedorov, N.V. 238, 239
financial deregulation 73–4, *75*, 84
financial programming: model 115–18, 122–9; and poverty alleviation 113–29; simulation 125–9
financial stabilization 226–7
fiscal deficit: and economic reform 147, 158; Russian 230–3, 234–5, 237
fiscal policy: contribution to market liberalization 57–62; and environmental concerns 93, 94; 'hidden budgets' 56–7; 'off-budget' techniques 56, 57–8; and privatization 34; Russian 229, 233–41 *passim*; simulation of effects on poverty 126–9
food stamps 174–5
foreign direct investment 74–5, 246–90; attracting 247–8, 249, 282–90; non-tax factors 248–51; tax factors affecting 251–9; and tax incentives 249, 251–90; and technology transfer 247–8, 273; uncertainty in 249–50
foreign investment 36, 42, 43, 74–7; fictive 270; portfolio investment

75–7; *see also* foreign direct investment; investment France 50, 207, 279
free trade zones 274–6

Gaidar, Igor 226, 227, 228, 238, 241
Galal, A. 9, 14, 16, 19
Galal, A., Jones, L., Tandon, P., and Vogelsang, I. 24, 25, 26–8
GATT 50, 274, 275, 276
Georgia *136*, *138*, 154, 155, 156
Germany 11, 40–1, 43, 50, 279
Gini coefficient 120, 129
Goulder, Lawrence H. 103–4
government debt 35, 47, 230–3
government expenditure: and environment taxes 93, 98–100; and proceeds of privatization 35; Russian 230–4, 235–6, 237, 238, 239, 242; on social safety nets 114, 128–9, 139, 157–9
government revenue: collection 141, 143, 151, *153*, 165, 229; effect of economic reform on 114, 164–5; effect of FDI tax incentives 260–1, 262, 268–9; effect of tax reform on 84–6; and environment taxes 96–8; monopoly as source of 54, 55; Russian 229, 234–6, 237, 239, 242; *see also* tax revenue
Greece *40*
Guinea 19

head count ratio 119, 124, 127, 129
Hetzel, R. 55
'hidden budgets' 56–60
Hills, John 29
housing tax relief 81
Hungary 135, *136*, 137, 154; excess wages tax *183*, 204–5, 206; privatization 20, 29, *40*, 42, 46, 48; social safety nets 29, *138*

income distribution 12–13, 60–1; rationing and 168, 169, 172–3; in transition economies 135–7, 164
income tax *see* taxes
incomes policies, tax-based 182, 186
India *16*, *17*
Indonesia *16*, *17*
inflation: excess wages tax and 185, 194–5, 206–7; and poverty 123, 124, 127; Russian 228–9, 234, 237–8, 240
interenterprise debt 229–30
International Monetary Fund (IMF) 4, 113
international trade 55
investment: effect of privatization on 34–5, 37; privatization proceeds used for 38, 39, 43, 47–8; share of public enterprises in 10–11, *22*; tax reform and 81–3; *see also* foreign direct investment; foreign investment
investment allowances 264–6, 268, 278–80
Ireland *40*
Israel *40*
Italy 20

Jamaica 19, *40*
Jones, L., Tandon, P., and Vogelsang, I. 21; *see also* Galal, A., Jones, L., Tandon, P., and Vogelsang, I.

Kazakhstan *136*, *138*, 155, *183*, 205
Kelang Container Terminal *27*
Kyrgyz Republic *136*, 137, 154; excess wages tax *183*, 205, 206; social safety nets *138*, 155, 157

labor supply: excess wages tax and 190–2, 193–4, 196–8, 199; tax reform and 79–81; *see also* employment; unemployment land, privatization of 38, 41, 46–7
Lao People's Democratic Republic 135, *136*, 137, *159* (Appendix); social safety nets *138*, 139, 155
Latvia *136*; excess wages tax 182, *184*, 186, 205, 206; social safety nets *138*, 139, 155, 156, 157
Layard, R. *see* Blanchard, O.J. and Layard, R.
liberalization policies 50–62, 74–7, 86; and fiscal policy 54–62; implementation 51–3; Russian 226, 227, 228, 242; in service sector 50–3; *see also* price liberalization
Lithuania *136*, *138*, 155
Little, I.M.D. and Mirrlees, J.A. 12
Lorenz curve 120, 121
losses: banking 74, *75*; tax treatment of 256–7, 269

Macedonia, FYR of *136*, 154; social safety nets *138*, 139, 154, 155, 156, 157
macroeconomic factors: affecting poverty 122–3, 125–9; and environment taxes 94, 101–6; in excess wages tax 181–2; in foreign direct investment 250; and impact of privatization 33–8
macroeconomic policies: coordination with tax reform 86–7; in Russian Federation 227–43; *see also* credit policy; fiscal policy; liberalization policies; monetary policy
Malaysia *27*, 28, 40, *40*
Malaysian Airline Systems *27*
management: advanced techniques 248; privatization by 38, 42, 45; self-seeking by 198–200, 210–11 (Appendix)
market failure 55–6
market liberalization 74–7; *see also* liberalization policies mass privatization 32, 38, 41, 43, 46
Mexicana de Aviación *27*, 28
Mexico *16*, *17*; privatization 19, *27*, 28, 40
Mirrlees, J.A. *see* Little, I.M.D. and Mirrlees, J.A.
Moldova *136*, *138*, 155, *184*
monetary policy and privatization 34; Russian 229, 233; *see also* credit policy
monopoly 51–2, 56, 58–60; as source of public revenue 54, 55; *see also* restrictions on competition
monopsony, and excess wages tax 189–94, 210 (Appendix)
Musgrave, Richard 100

National Freight 26–7
natural monopoly 56
Netherlands *40*
New Zealand 20, 40
Newbery, D.M. 20
Niger 19
Norway: effect of tax reform 79, 80, 82, 83, 84; financial deregulation 73; tax system 68–71 *passim*, 77, *78*, 79; *see also* Scandinavia

OECD countries: tax system in 251–9, 277, 279–80, 283, 290; use of tax incentives 246–7, 259, 260, 262–3, 269
'off-budget' techniques 56, 57–8, 233

payroll tax *see* taxes
pensions 29, 140, 141, 150–1, *153*, 157
pharmaceutical industry 59–60
Philippines *40*
Pigou, Arthur C. 93; Pigouvian taxes 93, 94–6, 99
Pinto, B. 202, 203
Poland 135, *136*, 154, 165; excess wages tax 181–2, *184*, 186, 200–3, 206, 207; privatization 20, 32, *40*, 44, 46; social safety nets *138*, 154, 155, 156, 157
pollution 94–6
population: poverty and size of 122, 124–5; and social safety net 139–40, 147–8
Posner, R. 54, 55
poverty alleviation 113–29; exchange rates and 122–3, 124, 127, 128–9; and financial programming 115–18, 122–9; inflation and 123, 124, 127; macroeconomic factors in 122–3, 125–9; measures of poverty 119–21; and population growth 122, 124–5; and structural adjustment programs 113–15; *see also* social safety nets
poverty gap 119–20, 124–5, 127, 129
poverty line 119, 124, 127, 129
price liberalization 137, 149–50, 164–76; 'big bang' or gradualist approach 165–6; Russian 227, 228, 242; and social safety nets 164–76; *see also* liberalization policies
private sector: and excess wages tax 186; impact of privatization on 33–8
privatization 9–29, 32–48, 228; case studies 25–9; cost–benefit evaluation 21–8, 29; in developed countries 18–19; extent of 19–20, 40–1; foreign investment in 36, 42, 43, 248; institutional factors 37–8; of land 38, 41, 46–7; macroeconomic impact 33–8; by management/employee ownership 38, 39, 42, 43, 45; mass 32, 38, 41, 43, 46; nontraditional approach to 32, 38–9; proceeds of 29, 35–9, *40*, 47–8; and restructuring 36, 37, 39, 43, 44; traditional approach to

32, 33–8, 42; in UK 11, 18–19, 20, *21–4*; voucher 38, 39, 43, 44–6; *see also* public/state-owned enterprises
profit maximization, and excess wages tax 187–95, 206, 207–9 (Appendix)
profit tax 234–5
protectionism 55
public goods 93, 98–100, 102–3
public/state-owned enterprises 9–19, 29, 185–6, 196–200, 207, 225; and break-up of Soviet Union 225; in developed countries 18–19, *21–4*; in developing countries 13–18; economic importance of 9–18, 20, *21–4*, 29; and excess wages tax 185–6, 196–200, 207; *see also* privatization

rationing 166–76; basic model 167–70; convertability 170–2; effect on income distribution 168, 169, 172–3; food stamps as alternative to 174–5; institutions and administration 173–4; modified form 166–74; *see also* poverty alleviation; social safety nets
reform *see* economic reform; liberalization policies; price liberalization; tax reform
regional development 272–3
regional tax avoidance 271
regulation: of competition 54–7; financial deregulation 73–4; framework to foreign direct investment 250
rent seeking 57
restrictions on competition 50–1, 53, 54–62; calculating budget of 57–60; legal 50–1, 53; and redistribution of income 60–1; role of fiscal policy 61–2; as tax and subsidy system 54–7, 60–2; *see also* competition; liberalization policies
restructuring: and foreign direct investment 248; and privatization 36, 37, 39, 43, 44; and unemployment 153
revenue *see* government revenue; tax revenue
rollover of business tax avoidance 270–1
Romania *136*, 137, 154, *159* (Appendix); social safety nets *138*, 154, 155, 156, 157
Russian Federation *136*, 154, *159* (Appendix), 223–43; defense spending 227–8, 230; economic cycles 227–41; first phase of cycle (STOP) 227–30; second phase of cycle (GO) 230–4; third phase of cycle (STOP) 234–6; fourth phase of cycle (GO) 237–8; fifth phase of cycle (BREAKS and STOP) 238–9; sixth phase of cycle (GO) 239–40; seventh phase of cycle (BREAKS) 240–1; economic reform 223–43; excess wages tax *184*, 205–6, 207; exchange rates 228, 238, 242; financial stabilization 226–7; fiscal deficit 230–3, 234–5, 237; fiscal policy 229, 233–41 *passim*; government expenditure 230–4, 235–6, 237, 238, 239, 242; government revenue 229, 234–6, 237, 239, 242; inflation 228–9, 234, 237–8, 240; land privatization 46, 240–1; liberalization policies 227, 228, 242; monetary/credit policy 228–9, 230–4, 236, 237, 238–9, 240; post-Soviet conditions 223–7; privatization 20, 43, 45–6, 228, 240–1; reform of subsidies 227–8, 235, *236*; social safety nets *138*, 155, 156, 157; tax reform 227, 229, 234; *see also* Eastern Europe and former Soviet Union (EEFSU); Soviet Union

sales tax 227, 234
savings 70–3, 83–6
Scandinavia: corporate taxes 69–70, 75–7, *78*, 81–2; financial deregulation 73–4; liberalization policies 74–7, 86; marginal tax rates 69–70, 80, 86; tax reform 67–87; taxation of capital income and savings 70–3, 77–9, 81, 86–7; unemployment 79–80
self-seeking management 198–200, 210–11 (Appendix)
Sen poverty index 120–1, 124–9
sequestration 239–40
service sector 50–3
Short, R.P. 10
Slovak Republic 155
social cost: of environment taxes 102–3, 104, 106–7; of pollution 94–6; of public enterprises 12–13

social safety nets 113–15, 122–3, 127–9, 134–59, 164–76; added to or integrated in financial programs 113–15, 122–3, 127–9; and economic reform 134–59; food stamps 174–5; and price reform 137, 149–50, 164–76; stylized model 139–43; targeting 137, 157; *see also* poverty alleviation; rationing
South Africa *40*
South Korea *40*
Soviet Union: break-up 224–5; price reform 165–6; rationing 174; social safety nets *138*, 139, 154, 155–6; tax revenue 234–5; *see also* Eastern Europe and former Soviet Union (EEFSU); Russian Federation
Spain 50, 59–60
Sports Toto Malaysia *27*
standards of living 135–7, 164
State Privatization Agency, Bulgaria 42–3
state-owned enterprises *see* public/state-owned enterprises
statutory tax rate 253–4; OECD countries 253
structural adjustment programs 113–15; simulation of 125–9
subsidies: cross 55, 61, 62; and economic reform 135–7, 139, *153*, 154–6, 158; and modified rationing 173, 175; regulatory 54–5; restrictions on competition as 54–7, 60–2; Russian reform 227–8, 235, *236*; and social safety net 140–3, 144, 149–50; 'unbudgeted import' subsidies 230–1
Sunley, E.M. *see* Dildine, L. and Sunley, E.M.
Sweden 40, 73–4, 93; effect of tax reform 79, 82, 83, 84; market liberalization 75; tax system 68–72 *passim*, 75–7, 79; *see also* Scandinavia

Tajikistan *136*, 137
Tandon, P. *see* Galal, A., Jones, L., Tandon, P., and Vogelsang, I.; Jones, L., Tandon, P., and Vogelsang, I.
Tanzi, V. 20, 72, 94, 164–5, 176, 233; list of publications 291–6
tax avoidance 259, 269–72, 283
tax base 254–5
tax credits 264–6, 268, 278–80; *see also* tax incentives
tax holidays 263–4, 267–8, 270–1, 283, 285–6; *see also* tax incentives
tax incentives: administration 261–2, 269–72; beneficiaries of 267–8; costs and benefits of 259–63; discretionary 276–7; domestic or foreign 277–8; and foreign direct investment 259–82; general 263–72; government revenue and 260–1, 262; income-tax-based 283–6; international aspects 278–82, 287–9; investment-based 264–6, 268, 278–80, 284–5; non-income-tax-based 267, 286–7; in OECD countries 246–7, 259, 260, 262–3, 269; purpose of 272–8, 289–90
tax reform 67–87, 227, 234; and financial deregulation 73–4; macroeconomic effects of 79–86; need for coordination with other policies 86–7; Russian 227, 229, 234
tax revenue: excess wages tax and 181, 186, 194; FDI tax incentives and 260–1, 262, 268–9; tax reform and 83–6; USSR and Russian Federation compared 234–5; *see also* government revenue
tax sparing 280–2; *see also* tax incentives
tax system: anti-avoidance rules 259; attracting foreign investment 249, 251–9, 282–90; breakdown in USSR 224–5; international aspects 75–7, 106, 278–82, 287–9; OECD and transition countries compared 251–9, 277, 279–80, 282–3, 290; optimal 60–2; transparency of 251–3, 282–3; *see also* tax incentives; tax reform; taxation; taxes
tax treaties 258, 269–70, 280–2, 287–9; *see also* tax incentives
tax-based incomes policies (TIP) 182, 186
taxation: competition restriction as 54–7, 60–2; excise 60–1; and foreign direct investment 246–90; of foreign-source income 278–80; limiting interest deductions 77–9; mortgage interest

relief 81; statutory tax rate 253–4; tax–GDP ratios 67–8; treatment of expatriates 255–6, 286–7; treatment of expenses 255–6; treatment of losses 256–7, 269; *see also* tax avoidance; tax incentives; tax reform; tax system; taxes
taxes: capital income and savings 70–3, 77–9, 86–7; carbon 93, 94, 102, 103–4, 106; corporate 69–70, 75–7, *78*, 81–2; customs duties 258, 287; energy 93, 103–4, 105, 106; environment 93–107; excess wages 181–207; income 72, 80, 86–7, 282–6; levels of 251; payroll 139, 141, 143, 151–2, *153*, 158–9; Pigouvian 93, 94–7, 99; profit 234–5; sales 227, 234; turnover 227; value added 227, 287; *see also* tax incentives; tax reform; tax system; taxation
technology transfer 247–8, 273
telecommunications 51, 59, 61
Teléfonos de México *27*, 28
Tobin, J. 166, 172, 175
Togo 19
transfer pricing 270
transition economies 135–7, *136*, 154, 164; excess wages tax 181–207; foreign direct investment (FDI) 246–90; inadequate capital markets 32, 41, 43, 44; privatization in 38–9; role of fiscal policy 61–2; social safety nets in 135–9, 164–76; tax system 251–9, 277, 279–80, 283, 290; unemployment 153–4, 159
Treuhandanstalt 20, 40–1, 43
Turkey *16*, *17*, *40*
Turkmenistan *136*, 137, *138*, *184*
turnover tax 227

Ukraine *136*, 137, 154; social safety nets *138*, 154, 155, 156
unemployment 79–80, 148–9, 153–4, 159; *see also* employment; labor supply
unemployment benefits 140–2, 149, 152, 153–4
UNIDO 13
United Kingdom 50, 279; privatization 11, 18–19, 20, *21–4*, 29, 40
United States 11, 50, 102, 104, 175, 279
Uzbekistan *136*, 137; social safety nets *138*, 154, 155, 156, 157

value added tax 227, 287
Venezuela 16, *17*, 40
Vogelsang, I. *see* Galal, A., Jones, L., Tandon, P., and Vogelsang, I.; Jones, L., Tandon, P., and Vogelsang, I.
voucher privatization 38, 39, 43, 44–6, 228

wages: curbing excessive awards 185, 189–94, 198, 206; liberalization 227; maximization of 197–8, 206; wage determination 185–6; *see also* excess wages tax
Weitzman, M. L. 172–3
welfare benefits of privatization 27–8, 29
World Bank 13, 29

Yeltsin, Boris 224–5, 226, 228, 230